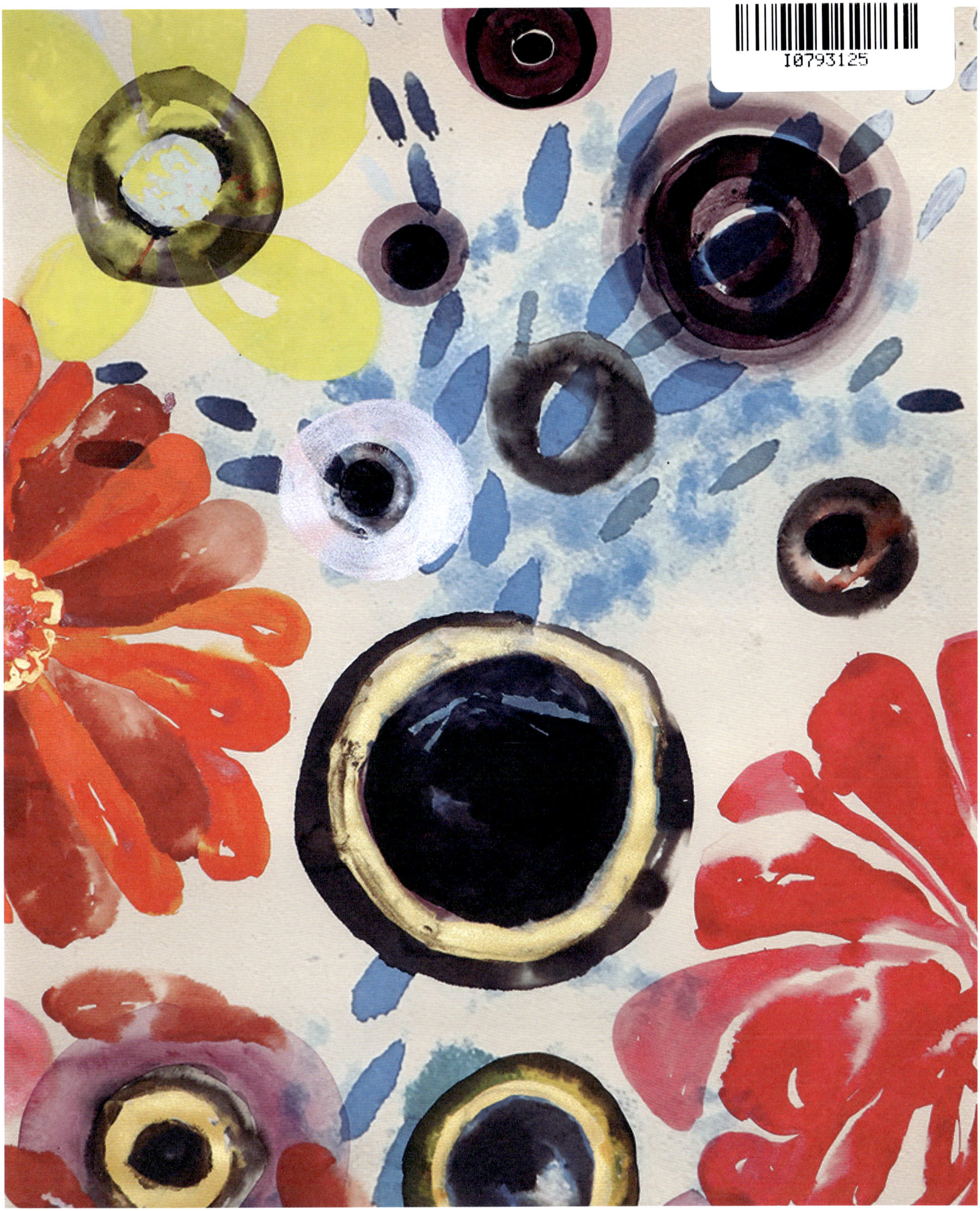

I0793125

MARÍA MAGDALENA CAMPOS-PONS
BEHOLD

EDITED BY
Carmen Hermo

WITH CONTRIBUTIONS BY
Mazie M. Harris
Amalia Mesa-Bains
Jenée-Daria Strand
Phillip Townsend
Selene Wendt

J. Paul Getty Museum, Los Angeles
Brooklyn Museum, New York

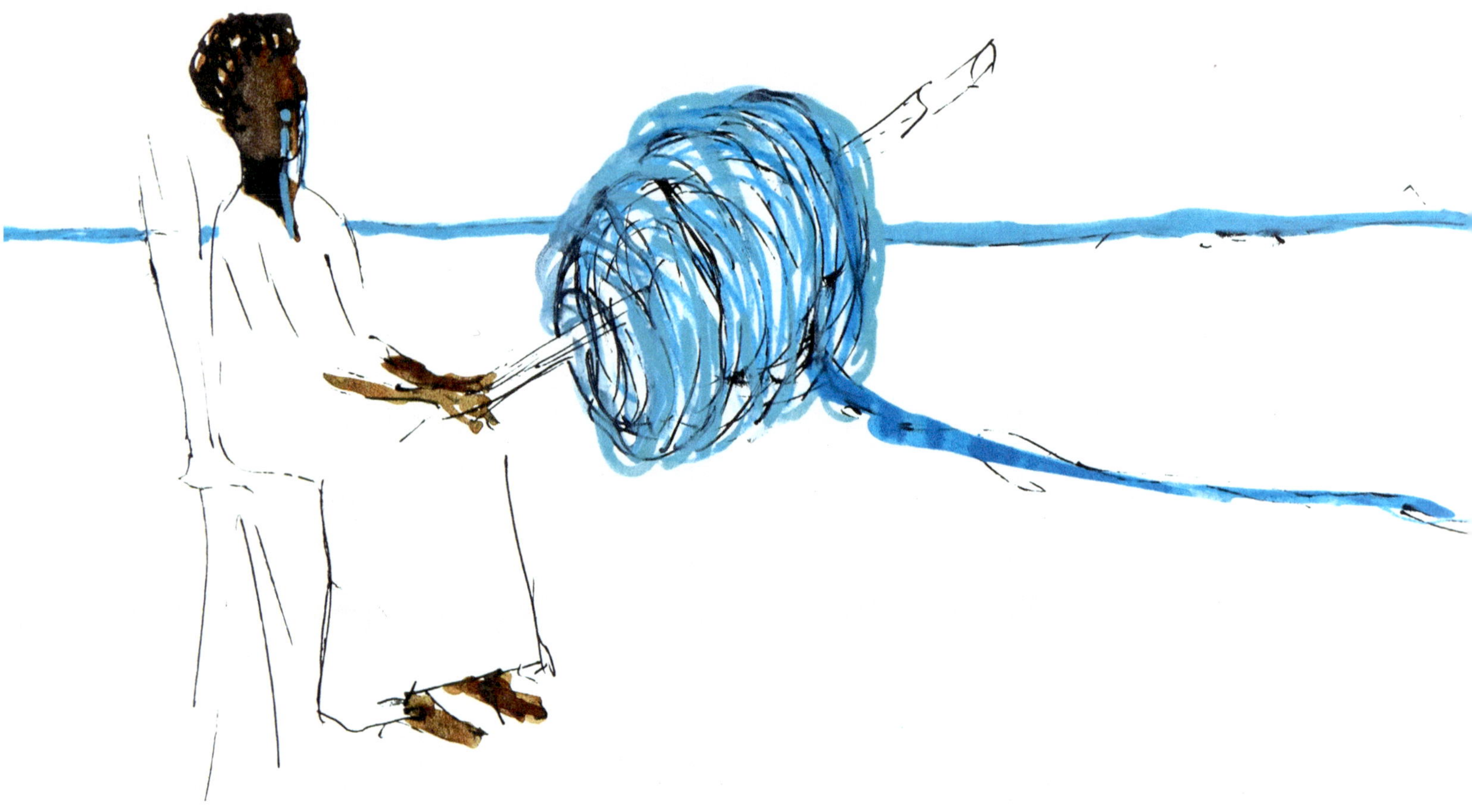

The Warrior Reservoir - Ocean (detail), 2022

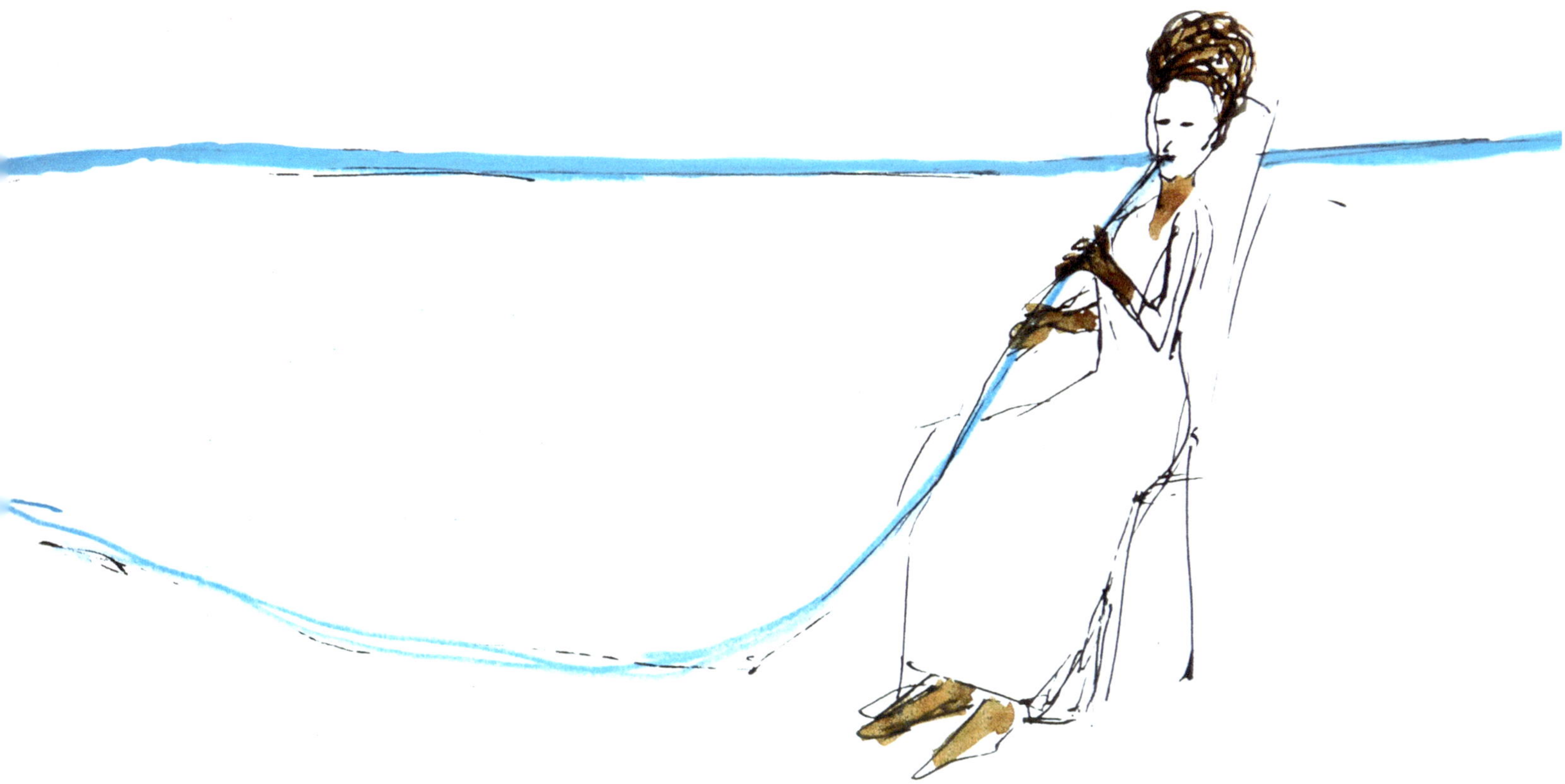

FOREWORD

The Brooklyn Museum and the J. Paul Getty Museum are proud to present *María Magdalena Campos-Pons: Behold*, the first multimedia museum survey since 2007 of the artist's prescient and powerful work.

María Magdalena Campos-Pons is a creative force, innovative in her cross-disciplinary approach to art and life. She makes sensorially stunning works of art: Polaroid emulsions drip with sumptuous, symbolic colors, videos ring out with potent performances and rituals, and installations combine and contrast objects and textures. She strives to create awareness, reconciliation, and action through her work, which represents the very best of art making—seeking, in her words, to create a "poetic, compassionate reading of our time."

Campos-Pons, who lives and works in Nashville, Tennessee, was born in Matanzas, Cuba, where the legacy of enslavement and colonial violence is palpable and pervasive, from its architecture to its social structures. Educated during a promising time of experimentation in post-Revolutionary Cuba, her artistic maturation coincided with the extremely difficult challenges of daily life during the Special Period, as well as heightened restrictions on artistic freedom—exacerbated by the contentious relationship between the governments of the United States and Cuba, which continues to impact their citizens. Campos-Pons's work draws on this complex history, as well as on her personal lineage. She was nurtured in a family that carried forth the cultural resilience, respect for ancestors, and sense of cosmological connectivity central to the Yoruba-derived Santería religion. Her oeuvre over the last four decades makes manifest how global histories and personal realities, tradition and experimentation, the past and the future interconnect. Expansive, formalist, and incisive, her work contends with the legacies of racial violence, the dislocations of migration, and the desire for connection.

A project of this scale comes to fruition through the work and talents of many people. We thank the curators: Carmen Hermo, editor of this publication and associate curator, Elizabeth A. Sackler Center for Feminist Art at the Brooklyn Museum; Mazie M. Harris, assistant curator of photographs at the J. Paul Getty Museum; and Jenée-Daria Strand, former curatorial associate, Elizabeth A. Sackler Center for Feminist Art at the Brooklyn Museum. We are grateful to the Nasher Museum of Art at Duke University and the Frist Art Museum in Nashville for their enthusiastic participation in this exhibition tour. For their generous support of the J. Paul Getty Museum's exhibition, we are grateful to Alicia Miñana and Rob Lovelace; for their support of the Brooklyn Museum's exhibition and this publication, we warmly thank Debbie and Mitchell Rechler and the Elizabeth A. Sackler Museum Educational Trust.

We extend our deepest gratitude to the artist herself. María Magdalena Campos-Pons inspires us not only with her artwork, but with her open embrace of collaboration and her boundless energy, kindness, and joy. We are thrilled to honor an artist whose work expresses a vision for new modes of understanding humanity, grounded in bold acts of beholding historical realities and inspiring compassion and action.

Timothy Potts
Maria Hummer-Tuttle and Robert Tuttle Director
J. Paul Getty Museum

Anne Pasternak
Shelby White and Leon Levy Director
Brooklyn Museum

ACKNOWLEDGMENTS

To all of our mothers

This publication, and the exhibition it heralds, is the outgrowth of collective labor and love, beginning with María Magdalena Campos-Pons—or Magda, as she is known to her friends, family, and collaborators—and her unabashed love for life, connection, and community that comes through so clearly in her work. Thank you, Magda.

I wish to thank my co-curator Mazie M. Harris for her sharp intellect, flair for curatorial diplomacy, and warm wit throughout this project, as well as Jenée-Daria Strand, whose depth of thought and careful approach shaped its genesis. Describing in words the multisensory, complex work of this artist is a particular challenge, and I am grateful for the ideas and visions gathered in this book by Harris, Strand, and contributors Amalia Mesa-Bains, Selene Wendt, and Phillip Townsend. We salute the scholars who built the foundation of writing and thinking around Campos-Pons's work; their contributions are honored in the "Further Reading" section at the end of the book. Rachel Barth, the conscientious and compassionate associate editor at Getty Publications, deftly and gracefully shepherded this book, in collaboration with Audrey Walen, director of publications, interpretation, and editorial services at the Brooklyn Museum. The captivating design of the publication was created by Wael Morcos, Jon Key, and the rest of the fantastic Morcos Key staff, especially Rouba Yammine and Chuck Gonzales.

Further thanks are due to the many collaborators and supporters who span and exceed the Brooklyn Museum and J. Paul Getty Museum, beginning with directors Anne Pasternak and Timothy Potts, for their support of this project. At Brooklyn, we are grateful to Gwen Arriaga, senior manager of touring exhibitions, who organized this institutional collaboration and exhibition tour; Melinda Zoephel, exhibition designer; Paloma Obregón, project registrar; Ellen Nigro, assistant paintings conservator; Catherine Morris, senior curator of the Elizabeth A. Sackler Center for Feminist Art, and Catherine Futter, director of curatorial affairs; Dolores Farrell, director of exhibition planning, for strategizing the project; and Carla Forbes for providing support. We are thankful for the contributions of Adam O'Reilly, director of graphic design; Danielle Reydon, director of institutional giving; danilo machado, public programs producer; Kathryn Johnson, senior development officer, individual giving; Lindsay C. Harris, director of education; Sarah DeSantis, director of digital collections and services; Sharon Matt Atkins, deputy director for art; Sonjie Solomon, assistant exhibition designer; Bon Hae Koo, graphic designer; and interns Sophia Abrams, D'Mia Britton, Zmira Stouber, and Alicia Vadillo. We greatly appreciate the labor of everyone who helped with the preparations, painting, electrical, and carpentry work that constructed the exhibition, as well as my colleagues and all those who guide our audiences to art.

At Getty, we thank Jim Ganz, Reena Antonishak, Cynthia Aquino, Miriam Katz, Sharyne Nagy, and Antares Wells in the Department of Photographs; associate conservator Ronel Namde; senior mountmakers David McDaniel, Jr., and Ron Stroud; Michael Mitchell and the Getty Museum preparations team for their work planning for and installing the exhibition; associate conservator Madeline Corona and senior mountmaker BJ Farrar for the careful review of the materials in the installation; Carolyn Marsden-Smith, Susan McGinty, Richard Rand, and Kanoko Sasao for their support and oversight of the project; Jes Harden and the exhibition design team; Tuyet Bach, Sahar Tchaitchian, and their colleagues in Interpretive Content; Sarah Cooper, Laurel Kishi, and Greg Sandoval in Public Programs; and the interlibrary loan coordinators at the Getty Research Institute. Special thanks are due to the members of Getty Publications whose rigor and efficiency shaped this publication: Kara Kirk, publisher; Nola Butler, editor in chief; Karen Levine, former editor in chief; Clare Davis, design and production manager; Leslie Rollins, rights manager; Nancy Rivera, rights assistant; and Michelle Woo Deemer, senior production coordinator. We thank the freelancers who provided careful editorial work: Lindsey Westbrook, copy editor; Deanna Lee, proofreader; and Do Mi Stauber, indexer.

Profuse thanks are due to Wendi Norris at Gallery Wendi Norris and Simon Tatum of the Campos-Pons studio, who greatly amplified the archive of Campos-Pons's work at this crucial moment, and to the closest supporters of her work—Giampaolo Abbondio, Barbara Thumm, Bernice Steinbaum—as well as Neil Leonard, Anais Daily, and Vivien Green Fryd.

This beautiful book emerged from a period of personal disruption, amid the churning state of the world around us. Mazie wishes to thank John and Joseph Carr, Marjorie Cohn, Stacey McCarroll Cutshaw, Barbara Hitchcock, Deborah Martin Kao, and Miriam Stewart. I especially wish to thank Ryan and Lucía, my dear friends for their tremendous support (particularly Debbie and Mitchell), and my parents, José and Sara, for their encouragement, example, and love—mil gracias.

Carmen Hermo
Associate Curator, Elizabeth A. Sackler Center for Feminist Art
Brooklyn Museum

In gratitude

to the Ancestors, the Seven Powers, Estervina and Sotero, my departed ones,

to my beloved son Arcadio,

to the Campos-Pons family,

to the Leonard, Macomber, Sheats, and Lloyd families,

the Steinbaum, Ladd, Rappaport, Hess, Pérez, and McCormack families,

to my mentors from Nelson Sanchez, Escuela Provincial de Arte, Escuela Nacional de Arte, and Instituto Superior de Arte,

from the Massachusetts College of Art and Design, from Harvard,

to my collectors, my gallerists,

colleagues at the School of the Museum of Fine Arts at Tufts and Vanderbilt,

to the tribe of peers, makers, thinkers, discontented trailblazers, and dreamers who inspire me,

to past and present curators, writers on my work, jurors who gave me awards and residencies, museum directors who championed my work,

to my students and studio assistants,

to all good energies and entities of the universe,

to the red soil of La Vega, I owe my work.

María Magdalena Campos-Pons

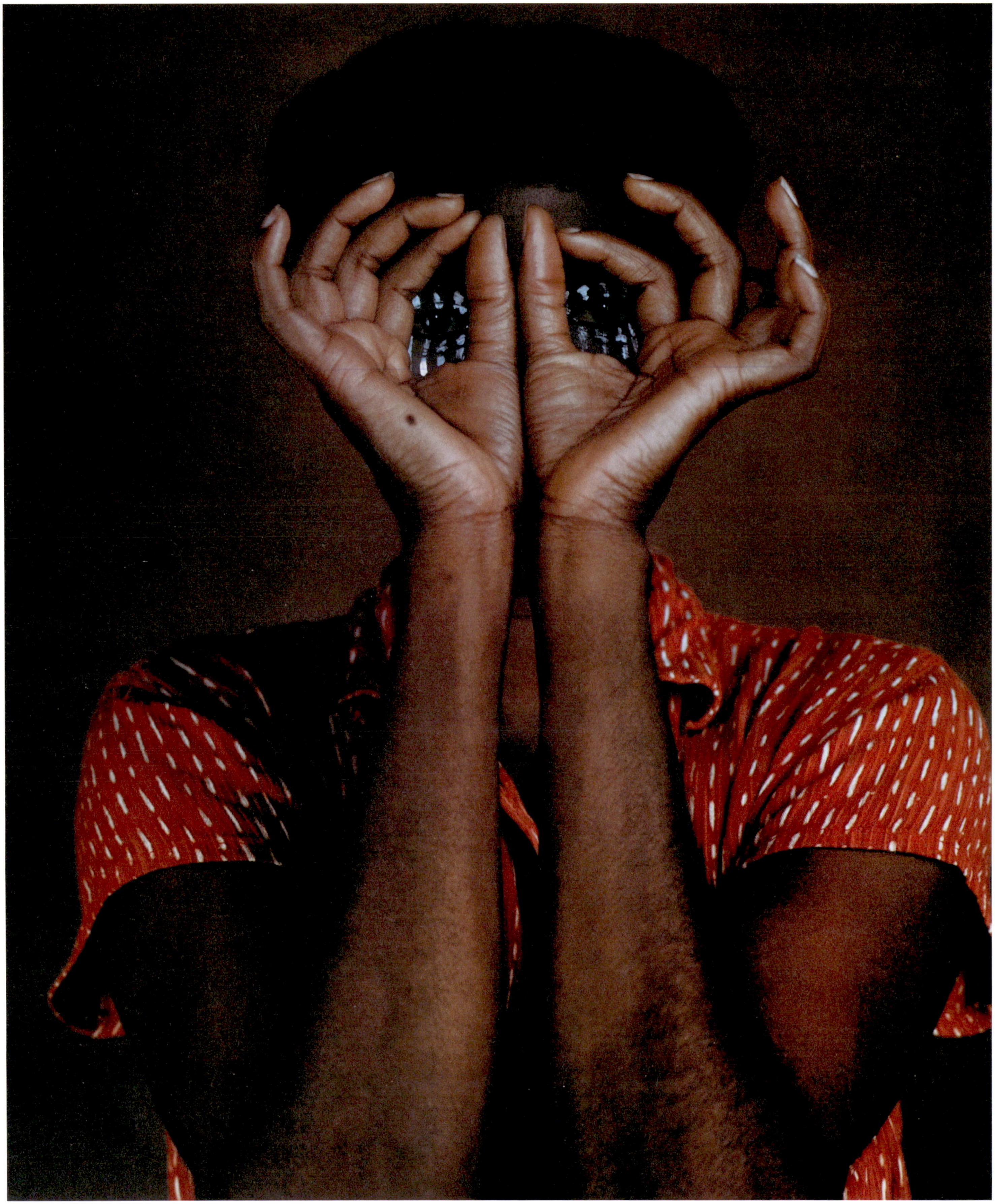

Nesting II (detail, plate 24), 2000

PREFACE: THE CALLING

Carmen Hermo
Mazie M. Harris
Jenée-Daria Strand

This book and the traveling exhibition it accompanies offer an overview of the four-decade-long calling of artist María Magdalena Campos-Pons. Campos-Pons was born in Matanzas, Cuba, in 1959, the year Fidel Castro came to power, and nurtured in a family and community that practices Yoruba-derived Santería religion. Her personal story intertwines with transnational histories of enslavement, indentured labor, domestic labor, and advocacy for bodily autonomy. Campos-Pons moved to the United States in 1991 and was unable to return to Cuba for many years due to the tensions between the two nations. Her artwork has often visualized the difficulties of being in multiple places at once: working and living in one geography while being emotionally and psychologically tethered to another, striving all the while for connection across distance.

Campos-Pons's installations, performances, photographic works, paintings, and videos have been included in exhibitions worldwide, bringing under-sung stories, shared through an incredible range of media, to the attention of many audiences. This spans the Sharjah Biennial (2023), documenta 14 (2017), the Venice Biennale (2013, 2001), the Havana Biennial (2012, 1991, 1989), the Guangzhou Triennial (2008), her traveling mid-career survey *Everything Is Separated by Water* (2007), the Dak'Art Biennial in Dakar (2004), and numerous university and college museum presentations—that last a context that resonates with her work as a professor and mentor to many artists, including those she has featured in projects she has organized for the Havana Biennial in Matanzas (2019) and the Tennessee Triennial (2023). Resources on Campos-Pons's career and the issues with which she engages can be found at the end of this book, and the authors of this volume gratefully acknowledge the foundational work of this scholarship.

While preparing this volume, the editor and authors sustained conversations not only about Campos-Pons's stunning, layered artworks but also about the art world and its impulse to categorize cultures and identities, flattening or glossing or—in the most generous sense—uniting nuanced, specific people, cultures, and geographies. Campos-Pons's work has always resisted categories, insisting instead on "the space in between," a confluence of identities, and what the artist calls "intangible material" that overlaps experiences. Artist, teacher, daughter, mother, Afro-Cuban, Caribbean, Latina, Black, American, feminist, woman—these are just some of the currents, realities, allusions, and experiences that run through her work. Magda shared with us how she grounds herself: "I am from many places. I live with that duality and multiplicity in my mind, and in my soul, and in my body. My roots are a bunch of dispersed fragments in the planet, in the universe, in this incredible miasma that is the world." She asks us to push past approaches to naming and classifying identity rooted in colonialism: "There is something yet to be defined, or understood, to have the complete language to grasp it."

Just as the artist's work is a visual grasping toward understanding, the essays in this book do not dwell on specific identity categories or language but instead surface the spaces, symbols, heritages, histories, and communities that Campos-Pons has engaged in her life and her travels as an artist, educator, and activist. The artist and cultural theorist Amalia Mesa-Bains opens the book with a heartfelt rumination that situates the generational legacies, shifting cultural contexts, and re-centering work of Campos-Pons's oeuvre to date. The exhibition's curatorial team each contribute essays: Carmen Hermo on the theme of replenishing cycles of tears and growth that circulate throughout the artist's work, Mazie M. Harris on her photographic experimentation combining conceptualism and cross-media play, and Jenée-Daria Strand on the spiritual and sensorial aspects of her performances and persona. They are joined by art historian and curator Phillip Townsend, who tracks the connections between Campos-Pons's video work and oral history traditions, and Selene Wendt, a curator, writer, and close collaborator of the artist across varied projects, who contextualizes Campos-Pons's commitment to not only mark but also advance social change.

Everyone involved in this publication has been moved and awed by Campos-Pons's creativity and compelled by her vision. Ultimately, the language we set down here cannot contain her work or her energy, and thus we hope that these writings inspire more people to seek out the source: her artworks, talks, and ideas.

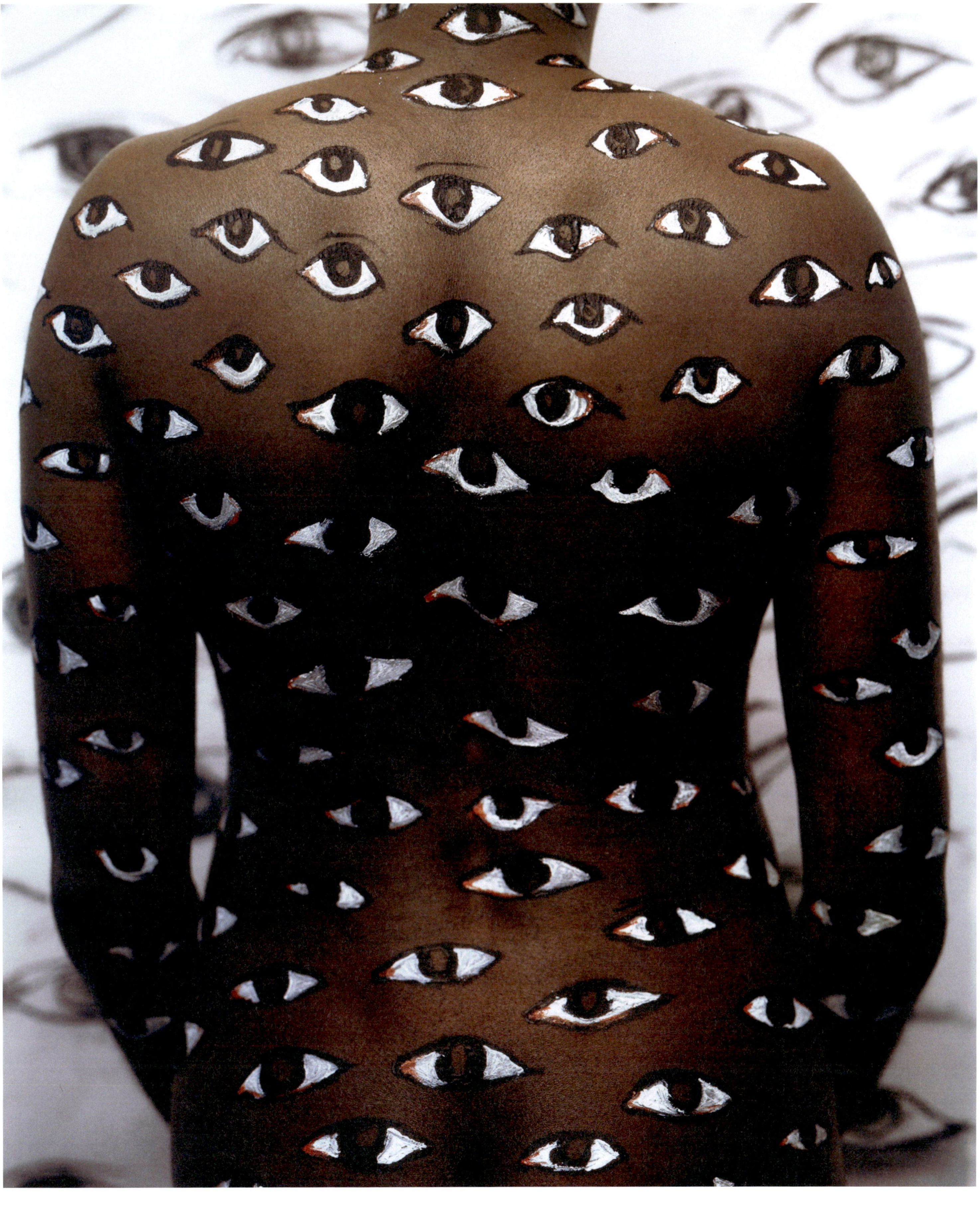

The Right Protection (detail, plate 22), 1999

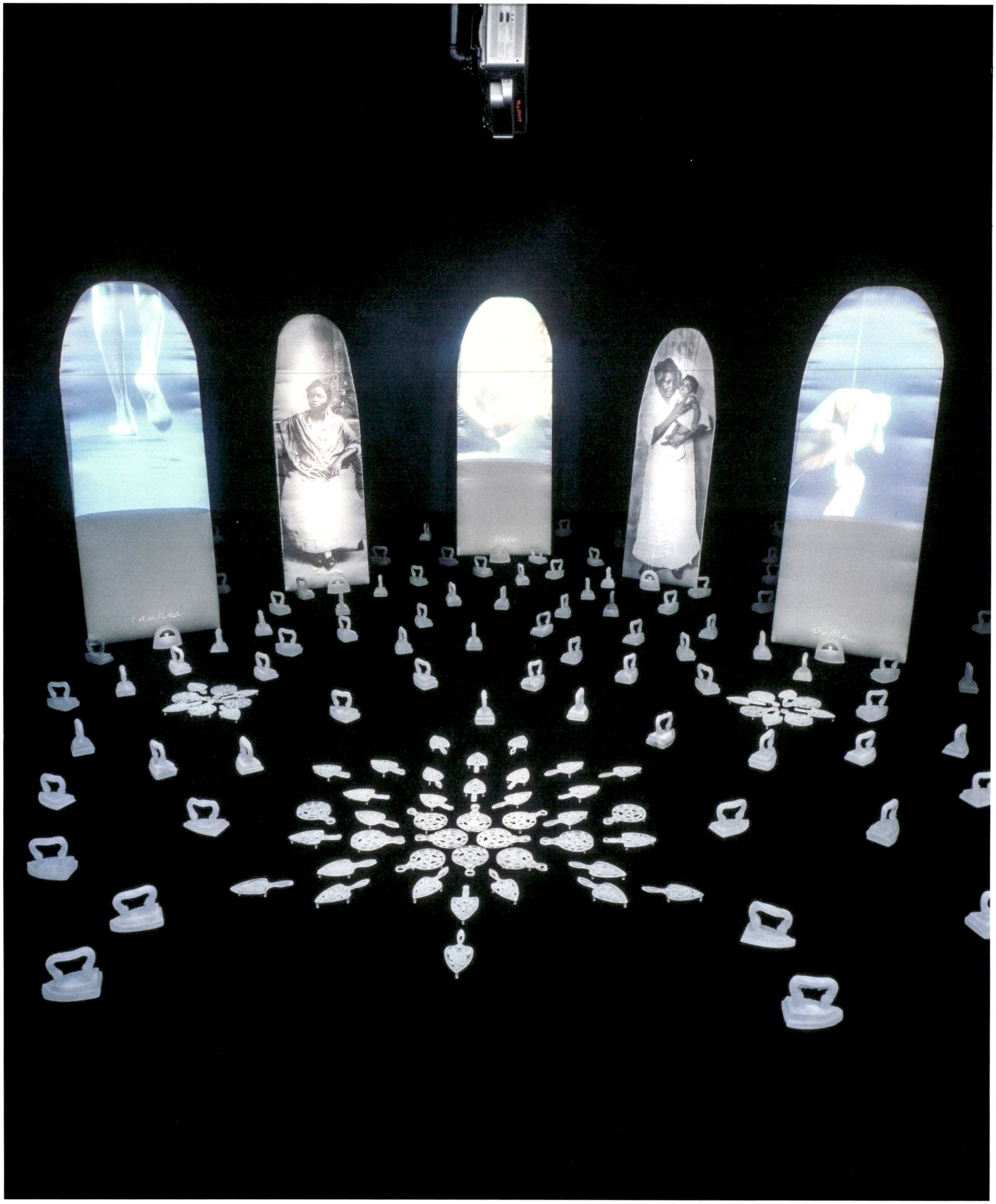

Spoken Softly with Mama (detail, plate 20), 1998

INTRODUCTION: LA ÚNICA

Amalia Mesa-Bains

María Magdalena Campos-Pons has established a unique multidisciplinary artistic practice that embodies ancestral spiritual traditions in installation, photography, painting, performance, and film. She is an African-descended Cuban woman capturing a complex odyssey that integrates the realities of race, gender, history, politics, and memory. Her interior journey is one of the psyche and the soul, and her physical journey has taken her across nations and landscapes, through rupture and displacement.

From her earliest days in Cuba, Campos-Pons manifested a deep artistic talent that was recognized by family and institutions. Her earliest works claimed the female body as a territory of debate, forefronting questions of control, freedom, and sexuality. Her work continued to express issues of the body as a site of feminism and racialized histories in Cuba during a time when the nation was beginning to lay claim to its own memory of the transatlantic slave trade, and Campos-Pons was drawing from her experience as the great-granddaughter of an enslaved man. As the artist moves through this collective memory, she enacts the process of embodiment that marks her work.

Campos-Pons's artistic career came about very soon after the feminist language of intersectionality was first enunciated by Black feminist scholars and thinkers, long before this idea entered the mainstream conversation. The artist made an awareness of the inseparability of race, gender, and sexuality central in her representations of the women in her family, including her grandmother, mother, and sisters, with whom she is particularly close. She introduced the role of spiritual practice and the traditions of her ancestors through imagery focused on the familial histories of Black Cubans. Individual and collective histories emerged from memories of her family home at La Vega in Matanzas, where they resided in the former barracks that held her great-grandfather on the sugar plantation. The poignant and powerful knowledge of her dwelling's violent history forever changed her sense of self and initiated many works focused on the slave trade and the economy of goods such as sugar and rum.

DOMESTICANA

> [*Domesticana* work] takes on a deeper meaning of domestic tension, as the signs of making do are both affirmation of the domestic life and resistance to the subjugation of the women in the domestic sphere. The domestic tension signifies the contradiction between the supportive aspects of the feminine and the struggle to redefine restrictive roles. Cherished moments stand side by side with examinations of self, culture and history in visions of a domestic chamber that is both paradise and prison.
>
> —Amalia Mesa-Bains, "'Domesticana': The Sensibility of Chicana Rasquachismo"[1]

Once Campos-Pons married, had a child, and began her journey to permanent residence in Boston, she learned that what is left behind is worth the new encounter. Yet she also experienced a sense of self-exile, as she saw issues differently once outside Cuba. The embargo and restrictions on travel to Cuba profoundly separated Campos-Pons from her family, and as a new mother she began a reexamination of her relationships with the women who had been closest to her. She began relating her personal history with women's work—the domestic labor that is done collectively and establishes a sense of connectedness in the home—and rituals of laundering, ironing, and folding clothes became a source of ceremony. Imagery of sheets folded and embroidered with the multiple languages she speaks brought a powerful domestic tension and a more reflective feminism to her oeuvre. Her body became the ground of a deeper collective memory and a more complex performative life, beyond gender and sexuality, at the site of an economy of labor tied to her experiences and feminism.

CUERPO Y CORPUS

Newly influenced by artists she was encountering, such as Ana Mendieta, Lorna Simpson, and Carrie Mae Weems, Campos-Pons also pushed forward her own sense of sensitively representing the Black body. She realized that, even in Boston, she was operating from the positionality of an African heritage lived in contemporary Cuba, which set her work apart from that of African Americans rooted in the racial capitalism of the United States. Drawing on ceremonial and spiritual traditions related to her Black diasporic identity—reaching out through and beyond the context of the Caribbean and United States to connect to Yoruba-derived traditions in Brazil, Haiti, and other places of syncretism—Campos-Pons honored and innovated, through allusions to Santería, artworks inspired by domestic altars as well as the healing powers of her father's Yoruba herbalism practice.[2] In much of her work, the body is the land and the soil, the corpus of culture, sometimes wounded or fragmented. The body carries the footprints of the one who left, the migrant.

In her performances and films, the power of the voice of silence, learned from her father—"He could stay for two hours without saying a word and still communicate[;] words were very important, you heard them for only a moment and the rest was silence"—balances fragility and vulnerability with expressive urgency.[3] Video and performance create a narrative of ambivalence where identities can be painful, restrictive, even dangerous. In the work, Africa is in her home in Cuba and has been lived through mother to daughter, from woman to woman, in the healing touch.

Campos-Pons's transculturation is evident in the multiple languages that express a memory of exile, held in the inner voices of her family. For instance, in *Alchemy of the Soul, Elixir for the Spirits* (2015, plate 66), the artist addresses the Middle Passage as a source of tobacco, sugar, and rum. In this undertaking, she not only alchemically mixes the elements of her ancestral home but heals the violence from the transatlantic and global trade, which created an economy of racialized suffering. Certainly during and even after Spain banned the slave trade, it built the tobacco, sugar, and rum industries on the backs of people whose lives were limited under plantation life and labor, filled as it was with violence and punitive treatment.[4]

Campos-Pons uses memory, both individual and collective, to bring about historical recognition and spiritual cleansing. For her, memory is never an exact replica of an original experience but rather a creative and mediated expression. Water acts as memory and a journey in her visual language, implying the incomplete, discontinuous, and often ambivalent nature of memory, its porous and permeable nature used by Campos-Pons as a bridge over time and distance, the past and the present, the painful and the hopeful. The possibilities of this interstice reflect the long journey of an artist on the edge of new discoveries of form and meaning.

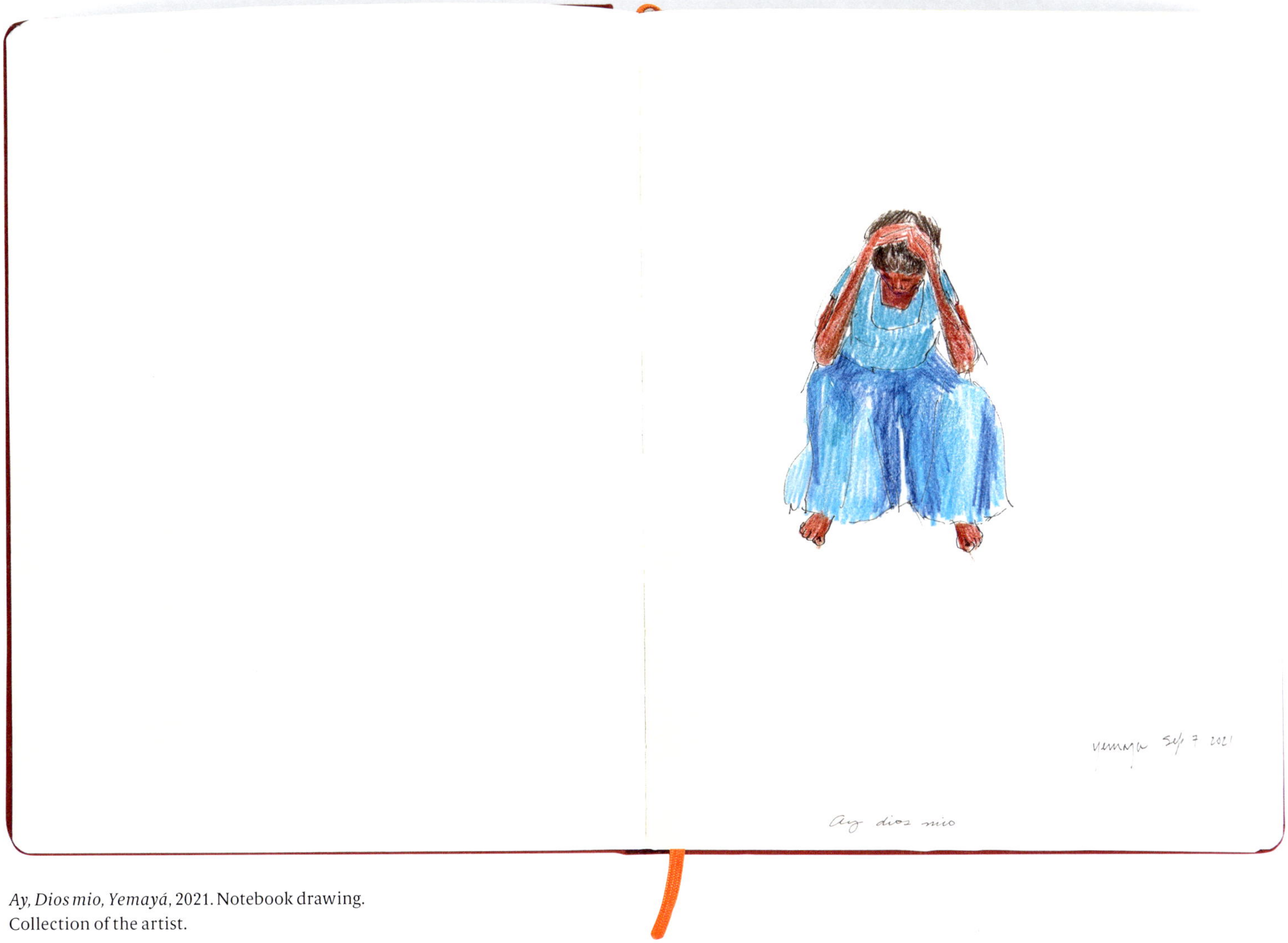

Ay, Dios mio, Yemayá, 2021. Notebook drawing.
Collection of the artist.

NOTES

1—Amalia Mesa-Bains, "'Domesticana': The Sensibility of Chicana Rasquachismo," in *Chicana Feminisms: A Critical Reader*, ed. Gabriela F. Arredondo et. al (Durham, NC: Duke University Press, 2003), 7.

2—Santería is a fusion of Catholic practices and West African spirituality. Its roots can be traced to the Lucumí religion, which was practiced by the Yoruba tribes of modern-day Benin and Nigeria. When people from West Africa were enslaved and forcibly transported to Cuba in the seventeenth century, they brought their religious traditions with them. As a belief system that emphasizes the linkages between spirituality and the body, Santería utilizes ritual cleansing of the body in order to maintain spiritual and physical well-being.

3—Lynne Bell, "History of People Who Were Not Heroes: A Conversation with María Magdalena Campos-Pons," *Third Text* 12, no. 43 (Summer 1998): 38.

4—Adriana Zavala, "Blackness Distilled, Sugar and Rum: María Magdalena Campos-Pons's Alchemy of the Soul, Elixir for the Spirits," *Latin American and Latinx Visual Culture* 1, no. 2 (2019): 11.

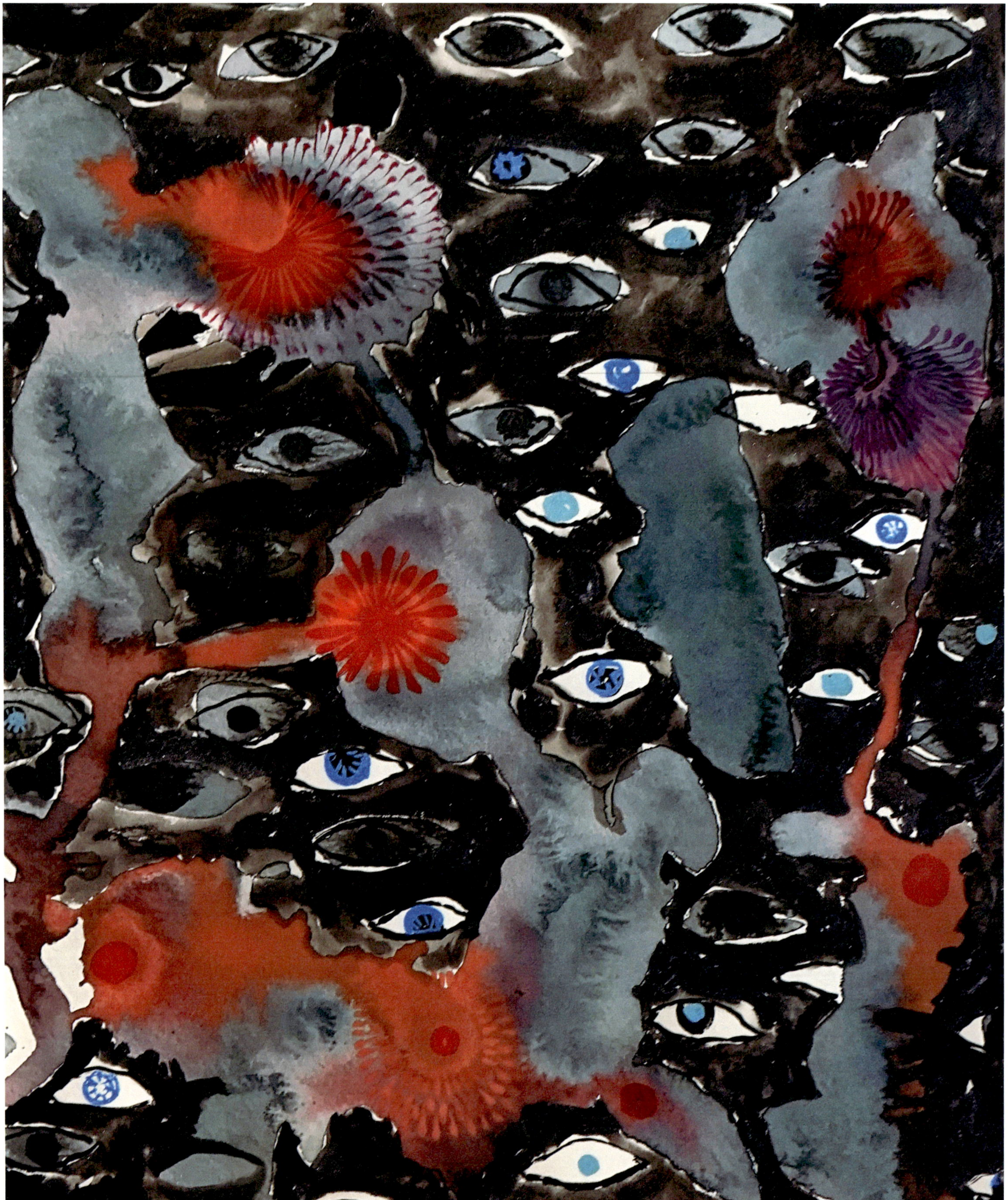

Miasma #7 (detail, plate 85), 2020

MARÍA MAGDALENA CAMPOS-PONS: BEHOLD

Carmen Hermo

> We are so privileged that we have been given tears, that we have been given taste, that we have been given eyes, that we have been given senses, the brain, and the machine that is the heart and this liver for alchemy. Our bodies themselves are a maker of alchemy. So, my unfolding desire is to find agency and to put all those things together and to keep working.
>
> —María Magdalena Campos-Pons[1]

An ebb and flow, interlocking circularities, one book with many chapters—in the work of María Magdalena Campos-Pons, themes, stories, and symbols blossom in recurring, recombinant ways. The artist describes her career, which now spans nearly four decades, as originating from an "undisciplined" approach to the traditional boundaries of media and performance. Her oeuvre presents a system of cyclical growth, where the watery wetness of the body germinates—through visual and physical acts of beholding, irrigated by tears—a flowering of truth.

In *Soy Una Fuente (I Am a Fountain)* (1990, plate 1), Campos-Pons presents bodily functions of flow and output: painted and shaped forms depict breasts spurting milk, legs opening to pass excrement and menstrual blood, an eye dripping a large teardrop, spiral-like forms emerging from a womb and heart-like lips. The declarative title marks all these secretions as self, as fountain—women's bodies in states of production and excess, the body as a water- and life-giving system. Campos-Pons developed these votive-like forms from the so-called Codex Mendoza, thought to have been painted around 1541 by Indigenous artist Francisco Gualpuyogualcal and commissioned by Spanish colonists to picture and describe the Aztec Empire's history and Spain's violent economic conquest begun two decades earlier. Adapting symbols from this hybrid source, Campos-Pons inscribes her experiences and bodily reality onto colonial stories and asserts the potential of her secretions to produce life and legacies. As depicted and evoked in her work from here forward, Campos-Pons has been "reclaiming women not just as body, but as intellectual entity and generator of knowledge," indicated by the spiral of potential emerging from the lips as well as by the fruit of tears, birth, and life.[2] While much of her work engages her body, it is always attuned to the spiritual, the internal; earlier works such as *Cinturón de Castidad (Chastity Belt)* (1984–85, fig. 1), which appeared in her 1985 thesis show, and *Anticonceptivo (Contraceptive)* (1987, fig. 2) reject patriarchal prohibition of women's pleasure and emphasize bodily autonomy, respectively.

The image of an open eye shedding a teardrop would return, repeating ten times in an array of Polaroid photographs, in *Voyeurs and Beholders of…* (2008/2015, plate 46), in which Campos-Pons suspended mobiles of hair, paper, and paint corresponding to iris colors in front of dripping, sepia-painted backdrops filled with more open eyes. The title's ellipsis leaves much to the imagination. What inspires these tears? Are they of mourning, or of joy? Campos-Pons's body of work shows us the ache of sublimated violence, the resilience of memory, the bittersweet beauty inherent in the fortitude of survival, continuation, and growth. The title also proposes two ways of seeing, of being: as a voyeur whose gaze is passive or even exploitative, and/or as a beholder, a word that contains *hold* and denotes associations of touch, support, and dignity. Campos-Pons works with her hands, her eyes (and the photographic eye of the camera), and her body, all united in the unseen core of the spirit. The stories, experiences, and communities that she upholds and beholds are myriad, encompassing her family and autobiography, which intertwine with the legacies of enslavement and ongoing extractivism from Afro-descendent people, especially women and migrants, with an early focus on Cuban and Caribbean histories that eventually expanded out to reflections of Boston, Padua, and Nashville in a transnational conversation.[3] For Campos-Pons, the work of making art in seemingly endless times of pain is tactile and body-based in both subject and gesture and calls for viewers to bear witness to and behold the truth.

Campos-Pons's family legacy is the foundation of her life experience and a conduit to the intersecting histories she honors in her work. In 1959, the same year that the Cuban Revolution crystallized into Fidel Castro's one-party Communist and nationalist system, Campos-Pons was born in Matanzas to Sotero Arcadio Campos-Suri and Estervina Pons-Leon. As "Campos" derives from her father's mother's name and "Pons" from her mother's, her name carries forward a matriarchal rupture to colonist-imposed patriarchal naming traditions. It also upholds her special connection with her paternal grandmother, an initiated Santería priestess who died sixteen days after her granddaughter's birth, but not before she named Yemayá and Oshun as Campos-Pons's guardian orisha deities.[4]

Santería, also known as Regla de Ocha or Lucumí in Cuba, is a religion derived from West African Yoruba beliefs and pantheons and syncretized, for survival during the religious and cultural oppression of colonialism, to correspond to Catholic saints. While this essay cannot fully explore Santería—which itself is only one of the many Afro-Cuban religions[5]—the energies, colors, and stories of individual orishas flow through Campos-Pons's visual references. Her Nigerian ancestors and their spiritual impression on her life show a persistence despite colonists' destruction of families, barring of the enslaved from public life, and bans on practicing Santería that persisted following the post-Revolution prohibition of religion, only lifted in 1992. Of paramount importance to the artist is Santería's emphasis on embodied knowledge in practices like ritual processions, herbalism, songs, and chants, and in the foundational Yoruba belief that existence spans two realms: the physical and tangible, and the spiritual. The symbolic colors associated with the orishas originate the color theory behind Campos-Pons's palette, directing color relationships as well as composition. In *The Calling* (2003, plate 29), Campos-Pons wears the traditional white of Santería and bends back, extending white flowers like an offering, her body flecked in cascarilla (a powder made from crushed eggshells, used in some cultures for protection against negative energy in a white-hued homage to Obatalá, the creator of earth and humanity). She has made clear she never received "the calling" to be a Santería priestess; instead, her calling is to the arts and creativity, which are revered in her artworks, in her work as a teacher, and in her organizing of artists and ideas as an activist.[6] The cascarilla, symbolizing purity and spiritual power in Santería, often appears in works that "call" back to ancestors.

In *Finding Balance* (2015, plate 65), her largest photography-based work to date, symmetry and asymmetry balance the eye across twenty-eight photographs of weights, screens, and birdcages. At center, Campos-Pons is resplendent in cascarilla and an antique Chinese theatrical robe—a reference to her Cantonese ancestors, who were coerced to Cuba as indentured laborers. Following the Haitian Revolution (1791–1805), Europe imposed a punitive embargo on the newly independent nation's sugar, and Cuba advanced in the cultivation and trade of its main export due, owing to its enslaved African labor force. By

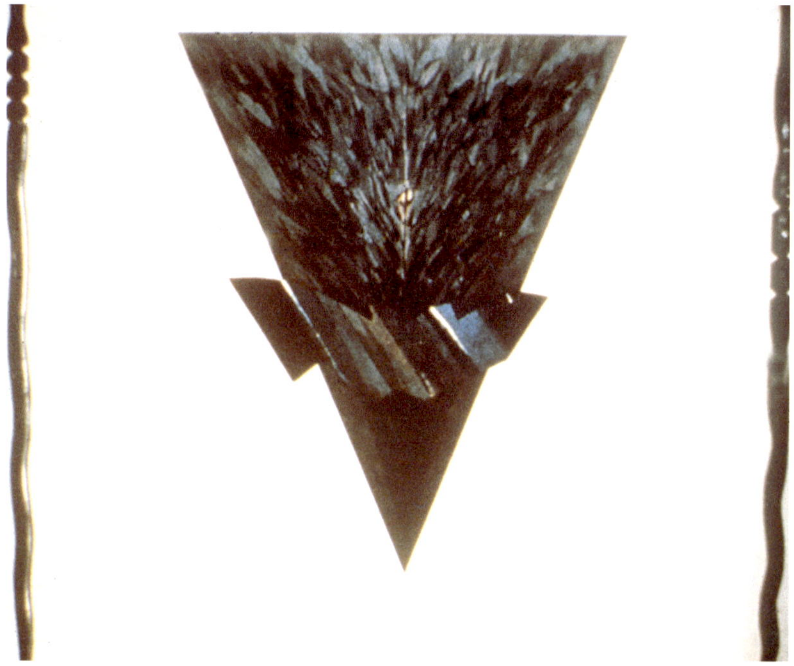

Fig. 1 María Magdalena Campos-Pons, *Cinturón de Castidad (Chastity Belt)*, 1984–85. Acrylic and oil on canvas and wood, approx. 200.7 x 299.7 cm (79 x 118 in.). Havana, Center for the Development of the Visual Arts

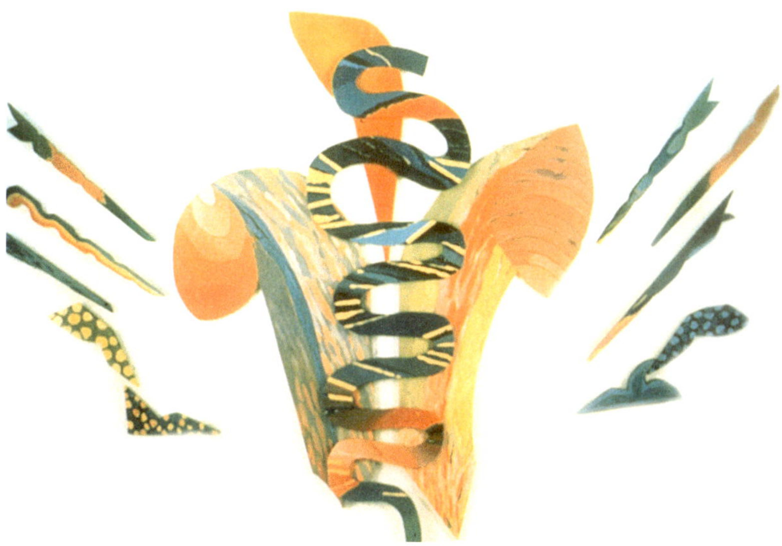

Fig. 2 María Magdalena Campos-Pons, *Anticonceptivo (Contraceptive)*, 1987. Acrylic on canvas and wood, approx. 398.8 x 500.4 cm (157 x 197 in.). Havana, National Cuban Foundation

the 1840s, when Chinese indentured laborers amplified the economy of coercion and exploitation, Cuba was the world's primary producer of sugar.[7] Matanzas, Campos-Pons's early home, gathers both Cuba's largest populations of descendants of enslaved Africans[8] and of Chinese people who comprised the entrapped "coolie" labor force.[9] Five generations after these ancestral lineages connected, Campos-Pons sits in majestic contemplation of the ongoing work of "finding" equilibrium in the multiplicities of one's self and heritage.

In the double self-portrait *De Las Dos Aguas (Of the Two Waters)* (2007, plate 43), twelve individual Polaroid panels assemble an image of female power in the Santería pantheon and practice. At left, Campos-Pons in blue evokes Yemayá, the mother of all orishas and all people, the goddess of the ocean who represents fertility; at right, in yellow, she represents Oshun, the orisha of rivers, associated with love, beauty, and destiny. These sisters are her protectors, and here her body stands in for these goddesses of water to symbolize the divine protection granted to people migrating by force, choice, or lack of choice, as represented by the wooden boat held aloft at center. Paper bags tied shut and marked with a stamp reading "this is not art" dangle from braids and twists of hair: what swirls beneath the boat, what protectors carry, is beyond the imagination, beyond the capacity of art to depict.

Campos-Pons catalyzed her art making as a way to visually enunciate the unspeakable, particularly in her large-scale installations centering personal and transnational histories of enslavement. This first appeared in *TRA* (1991, plate 5), in the fourth edition of the Havana Biennial under the theme "The Challenge to Colonialism," in a moment when many Western institutions were "celebrating" the five hundredth anniversary of Christopher Columbus's 1492 landing. The biennial positioned itself (and, by extension, Cuba) as an alternative, re-centering voice to neocolonial culture-washing, and Campos-Pons brought her community forward—their images, their history, her history—in a multipart installation visualizing and beholding those usually left out of the story of Cuban culture. Sixty everyday black-and-white portraits of three generations of Afro-Cubans from Matanzas are paralleled in three planks carved with what Cheryl Finley described as the "slave ship icon," depicting the intentionally cruel organization of kidnapped African people that represents for many "the elements of a complex system, the business of the slave trade, in abstract form," yet in the hands of Campos-Pons becomes "a rich source for making claims for the survival and transformation of Yoruba religious beliefs in Cuba and North America . . . convey[ing] a sense of spiritual and familial will, transformation, and renewal."[10] By combining the everyday beauty of Matanzas's present-day community and text describing the *travesía* (crossing), *trata* (trade), and *tragedia* (tragedy) as a global history, Campos-Pons pictures "the Crossing" as theorized by M. Jacqui Alexander as a connection through the Middle Passage across generations, places, and powers where "not only humans made the Crossing . . . Grief traveled as well." It is a "confrontation with history," effectively a counter-monument to the suppression of these stories.[11]

Much has been written on the artist's monumental, sensorial installations that bring forward multivalent auto- and community-biographies.[12] As *TRA* presented the circularity of history and the proximity of "then" and "now," *The Seven Powers Come by the Sea* (1992, plate 6), an installation adapted into *The Seven Powers* (1994, plate 9), recontextualizes *TRA*'s portraits of Matanzas, now divinely escorted by painted orishas. Oggún, Oshun, Yemayá, Obatalá, Changó, Ochosi, and Oyá stood first as silhouettes among slave ship icons in the 1992 work, then in 1994 as figures embedded in soil gathered in Cuba and Boston, arranged as if the work is one large altar, with letters spelling out in Spanish and English, "Prohibido Olvidar / Let Us Never Forget." Among these portraits is a photograph of Gabriel, the artist's great-grandfather, a Yoruba man kidnapped from West Africa and enslaved in Matanzas's sugar industry in the final waves of forced migration before Cuba stopped participating in the slave trade in 1867. Slavery as an institution was not abolished there until 1886. Cuba was one of the last countries to do so due to the country's reliance on sugar; its economy combined coerced and indentured labor with the social disenfranchisement of Chinese and Afro-descendent people.

Speaking with her family while developing *A Town Portrait* (1993, plate 8), the first installation in the *History of a People Who Were Not Heroes* trilogy, Campos-Pons learned a horrible truth: after Castro expropriated private property and her family lost their home in Colón and resettled in La Vega, they moved into apartments created inside former barracks that had housed enslaved people at the Tirso Mesa y Hernandez sugar factory—the very structure where her father's grandfather Gabriel had been confined. "I cannot describe what I felt when I finally found this out," she reflected in 1998.[13] As words failed her, Campos-Pons processed this architectural and generational haunting by reproducing in sculpture and videos the sites and markers of La Vega that her family associated with home—a doorway, a wall, a fountain, and the tower of the sugar distillery—giving permanence to their memories and retellings relayed from Cuba to Boston through letters and phone calls. Campos-Pons's installations around this time incorporated sound and video in collaboration with the musician and sound artist Neil Leonard,[14] commanding attention in multiple modalities.

Campos-Pons summarized her trilogy, the "unofficial history of her hometown,"[15] as a crux of personal and global narratives: "I focus on my own experience. . . . It gives me some authority *then* to sketch the larger portrait. In *History of a People Who Were Not Heroes*, I focus on my family but it's also a monument to the history of every single Black family in Cuba."[16] Beginning with architecture and institutions built for enslavement that shape and hold contemporary life, the installations focus on the experiences of women and children. *Spoken Softly with Mama* (1998, plate 20), the trilogy's second part, takes the form of a massive altar, adapting Santería's sensorial and performative rituals of Santería to honor women who continue to pray in this way. It also amplifies the hushed and invisibilized experience of Afro-Cuban women working as domestic laborers. The reality that the women in her family—except Campos-Pons, the only one who left Cuba—continued to be relegated to domestic labor generations after enslavement impacted the forms of the artwork: seven ironing boards parallel slave ship icons, and cast-glass irons are arranged like a flotilla. This work ascribes a sacred beauty to Afro-descendent women in their survival and mourns the time and creative potential lost laboring for others, rerouted to domestic arts. Unable to return to Cuba at this time, Campos-Pons took a layered, intensive approach to reach the women in her life when proximity was impossible, entangling the twentieth-century pain of U.S.-Cuban relations, as the U.S. embargo on travel and trade impacted Cuba's citizens horribly, curtailing economic growth and blocking them from receiving food and medical equipment. In one video in the installation, the artist clicks her heels together three times, wishing for Dorothy-like magical transport back home, yet she is thwarted by distance, the bureaucracy of immigration, and exile.[17]

Meanwhile the Girls Were Playing (1999–2000, plate 21), the final work in the trilogy, reflects on the unknowing innocence of childhood through abstraction and movement. The colors evoke the yellow, green, and blue dresses Campos-Pons's mother made for her and her two sisters, Amparo and Marta, in patterns splayed in circles with embroidery details rendered in glass. Videos allude to spinning games, songs, and childhood memories of pleasure, play, and candy. The title gives a foreboding sense of the ever-present reality of growing up in a slave barrack and the precarious lives of Afro-Cuban women amid misogynoir and colorism, since cherished candy is effectively a symbol of enslavement; after all, the global demand for sugar drove the inhumanities of the slave trade, chattel slavery, and indenture in the Caribbean.

Sugar/Bittersweet (2010, plate 51), a work from a decade later, focuses more closely on sugar production, using two dozen ready-made African spears to penetrate circles of real sugar, simulating the "brutality of the math of the sugar fields."[18] Here, violence underpins sweetness, underscored by the selection of three types of sugar that point to the persistence of anti-Blackness and colorism today, spanning from dark brown natural molasses; to the flaxen in-between color of turbinado sugar; to refined sugar, or *cristal*, where refinement means whiteness. They all taste more or less the same, but they demand increasing labor and risk, and the tall cane plant therefore becomes "a weapon against certain bodies."[19] Spanish colonists codified colorism into social class, effectively curtailing the lives and possibilities for people with rich melanin for generations after their enslavement, with a particular impact on the divisions and debates around *latinidad*'s relationship to whiteness and historic ties to social pigmentocracy. In a 2006 performance in Milan titled *Habilitation, Mojitos, and Crocodile's Tears* (plate 42), Campos-Pons carried a tray of fresh rum-and-sugar mojitos, urging viewers to "drink the mojito, and as you do, sip in the pain of unseen tears that I/we have dropped into it . . . . Today you are a witness to the future," before smashing the drinks onto the old stones of the courtyard, rejecting the invisibility of the trauma of the sugar and rum industries.[20]

In *Matanzas Sound Map* (2017, plate 71), a sprawling ten-channel sound composition of field recordings made in the province, the voices of the Cuban rumba ensemble Los Muñequitos de Matanzas, along with Neil Leonard's alto saxophone, are timed with pauses of full breaths, encouraging the viewer to slow down and absorb the sight and sound. Collected dried flora in a state of beautiful decay, displayed among found wrought-iron screens and wooden stools, contrast with the smooth surfaces of monumental blown and cast glass unguentarium, or tear-catching bottles, whose forms derive from ancient Roman and Greek glass salve jars. Reflecting on the disenfranchisement of Matanzas—a thriving port during enslavement—as well as current-day events such as the Mediterranean refugee crisis that drove headlines in 2017, Campos-Pons mourns in this work that "there is not capacity enough to collect all of the tears," as evoked in the perilously, delicately elongated necks of the vessels.[21]

What can we make of all this pain, all these tears? For Campos-Pons, the water of the body connects to the water of the Earth, keeping us all sustained and living, and brings us together even as it can drive us apart. *Baño Sagrado (Rite of Initiation, Sacred Bath)* (1991, plate 4) is an early collaboration with Leonard in which Campos-Pons interprets Yoruba-derived rituals of cleansing and explores the energies of Yemayá and Oshun in her body and life, drawing on African proverbs that seem to summarize the challenges of exile, immigration, and interracial love. "I came to the water to find rest," a woman's voice intones, after the artist uses herbs and plants to cleanse her own feet, as she once did for her father, a practicing herbalist.[22] She rests in a bathtub, far away from Cuba, but a stitched video brings tropical fish to swim at her feet. In another scene, water cupped in her hand acts as a screen showing shimmering waters in Baracoa, where three ships of armed Spanish settlers first landed in Cuba in 1492, beginning their genocide of Indigenous people and campaign of colonial violence. A mound of dirt between her breasts seems to sprout plant life, wet and running into her belly button, suggesting that no matter where the body goes, or cannot go, the water memory remains.

In the only singular photograph (plate 11) from Campos-Pons's When I Am Not Here / Estoy Allá series (1994–96), the artist's body is painted in stylized blue waves evoking Yemayá and she holds a carved wooden boat. Protection and nourishment intertwine in this image of fertility—a "self-possessed and self-constructed" portrait that refuses the voyeuristic white male gaze.[23] The bottles draped around her neck drip breast-milk tears. Breast milk in this oceanic context points to chattel slavery's abuse of African and Afro-descended women, as life-giving birth became weaponized as reproductive labor, eradicating the continuity of family in favor of profit and forcing Black women to wet-nurse and raise white children. In his exploration of identity across the African diaspora, Michael Gomez describes the Middle Passage as "a birth canal" for a "prolonged struggle between slaveholder and enslaved over rights of definition."[24] In charting waters of connection and familial survival, Campos-Pons points to what could be, a view of the future, as the bottles contain her actual breast milk for her son (she was pumping constantly while creating this series).

In *She Always Knew of the Space in Between* (2019, plate 73), Campos-Pons looks back as a mother on her own mother. Depicted in watercolor on an immense scale, an expanse of water extends across five panels, from afar to inside its thriving depths. Her mother appears in yellow in the second panel, emanating celestial energies similar to those that swirl around the central image of a Dogon sculpture of water guardians. In looking back on her mother's wisdom, Campos-Pons's retrospective title evokes Homi Bhabha's third-space theory of hybridity and "in-betweenness" across intersections of cultural identity engendered by migration and colonialism.[25] Her mother—who never left Cuba and presumably never read Bhabha, and now communes with her daughter between the spiritual and living realms—nonetheless always knew this truth, not from theory but from her own lived experience. Campos-Pons, too, always knew of her connection to Yoruba culture, to Africa. She contrasts her immersion in Afro-Cuban culture with conversations around Black life in the United States that "focus on displacement"; for her, "Africa was in my backyard."[26] In *Replenishing* (2001, plate 26), made once Campos-Pons was finally able to return to Cuba after eleven years away, connotations of watering, irrigation, and fulfillment title an image of physical reconnection and rejuvenation. Seven photographs, echoing the seven orisha powers, are arranged in an H shape, representing home (*hogar* in Spanish), and colorful African beads, or *collares*, link the hands, bodies, and lives of the artist and her mother.

Water as a metaphoric memory—of the distance and dislocation of migration, or of the grief and tears shed over the deaths at sea and on land from the transatlantic slave trade—has long been key to Campos-Pons's artistic cosmology, and this theme continues in the 2019 series Un Pedazo de Mar. In *Floating between Temperature Zones* (plate 76), blue watercolor soaks to the edges of the paper, and sea creatures—a feathery nudibranch, an owl-faced seal—swim in watery suspension near a chorus of thirteen submerged angels, their simplified forms referring to the figures on slave ship icons. *Descending Angel* (plate 78) focuses in on one such figure, a visitation from spirits lost to the depths of history, and a mourning of the ones we are losing now, as is also seen in *Untitled* (plate 77), where asylum seekers in orange lifejackets flail into the distance of the watercolor's splash. In *Wet All Day* (plate 74), haloed beings nestle into the ribs of a figure evoking a crucified Jesus Christ, a tribute to the sacrifice of migrating people who change their lives and, by extension, the lives of their descendants. In *An Army of Angels* (plate 75), these ancestors arise from pooled and sprayed accumulations of watercolor, their bodies elongated and stylized in forms reminiscent of the figures of Afro-Cuban Chinese artist Wifredo Lam (fig. 3).[27] In an earlier work from another series that presages the depth and breadth of this shade of cerulean blue, *Nesting IV* (2000, plate 25), Campos-Pons's self-portrait is bifurcated by a monolith of blue, indicating her preoccupation with the water and its stories welling up in her psychic space, between and in her eyes.

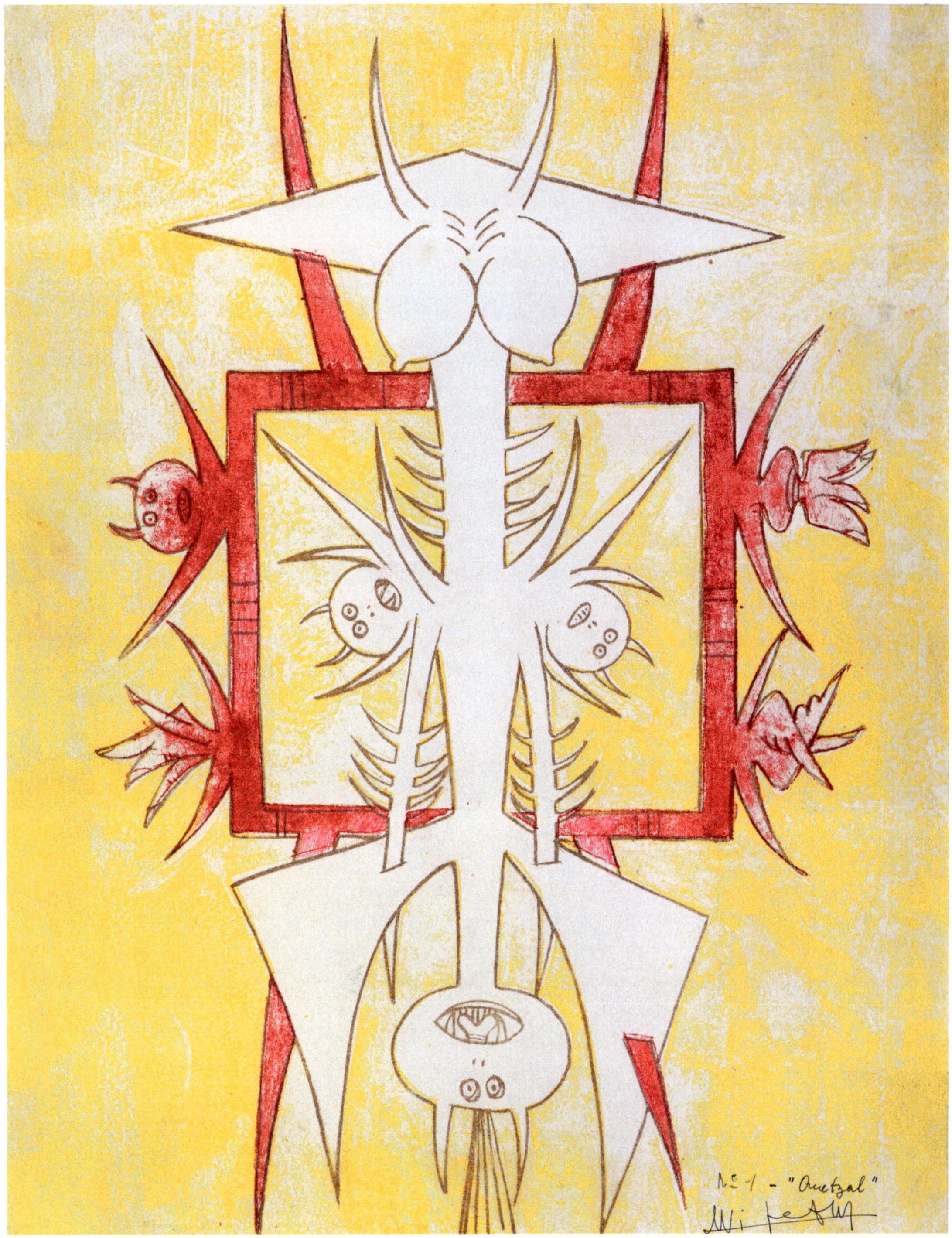

Fig. 3 Wifredo Lam (b. 1902, Sagua la Grande, Cuba; d. 1982, Paris), *Quetzal*, from Brunidor Portfolio, no. 1, 1947. Lithograph, edition of 70, 42 x 33.1 cm (16 9/16 x 13 1/16 in.). New York, Museum of Modern Art, Purchase Fund, 342.1947.3

What are the fruits and flowers of all this watering? The irrigation of tears nourishes the blooms of generational growth. In *Backyard Dreams #8* (2005, plate 33), the artist embraces her son, Arcadio, in their Boston backyard, lush with well-watered plants. Behind them, a painted portrait of the artist's mother amid verdant brushstrokes brings the space of her Matanzas curative herbal and food garden into an intergenerational continuation, indicated by Arcadio and his mother holding a skein of beads reminiscent of those connecting the artist and her mother in *Replenishing* (plate 26).

Just one year later, the artist's family temporarily moved to Padua, Italy, where Campos-Pons started fresh with no studio materials and at first, in her words, "intentionally steered clear of anything and everything that had to do with work."[28] Following that rest and fresh start, she began to gather scraps of the city—greasy remnants of great sandwiches, snippets of stories from Nigerian street vendors, and leather and cloth from the former tanning factory she used as a studio. In *El Nacimiento de la Flor de Cardi* (2006, plate 34), fragments of crochetwork by nuns, collaged onto a globe-like mound resembling a belly and adorned with tiny uterus-like forms, hover above two spread legs, from which grows an enormous stalk of milk thistle, a hardy seed that thrives wherever it is planted—even, as in the idiom *hierba mala nunca muere* (a bad weed never dies), in the face of adversity. Sometimes known as Mary or holy thistle, it has been used for medicinal purposes for centuries, most notably to promote breast milk production. It is also known as "viajera," or traveling plant, as its decay and eventual toppling lead seeds to take root further into the landscape, journeying forward in its cycle of death and renewal.

The assemblages created in Padua heralded a new modality for Campos-Pons, beginning a process wherein natural materials are integrated directly into works on paper. *The Warrior Reservoir* (2010–11, plate 52) enmeshes a drawing by Arcadio, natural bark, ribbon, and wooden figures and spears with watercolor and ink. In *The One That Carried the Fire* (2011, plate 53), Arcadio's painting of a yellow orb alights into a pink and orange conflagration of fire and thistles and flowers amid coiled collaged human hair, perhaps alluding to the purifying rage of the orisha Changó, boiling under a placating facade. Continuing and furthering this work during her 2016 Rauschenberg residency in Captiva, Florida, Campos-Pons used living and dying plants, for instance pressing the pulpy sapote fruit into *Jungle* (2016, plate 68) and later making prints directly from the cores of tree trunks, as in *Because the human body is a tree, Spring Awakening II* (2019–20, plate 80). In *Angels' Trumpets, Devils' Bells* (2019, plate 72), baggage tags, packing tape removed from art shipments, and TSA inspection tape float like flotsam around a descending figure whose hair and hands are full of dried, pressed flowers, as her body moves through and past the surveillance and detritus of contemporary travel. These traces of the flora and fauna of specific places connect art to its context, flowering from the land itself as much as from Campos-Pons's own hand.

The transformation of the everyday into the ethereal relies on the alchemy of the artist's vision. Campos-Pons and Leonard's largest and most complex collaboration, *Alchemy of the Soul, Elixir for the Spirits* (2015, plate 66), encompasses large-scale blown-glass sculptures, photographs, paintings, and a ten-channel sound composition. Commissioned by the Peabody Essex Museum in Salem, Massachusetts, its display wound through various gallery spaces. The glass sculptures—bulbous, interlocking, thrumming, odoriferous—corresponded conceptually to the structures and sensations of sugar mills and rum factories, the engines and sites of Caribbean slavery. Steel armatures referenced the unseen structure of human labor behind the industries, the breath involved in the glass's creation echoing the pauses of the sound element. The *elixir* in the title refers to the result of sugarcane distilled into rum, but the word *spirits* also operates on a ritualistic level, as the alchemical installation was itself an offering, a libation poured, tears spilled for the artist's ancestors. The blue glass sculpture interprets the art historical antecedent set by Remedios Varo, the Spanish Mexican Surrealist artist who painted *Creación de las aves* (Creation of the Birds, 1957, fig. 4), in which an anthropomorphic owl, understood to be a self-portrait, harnesses moonlight, magic, and color to create living birds.[29]

The motif of the owl, first introduced in *Nesting II* (2000, plate 24), a Polaroid triptych in which the artist uses her hands to evoke the bird's hypersensitive night vision, takes on a monumental scale and merges with Campos-Pons herself in *Secrets of the Magnolia Tree* (2021, plate 94). Part of a body of work honoring women in her life as owl-like guardians, in this self-portrait Campos-Pons's eyes are enlarged and exaggerated, her hair gray with experience as she rests her head in her hands, perceiving and pondering, crouched in anticipation of movement or action. The magnolia tree, emblematizing the flora of Nashville, where the artist moved in 2018, is partially digitally printed from a photograph taken by the artist, and then painted in watercolor. What does this owl witness, what does she behold? What have the trees themselves seen, their lives extending far longer than ours? Irrigated by the actions and inactions of humans as much as the water cycle, these trees hold memories, too. Working from Nashville, Campos-Pons beholds the legacy of slavery from a new perspective in the southern United States in a time of both unveiling and retrenchment of white supremacy, the control and silencing of women's bodies and experiences, and ongoing, persistent loss.

Eyes behold and perceive. They can also offer protection, as in the uncannily beautiful eyespots of butterflies that ward off predators. The series The Rise of the Butterflies (2021, plates 88–91) is dedicated to Breonna Taylor, a Black woman killed in 2020 in her own home with impunity by Louisville police officers. Taylor's story and photograph were shared and seen by millions during the resurgence of the Black Lives Matter movement. Campos-Pons, sheltering in place during the COVID-19 pandemic and also at work on her intimate series Miasma (2020, plates 82–85), memorialized Taylor with lush, colorful flowers and rounded, all-seeing butterfly eyespots in *Butterfly Eyes (for Breonna Taylor)* (2021, plate 87).[30] Ruminating on Taylor's brown irises—and the horrific way she was denied protection by police and courts—Campos-Pons's tears in the face of this loss crystallize in The Rise of the Butterflies into blown-glass mobiles. Brown glass, symbolizing Taylor's eyes, takes the shape and surface qualities of minerals, gemstones, and blue glass *nazars* (amulets believed to ward off the evil eye). The butterfly eyespots act almost as the opposite of the *nazar*: rather than ward off evil, they seem to welcome and demand community protection, witnessing, and care, as they elongate into dripping tears, swaying in a precarious balance.

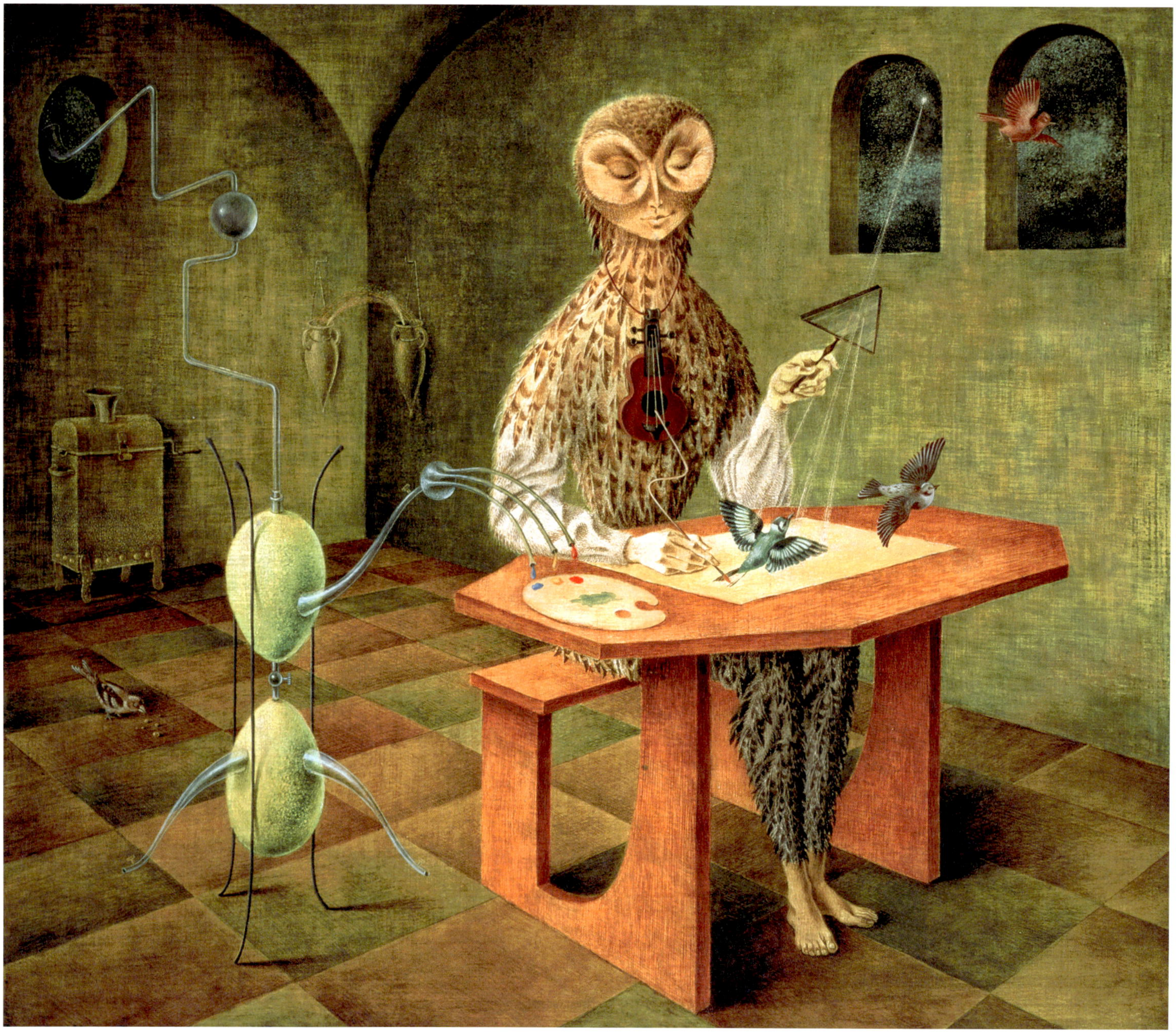

Fig. 4 Remedios Varo (b. 1908, Anglès, Spain; d. 1963, Mexico City), *Creación de las aves* (Creation of the Birds), 1957. Oil on Masonite, 54 x 64 cm (21 1/4 x 25 1/4 in.). Mexico City, Museo de Arte Moderno de Mexico

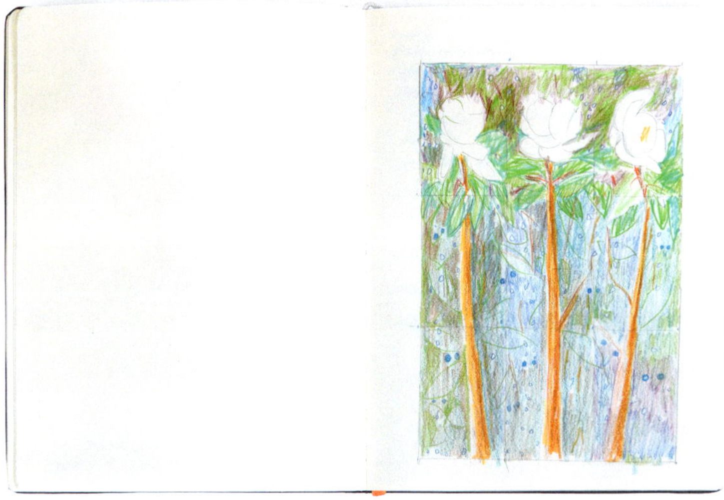

Untitled [Magnolia Tree Study], 2022. Notebook drawing. Collection of the artist

NOTES

1—Sarah Lewis-Cappellari, "On the Art of Alchemy and Unfolding Desires: A Conversation with María Magdalena Campos-Pons," *Theatre Journal* 72, no. 3 (September 2020): 7.

2—Tatiana Flores, "Sea and Self," in *María Magdalena Campos-Pons: Sea and Self* (Milwaukee: Haggerty Museum of Art, Marquette University, 2021), 10.

3—Campos-Pons lived in Boston from 1991 to 2017, after leaving Cuba and spending one year in a holding pattern in Canada in 1990. In 2006 she lived in Padua and created the Sono Qui series featured in this book; this is the first time this series has been seen in the United States. In 2018 she moved to Nashville, where she is the Cornelius Vanderbilt Endowed Chair of Fine Arts at Vanderbilt University.

4—"I don't have initiation [into Santería]," Campos-Pons explains. "What I learned is from my family, and against my will." Her grandmother told her parents not to initiate her, but they instilled in their daughter a respect for the orishas, despite her adolescent embarrassment. They bought her blue and yellow undergarments to ensure Oshun and Yemayá's protection, marked her shoes with a white cross in cascarilla without her knowledge, and imparted her father's care for the Earth and knowledge and respect for plants. Conversations with the author, December 2, 2021, and June 17, 2022.

5—Okwui Enwezor, "The Diasporic Imagination: The Memory Works of María Magdalena Campos-Pons," in *María Magdalena Campos-Pons: Everything Is Separated by Water*, ed. Lisa D. Freiman (Indianapolis: Indianapolis Museum of Art; New Haven, CT: Yale University Press, 2007), 74. Enwezor reminds the reader that Afro-Cuban spirituality can also refer to Palo Monte (derived from Kongo people), Regla Arara (Ewe-Fon), and Abakuá (Calabar) cultures. Enwezor's essay also describes Campos-Pons's work as accessing "classical material" in the Yoruba pantheon.

6—Conversation with the author, December 2, 2021. For more on the latter, see Selene Wendt's essay in this book.

7—Lisa Yun, *The Coolie Speaks: Chinese Indentured Laborers and African Slaves in Cuba* (Philadelphia: Temple University Press, 2008), 11.

8—Cheryl Finley, "Schematics of Memory," *small axe* 35 (July 2011): 100.

9—Yun, *The Coolie Speaks*, 16. As Yun's book elucidates, "In the case of Cuba, coolies were directly installed into a social and economic system where slavery had not been abolished. In fact, African slave importation to Cuba increased during the coolie period" (7).

10—Finley, "Schematics of Memory," 97, 99.

11—M. Jacqui Alexander, *Pedagogies of Crossing: Meditations on Feminism Sexual Politics, Memory, and the Sacred* (Durham, NC: Duke University Press, 2005), 7–8, 289.

12—For more resources on Campos-Pons, see "Further Reading" at the end of this book.

13—Lynne Bell, "History of People Who Were Not Heroes: A Conversation with María Magdalena Campos-Pons," *Third Text* 12, no. 43 (Summer 1998): 34–35.

14—Campos-Pons's former husband.

15—Freiman, *Everything Is Separated by Water*, 44.

16—Bell, "History of People Who Were Not Heroes," 33.

17—Sally Berger, "María Magdalena Campos-Pons, 1990–2001," in *Authentic/Ex-Centric: Conceptualism in Contemporary African Art*, ed. Salah M. Hassan (Ithaca, NY: Forum for African Arts, 2001), 138.

18—Conversation with the author, December 3, 2021.

19—Lewis-Cappellari, "On the Art of Alchemy and Unfolding Desires," 5.

20—María Magdalena Campos-Pons, *Habilitation, Mojitos, and Crocodile Tears* (Pontedera, Italy: Bandecchi e Vivaldi, 2006), 26.

21—Conversation with the author, December 3, 2021.

22—Conversation with the author, December 2, 2021. The respect and medicinal practices of plants that are central to Yoruba spiritual beliefs were passed on from father to daughter, who honored this in the sprawling aromatic installation *The Herbalist's Tools* (1994, plate 10).

23—Kimberly Wallace-Sanders, "The Body of a Myth: Embodying the Black Mammy Figure in Visual Culture," in *Black Womanhood: Images, Icons, and Ideologies of the African Body*, ed. Barbara Thompson (Seattle: Hood Museum of Art, University of Washington Press, 2008), 172.

24—Michael Gomez, *Exchanging Our Country Marks: The Transformation of Colonial Identities in the Colonial and Antebellum South* (Durham: University of North Carolina Press, 1998), 14.

25—Homi K. Bhabha, *The Location of Culture* (London and New York: Routledge, 1994).

26—Freiman, *Everything Is Separated by Water*, 27.

27—As an artist with ties to Western avant-gardes who exhibited frequently in New York and Europe, Wifredo Lam is a well-known figure of twentieth-century Cuban art. While his African, Chinese, and Spanish heritage was often flattened in those contexts, Lam was dedicated to fighting corruption and poverty in Cuba and brought Afro-Cuban forms into his Surrealism-inflected work.

28—Sergio Risaliti and Martina Cavallarin, *Sono Qui* (Milan: Galleria PACK, 2006), 35.

29—Campos-Pons has been inspired by the mystic maker Varo since encountering her work in 1988 while visiting the United States for the first time.

30—Taylor's sister, Ju'Niyah Palmer, released butterflies in her sister's honor after a grand jury declined to charge the officers. Palmer was also involved in conversations with the artist around Campos-Pons's tribute being included in the 2021 exhibition *Promise, Witness, Remembrance* at the Speed Art Museum, Louisville.

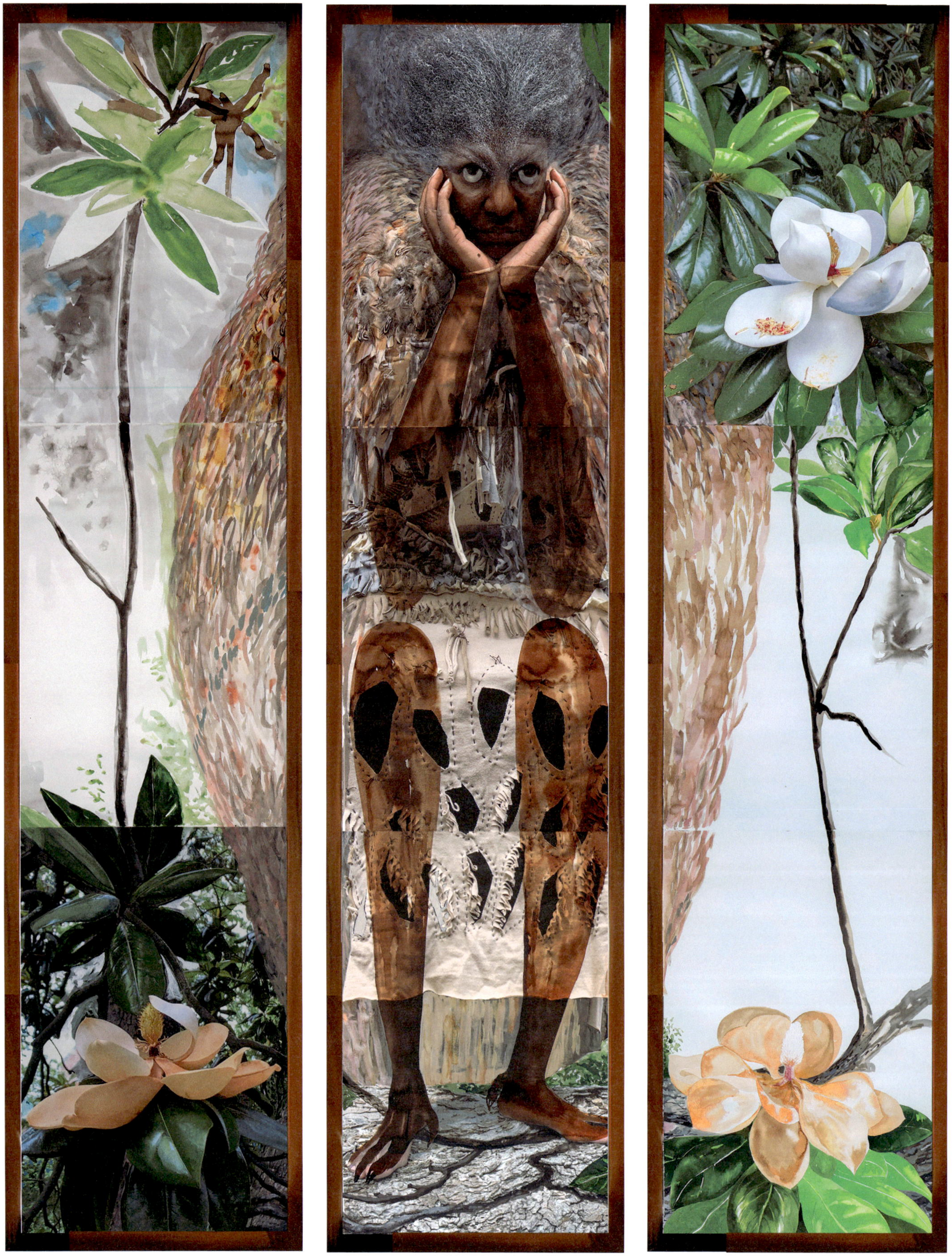

Secrets of the Magnolia Tree (plate 94), 2021

ROOTED IN CUBA AND CONNECTED TO THE WORLD

Selene Wendt

It seems kismet that my first introduction to the work of María Magdalena Campos-Pons was related to her mother, who played such a crucial role in shaping the artist's worldview. This was in 1998, when Campos-Pons's multimedia installation *Spoken Softly with Mama* (plate 20) debuted at New York's Museum of Modern Art.[1] Little did I know that this initial encounter would evolve into a lifelong friendship and numerous collaborations in locations around the world.

Spoken Softly with Mama pays homage to the generations of women who have supported the Campos-Pons family through domestic work. The installation features performative videos of Campos-Pons and old sepia-toned portraits of her family members projected onto seven silk-clad replicas of ironing boards and several stacks of meticulously folded sheets. The work recreates and transforms the everyday tools that her ancestors used into exquisite sculptural elements, including luminescent glass trivets and irons. The result is an enigmatic, dreamlike environment where past and present, fact and fiction, meld seamlessly. This immersive family portrait conveys the tremendous impact that women ancestors have had on Campos-Pons. Their caretaking seems to have helped guide her on a path toward social justice.

Spoken Softly with Mama came at a stage in Campos-Pons's career when she was most widely recognized for her monumental photographs and multimedia installations. She would later become equally renowned for performance works, paintings, and mixed-media works on paper as well as sculptures made in polymer and glass. In retrospect, it is easy to see how the diverse threads of her art became interwoven with her work as an artist dedicated to creating societal change, but it took a few more years, even decades, before her role as an artist-activist became fully evident.

As early as 2003, Campos-Pons took a tremendous leap of faith when she decided to open an experimental gallery in Brookline, Massachusetts. GASP, an acronym for

Gallery Artists Studio Projects (fig. 5), was an alternative project space where one might cross paths with curator Okwui Enwezor, see an early work by Carrie Mae Weems, or discover a promising young local artist. GASP was an alternative art space where Campos-Pons highlighted the work of others—a place she often referred to as an engine.[2] There, a seed was sown for what would evolve into the Engine for Art, Democracy and Justice, which she founded in 2018 at Vanderbilt University, where she is now a professor of fine arts and the Cornelius Vanderbilt Endowed Chair of Fine Arts.

Campos-Pons has addressed racial and sociopolitical injustices throughout her career. *Windows of Opportunity* (2001, fig. 6), a site-specific textile installation, was created in response to the tragic death of Amadou Diallo, a twenty-three-year-old immigrant from Guinea who was shot and killed in 1999 by police officers in the Bronx.[3] Campos-Pons was inspired to make the work when she saw a photograph of a window shattered by one of the forty-one bullets fired at Diallo. Using this as a point of departure, she silkscreened the image of the star-like pattern of broken glass onto diaphanous white organza fabric, then embroidered the pattern onto the fabric with hair extensions.

Although police brutality was its primary theme, *Windows of Opportunity* also directed attention to issues of immigration and the burden of marginalization. Situated as they are between inside and outside, windows evoke a space in between and an implied division between private and public, center and periphery. In general, Campos-Pons's work often challenges us to question the implications of "here" versus "there." When she created *Windows of Opportunity*, "here" related to her life in the United States, and "there" alluded to her persistent longing for Cuba and her family roots. During the past decade, she has reversed this equation and now spends more and more time in Cuba.

Wherever Campos-Pons is in the world, she always finds a way to connect with the people around her. Beyond her exceptional sociability, it is her ongoing commitment to making a societal impact that has inspired her to connect people and places through the common cause of social justice. In equal measure, the sociopolitical underpinnings of her visual art practice have become ever more visible through the years, as conveyed in such key works as *Pied-à-terre, Everyone Needs His Oba Oba* (2006, plate 36), part of the mixed-media series Sono Qui, and *Llegooo! FeFa!* (2012, plates 56, 57). Both artworks exemplify the highly collaborative approach that has defined much of her work.

Sono Qui addresses the predicament of African immigrants all over Europe whose livelihoods are dependent on the sale of counterfeit goods. These works unveil the beauty, humanity, and individuality of those who suffer the double injustice of being denied access to the economic and social privileges that Europe has to offer while they are also relegated to an illegal trade built in turn on crime, terrorism, and child labor. Richly embellished portraits of street vendors she met in Italy include colorful woven threads, remnants of counterfeit goods, and cutouts from luxury-brand shopping bags. The artist uses her success and privilege to offer sharp criticism of the global, social, and cultural inequities that exclude so many individuals from a just and fair existence.

The collaborative performance *Llegooo! FeFa!*, featured in the 11th Havana Biennial, was an equally important step on this path. *Llegooo* is a sonic extension of *llegar*, the Spanish verb for "to arrive," while FeFa is the name of her artistic alter ego, an acronym that combines the Spanish *familiares en el extranjero* with its English translation, "family abroad." An important aspect of this performance involved the distribution of baked goods, T-shirts, soap, fabric bags, and other items to the audience. The performance also featured eighteen *pregoneros* (street vendors) dressed in colorful outfits and calling out in their typically Cuban singsong sales pitches, advertising peanuts, flowers, garlic, gold trinkets, and other goods. Prior to the opening, in true Campos-Pons style, she had arranged the first-ever national *pregonero* competition to select the voices that would greet the chanting FeFa's arrival at the opening and follow her during her performance. In the same way that she had humanized street vendors in Italy, she helped to empower and legitimize *pregoneros* in Havana. The exchange of goods integral to this intervention reflected her ongoing interest in the wider implications of the global economy and its effects on society and politics.

Campos-Pons returned to aspects of *Llegooo! FeFa!* for her participation in the Cuban Pavilion at the 55th Venice Biennale. In collaboration with Neil Leonard, she created *53+1=54+1=55 / Letter of the Year* (2013, plate 59), a multimedia installation featuring dozens of birdcages hewn from rattan and a mash-up of sounds recorded in the streets of Havana. This tapestry of visual and sonic elements was conceived to emphasize the importance of sound as it relates to architecture. Inside the birdcages, individual stories are conveyed in documentary-style videos of interviews with Cubans who have never left the island. No birds fill the cages; instead, they are filled with the captured remnants of hopes and dreams, traces of everyday life, which continue to unfold even in a constant state of entrapment. The work celebrates the capacity to aspire to a better future

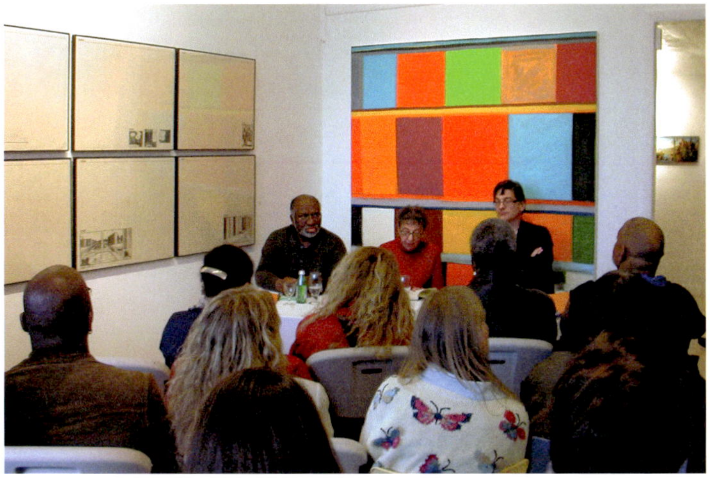

Fig. 5 Public program, *Image/Text*, curated by Maxine Yalovitz-Blankenship and Campos-Pons, Gallery Artists Studio Projects (GASP), Brookline, Massachusetts, 2005

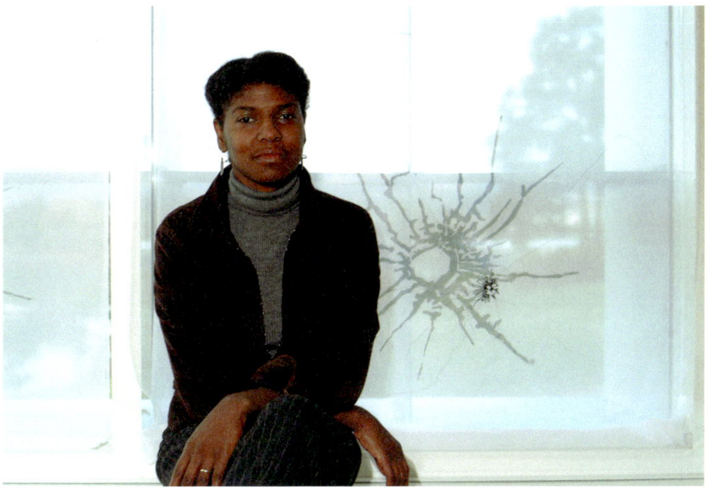

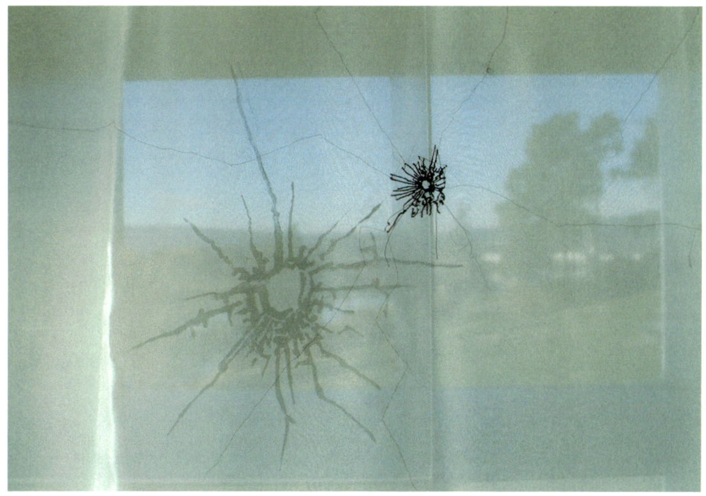

Fig. 6 María Magdalena Campos-Pons, *Windows of Opportunity*, 2001. Site-specific embroidered textile installation created for *Art through the Eye of the Needle*. Henie Onstad Art Center, Høvikodden, Norway, 2001

under almost any circumstances. In its cacophony of voices and sounds, this work extends beyond physical, political, and geographical boundaries to address migration in a poetic and metaphorical sense. Like birds, humans construct temporary homes, and at times they find their wings clipped by the constraints of invisible cages. Yet even in the face of despair, they sing songs of hope and freedom, and this is the underlying message that resounds through this pivotal work.

In 2018, when Campos-Pons was asked to participate in the 13th Havana Biennial, she took it as an invitation to realize her most ambitious collaborative initiative to date. Instead of producing an artwork for an exhibition space in Havana, she decided that the biennial needed to come to Matanzas, her home city. She was intent on creating a project that would inspire meaningful transcultural collaborations, revive the local art community, and encourage cross-cultural dialogues between Cuba and the United States. She seized this opportunity to reimagine the city of her youth and think about its history in relation to the present by shedding light on local concerns and challenges. In 2019, she made it all happen with *Ríos Intermitentes* (*Intermittent Rivers*) (figs. 7, 8), a multidisciplinary exhibition project that featured more than sixty local and international artists, directed by Campos-Pons and curated by Salah M. Hassan, Octavio Zaya, and me.

This collective effort displayed the extent to which Campos-Pons's upbringing in Matanzas influenced who she is as an artist and activist. To stand along the banks of the San Juan River in Matanzas is to experience the paradoxical place that so fundamentally shaped her artistic vision. On one side of the river, newly restored artist studios and a refurbished walkway, supported with funding from the *Ríos Intermitentes* exhibition budget, are prime examples of what she achieved. The other side of the river, crowded with colorful fishing boats, evokes another time and place. Standing there gave me a strong sense of being in two places at once, echoing the ongoing theme in her work of being situated between here and there, yet inexplicably in both simultaneously. Listening carefully to all the sounds—the motorboats and the children playing, the call of the street vendors, reggaeton from a small nearby outdoor bar, the constant rumbling of cars—I could hear the endless cry of poetry and feel the musicality of everything around me. I was struck, in a deep Glissantian sense, by the interconnectivity between all things and was equally mesmerized by this city, where everything seems to be reverberating with rhizomatic intensity, where even the landscape seems to speak. Édouard Glissant's concept of *échos-monde*, understood as the world of things resonating with each other, came powerfully to life.[4]

If I were to describe the duality of Matanzas in one word, it would be *baroque*. From the ornate metalwork of the doorways and windows, to the decorative tiles found everywhere, to the busy, bustling streets, there is nothing simple or minimalistic about Matanzas. This is a place where past and present collide beautifully and unexpectedly and where every corner somehow comes alive with magic realism. It's no wonder that Campos-Pons often describes her work as "baroque minimalism." She elaborates on this term, which I would argue ultimately defines her entire artistic practice, as a "hybrid, a juxtaposition of contrasting elements, a place of contradiction where there is beauty deeply inscribed in the paradox."[5]

The specificity of place that was so integral to *Ríos Intermitentes* is evident throughout Campos-Pons's artistic practice. Her vividly detailed descriptions of growing up in Matanzas provide valuable insight into her creativity. For instance, escaping reality through books opened her mind to literary worlds where past and present, fantasy and reality, merged. Reading gave her a sense of freedom and the words to describe her specific world—the history, architecture, and spirit of Matanzas:

> My sensibilities lie between the complex and luxurious grandeur of Cuban architecture, the voluptuousness of Cuban curvilinear furniture, beautiful women and suave men walking in the hustle and bustle of the city, as contrasted with the austerity and rigor of the blue of the ocean horizon on a calm day, or the flatness and rationality of a sugarcane field. As a girl I wandered in the sugarcane fields not knowing yet I was walking within a grid, but I loved the pattern and simplicity of the walls of delicately moving green sugarcane all around me, and the straight, red dusty path. This was the place where I found relief reading Rainer Maria Rilke, Thomas Mann, Chinua Achebe, and Immanuel Kant.[6]

If Campos-Pons found freedom in books as a young girl, she now possesses the freedom and resources to provide opportunities and hope for others, and her unwavering belief in the power of art to create societal change was abundantly evident in *Ríos Intermitentes*. With this project she broke down barriers between art and life, public and private, art world elite and civic society. Perhaps above all, the project offered an unprecedented opportunity to showcase

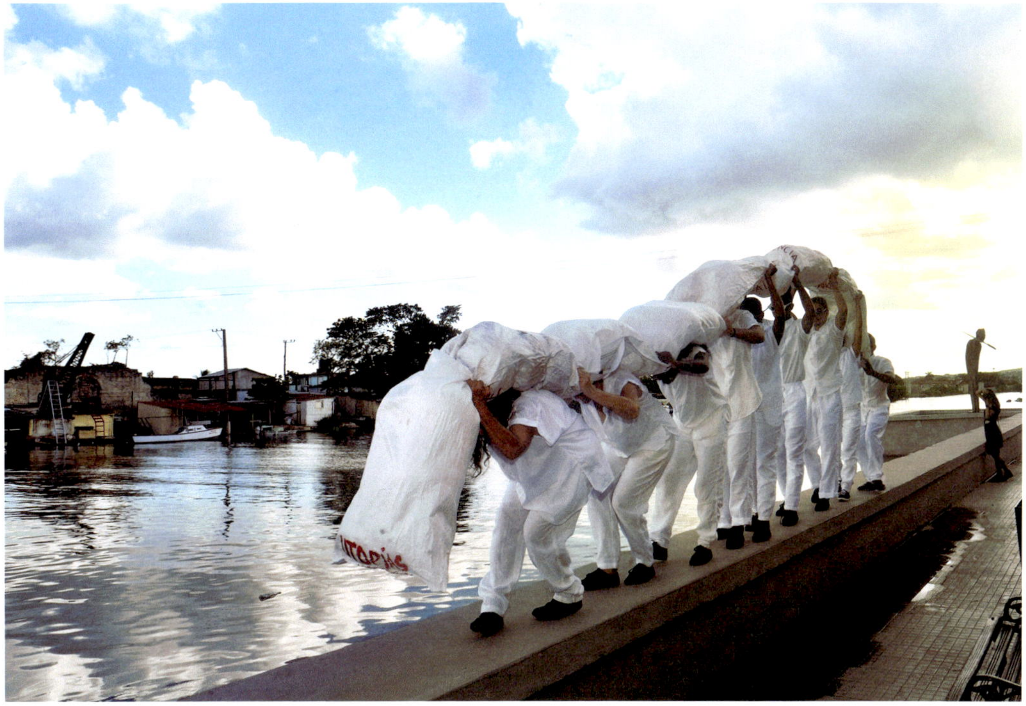

Fig. 7 Jana Harper, Lilian Padrón, and Moksha Sommer, *Cargas*, a performance at *Ríos Intermitentes (Intermittent Rivers)*, by the Danza Espiral group in which the performers carried ration bags, representing the range of burdens experienced by Cubans, through Matanzas to the Palace of Justice. Performance documentation, 13th Havana Biennial, Matanzas, Cuba, 2019

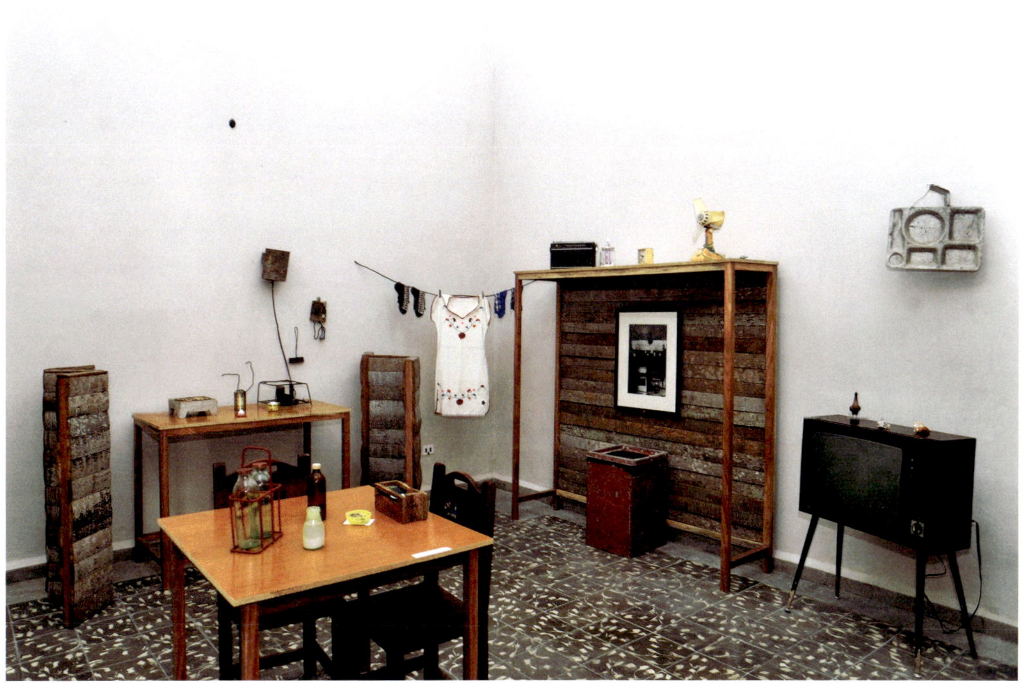

Fig. 8 Ramón Pacheco (b. 1954, Villa Clara, Cuba), Installation with objects from Cuba's "Special Period," part of *Ríos Intermitentes (Intermittent Rivers)*, 2019. Installation view, 13th Havana Biennial, Palacio de Justicia, Matanzas, Cuba, 2019

the work of legendary local artists such as Ramón Pacheco and Augustín Drake Aldama; the artist-run book collective Ediciones Vigía; younger, emerging artists; and more internationally renowned artists such as Olu Oguibe and Dawit L. Petros, resulting in cross-cultural collaborations and dialogues that continue to resonate today.[7]

At the time, Campos-Pons had one foot in Matanzas and the other in Nashville, where she had initiated the Engine for Art, Democracy and Justice at Vanderbilt University, her most ambitious social justice initiative yet. She launched the first edition in 2018, with Fisk University, the Frist Art Museum, and Millions of Conversations as institutional partners.[8] The event included lectures by Adam Szymczyk, documenta 14 artistic director; Holland Cotter, co-chief art critic of the *New York Times*; and artist Olu Oguibe. The 2020 edition, which was curated by Marina Fokidis, featured online panel discussions and a site-specific installation by artist Ibrahim Mahama, known for works that often involve covering entire buildings with jute sacks.

In keeping with Campos-Pons's overriding vision, the goal of the Engine for Art, Democracy and Justice is to make a real and lasting impact through transcultural dialogues and collective action.[9] Campos-Pons's ongoing commitment to the Engine for Art, Democracy and Justice is testimony to her taking every opportunity to extend beyond her own studio practice, to use art as a tool for societal awareness, and to create change through artistic collaborations and social justice initiatives.

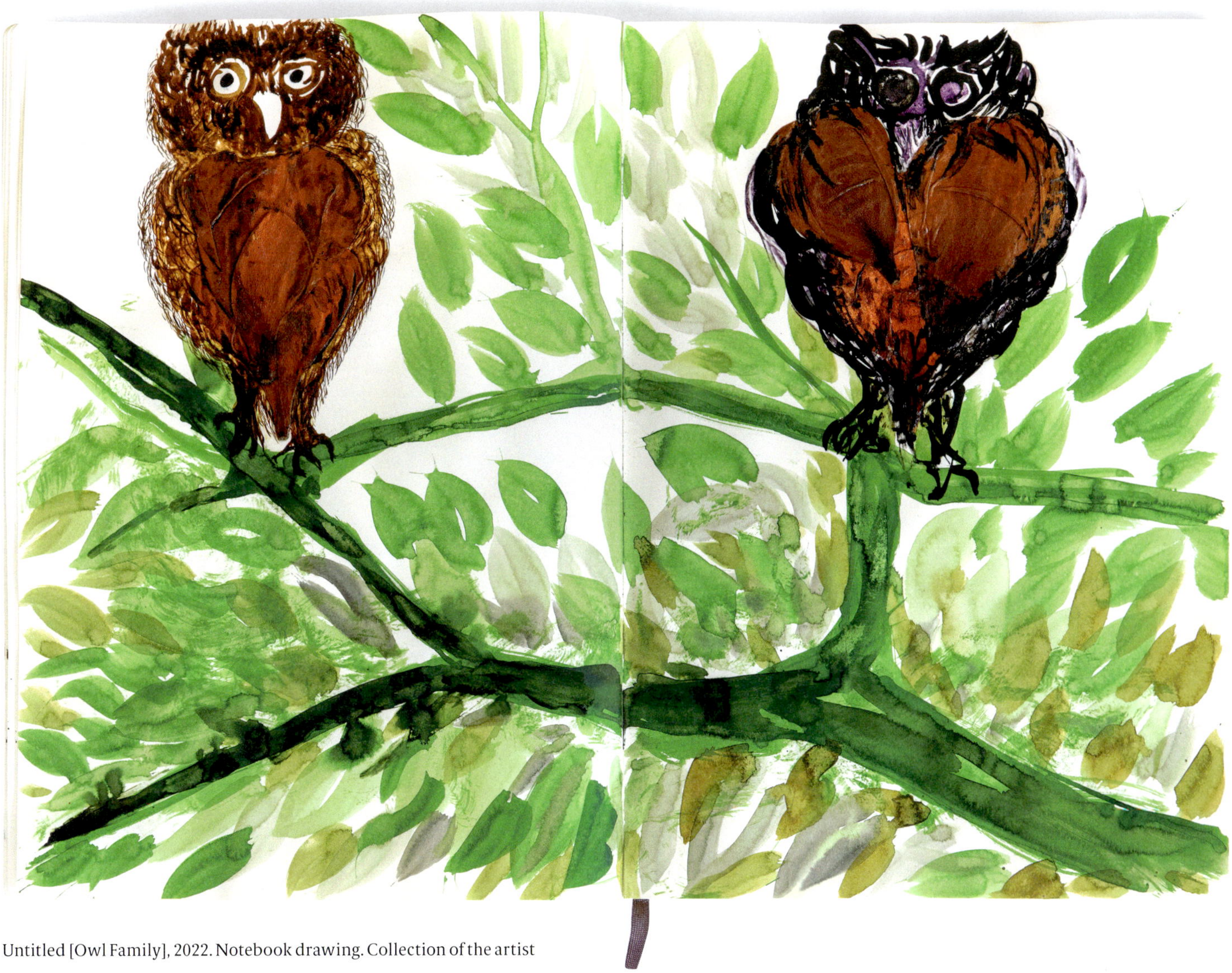

Untitled [Owl Family], 2022. Notebook drawing. Collection of the artist

NOTES

1—*Spoken Softy with Mama* was also featured in *Authentic/Excentric*, an exhibition curated by Salah M. Hassan and Olu Oguibe for the 49th Venice Biennale (2001), marking the artist's first participation in the Venice Biennale.
2—Campos-Pons owned and directed GASP from 2003 until it closed in 2012.
3—*Windows of Opportunity* is a site-specific work created for her participation in the 2001 exhibition *Art through the Eye of the Needle*, Henie Onstad Art Center, Høvikodden, Norway.
4—Edouard Glissant's (1928–2011) influential novels, poems, and theories established the idea of a "poetics of relation" that sites a generative future in the imaginative potential of Caribbean sensorial and communicative experience.
5—Conversation with the author, September 1998.
6—Conversation with the author, July 2011.
7—In addition to supporting local artists and providing them with a platform to present their art to an international audience, *Rios Intermitentes* provided several opportunities for urban renewal, including the complete restoration of the Palacio de Justicia.
8—Millions of Conversations is a Nashville-based organization that seeks to transcend critical divides by promoting positivity and inclusion.
9—I was honored to have been selected as the curator of the 2022–23 program "Artistic Activism and the Power of Collective Resistance."

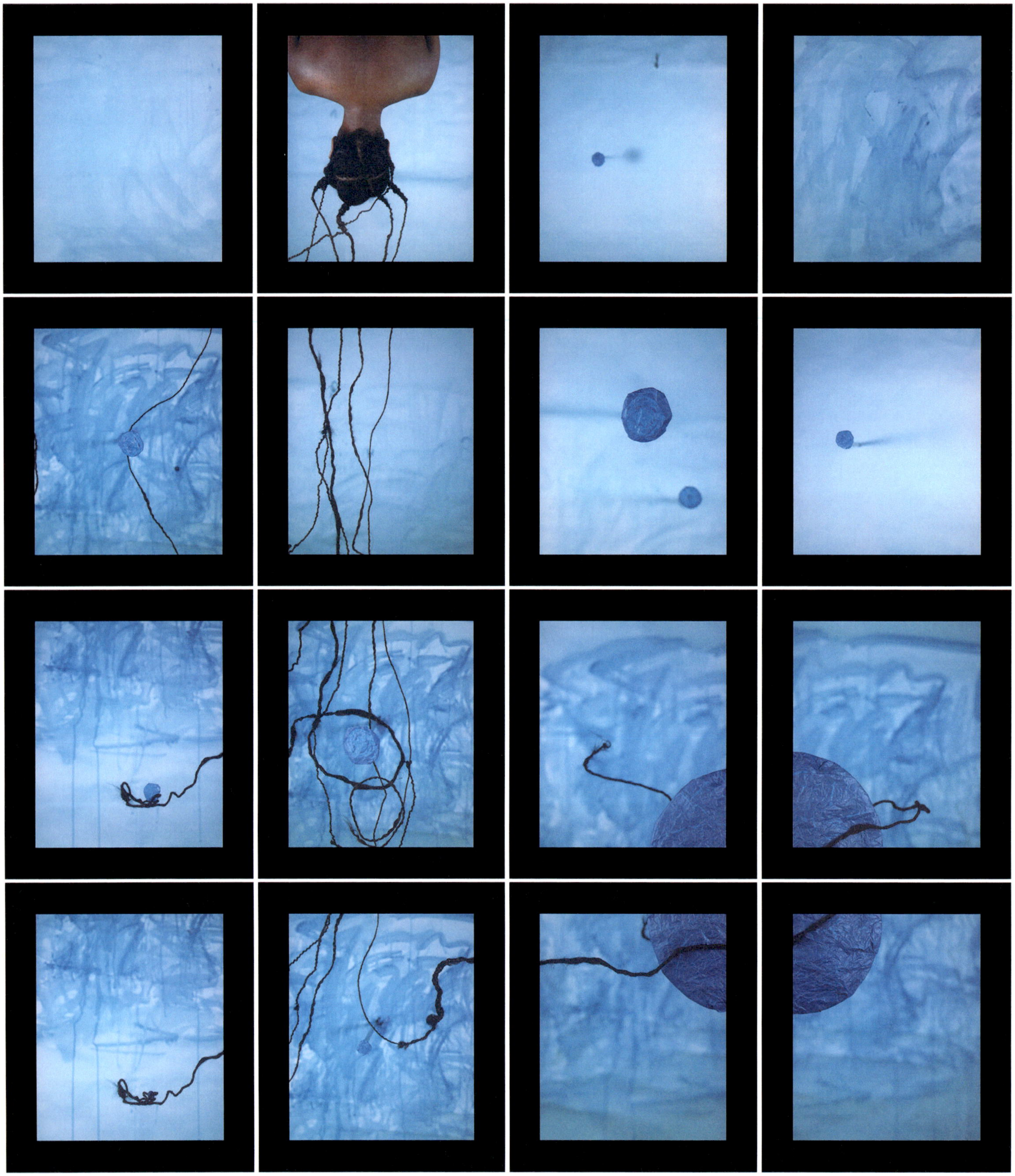

Elevata (plate 27), 2002

"THIS, THIS, THIS, THIS, THIS": PHOTOGRAPHY IN PIECES

Mazie M. Harris

We take photographs to remember individual moments, but it is in their accumulation that stories are told. María Magdalena Campos-Pons had already been working with photography for many years when in the 1990s she began making large-scale, multipart, narrative photographic compositions. She found that clustering photographs in groups of two or three and, later, mounting images together in enveloping grids created dialogue through juxtapositions. Her sometimes-confrontational portraits evoke the emotional tenor of her own experiences as a woman, mother, migrant, and artist of color, encouraging awareness of the ways that distance serves not only to divide but also at times, perhaps counterintuitively, to deepen connection. The pieced-together images foreground the complexities of filmic technologies developed for light skin and by white people, channeling both the capacities and the limitations of photography.

"Photography was an elusive presence in my childhood," the artist explains.[1] The town in Cuba where she grew up in the 1960s had no photography studios, and photographic equipment was a prohibited luxury. A photographer from a studio several towns over would come to Matanzas on rare occasions—events so special that they became seared into the artist's memory. She recalls the arrival of the truck full of materials as a festive affair. The cameraman would set up the equipment outside, draping up a backdrop to create a makeshift space for family portraits, and she and her neighbors gained glimpses of the process in action. Those times felt, for Campos-Pons, like magical moments. In that era of scarcity, for many families such photographs were their only portraits of loved ones.

One particular family photo holds a special place in the artist's recollections. She is seven years old, posed with a younger sister. Though the image is in black and white, the colors remain vivid in her mind. The dresses the girls wore have become a touchstone in her work, inspiring the green, blue, and yellow palette of her 1999–2000 installation *Meanwhile the Girls Were Playing* (plate 21). The same elements that animate her memory of that portrait—the power of photography to summon sense memories, the importance of clothing and color in marking significance, and the ability of pose and proximity to signal relationships—continue to inform her work today.

When Campos-Pons traveled to Boston in 1988 for an exchange semester at the Massachusetts College of Art (MassArt), she was initially overwhelmed by the availability of photographic materials. At Cuba's Instituto Superior de Arte (ISA), she and her peers had pleaded with their professors to incorporate photography into the program. They were attuned to the sway that photographs held in Cuban politics and had been further motivated by discussions with students from Mali who described the rich photographic tradition in West Africa, which often incorporated painted backdrops and stylized poses to create heightened renderings of everyday life. ISA professors and administrators, though, insisted that photography was a commercial medium, and the students' requests were refused.

Scholar Rachel Weiss characterizes the work of Campos-Pons and her contemporaries who began making art in Cuba in the 1980s as "a reaction to the prescriptions and proscriptions of official culture. But it was also, crucially, the dynamic entry of a group of young people, born about the time of the Revolution and formed not only by its encroaching orthodoxies but also by its poetic idealism and dedication to independence."[2] After her semester in Boston, Campos-Pons returned briefly to Cuba, but political upheaval prompted her to accept a fellowship in Canada, where she stayed until she was allowed to reenter the United States in 1991.[3] At that point, the U.S. embargo made it uncertain whether she would ever again be permitted to return to Cuba and her family. In exile, she experimented with film, photography, performance, and other disciplines that had not been taught at ISA, which proved useful in her efforts to craft forms of connection to people and places she was unable to visit.

The work of Abelardo Morell in particular propelled Campos-Pons's embrace of photography. Morell was born in Cuba only a decade before her and had fled the country with his family in 1962, when he was just an adolescent. By the time they crossed paths in Boston, Morell had begun experimenting with immersive photographic images that toyed with the basic properties of the medium. Creating small holes in the window coverings of darkened rooms, he turned the spaces into chambers in which images of the outside world were projected upside down through the tiny apertures, then used a large-format camera to photograph the inverted world. Shimmering with the light of the outside, otherwise mundane rooms were transfigured (fig. 9). Campos-Pons was mesmerized, reminded of the sense of magic she had experienced when the traveling photographer came to call in the fields near her home. But rather than use cameras to show the world as it was, she was determined to elicit emotional realities. While Morell's work is rarely populated, hers is insistently figural. She gleaned from Morell the power of immersion, the impact of conjuring a new perspective of one's surroundings.

Other artists and artworks also made an impression on Campos-Pons in her early years in the United States. Carrie Mae Weems was an assistant professor at Hampshire College in Amherst, Massachusetts, and lectured at MassArt while Campos-Pons was studying there. By the late 1980s Weems had begun pairing photographs with expressive captions to call forth a sense of aurality and intimacy, and she had begun centering her compositions on herself as a stand-in for other Black women (fig. 10). Campos-Pons, too, began to use her own body as a means of channeling collective experience and intensified her interest in staged pictures.

But while Morell and Weems became known for works using black-and-white photography, in Boston Campos-Pons found herself drawn to a local color product: Polaroid. Founded in Cambridge, Massachusetts, in 1937, Polaroid popularized instantaneous processes in which images are developed within the camera itself. To help launch its new eight-by-ten-inch Polacolor film in 1976, the company introduced extremely large-scale Polaroid cameras to showcase the capacity of its film at attention-grabbing scale (fig. 11). Eventually, five such massive cameras were built and drew publicity when artists such as Andy Warhol used them to produce twenty-by-twenty-four-inch photographs notable for their rich tones and the vibrancy and flow of the colors.[4] Polaroid cameras were popular among commercial and professional practitioners because they were easy to use, but there is nothing easy about making a twenty-by-twenty-four-inch Polaroid. The device is several feet tall and weighs more than two hundred pounds, with a lens that can extend up to five feet. Working with the process requires careful technical oversight, and each individual image is time-consuming to produce. Artists granted access to one of the Polaroid studios—at MassArt, in New York, or abroad—had to collaborate with at least two skilled in-house technicians.

Campos-Pons's interest in making narratives using Super 8 film—and in the video work of artists such as Dara

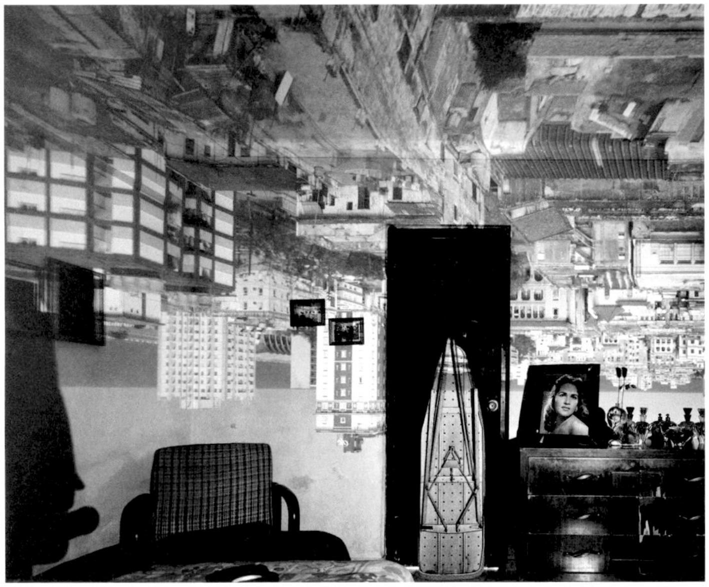

Fig. 9 Abelardo Morell (b. 1948, Havana; active in the United States) *Camera Obscura Image of El Vedado, Havana, Looking Northwest*, 2002. Gelatin silver print, 45.7 x 57.1 cm (18 x 22 1/2 in.). Los Angeles, J. Paul Getty Museum, gift of Daniel Greenberg and Susan Steinhauser, 2016.186.3

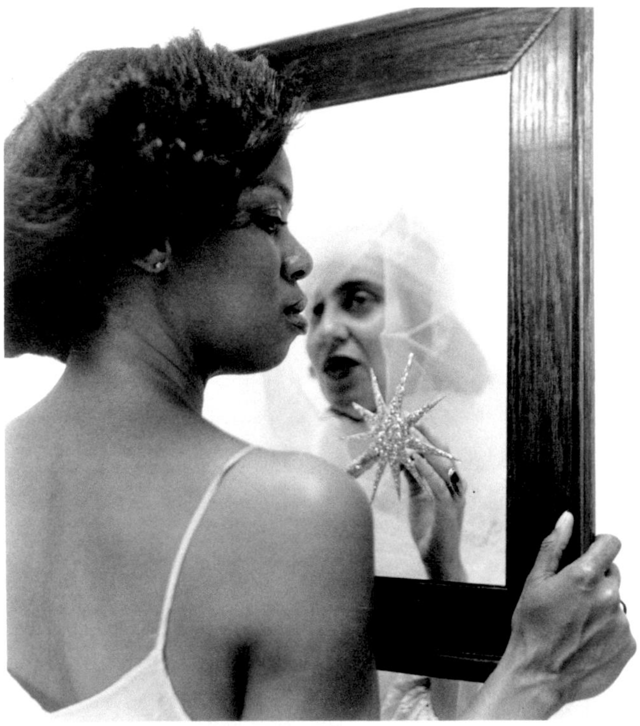

Fig. 10 Carrie Mae Weems (b. 1953, Portland, Oregon), *Mirror, Mirror*, 1987–88. Gelatin silver print with text panel, 42.2 x 36.5 cm (16 5/8 x 14 3/8 in.). Modern Art Museum of Fort Worth, museum purchase made possible by a grant from the Burnett Foundation, 1995.24.2

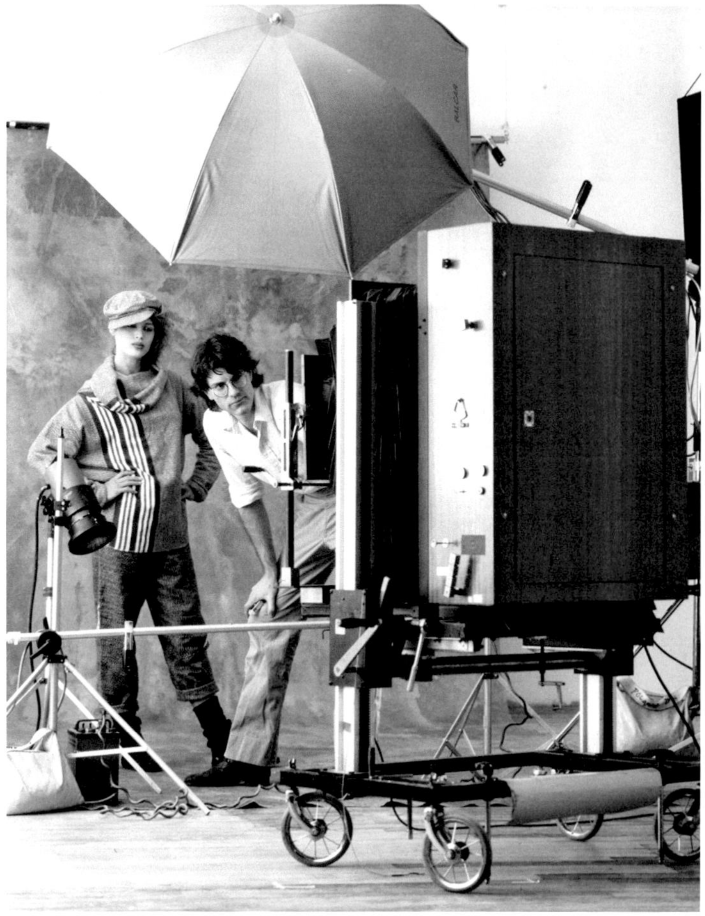

POLAROID'S 20x24-INCH CAMERA
USED TO CREATE PHOTO-ART

A Boston-based photographer uses Polaroid's ultra-large format camera to produce instant 20x24-inch black-and-white or color photographs in 80 seconds. The camera, containing a 60-inch bellows extension and a lens board with all the standard swings, tilts and shifts of a view camera, is primarily used by internationally renowned and emerging artists to produce creative imagery in studios located in Boston, Massachusetts; Offenbach, Germany and Tokyo, Japan.

###

Fig. 11 Promotional image of Polaroid 20 x 24 camera, ca. 1982. Boston, Polaroid Corporation records, Baker Library Special Collections, Harvard Business School

Birnbaum (fig. 12)—had been transposed to her work in photography, in which she thought carefully about each frame and about the story implied when multiple images are sequenced together. Thus, she had already developed a robust practice of photographic installation and performance when in 1994, while teaching at the School of the Museum of Fine Arts in Boston, she was granted access to the large-format Polaroid camera at MassArt. She found that the equipment enabled her to fuse immersive scale and bodily engagement in novel ways. Campos-Pons relied on the studio team's help but came to each session with fully fleshed-out ideas regarding what she wished to accomplish. For an artist for whom color is such a crucial carrier of symbolic meaning and emotional import, the transition was a significant step from the black-and-white images she had relied on in her earlier installations, which she had mostly sourced from friends and family and printed at commercial photography labs. The rich colors of the twenty-by-twenty-four-inch Polaroid process were well suited for the stories she sought to share. In these vivid images, the artist's own body became ever more central. Even when her figure is only partially represented—a torso, a head—the female form is determinedly the focus.

Returning to the liquid imagery of her early panel paintings like *Soy Una Fuente (I Am a Fountain)* (1990, plate 1), as well as her early sculptural work depicting body extrusions, one of Campos-Pons's earliest Polaroids (plate 11) from the series When I Am Not Here / Estoy Allá focuses on lactation. Her breasts overlaid with bottles dripping milk, the artist depicts herself as a body of liquid, a source of nourishment. Painted blue, the color associated with Yemayá, the orisha of motherhood and the sea, Campos-Pons embodies maternal care. Yemayá and Oshun had been deemed her guardian orishas by Campos-Pons's grandmother, so their colors channel protection for the artist. A new mother herself at the time, the artist regularly pumped her breast milk so that her husband could feed their son while she worked. But the dripping milk represents not only the life she was directly sustaining but also more generally the ancestors who had nurtured earlier generations. Liquid excretions continue at the edges of the photograph, where the residue of the Polaroid process is visible. The piece comprises just one print, but most of the artist's photographic works aggregate multiple images to more explicitly suggest the close relationships through which identities are refracted. The photographs in *Umbilical Cord* (1991, plate 2) are physically linked with a connective wire, but most others rely on the power of juxtaposition to mobilize interrelationships.

Another of the When I Am Not Here / Estoy Allá works (plate 13), for example, groups multiple images into a grid to register the capacities and limitations of the photographic medium and allude to the insidiousness of colorism.[5] While many of Campos-Pons's Polaroid works benefit from the process's saturated color palette, here the artist relies on her own body to establish the tones. She coated herself in cascarilla, an eggshell powder used for protection and purification, and scrawled "Identity Could Be a Tragedy" on her chest. The words convey the extent to which skin tone impacts one's fate. Underscoring the message, each subsequent image was made with a brighter and brighter flash, gradually washing out her skin, exactly as a camera instruction manual would warn against. The piece points to how photography impacts our perception, what we think we are seeing. Each frontal image evokes not only an ID or passport photo but also a mug shot, albeit with the identifying information typically held at chest height replaced by the text inscribed into the pigment. Together the images suggest the ways that governmental agencies and other bureaucratic systems delimit possibilities and restrict opportunities.

Polaroid, like other photography corporations, struggled to produce film able to register a wide range of skin tones. Historian Sarah Lewis has noted, "By categorizing light skin as the norm and other skin tones as needing special corrective care, photography has altered how we interact with each other without us realizing it."[6] Lewis's work is an important reminder that for most of its history, photographic technology operated with a built-in bias, skewing perceptions so that light and white skin was treated as a normalized standard. It is only recently that still and moving images have been better able to capture a darker range of skin tones. In its earliest iterations, Polaroid films were tested exclusively by fair-skinned scientists using light-skinned subjects. Hundreds of SX-70 test images in the company archives show a range of men and women scientists in their offices, posed with a crocheted blanket in a range of colors, and in some cases also a reproduction of a Pierre-Auguste Renoir painting and an abstract artwork (fig. 13).[7] Variation upon variation is annotated with the different filters, chemical compositions, and substrate configurations used. Employees also tested the equipment around their homes, making images much as their customers would—of children, pets, office parties, sunsets. But because the majority of the staff were pale in complexion, few trials focused on a wider range of pigmentation. The company also relied on the help of professional photographers to refine and market their products, but again, markedly few photographed non-white subjects.[8]

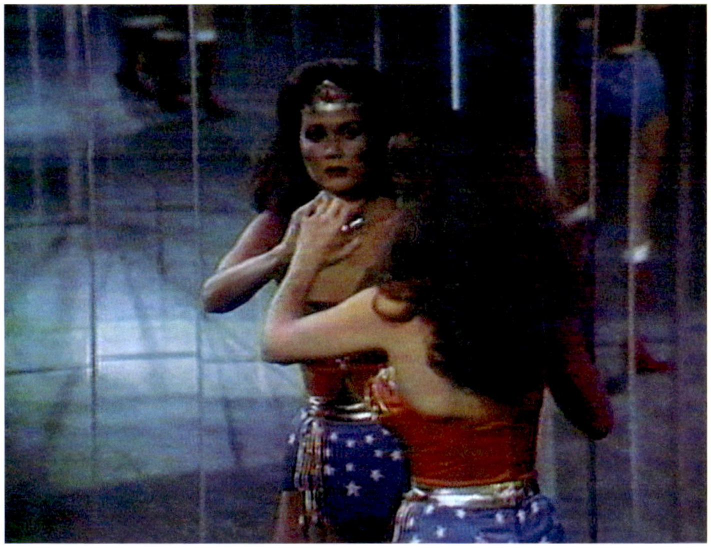

Fig. 12 Dara Birnbaum (b. 1946, New York), *Technology/Transformation: Wonder Woman*, 1978–79. Video, color, sound, 5:50 min. New York, Museum of Modern Art, Committee on Media Funds, 1161.2007

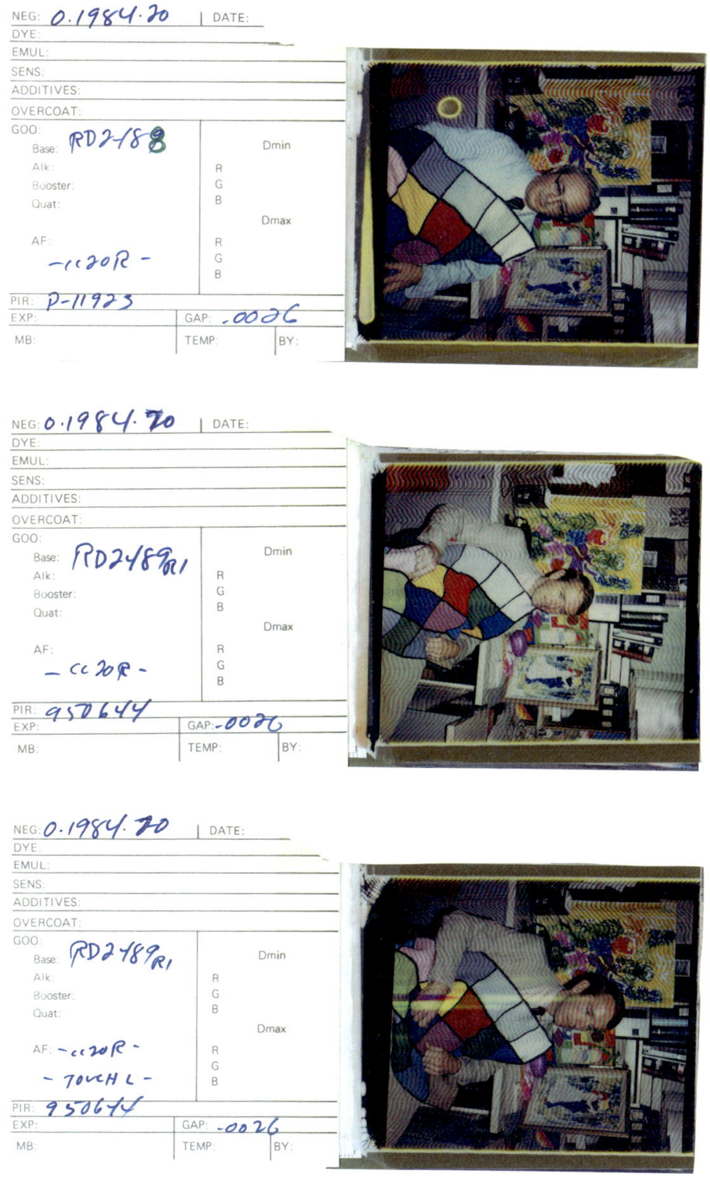

Fig. 13 Unidentified photographers, Polaroid Corporation Research and Development test images, 1970s. Dye diffusion prints and attached cards, each approx. 20.3 x 10.8 cm (8 x 4 1/4 in.). Boston, Polaroid Corporation records, Baker Library Special Collections, Harvard Business School

The rare photographs of persons of color in the Polaroid archive reveal the difficulties the products continued to have in adequately capturing darker skin tones and make clear the strategies photographers were forced to use to compensate (fig. 14). When editorial photographer Art Kane made a series of SX-70 test photographs in Haiti, for example, the medium brightly registered reds and blues but the features of his darker-skinned subjects were often illegible unless he turned them to the light or used artificial lighting strategically (fig. 15).[9] In any case, feedback from field trials seems not to have prompted Polaroid to change the chemical compositions of its film but was instead integrated into customer instruction manuals. Camera instructions did not address race directly but guided users to use a flash or otherwise adjust lighting in shadowy situations.[10]

Campos-Pons's images are not direct references to the company's products or history, but her artworks call to mind legacies of commercial and cultural efforts to regulate bodies. Yet Campos-Pons also deploys the medium toward recuperative agency, indicating potential for progress. Two triptychs in the When I Am Not Here / Estoy Allá series (1996, plates 14, 15) are bookended by frank observations: "Patria una trampa" (Homeland a trap) and "Identity could be a tragedy." But the center panel in each shows the artist without a protective cascarilla coating. She stares straight at the camera, her hair bound with branches that have double symbolism. Turned to their side, they resemble Cuba, but they also look like the hooked *garabato* staffs used by farmers, herbalists, and the orisha Elegua, "the one that allows you to find your destiny" by clearing pathways.[11] When she returned to the composition years later (plate 15), her body had changed but her determination remained unwavering. In preserving space between each image, she suggests both self-sufficiency and the ways that varied versions of one's self, even when they feel disparate, are part of a whole.

As the paths the artist forged began to broaden, the worlds she constructed deepened. Increasingly her imagery began to flow out from each frame. She continued to cluster her Polaroid prints, but the compositions began to bridge the interstitial spaces, crossing borders, unfurling from frame to frame like richly hued puzzle pieces. She built multilayered spaces and more elaborate compositions to photograph, moving away from the insistently frontal positioning of her earlier portraits. Given her limited windows of time in the Polaroid studios, she prepared more and more elaborately in advance of each session, sketching out ideas and constructing the various elements she would use. Her studies for *Elevata* (fig. 16, 2001; plate 27, 2002) give a sense of her working process. Envisioning her hair as an energetic swirling whirlwind, she pictured her extensions and her person as connective threads holding a universe in orbit. In Kobena Mercer's description, "Campos-Pons slips away from monologic self-centering to evoke a rhizomorphic subject constituted in a network of affective ties to others, along the lines of dreadlocked strands of hair which resemble plant roots equally at home in soil or water."[12] She reframes perceptions of Black hair as unruly by transforming it into a powerful, flourishing force.

The connective locks of hair from *Elevata* and other works from this period serve as a bridge, a lifeline, an unfurled anchor rope. *De Las Dos Aguas (Of the Two Waters)* (2007, plate 43) calls to mind families separated by immigration or forced migration. The strands tether each figure, suggesting that relatives are both burdened and buoyed by familial ties. In subsequent Polaroids, the artist began to activate the backgrounds of her images, conjuring the natural world. Her photographic works took on the scale of installations. The liquid, flowing compositions and large size of *Dreaming of an Island* (2008, plate 47) envelop the viewer much as the artist recalls being enveloped in the sugarcane fields of Cuba, with the blue sky overhead, yet the island she contemplates is off Maine.

As changes in the industry made Polaroid materials and studio time increasingly scarce, Campos-Pons—like so many other artists in the 2000s—began experimenting with digital photography, which enabled her to work more spontaneously. Her early digital works have the feeling of sketches and indeed often depict materials of everyday life that also appear in the notebooks she always carries: tools of labor and daily experience such as laundry lines (plate 39) and buckets (plate 40). In recent series she utilizes digital photographs as foundational sketch-like elements, building them out with layers of handwrought drawing and painting. She likens such collisions to the process of making *ajiaco*, a stew that combines a wide variety of ingredients.[13] In *Carta Natal 7/26/1953, 7/22/1959, 7/13/1989, 7/11/2021* (2021, plate 86), photographic images are overlaid with watercolor, ink, and gouache in a densely layered composition that melds the filmic and the handmade. The piece references key July dates of birth and rebirth from the Cuban Revolution and the artist's life: the failed coup that brought Fidel Castro's revolutionary ideas to international attention; the artist's birth just months into Castro's regime; the execution of Cuban general Arnaldo Ochoa by firing squad, which renewed focus on Castro's resistance to political reform; and the 2021 protests in Havana that led to mass arrests of demonstrators. The warmth of the summer sun fosters both protests and plants, as faces and sunflowers—some drawn,

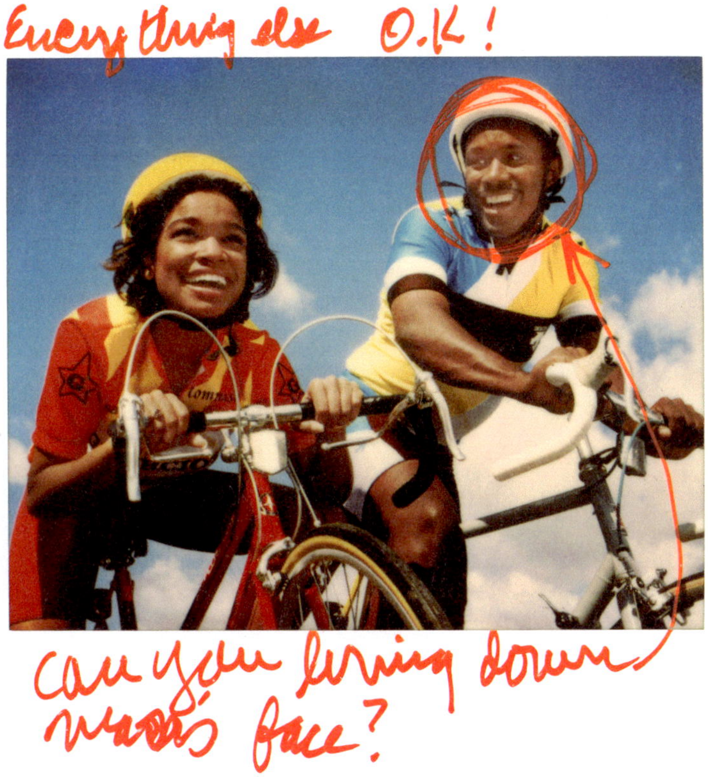

Fig. 14 David Franklin and Robert Alpe (dates unknown), Spectra promotional image, June 25, 1987, "Can you bring down man's face? Everything else O.K.!" 10.8 x 8.9 cm (4 1/4 x 3 1/2 in.). Boston, Polaroid Corporation records, Baker Library Special Collections, Harvard Business School

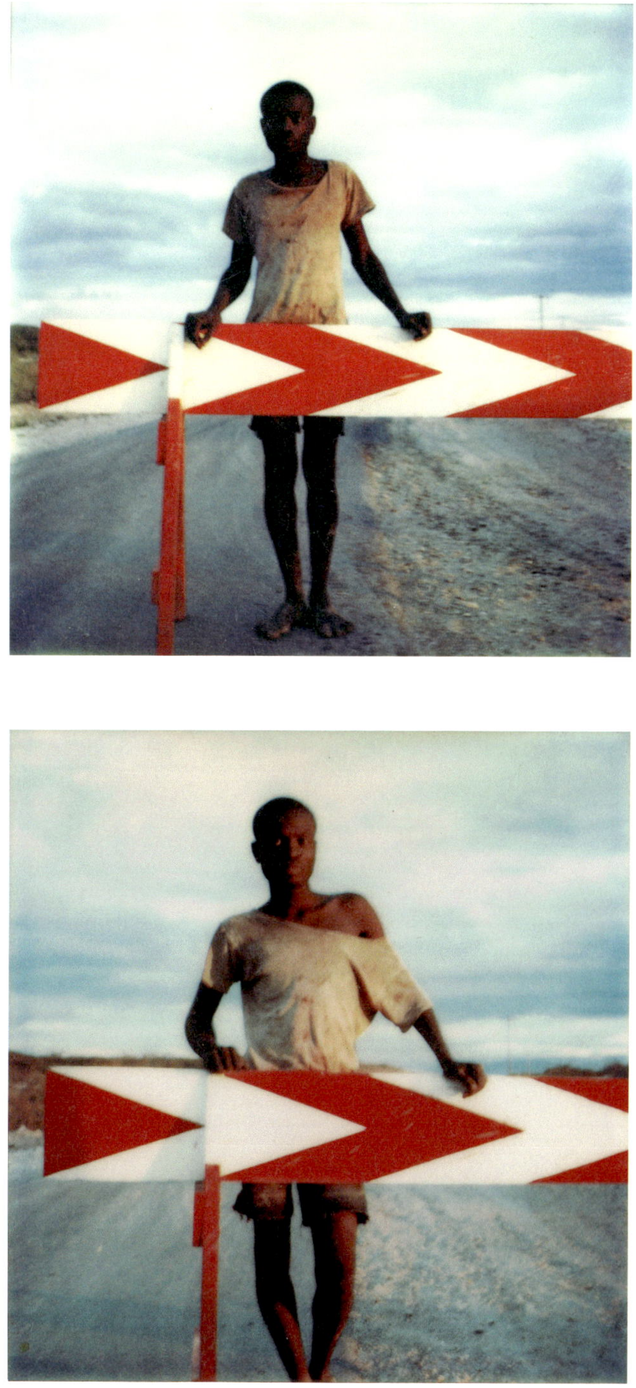

Fig. 15 Art Kane (b. 1925, New York ; d. 1995, Garrard County, Kentucky), SX-70 Time Zero test prints made in Haiti, early 1980s. 10.8 x 8.9 cm (4 1/4 x 3 1/2 in.) each. Boston, Polaroid Corporation records, Baker Library Special Collections, Harvard Business School

some photographed—intermingle. While the strict spacing in most of her Polaroid grids necessitates that a viewer piece together meaning, the 2021 iteration of *Carta Natal* collapses easy legibility, demanding greater time, greater attention, to parse out component parts and their interrelationships.

We are inundated these days with news imagery and often turn to nature as a respite from the media, but Campos-Pons's photo-based works of the 2020s disallow any imagined distance between nature and human struggles. They suggest that violence is inescapable, and so we must attend carefully—not avert our gaze but look, behold, react, act. The vivid colors of *Butterfly Eyes (for Breonna Taylor)* (2021, plate 87) urge us to remember a life that was flourishing, then cut tragically short. Intermixed photographic and drawn florals are a reminder that the violence enacted on one generation sows the seeds of trauma in the next. Campos-Pons continues to gather photographic images to construct worlds, but they are ever denser and more challenging to navigate. She describes her work as a way of thinking about both the perils of being human and the perils of our times: "How are we to deal with this pain, this sorrow, this history, this, this, this, this, this? We are responsible."[14] In her iterative practice, merging photographic elements with other media helps build narratives from component parts, but it is up to each viewer to piece together a path forward.

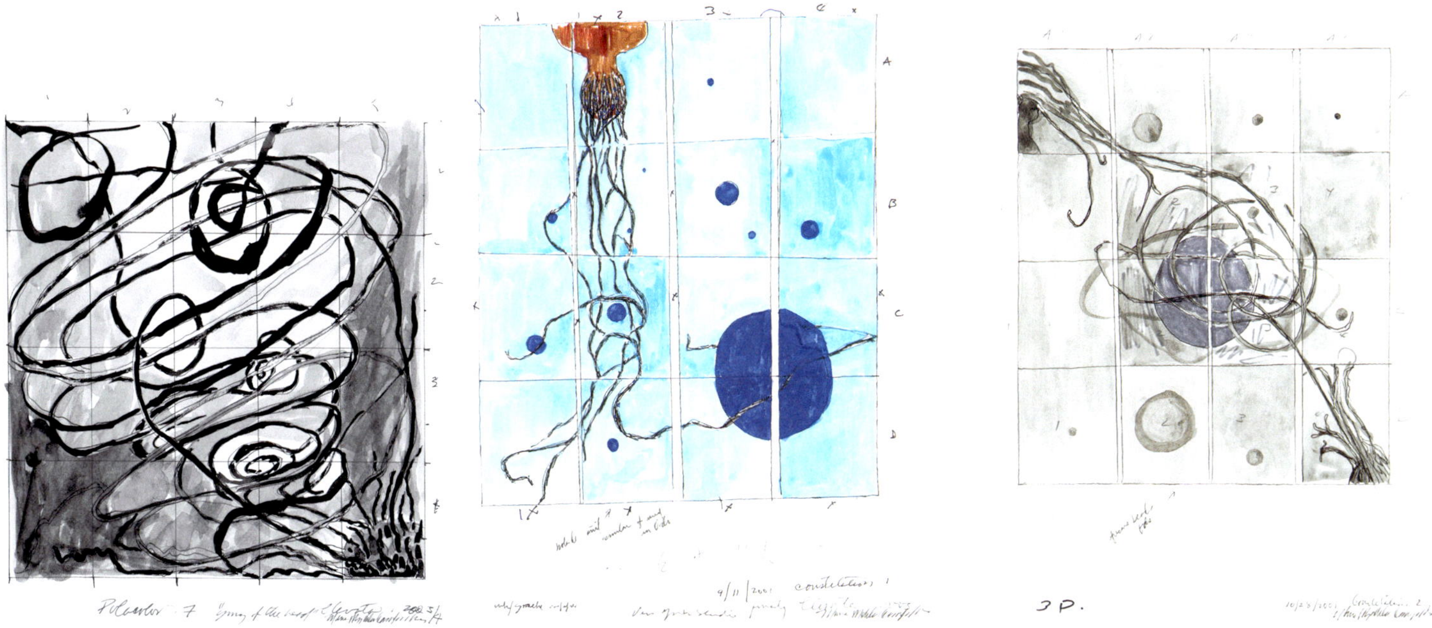

Fig. 16 María Magdalena Campos-Pons, Studies for *Elevata*, 2001. Ink, watercolor, wash, and graphite on paper, 27.7 x 21.3 cm (10 7/8 x 8 3/8 in.), 27.7 x 21.2 cm (10 7/8 x 8 3/8 in.), 18 x 20.5 cm (7 1/16 x 8 1/16 in.). Cambridge, Massachusetts, Harvard Art Museums/Fogg Museum, gift of the artist in memory of Michael Silver, 2004.56–.58

NOTES

1—Conversation with the author, May 27, 2022.
2—Rachel Weiss, *To and From Utopia in the New Cuban Art* (Minneapolis: University of Minnesota Press, 2011), xiii.
3—For a thorough chronology of this period see Joshua Basseches, "Leaving Cuba for the North," in the online publication *Alchemy of the Soul* (Salem, MA: Peabody Essex Museum, 2016), http://alchemy.pem.org/leaving_cuba/.
4—Large-format 20 × 24 Polaroid equipment relies on the same process as smaller consumer Polaroid instant cameras: a sealed packet holding developing fluid breaks when passed through two rollers, diffusing its dyes across photographic paper. Therefore, while "Polaroid" is the proprietary brand name for the equipment and process that Campos-Pons used to produce her large-scale works of the 1990s and 2000s, the technique is sometimes more generically referred to as the dye diffusion process.
5—On colorism in Campos-Pons's work and background, see Adriana Zavala, "Blackness Distilled, Sugar, and Rum: María Magdalena Campos-Pons's *Alchemy of the Soul, Elixir for the Spirits*," *Latin American and Latinx Visual Culture* 1, no. 2 (2019): 8–32; Ilan Stavans and Jorge J. E. Gracia, "American America: María Magdalena Campos-Pons, *Above All Things*," in *Thirteen Ways of Looking at Latino Art* (Durham, NC: Duke University Press, 2014), 181–94. For a series of essays on colorism within the African diaspora more generally, see Leigh Raiford and Heike Raphael-Hernandez, *Migrating the Black Body: The African Diaspora and Visual Culture* (Seattle: University of Washington Press, 2017).
6—Sarah Lewis, "The Racial Bias Built into Photography," *New York Times*, April 25, 2019, https://www.nytimes.com/2019/04/25/lens/sarah-lewis-racial-bias-photography.html.
7—Polaroid Corporation Research and Development test images, Baker Library Special Collections, mss: 658 1905-2005 P762, Polaroid Corporation records, box X.538.
8—Under the supervision of Ansel Adams and Meröe Marston Morse, a loose association of photographers used Polaroid products in the field, sending in notes in exchange for new supplies of materials. See Polaroid Corporation records, series IV, mss: 658 1905-2005 P762 IV.
9—Polaroids by Art Kane, sports photographer Walter Iooss, William Albert Allard, a documentary photographer known for his nuanced work with color film, and others can be found in the Polaroid Corporation records, series X, Baker Library Special Collections, mss: 658 1905-2005 P762, box X.734.
10—There was, however, urgency to widen the capacity of the products to expand their commercial potential, though not necessarily with altruistic motivations. In 1970, Caroline Hunter, a Black Polaroid research chemist, realized that the company was profiting by producing passbook photographs for the South African apartheid government. See Ainissa Ramirez, "Captured," in *The Alchemy of Us: How Humans and Matter Transformed One Another* (Cambridge, MA: MIT Press, 2020), 108–19.
11—Conversation with the author, June 24, 2022.
12—Kobena Mercer, *Travel and See: Black Diaspora Art Practices since the 1980s* (Durham, NC, and London: Duke University Press, 2016), 16.
13—Conversation with the author, June 24, 2022.
14—Conversation with the author, June 24, 2022.

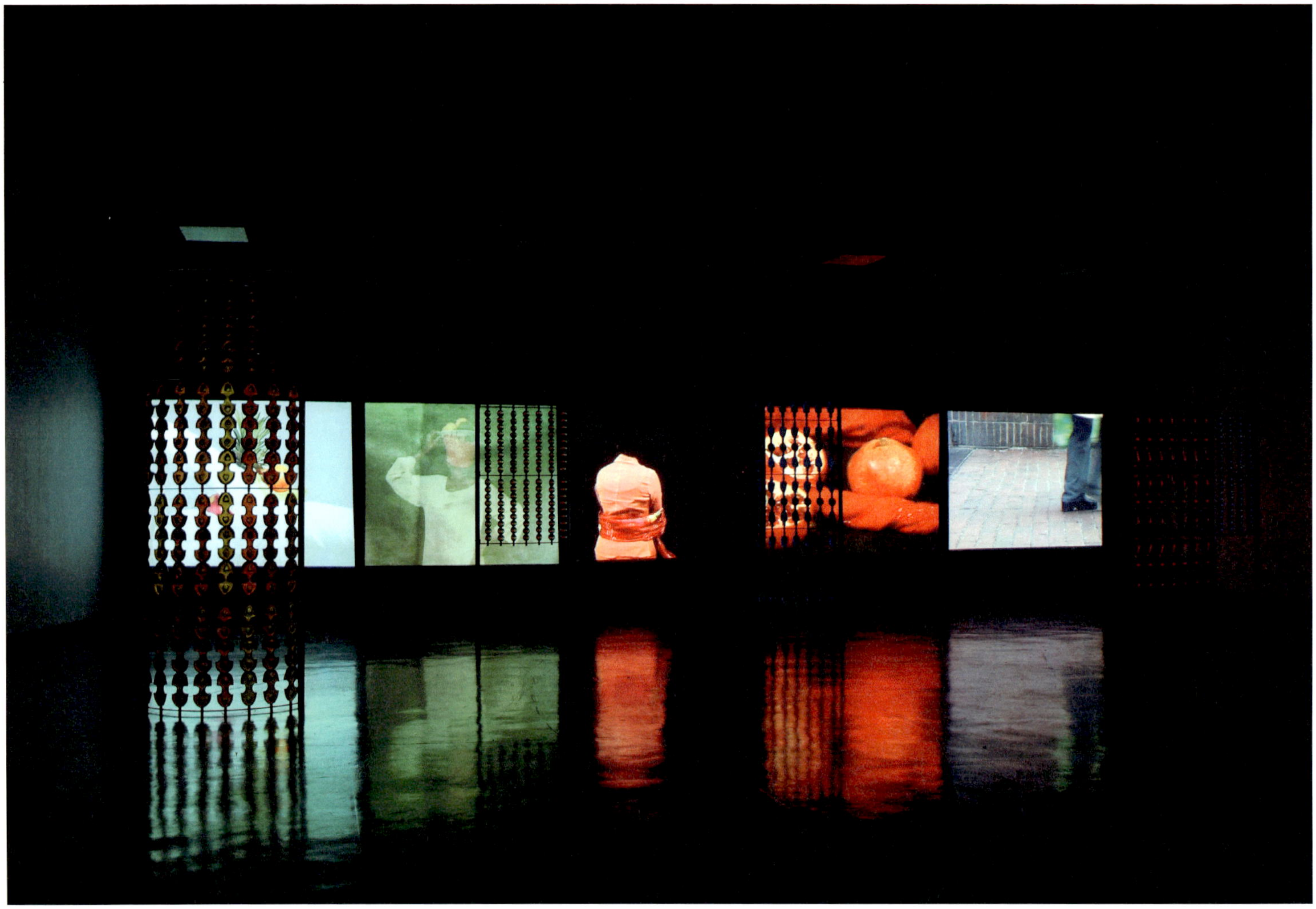

One Thousand Ways to Say Goodbye / Mil maneras para decir adiós / Threads of Memory (plate 30, detail), 2003

MARKING AND MAPPING: THE VIDEO ART PRACTICE OF MARÍA MAGDALENA CAMPOS-PONS

Phillip Townsend

The genesis of María Magdalena Campos-Pons's filmic work stretches back to the storytelling practices of her Nigerian ancestors—West African griots, whose oral traditions date back more than two thousand years—who passed them on to her father, who then taught them to her.[1] These oral narratives contain fine details of ancestry and ancestral experiences. They are important modes of transmitting knowledge, especially as they illuminate histories not present in archives, books, and other literary traditions. Often told through idioms and captivating storytelling, oral histories link present and past, serving as essential cultural preservation tools. Griots memorize important aspects of the history of their people, which they arrange in verses, recite often, and transmit from generation to generation by teaching their younger apprentices. Campos-Pons's film and video art practice considers, however, the deficiencies of oral traditions, such as the slippages that often occur with language translation, gaps in memory, and interculturalism. As such, we can think of her works as seeking to memorialize and retell her family's histories as they pertain to the experiences of Black people in white spaces, including her own biography.

Campos-Pons's artistic journey began in Cuba, where she was born in 1959 in Matanzas and then continued in the United States when in 1988 she was invited to study at Massachusetts College of Art (MassArt), taking film classes with Mark LaPore. During her time there, the artist learned to work with sound, film, and video—media not offered at Havana's Instituto Superior de Arte (ISA), where she received her earlier art training. At MassArt, she also met Carrie Mae Weems and other African American visual artists exploring the politics of Black women's identity. Campos-Pons's first yearlong stint in the United States also included repeated visits to the Harvard Film Archives—one of the largest and most significant university-based motion picture collections in the United States—and New York's Museum of Modern Art (MoMA), where she saw *For 25 Years: Crown Point Press* (1988) and *Arts for Television* (1989), both of which included work by U.S. performance and video art pioneer Joan Jonas.

Campos-Pons credits Jonas as well as Adrian Piper, David Hammons, Bruce Nauman, Chris Burden, and Louise Bourgeois, whom she would later see together in Robert Storr's 1991 monumental exhibition *Dislocations* at MoMA, as critical influences on her early video art practice.[2] Between 1990 and 1991, Canada played an essential role in the continuation of Campos-Pons's training in new media thanks to an artist residency at Banff Centre for the Arts in Alberta. While there, supported by video and performance artist Kate Craig, she created *Baño Sagrado (Rite of Initiation, Sacred Bath)* (plate 4) at Western Front, a nonprofit artist-run center, and was a visiting artist at Video-Inn, a video resource space with a library, both in Vancouver.[3] Her time away from Cuba enabled her to develop sophisticated content and the editing skills necessary to transform spliced film and video images into powerful meditations and visual metaphors on issues of race, gender, time, space, memory, and the power of the moving image itself.

Campos-Pons's interest in film, materiality, capturing time and memories, and storytelling is a product of her love of cinema. These ideas are present in *Baño Sagrado*, which also marked the beginning of the artist's more "sustained reflection on race and ethnicity."[4] This piece was an early collaboration between Campos-Pons and the experimental musician and composer Neil Leonard. During the subsequent thirty years, Leonard and Campos-Pons collaborated on what writer Nancy Pick describes as a "synthesis of art and music, Afro-Cuban and American, ancestral and electronic." Incorporating sound as a constant, critical component of her video art practice, Pick writes, they "created something new and entirely their own, as syncretic as the cultural intermingling that has taken place in Cuba itself between Europeans, Asians, and Africans."[5] Seeking a sonic analog for the work's visual poetry and spirituality, Leonard drew on sounds such as bells, synthesized percussion, flowing water, and even a sample from Jimi Hendrix. This protean soundscape enriches the experimental impact of the film.

In *Baño Sagrado*, Campos-Pons addresses the power and symbolism of a woman's bodily cycles through an interpretation of Santería and Yoruba rituals.[6] The central figure, played by the artist, references these rituals, "using water, milk, and blood as symbols of cleansing, sustenance, sexuality, pleasure, and nourishment connected with the cycles of life," in a work that "traces the journey from childhood to womanhood of a Black Cuban woman. In the piece I used nudity as a celebration of the body and the purity of the naked self. Also, as a mark of difference with the credo of the time in which Western feminists were very concerned with the representation of women's bodies. One idea was self-representation in a symbolic realm and empowering the body."[7] By presenting a Black woman's body, Campos-Pons claims ownership of her form and uses it as a vehicle to investigate her identity. Rather than mere personal introspection, this bodily performance suggests an investment in concepts beyond the artist herself such as spiritual hybridity, the scale of the universe, and humankind's position in it. *Baño Sagrado* also deploys stylistic and technical strategies indicative of early video art that stand in opposition to certain cinematic conventions such as linear narrative and character development.[8]

The emergence of video art in Latin America coincided with the region's uneven socioeconomic and political development. In many countries, its evolution was influenced by television, but in Cuba, cinema was the main pulse behind its rise. The Instituto Cubano del Arte e Industria Cinematográficos (ICAIC), also known as the Cuban Film Institute, formed shortly after the Cuban Revolution of 1959 and was part of a nationwide effort to educate the public by providing access to the arts. By 1961, the *cine móvil* (mobile cinema) program was sending mobile projection units to remote areas of the countryside, where illiteracy was prevalent (fig. 17). Film screenings were immensely popular and widely accessible, costing only one peso. The Instituto Superior de Arte, where Campos-Pons studied, developed a rigorous training regimen for the critical analysis of cinema.

But while the Revolution fostered debate about the role of cinema and the kinds of films best suited to the needs of the people and the state, Campos-Pons and other contemporary Cuban artists were regarding film as a vehicle for creativity and self-representation. To make *Baño Sagrado*, Campos-Pons distorted and played with various single frames she recorded over several weeks. She remixed and layered images and sounds to create a new artistic language that would permeate her subsequent video art practice. Video allowed her to use a medium previously regarded as embodying the literal to explore invisible phenomena and examine the gaps between the seen and the unseen, the spoken and the unspoken.

The unseen is central to Campos-Pons's 2012 video *Cuba Walk* (plate 55), which employs fragmented images of the artist's body to evoke the relationship between identity and the physical experience of place. The film shows only the artist's legs and feet as she promenades down a sidewalk

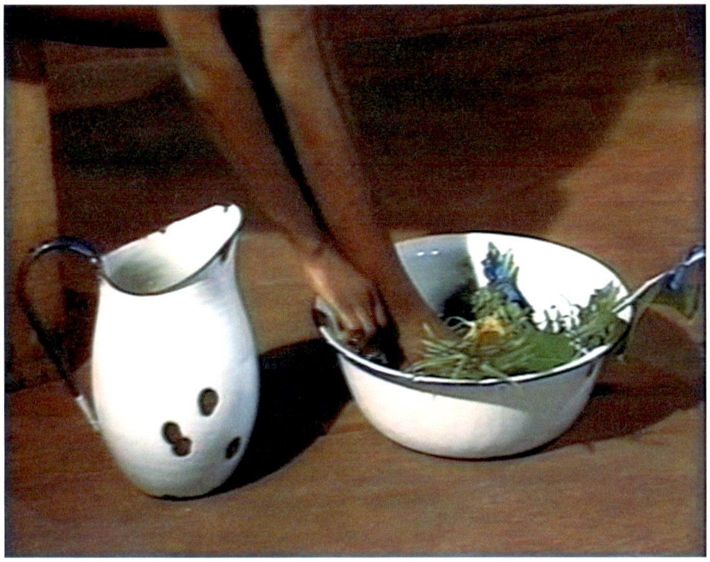

María Magdalena Campos-Pons, Still from video, *Baño Sagrado (Rite of Initiation, Sacred Bath)* (detail, plate 4), 1991

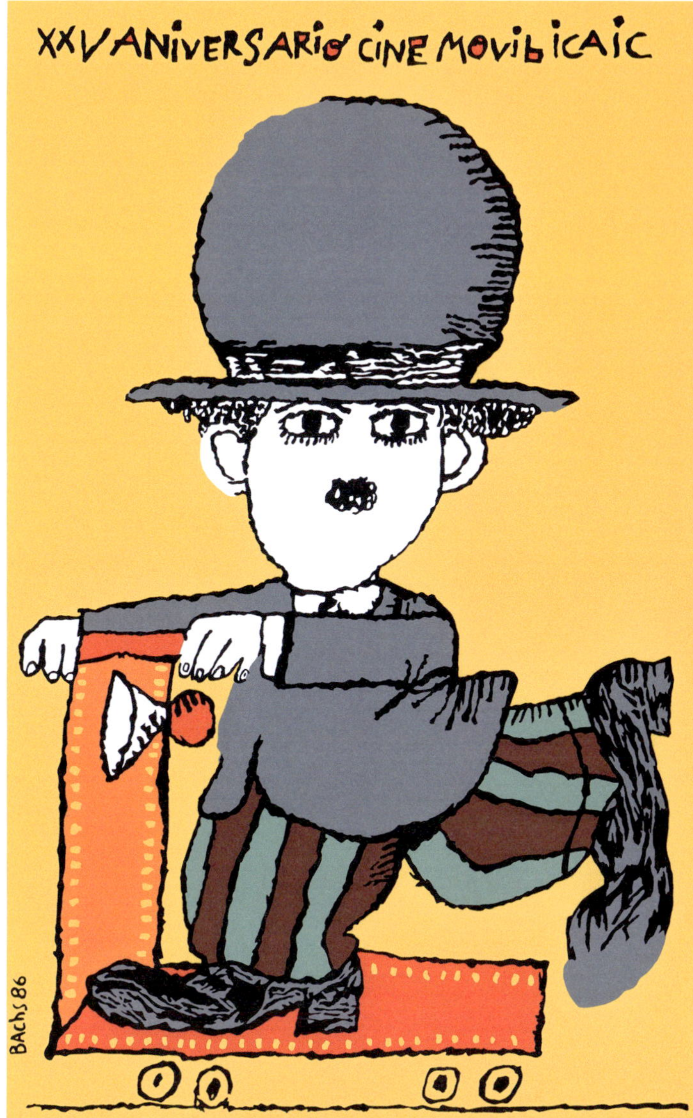

Fig. 17 Eduardo Muñoz Bachs (b. 1937, Valencia, Spain; d. 2001, Havana), *XXV Aniversario Cine Móvil ICAIC*, 1986. Screenprint, 76 x 51 cm (29 15/16 x 20 1/16 in.). Williamsburg, Virginia, Cuban Film Poster Collection, Special Collections Research Center, William & Mary Libraries

in Cuba. Voices and car engines and horns—a familiar urban soundscape—are audible, and for some listeners "nostalgic."[9] The stroll, with limited visual references, heightens the aural sensorial activation that walking can generate. The video highlights exilic bodies' simultaneous presence and invisibility in postrevolutionary Cuba—in other words, the partial display of Campos-Pons's body suggests a fragmented return to her home country. It harkens back to *Baño Sagrado*, in which the measured and careful movements of the artist's bare feet address the challenges and dynamism of self-representation. Near the end of *Cuba Walk*, the camera angle shifts from Campos-Pons's feet to her point of view, looking fixedly down at the sidewalk as she marches forward. In a way, the picture's shakiness puts the viewer in her position: pushing through the wind with a determined gait.

While the gesture of walking may seem mundane, walking as art has a rich history. Dadaist excursions in 1920s Paris were inspired by nineteenth-century French artists who painted pedestrians moving about the city, whose recent urban reconstruction involved the creation of new parks, squares, and boulevards. Art historian Nancy Forgione writes that in "recording the altered look of the city, painters also aimed to depict the everyday practices through which human life renegotiated its relation to the city. Its thematization in art focused not simply on the flâneur's specialized stroll but also on pedestrian activity as a wide-ranging modality of lived experience."[10] Using the country's colonial architecture as a backdrop, many contemporary descriptions of Cuba tend to highlight its aging infrastructure, lagging economy, and decaying urban landscape. But in *Cuba Walk*, Campos-Pons offers a sensorial view of the country that many fail to see. Here, walking is a generative gesture that marks and tracks time and presence and allows for contemplation.

In Campos-Pons's installation *Madonna Pellegrina - La Viajera* (2006, plate 41), stylized gold and green pavers, modeled after those typical of the Veneto region of Italy, bear gold impressions of Campos-Pons's footprints, which lead the viewer's eye to an accompanying video that documents the artist's daily walks in the city of Padua, where she resided at the time she made the piece. To a soundscape of footsteps, tintinnabulation, and moving cars, Campos-Pons traverses various surfaces—ancient and contemporary stone pavers, tiles, cobblestones, newly paved asphalt roads. The pavement, the shoes, the colors, and the feel of the seasons all change as she continues her journey through space and time. Walking becomes a meditative mode to question who has and has not inhabited the spaces one passes through, and to explore the specificity of territory, with all its contradictions, local conflicts, and constant transformations.

Madonna Pellegrina - La Viajera focuses on the repetition of the Black woman marking her journey, the simplicity of walking, and the complexities of marking territories. It also asks viewers to consider the historical presence of Black people in the Veneto region. The work belongs to a series that Campos-Pons calls Sono Qui, which in Italian means "I am here." There are scant artistic representations of people of African descent in Veneto, but two examples stand out: Vittore Carpaccio's *Miracle of the True Cross at the Ponte di Rialto* (ca. 1496, fig. 18) and *Hunting on the Lagoon* (ca. 1490–95, fig. 19). The presence of the Black gondoliers in Carpaccio's paintings is confirmed in scholarship by Dennis Romano, who found significant archival materials advertising their presence in Renaissance Venice.[11] However, as Kate Lowe suggests in her 2013 essay "Visible Lives: Black Gondoliers and Other Black Africans in Renaissance Venice," it is not currently possible to know the precise legal and social status of the Black gondoliers, or for that matter many of the Black servants in the Veneto region. The circumstances of much of their lives remain unknown.[12]

Madonna Pellegrina - La Viajera parallels *Carta Natal (Birth Certificate)* (1991, plate 3), an earlier wall installation by Campos-Pons that uses her own inked handprints to explore indexicality and the complexities of her journey from Cuba to Canada and ultimately to the United States. It also connects to *Cuba Walk* and *Baño Sagrado*, as they each mark and map the journeys of Black people traversing rural, urban, imagined, and real spaces: "I . . . collect and tell stories of forgotten people in order to foster a dialogue to better understand and propose a poetic, compassionate reading of our time."[13]

While Campos-Pons's prior video works embody her African ancestry, *My Mother Told Me I Am Chinese: China Porcelain* (2008, plate 44) illuminates the artist's familial connections with Chinese indentured laborers in Cuba. It attempts to visualize the complex web of experiences, nationalities, and histories that comprise her subjectivity and forces us to revise our understanding of the processes that led to the formation of her transnational identity. The video opens with Campos-Pons sitting in front of a mirrored red and black Chinese-style cracked-ice lattice panel (fig. 20). She places a *gelede* headdress—a headdress worn during masquerades staged in Yoruba villages and towns to pay homage to women—atop her dreadlocked head, then slowly removes the headdress and ritualistically applies white cascarilla (eggshell) powder to the parts of her body not covered by the Chinese robe she wears. She then draws stylized eyebrows and applies red lipstick. In a series of jump cuts, she flashes before the screen alternately holding the

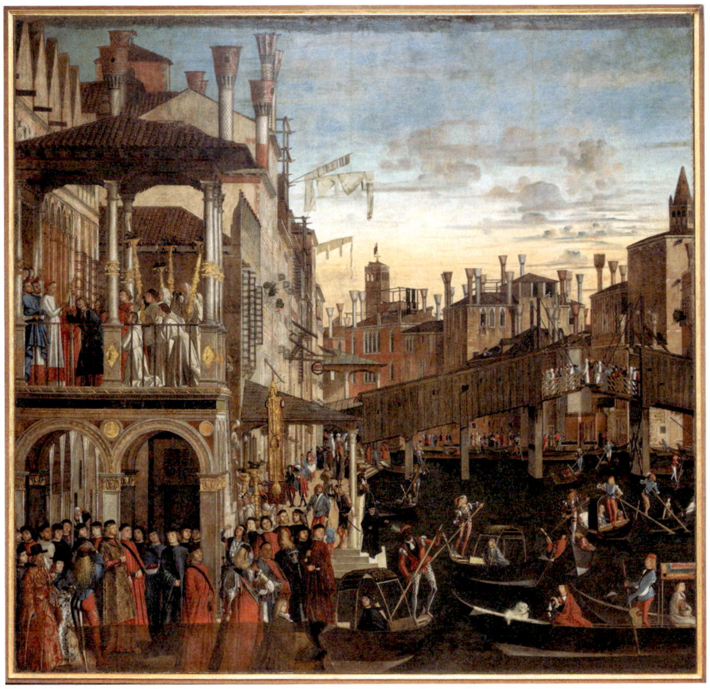

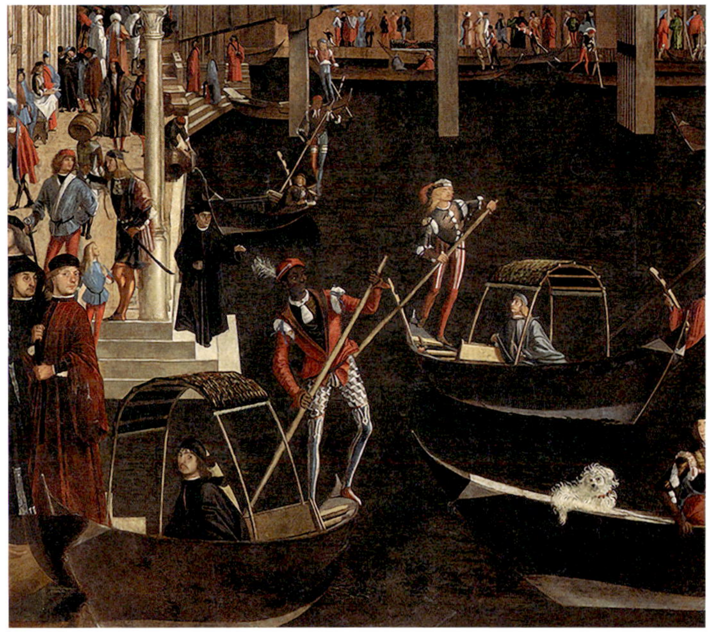

Fig. 18 Vittore Carpaccio (b. ca. 1460, Venice; d. 1526, Venice), *Miracle of the True Cross at the Ponte di Rialto* (and detail, top right), ca. 1496. Tempera on canvas, 371 x 392 cm (146 x 154 in.). Venice, Gallerie dell'Accademia

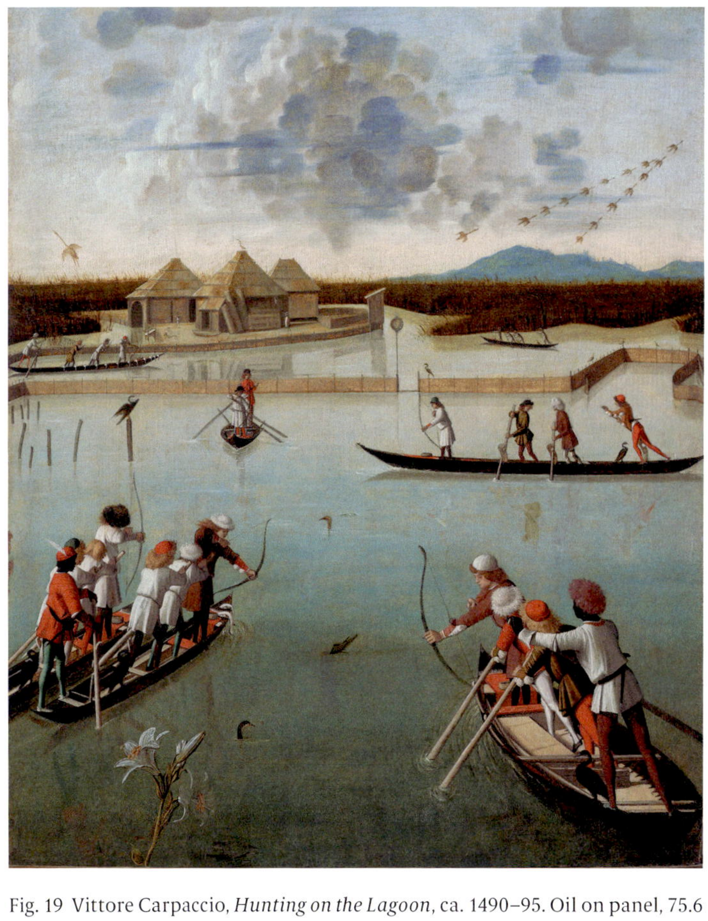

Fig. 19 Vittore Carpaccio, *Hunting on the Lagoon*, ca. 1490–95. Oil on panel, 75.6 x 63.8 cm (29 3/4 x 25 1/8 in.). Los Angeles, J. Paul Getty Museum, 79.PB.72

gelede headdress and a golden floral-patterned Chinese porcelain vase. Suddenly, the camera zooms in on a Chinese porcelain figurine of Guanyin, goddess of mercy and compassion, and transitions between it and the artist. Leonard's sound component incorporates Nigerian and Chinese sonic elements. The video ends with Campos-Pons standing in front of the Chinese panels, facing out at the viewer. She is not simply constructing an identity-laden self-portrait; she also presents hybridized Cuban, African, and Chinese cultural and historical references to the interracial alliances between Chinese indentured laborers and enslaved Africans. As historian Kathleen López notes, "African slaves and Asian coolies became . . . kinsmen and kinswomen in that world created by European masters."[14]

As with the griot tradition passed on to Campos-Pons by her father, the work's title emphasizes the importance of oral traditions to her matrilineal side. The artist recalls stories of an aunt nicknamed *la china* (the Chinese woman) and remembers a robust Chinese presence in her youth:

> I grew up aware of my Chinese ancestors, there was significant consumption of Chinese food at home. In fact, one of my favorite desserts was something we called at home "calabazita china," still, you could find it in Matanzas. . . . I was aware of the Chinese influence in Santería objects of the workshop and [it] just was a very common layer of everyday life. . . . What I know about them is that they were in the west of the island [originally] in Pinar del Rio, in a town called Guane. I believe the work there was centered on tobacco and railroad. . . . When I was young I visited some of my Chinese relatives in Havana City.[15]

Despite Campos-Pons having personal interactions with her Chinese relatives in Cuba, the first part of the work's title, *My Mother Told Me I Am Chinese*, underlines the revelatory importance of the oral tradition on Campos-Pons's matrilineal side. The artist's mother's disclosure of her Chinese heritage was just as profound as those stories taught by her father. Campos-Pons's artistic engagement with the Chinese contribution to her family's and Cuba's history emerged through conversations with relatives and a deeper probing of her memories and background.[16]

The history of Chinese migration to the Caribbean began in 1565 with the silver and chinoiserie trade, and the importation of indentured laborers from southern China to Cuba began in 1847. Chinese workers, referred to derogatorily as *los culíes chinos* (Chinese coolies), worked in urban areas and on sugar plantations alongside enslaved Africans.[17] This corresponded with an increased demand for sugar, which required an expansion of Cuba's labor force. Scholar Lisa Yun notes that between 1840 and 1847, an increase in Chinese indentured laborers, coupled with the rigorous enforcement of the transatlantic slave trade ban, led to a 90 percent decrease in the importation of slaves from Africa to Cuba.[18] Chinese laborers and enslaved Africans were a part of a "coproductive" economy until the abolition of slavery in Cuba in 1886.[19] *My Mother Told Me I Am Chinese: China Porcelain* not only highlights a personal history but also draws attention to the broader history of people and labor throughout the Caribbean.

Remarkable intersections of personal and communal histories are central to Campos-Pons's video art practice. Merging Eastern and Western technologies, symbols, cultural languages, and her own body, the artist creates moving images that function as loci of identity, relying on many facets and branching connections to her multilayered cultural heritage. Carrying her past with her, she remains steadfast in capturing the unstable, the fleeting, and the evasive, always in a poetic manner. Campos-Pons's film and video art practice is an ongoing investigation into and reconstruction of sensibilities and memories and shared culture, retracing of places and spaces, and evocation of personal and collective narratives. It articulates and resurfaces the tensions and commonalities in seemingly disparate diasporic histories and memories.

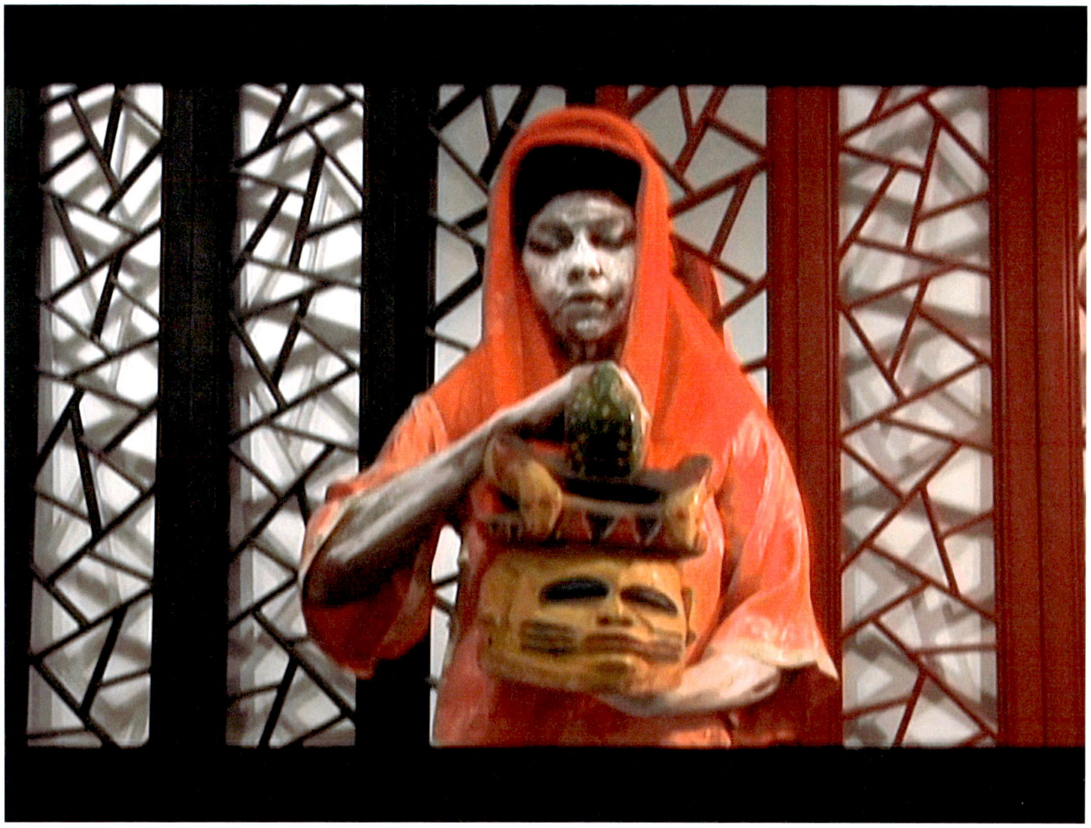

Fig. 20 María Magdalena Campos-Pons, Still from video, *My Mother Told Me I Am Chinese: China Porcelain* (detail), 2008. Hand-painted Chinese porcelain, Plexiglas shelf, single-channel video projection (color, sound, 5:48 min.), two-channel electroacoustic composition, approx. 228.6 x 231.1 x 139.7 cm (90 x 91 x 55 in.). Sound by Neil Leonard

NOTES

1—Griots are West African storytellers, oral historians, and poets trained to keep records of births, deaths, marriages, and significant events through the generations of a village or family. They are considered repositories of oral tradition, as the records they maintain are not written but learned, recited, and passed on orally, often with music.

2—Conversation with the author, July 6, 2022.

3—Western Front was founded in 1973 by architect Mo van Nostrand, writer Henry Greenhow, composer Martin Bartlett, and artists Kate Craig, Glenn Lewis, Eric Metcalfe, Michael Morris, and Vincent Nostrand. Campos-Pons has also carried out Canadian artist residencies at Nova Scotia College of Art and Design, Halifax (1990); Concordia University, Montreal (1990); Ontario College of Art, Toronto (1990); Fanshawe College, London, Ontario (1990); Simon Frasier University and Satellite Exchange, Vancouver (1990); and Western University, London, Ontario (1990).

4—Lisa D. Freiman, "María Magdalena Campos-Pons: Everything Is Separated by Water," in *María Magdalena Campos-Pons: Everything Is Separated by Water*, ed. Lisa D. Freiman (Indianapolis: Indianapolis Museum of Art; New Haven, CT: Yale University Press, 2007), 27.

5—Nancy Pick, "Cuba Distilled: Bringing Sound to the Alchemy of the Soul," Peabody Essex Museum website, http://alchemy.pem.org/cuba_distilled/. See also Phillip Townsend, "Like the Lonely Traveler: Video Works by María Magdalena Campos-Pons," in *Notes on Sugar / Like the Lonely Traveler: María Magdalena Campos-Pons* (San Francisco: Wendi Norris Gallery, 2018), 8, published following the exhibition *Notes on Sugar: María Magdalena Campos-Pons*, Art Galleries at Black Studies, University of Texas at Austin.

6—The Santería ritual that inspired *Baño Sagrado* is called *limpieza*. According to Solimar Otero, associate professor of folklore at Indiana University, "the *limpieza* may be used to open the way for other rituals or may be performed on its own. Usually, an adherent's godmother or godfather (*madrino* or *padrino*) takes an object, blesses it by calling upon Yoruba deities named *orisas* [*sic*], and passes it all over the adherent's body. The object is then removed and thrown out of a doorway, or taken to a crossroads for disposal. Objects that may be used include (but are not limited to) white cloth, live fowl, herbs, flowers, and blessed liquids. The *limpieza* ritual is arguably a focal point where body and spirit can actively be remedied at the same time." Solimar Otero, "Santería Health Systems: Looking at '*La Limpieza*,'" in *Folklore in Louisiana: Louisiana's Living Traditions* (Baton Rouge: Louisiana Office of Cultural Development, 2008), https://www.louisianafolklife.org/LT/Articles_Essays/LFMsanteria.html.

7—Freiman, *María Magdalena Campos-Pons: Everything Is Separated by Water*, 27.

8—While *Baño Sagrado* eschews narrative construction, it is central to many of Campos-Pons's filmic and video works, including *Spoken Softly with Mama* (1998, plate 20), *Meanwhile the Girls Were Playing* (1999–2000, plate 21), *One Thousand Ways to Say Goodbye / Mil maneras para decir adiós / Threads of Memory* (2003, plate 30), *Interiority or Hill-Sided Moon* (2003), and *53+1=54+1=55 / Letter of the Year* (2013, plate 59).

9—Louis A. Perez Jr., "The Nostalgia of Empire: Time Travel in Cuba," *International*

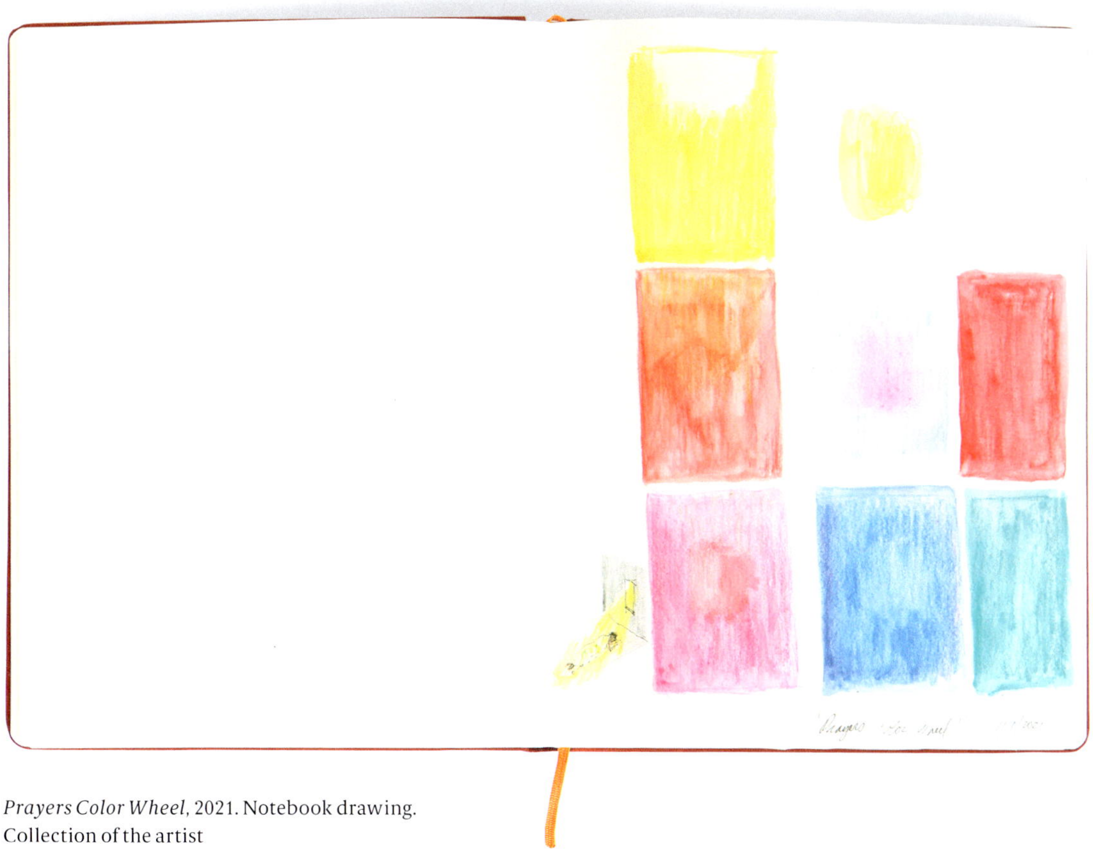

Prayers Color Wheel, 2021. Notebook drawing.
Collection of the artist

Journal of Cuban Studies 10, no. 1 (Spring 2018): 8–11. Perez argues that representations of Cuba in North American popular culture (blogs, travel guides, television documentaries, newspapers, travel company websites and brochures, music videos) establish the country as a "site of nostalgia." Images and sounds of classic cars—especially American automobiles from the 1940s and 1950s—serve as the dominant iconographic representation of Cuba.

10—Nancy Forgione, "Everyday Life in Motion: The Art of Walking in Late Nineteenth-Century Paris," *Art Bulletin* 87, no. 4 (December 2005): 664.

11—Dennis Romano, "The Gondola as a Marker of Station in Venetian Society," *Renaissance Studies* 8, no. 4 (1994): 359–74.

12—Kate Lowe, "Visible Lives: Black Gondoliers and Other Black Africans in Renaissance Venice," *Renaissance Quarterly* 66, no. 2 (Summer 2013): 413.

13—"When We Gather," CreativeTime.org, January 2021, https://creativetime.org/when-we-gather-mmcp-artists/.

14—Kathleen López, *Chinese Cubans: A Transnational History* (Chapel Hill: University of North Carolina Press, 2013), 5. See also Gary Okihiro, *Margins and Mainstreams: Asians in American History and Culture* (Seattle: University of Washington Press, 1994), 42; Lisa Lowe, "The Intimacies of Four Continents," in *Haunted by Empire: Geographies of Intimacy in North American History*, ed. Ann Laura Stoler (Durham, NC: Duke University Press, 1996), 191–212; Sean Metzger, "Ripples in the Seascape: The Cuba Commission Report and the Idea of Freedom," *Afro-Hispanic Review* 27, no. 1 (2008): 105–21; Lisa Yun, *The Coolie Speaks: Chinese Indentured Laborers and African Slaves in Cuba* (Philadelphia: Temple University Press, 2008).

15—"Art Imitating Life: An Exploration of the Chinese Caribbean Diaspora," Chinadaily.com.cn, March 20, 2018, https://global.chinadaily.com.cn/a/201803/20/WS5ab0c666a3106e7dcc143e63_3.html.

16—Heather Shirey, "Life Has Not Even Begun," *African Arts* 43, no. 4 (2010): 84–87. This shift in her gaze was also in part spurred by an invitation to participate in the 2008 Guangzhou Triennial, China.

17—"Coolie" was the bureaucratic term the British used to describe indentured laborers, but it became a highly charged slur. The label *los culíes chinos* refers to the thousands of East and South Asians who traveled to the Americas as part of a system of indentured labor used throughout the British colonies. Although the word "coolie" is primarily associated with histories of the Caribbean and South America, the term was long used as a slur against low-wage immigrant laborers in the United States. In fact, President Abraham Lincoln signed "An Act to Prohibit the 'Coolie Trade' by American Citizens in American Vessels" in 1862. See United States Congress, "1862 Anti Coolie Act," Asian American Digital History Archive, https://aadha.binghamton.edu/items/show/209.

18—Yun, *The Coolie Speaks*, 6.

19—Yun, *The Coolie Speaks*, 6. The term "co-production" was originally coined in the late 1970s by economist Elinor Ostrom to designate a process in which contributions from "individuals who are not 'in' the same organization are transformed into goods and services." Elinor Ostrom, "Crossing the Great Divide: Coproduction, Synergy, and Development," *World Development* 24, no. 6 (June 1996): 1073–74.

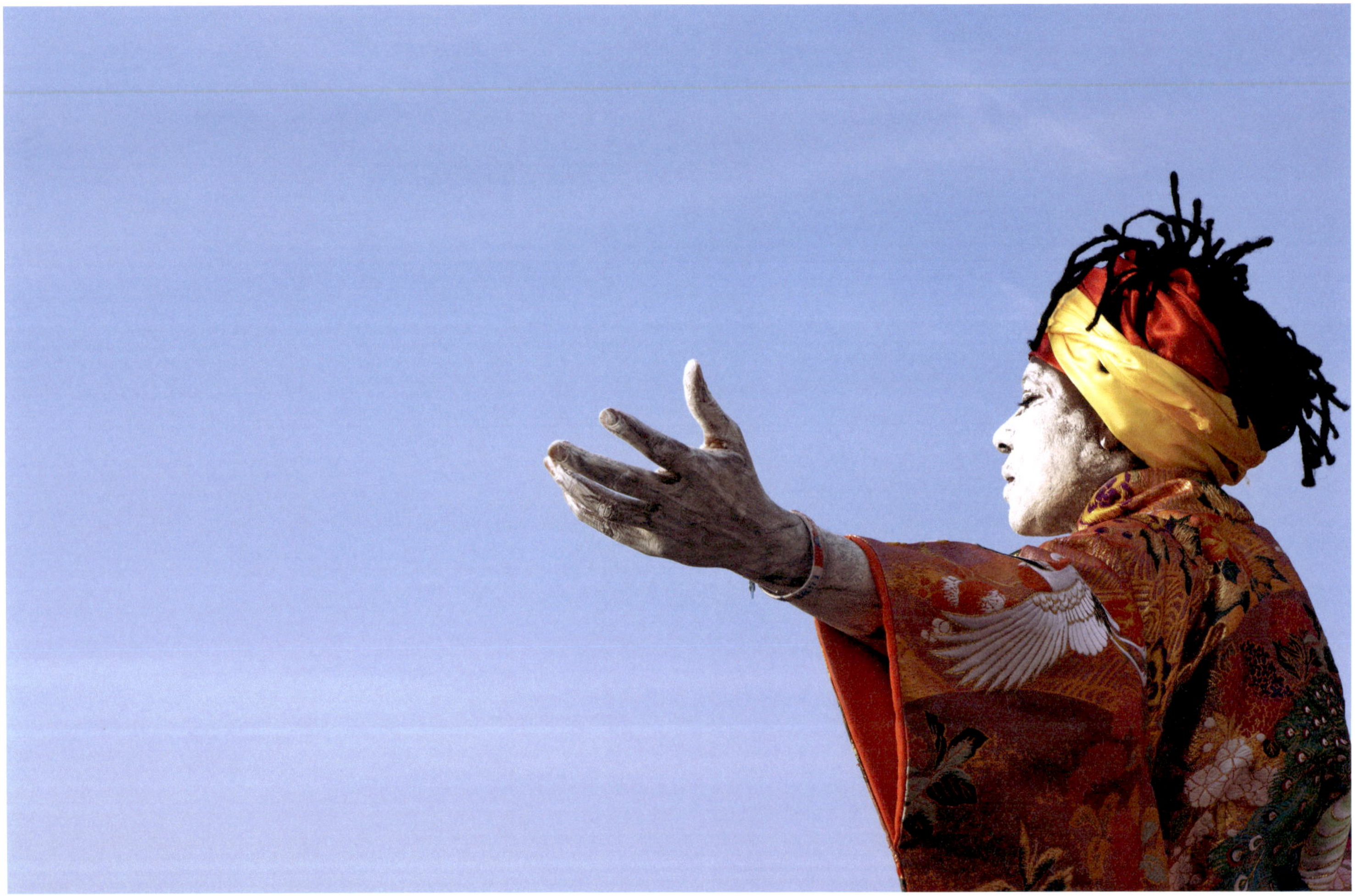

FeFa, 2012

FOLLOW FEFA

Jenée-Daria Strand

Prince as Camille, Beyoncé as Sasha Fierce, Lorraine O'Grady as Mlle. Bourgeoise Noire—what compels an artist to create an alternate self, an alter ego? For some, like Lorraine O'Grady or Nick Cave, the alter ego acts as a partition between the natural self and the performative self. In O'Grady's other persona, The Knight, enacted in *Announcement of a Persona (Performances to Come!)* (2020, fig. 21), the artist visually separates herself from her persona by concealing her markers of identity (race, gender, age) behind a custom-made plated-steel suit of armor. The same can be said for Nick Cave's soundsuits (fig. 22)—densely textured and richly colored garments that, aside from their limbs, almost entirely obscure the bodily form. Such separation ensures that the process of embodying the alter ego is a space of transformation, where the natural self can be erased and the alternate self may emerge with a newly defined past, present, and future. For others, as for example in the case of performance artist Vaginal Davis, elements of the natural self remain present, yet the alter ego provides a conduit through which liberation is seized and the boundlessness of emotivity is explored.[1]

For María Magdalena Campos-Pons, the latter rings truest. The artist's alternate self, FeFa, operates as a perennial counternarrative to constructions of power and bureaucracy, dwelling in liminal temporalities that collapse tradition, modernity, family history, Santería practices, and contemporary art theories.[2] Such ideas have been present in her work since the foundational *Umbilical Cord* (1991, plate 2), although FeFa did not officially appear until a 2012 performance in conjunction with Campos-Pons's first exhibition in Cuba since 1989, *1478 MB*, titled after the distance in miles between Matanzas and Boston and held at Havana's Casa de las Américas. FeFa would emerge again later that year in a performance at the Havana Biennial (plate 56). The name FeFa is an acronym combining the Spanish phrase *familiares en el extranjero* with its

English translation, "family abroad." FeFa supplies a conduit through which Campos-Pons can emote the fullness of her frustration, the multiplicities of all whom she represents, and the potentialities of new ways forward. When FeFa calls, you respond. Where FeFa goes, you follow.

Dressed in white (the signature garment color of Santería) with accents of blue (the color of Yemayá), seven women processed through the entrance to the court of the National Gallery of Art in Washington, DC, on April 30, 2022, chanting the names of their ancestors and alternate selves: *llegó Alma, llegó FeFa* (Alma arrived, FeFa arrived). The chants coalesce with the performers' commanding presence to usher in potent energies. Led by Campos-Pons and part of a performance titled *When We Gather* (2022, plates 92–93), the women create circular paths with their bodies and spatial patterns, transcending their physical state to connect with Yemayá, the Yoruba orisha of the sea. Yemayá is a representation of life, both present and ancestral, and performances in her honor recall her maternal essence through movement, voice, percussion, and communal gathering. The dancers' cyclical patterns are rhythmic, accented by the syncopation of a conga and imitating the cadence of crashing waves or an oar pushing against oceanic resistance.[3] Above all, performances in homage to Yemayá portray a spirit that is not easily broken. For the viewer, the procession is powerful, reverent, and timely. For Campos-Pons, it is often painful.

"It is not that I am *in* pain, but I *have* pain," the artist explains.[4] The pain she holds lingers from generations of colonialism and enslavement—she is amply aware of the intersections of her own familial and cultural history with larger global narratives of violence, forcible displacement, and slavery. The National Gallery performance is exemplary of Campos-Pons's enlacing of traditional African diasporic practices with contemporary artistic expressions in works that transcend temporal bounds.[5] Such alchemy thoroughly characterizes an oeuvre that is strikingly multifaceted yet notably harmonious; it is both traditional and contemporary, autobiographical and communal, present and historic, celebratory and critical. *When We Gather* commenced with an offering to the past—the extension of an invitation from the performers to their ancestors: "Ancestors, in this day, give us permission to mark this particular building, this particular site."[6] Decades earlier, a similar invitation began Pearl Primus's performance titled *Pearl Primus: Omowale (Child Returned Home)*, which was later restaged for the Alvin Ailey American Dance Theater and performed by Judith Jamison in 1974.[7] Primus (fig. 23) starts her performance with a downward gaze and outstretched arms as she recites an incantation of her own: "Oh earth, you who embrace the bones of our ancestors, help me—lend me your strength." Both proclamations are as intimate as reciting grace before a meal or gesturing the sign of the Cross during times of anxiety. Such gesticulations suggest that the body is a conduit for spiritual fulfillment—the spirit must take precedence, and the body will follow.

Traditions of African diasporic reverence are rooted in notions of liberating the physical, abandoning the constraints of the body and the anxieties of the mind to welcome the will of the spirit. African diasporic traditions embrace holistic sensorial embodiments. Touch, taste, sight, sound, and smell combine in practices that are often marginalized in Western traditions. Whereas Western modes of engagement, from religious interpretation to artistic spectatorship to early education, divide the mind from the body, in diasporic traditions the mind and the body are one and coalesce in displays of deep refusal, protest, and transcendence.[8]

Refusing this nonexistent divide is a practice Campos-Pons inherited by witnessing Santería ritual manifestations of the spirit in Matanzas, Cuba, as a child. Watching bodies travel across metaphysical planes and transcend into dimensions not yet comprehensible, the future artist knew that she was holding space for the fruition of an enchanted experience despite an inability at that time to verbalize her encounters.[9] Only later did she intuit that such ephemeral displays of cultural experience are, in fact, performances. Such spiritual intensities are the essence of Santería rituals, which deeply inform Campos-Pons's practice (although she intentionally avoids direct appropriation). A reverence for the orishas of Santería is integral to Campos-Pons's life, as in Oshun's role as goddess of the river, embodying replenishment and restoration through cyclical patterns of life. Campos-Pons creates work that honors this energy while disrupting temporalities and art historical traditions to advance contemporary performance practices.

Campos-Pons's performative practice conflates the sacred and the secular and connects the artist's biographical narrative to the revolving satellites of a larger transnational rendering. The artist contests the extractions and erasures of stories and bodies deemed peripheral, outsider, or subaltern from the master narratives of historical retellings.[10] The subaltern is normatively "relegated to the margins of intellectual discourse by being constructed as myth and/or folklore."[11] For Campos-Pons, the subaltern is nuclear; it is her subject, and the performance is her protest. "I am a conduit to capture the discomfort," she proclaims.[12] Discomfort does not wait for permission, nor does it have the privilege of time when pain is palpable and death is imminent.

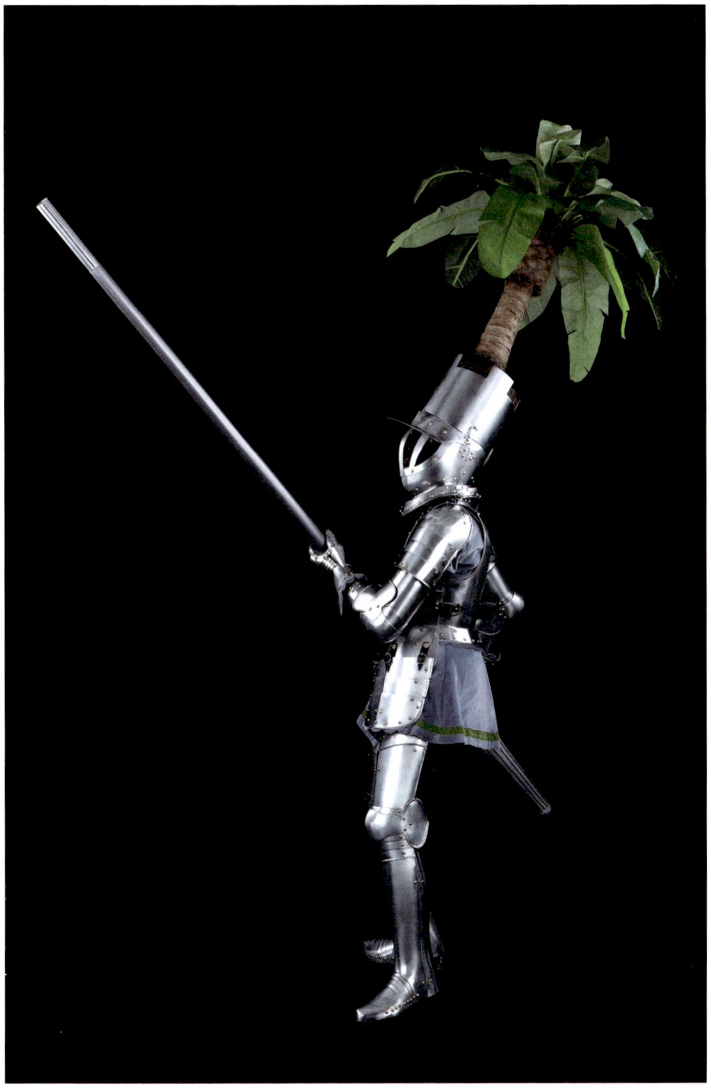

Fig. 21 Lorraine O'Grady (b. 1934, Boston), *Announcement Card 1 (Banana-Palm with Lance),* from Announcement of a New Persona (Performances to Come!), 2020. Digital print, 127 x 84.8 cm (50 x 33 3/8 in.). Alexander Gray Associates

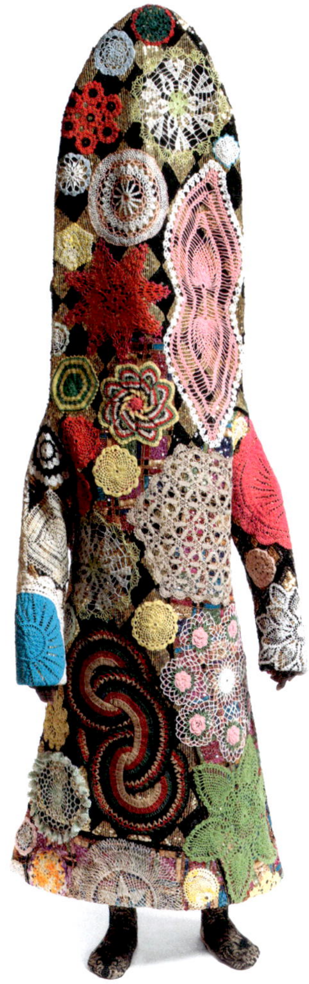

Fig. 22 Nick Cave (b. 1959, Fulton, Missouri), *Soundsuit*, 2009. Mixed media, 243.8 x 66 x 50.8 cm (96 x 26 x 20 in.). Jack Shainman Gallery, New York

Discomfort requires an intervention. It resists, abandons, and contests until it is free.

Embodied resistance is often difficult to imagine and enact within atmospheres that spatially demand objective education and tedious procedural requirements, such as museums.[13] Campos-Pons, however, has no shortage of imagination, and for the artist, performance is resistance to institutional structures seen and felt. In such early works as *The Seven Powers Come by the Sea* (1992, plate 6), she catalyzed guerrilla-style subversions of her prominent exhibition sites to "call attention to the artist as a body" in what the artist calls a "condition beyond theatricality."[14] Through FeFa, Campos-Pons creates performances that speak on behalf of others who do not have the privilege of mobility or access to certain spaces, and calls attention to pressing issues that are not celebratory. This emotional depth intentionally disrupts the superficial pleasantries of social interactions at "art world" events—as the artist has summarized, "Trust me, I am not entertaining you."[15]

While FeFa did not become a distinct part of Campos-Pons's practice until 2012, I perceive this alter ego's presence as early as 1991 in *Baño Sagrado (Rite of Initiation, Sacred Bath)* (plate 4), a collaboration between the artist and Neil Leonard. It depicts the maturation of a Black Cuban woman, played by the artist, who enacts a cleansing ritual interpreted from Santería and Yoruba traditions using water, milk, and blood, "which symbolize sustenance, sexuality, pleasure, and nourishment."[16] Simultaneously at play in Campos-Pons's conception of the work is an interrogation of Western feminist ideologies during a time in which "Western feminists were very concerned with the representation of women's bodies."[17] Campos-Pons uses the woman figure to embody self-representation and bodily autonomy through symbolism and ritual; the essence of the performance is for a purpose larger than her own concerns. The woman in this particular piece, though unnamed, engages in a framework that is now linked to FeFa. Decades later, the artist proceeded to develop FeFa as "both an artistic persona and a metaphor for the immigration, exile, family and community separation experienced by numerous Cuban families."[18] At the 2012 Havana Biennial, the opening performance at the Wifredo Lam Center involved one of Campos-Pons's and Leonard's multimedia collaborations and was the second official appearance of her alter ego. It was titled *Llegooo! FeFa!* (plate 56), and at the outset eighteen Cuban street vendors (*pregoneros*) from the Malecón vibrantly greeted FeFa; each had successfully impressed the judges of the first-ever *pregonero* competition, arranged by Campos-Pons in a manner after *American Idol* and juried by notable music specialists in honor of the musical cries of the vendors characteristic of Cuba to this day.[19]

The melodic and rhythmic chants known as the *pregón*, or seller's cry, are a sound unique to the streets of Cuba, although the *pregón* did make its way to the United States in 1931 after Louis Armstrong and His Sebastian New Cotton Club Orchestra sampled the iconic Cuban song "El Manisero" (The Peanut Vendor).[20] Back in the Wifredo Lam Center, the *pregoneros* beckoned to FeFa, who responded with her own chants and led the *pregoneros* around the pavilion in a procession—now one of her trademarks.

"The procession employs distinctive elements to distinguish it from everyday movement through space. . . . [It] is designed to compete with the existing environment around it, becoming for a time the dominant element."[21] Processions are integral to many groups and cultures but remain particularly relevant in African diasporic traditions, as for instance in American jazz funeral dirges and second-line parades (fig. 24). The procession is not simply a means of moving from one place to another but rather movement through a space in ceremonially and symbolically important ways. Through this procession, FeFa pointed to the *pregoneros*' survival across centuries despite the erasure of free-market enterprises after the 1959 Cuban Revolution and Fidel Castro's enactment of a centralized economy, which *pregoneros* disrupt in a prolific caveat to state ownership of capital and resources. In proclaiming their voices at the Havana Biennial, the *pregoneros* reiterated their presence as integral to the cultural fabric of Cuba—one that had prevailed despite prolonged attempts to efface their labor and financial freedom. FeFa's performance resulted in the social legitimation of the *pregoneros*, ultimately easing the sustained police harassment they faced in Cuba.

The *pregón* continued to reverberate in 2013 when the artistic trio of Campos-Pons, FeFa, and Leonard created the multisensory installation *53+1=54+1=55 / Letter of the Year* (plate 59) in conjunction with the Cuban Pavilion at the 55th Venice Biennale. An amalgamation of sounds recorded in Havana overlaid the sculptural presence of one hundred interconnected birdcages housing documentary-style videos streaming on numerous custom video screens. Birdcages have been used for millennia by imperials and ordinary people alike as a means of capturing beauty for personal enjoyment. The metaphorical resonances of the birdcages aptly confronted the peering gaze of Roman imperial busts installed nearby. Leonard's sound score combined *pregonero* chants with interviews in which Cubans describe the economic and material support they wish to receive

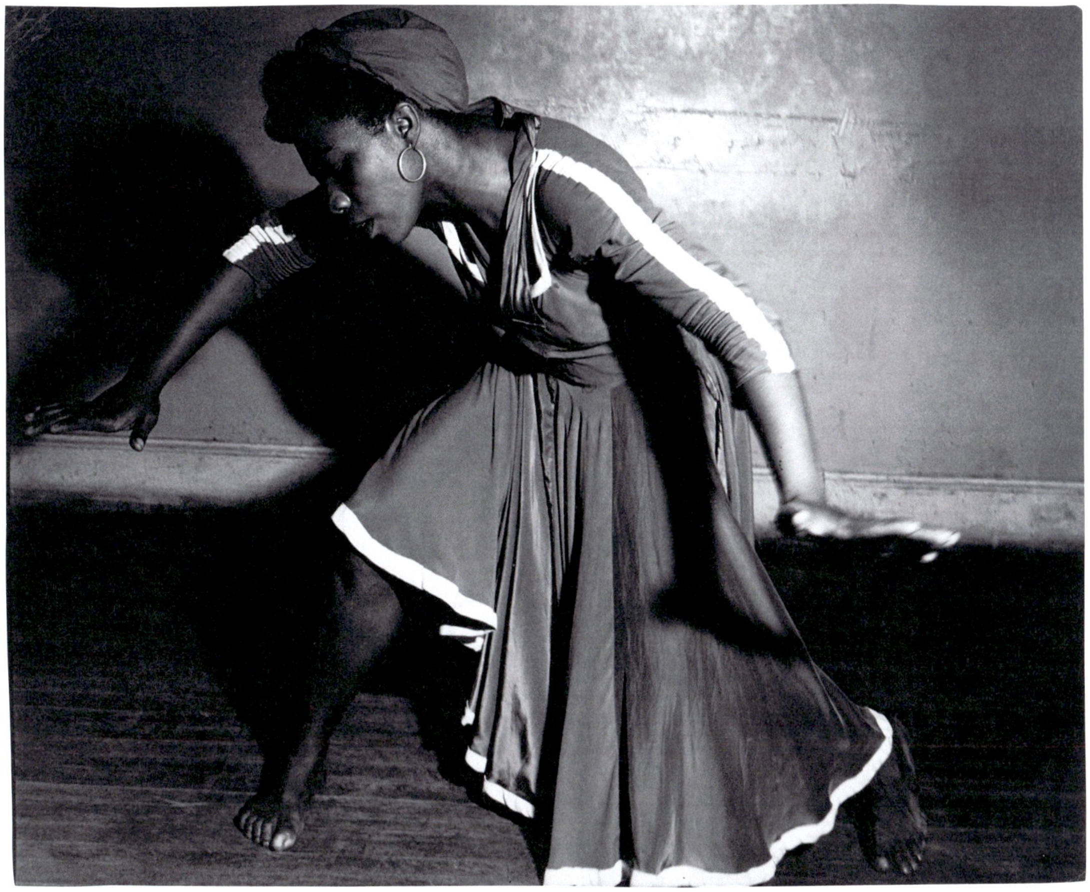

Fig. 23 Lisette Model (b. 1901, Vienna; d. 1983, New York), *Pearl Primus*, 1943. Gelatin silver print, 27.7 x 34.8 cm (10 7/8 x 13 3/4 in.). Washington, DC, National Portrait Gallery, Smithsonian Institution

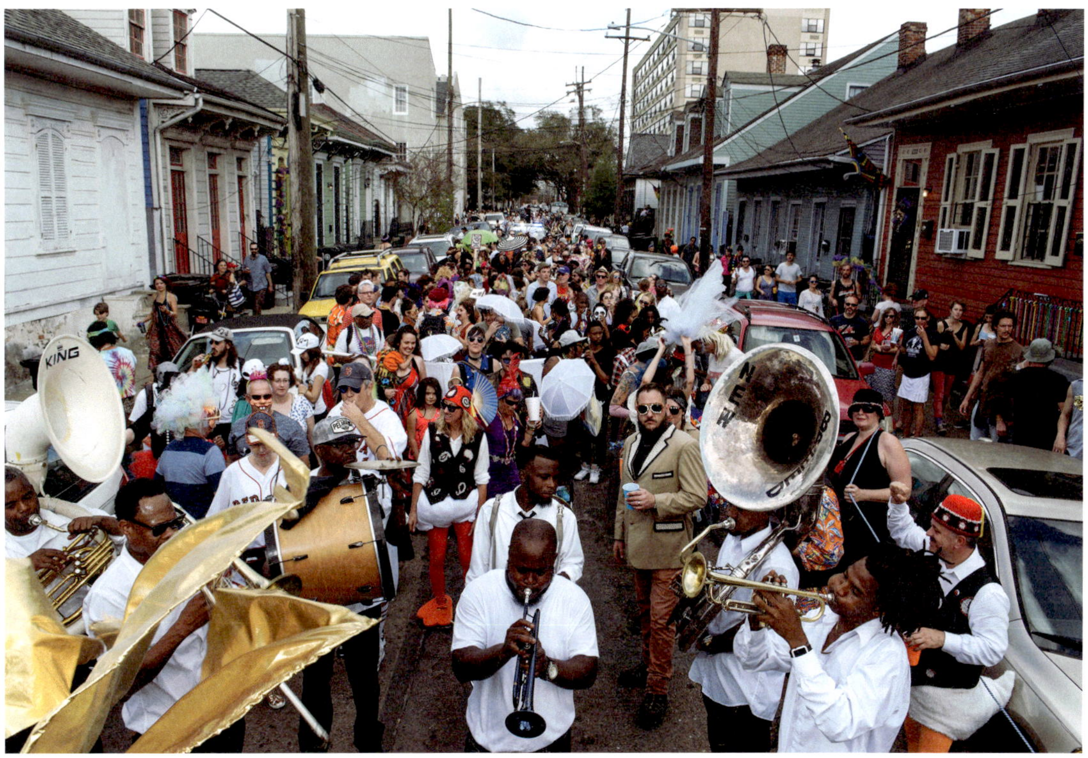

Fig. 24 Ryan Hodgson-Rigsbee (b. 1981, Chicago), *Krewe of Red Beans Parade on Lundi Gras, New Orleans*, 2020

from their families abroad. The result was a cartography of Havana's sonic cacophonies.

The installation was representative of Campos-Pons's self-appointed duty to use her access and art-world clout to represent Afro-Cubans in triumph and in tribulation. The narratives and cultural references the artist invokes are pointed, specifically considering the ways in which European Communist bloc regimes profited from the legacy of the labor of those enslaved and forced to work on sugar plantations in Cuba. For three decades, the Soviet Union acted as Cuba's primary trading partner, enforcing monoculture to the detriment of other potential exports, while sheltering its sugar industry with monetary subsidies. The collapse of Communist regimes in Eastern Europe in 1989, and the subsequent fall of the Soviet Union in 1991, sparked a crisis in Cuba's economy. As the exchange of oil for sugar between the Soviets and Cuba evaporated, the Cuban "Special Period" commenced—a time also known as the Special Period in the Time of Peace, marked by severe food shortages and a scramble for new ways to diversify agricultural production. Through FeFa, Campos-Pons engages in histories that call her personal proximity to enslavement to the fore while illustrating transnational relations through histories of enslavement, labor, and our global economy.[22]

53+1=54+1=55 / Letter of the Year is a complex commentary on lives, hopes, and dreams that reverberate well beyond the limitations of their confinement, an audible performance enacted through the limitations and freedoms of architecture. The title alludes to the sacred Yoruba ceremony held between the evening of December 31 and the morning of January 1, which through consultation with the Santería orishas predicts what the coming year will bring. Campos-Pons's nod to the Letter of the Year ceremony beckoned FeFa to lead the way forward in an unforgettable, and unannounced, performance (plate 60). Dressed in a decadently designed Chinese robe with Italian shoes and a reinterpreted Yoruba headdress, FeFa moved through the crowd in Venice's Piazza San Marco. Accompanied by the Cuban band Los Hermanos Arango, who were on this occasion dressed in Santería whites, FeFa performed a call and response of Yoruba chants and Abakuá dances (Abakuá is a Nigerian-derived esoteric society that is traditionally closed to women). FeFa knows how to make an entrance.

The artist's unsolicited invasion, her self-announced arrival, engaged in what scholars Stephanie Sparling Williams and Michelle Wallace argue is "the only 'tradition' available to the Black female critical voice."[23] It harnesses the strategies of the most notable political demonstrations and distills them into a practice of survival—"speaking out of turn."[24] Speaking out of turn is a methodology developed out of the historical condition of being silenced and rendered invisible. FeFa bypasses governances and bureaucracies to agitate structures of power and suppression. Museums and other exhibition sites, in particular, have restricted critique to performances of observation in which objective education is permissible but demonstrations of resistance are subject to policing. FeFa, for her part, challenges sites and entities that have historically surveilled bodies and curtailed liberties. Campos-Pons's practice rejects objective education via the amplification of embodied performance.

Acutely aware of the aura of spectacle that can ensue from witnessing a performance, Campos-Pons refuses canonical structures of performativity so as to disrupt the impression of theatricality. For instance, spatial distance between "performer" and "spectator" is reduced to create intimacies unavailable in typical theater architecture. Campos-Pons often performs "in the round," another method of disrupting spatial hierarchies between self and other—a circuitous energy that recalls the unification of spirit and body in Santería practices. FeFa's explorations of the body "in a condition beyond theatricality" from within African religious praxis, which requires full engagement in ceremonies and rituals to animate spiritual traditions.[25] Observation is not enough, and thus her performances are both presentation and invitation. "We gather for love, we gather for hope, we gather for peace," FeFa urges.[26] When we gather, possibilities emerge; when we gather, differences are set aside; when we gather, there is hope for our collective futures.

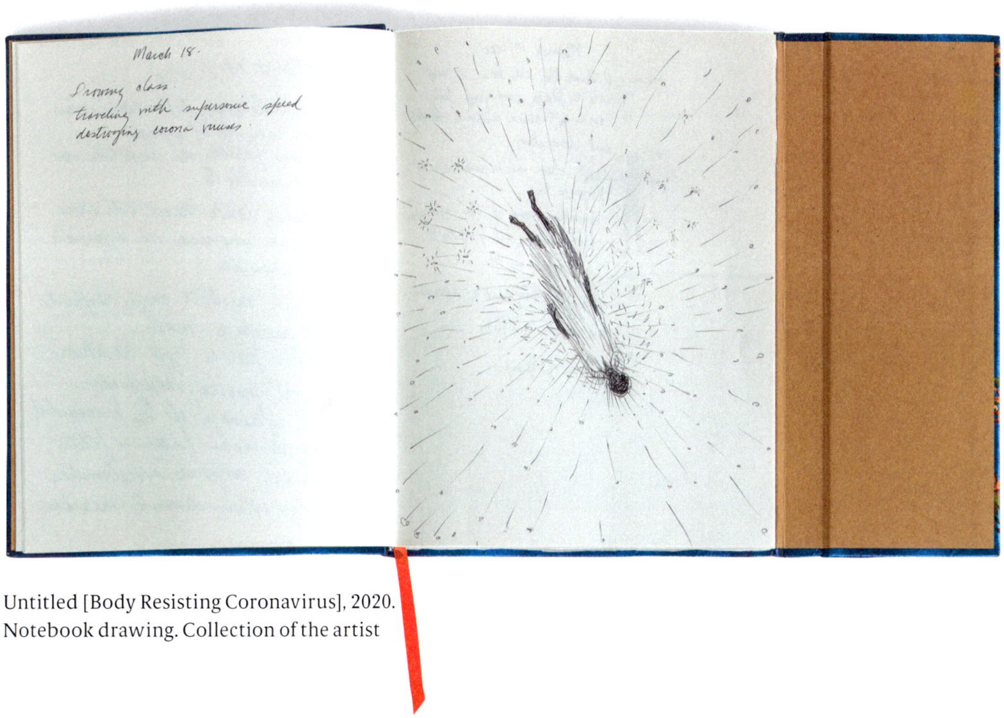

Untitled [Body Resisting Coronavirus], 2020.
Notebook drawing. Collection of the artist

NOTES

1—Vaginal Davis is a multidisciplinary artist whose work intentionally defies media classifications. Best known for her performance and experimental film practice, Davis creates provocative work that interrogates her cultural otherness. Davis's persona is not a part of her; it is who she is.

2—Flora M. González, "Possession and Altar Making: Reconstruction of Memory as Artistic Performance in the Multimedia Installations of María Magdalena Campos-Pons," *Cuban Studies* 31 (2000): 102–17.

3—Claudia Rodríguez, "The Dance of Yemayá, the Dance of the Waves," *Ashé pa mi Cuba*, August 3, 2020, https://ashepamicuba.com/en/el-baile-de-yemaya-la-danza-de-las-olas/.

4—Lynne Bell, "History of People Who Were Not Heroes: A Conversation with María Magdalena Campos-Pons," *Third Text* 12, no. 43 (Summer 1998): 40.

5—González, "Possession and Altar Making," 104.

6—"María Magdalena Campos-Pons's *When We Gather*," National Gallery of Art, 2022, YouTube, https://www.youtube.com/watch?v=yVxd9bi_mmU.

7—Jennifer Dunning, "Pearl Primus Is Dead at 74; A Pioneer of Modern Dance," *New York Times*, October 31, 1994, https://www.nytimes.com/1994/10/31/obituaries/pearl-primus-is-dead-at-74-a-pioneer-of-modern-dance.html.

8—Yolanda Covington-Ward, Jeanette S. Jouili, and Jacob K. Olupona, "Foreword," in *Embodying Black Religions in Africa and Its Diasporas*, ed. Yolanda Covington-Ward and Jeanette S. Jouili (Durham, NC: Duke University Press, 2021), vi–xiv.

9—Conversation with the author, July 17, 2022.

10—The term "subaltern," in the context of critical theory and postcolonialism, refers to populations that are socially, politically, and geographically denied access to hegemonic power.

11—Nikki Sullivan and Craig Middleton, "From LGBTQ+ Inclusion to Queer Ethics," in *Queering the Museum* (London: Routledge, 2019), 35.

12—Conversation with the author, July 17, 2022.

13—Jennifer Tyburczy, "All Museums Are Sex Museums," in *Sex Museums: The Politics and Performance of Display* (Chicago: University of Chicago Press, 2016), 1–38.

14—Conversation with the author, July 17, 2022.

15—Conversation with the author, July 17, 2022.

16—Lisa Freiman, ed., "María Magdalena Campos-Pons: Everything Is Separated by Water," in *María Magdalena Campos-Pons: Everything Is Separated by Water* (Indianapolis: Indianapolis Museum of Art; New Haven, CT: Yale University Press, 2007), 27.

17—Freiman, "María Magdalena Campos-Pons: Everything Is Separated by Water," 27.

18—Dayara Bernal Roque, "María Magdalena Campos-Pons + Neil Leonard." In *Artists' Prospectus for the Nation*, July 2013, trans. Rebeca Hey-Colón, http://www.artistsincontextprospectus.org/2013/07/23/maria-magdalena-campos-pons-neil-leonard/.

19—Neil Leonard, "True Bread: The Sounds of Change in Cuba," *Leonardo Music Journal* 25 (2015): 95–96.

20—Louis Armstrong infused the distinctive Cuban sound with elements of jazz vocal scatting.

21—Barbara Kirshenblatt-Gimblett and Brooks McNamara, "Processional Performance: An Introduction," *Drama Review: TDR* 29, no. 3 (1985): 2–5.

22—FeFa often leaves her audience with a gift, involving an exchange of goods—for example, at the Havana Biennial, the performance concluded with the distribution of fresh bread, made in collaboration between Cuban and American bakers in a culinary ritual of reconciliation.

23—Stephanie Sparling Williams, "'Frame Me': Speaking out of Turn and Lorraine O'Grady's Alien Avant-Garde," *Stedelijk Studies*, June 23, 2021, https://stedelijkstudies.com/journal/frame-me-speaking-out-of-turn-and-lorraine-ogradys-alien-avant-garde/, citing Michele Wallace, "Variations on Negation and the Heresy of Black Feminist Creativity," in *Invisibility Blues: From Pop to Theory* (New York: Verso, 2009).

24—See Sparling Williams, "'Frame Me.'"

25—Conversation with the author, July 17, 2022.

26—"María Magdalena Campos-Pons's *When We Gather*," 2022, National Gallery of Art YouTube.

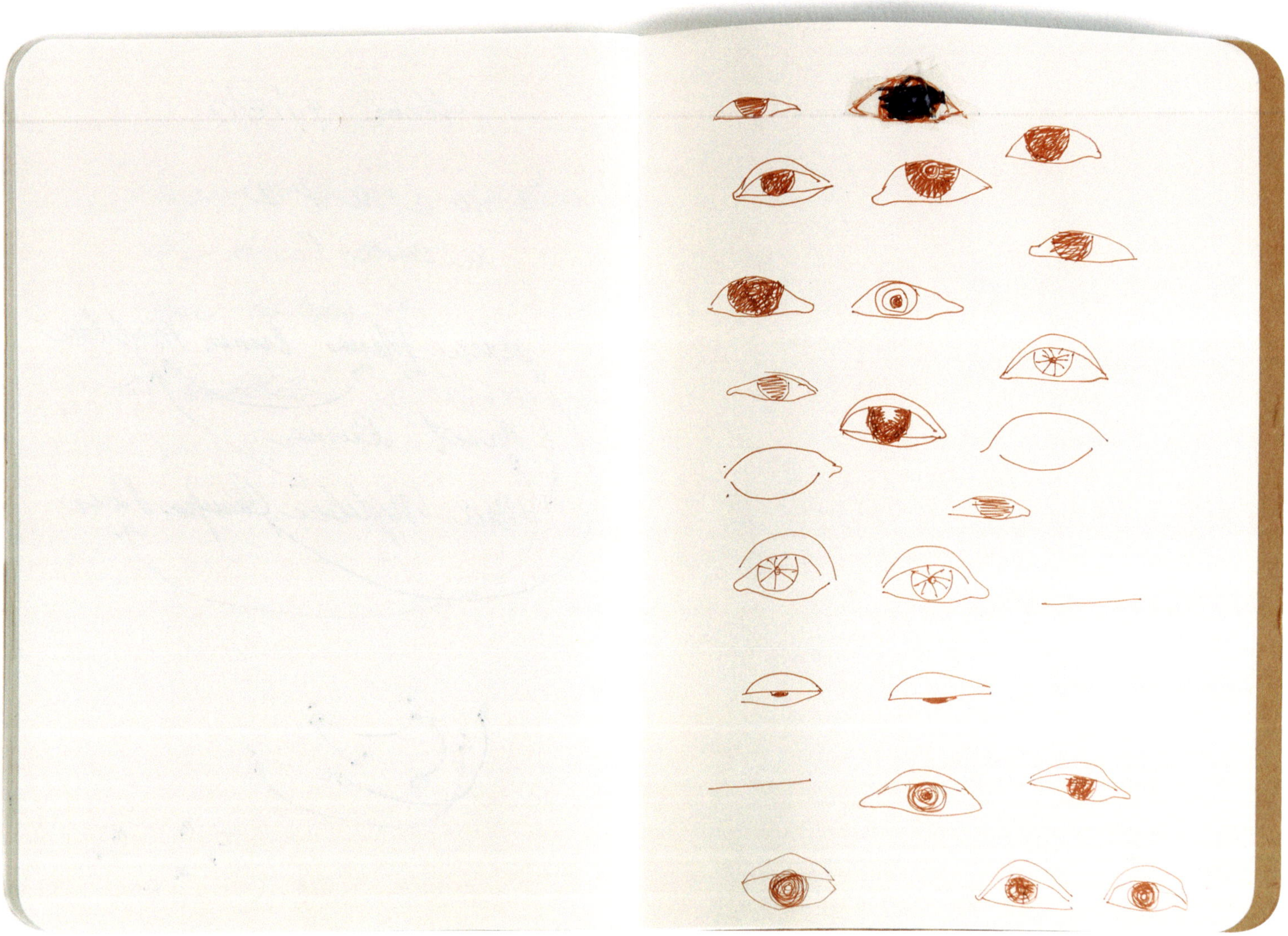

Untitled [Eyes in Brown Ink across Page], 2017. Notebook drawing.
Collection of the artist

PLATES

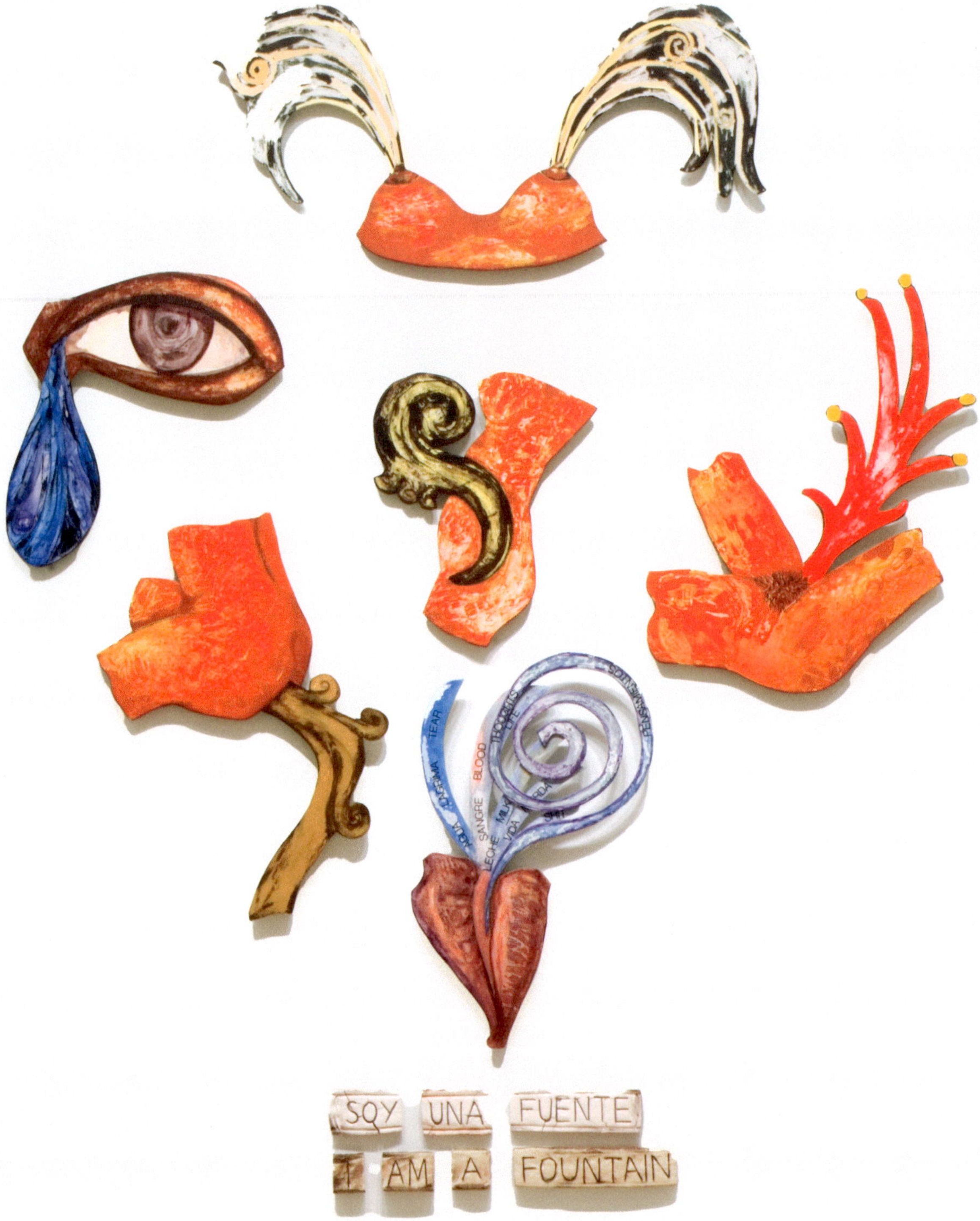

PLATE 1 *Soy Una Fuente (I Am a Fountain)*, 1990

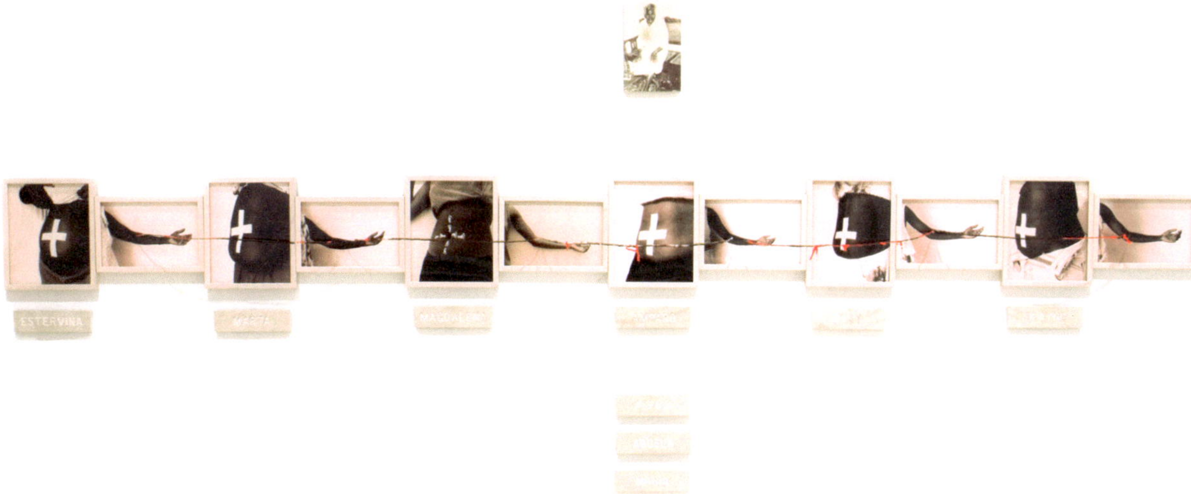

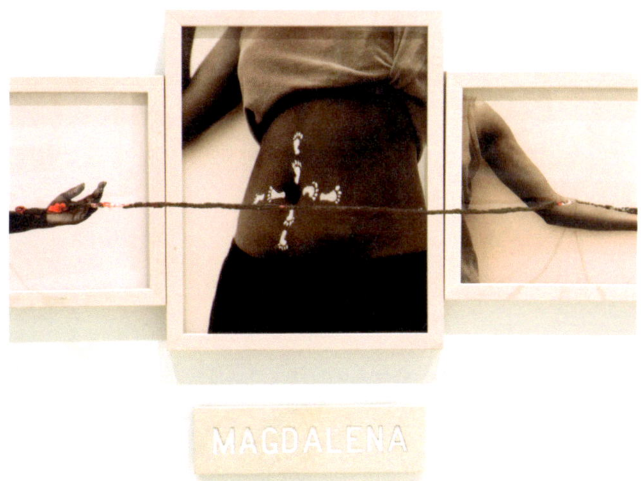

PLATE 2 *Umbilical Cord* (with detail), 1991

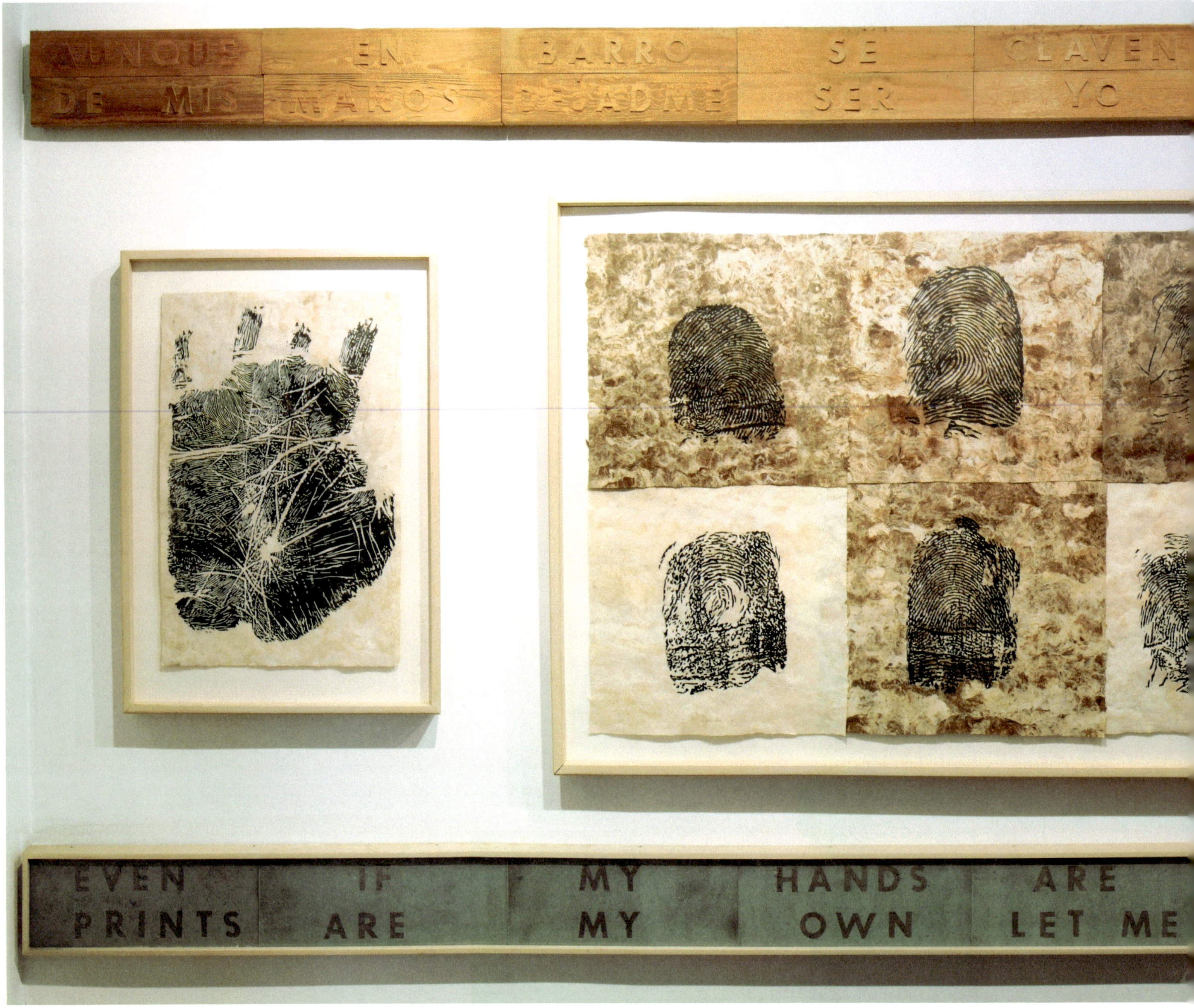

PLATE 3 *Carta Natal (Birth Certificate)*, 1991

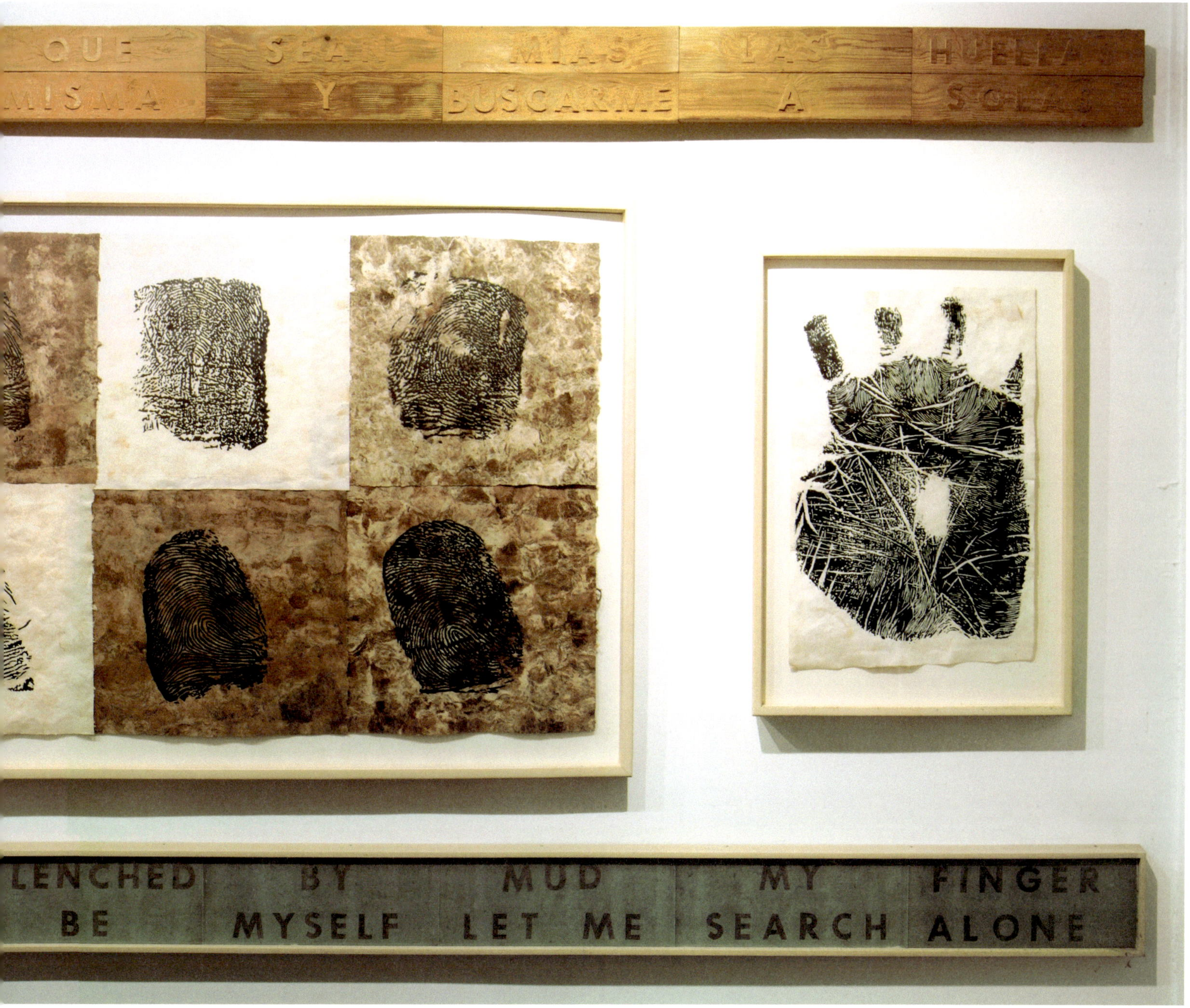
QUE SEAN MIAS LAS
MISMA Y BUSCARME A
LENCHED BY MUD MY FINGER
BE MYSELF LET ME SEARCH ALONE

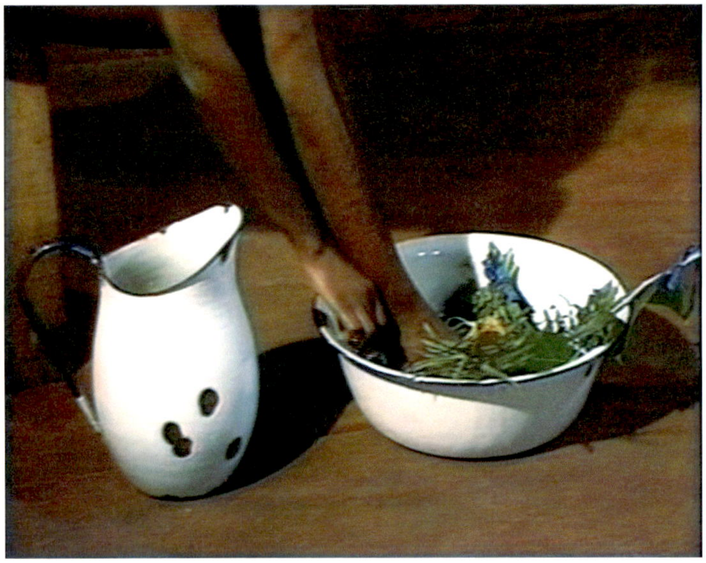

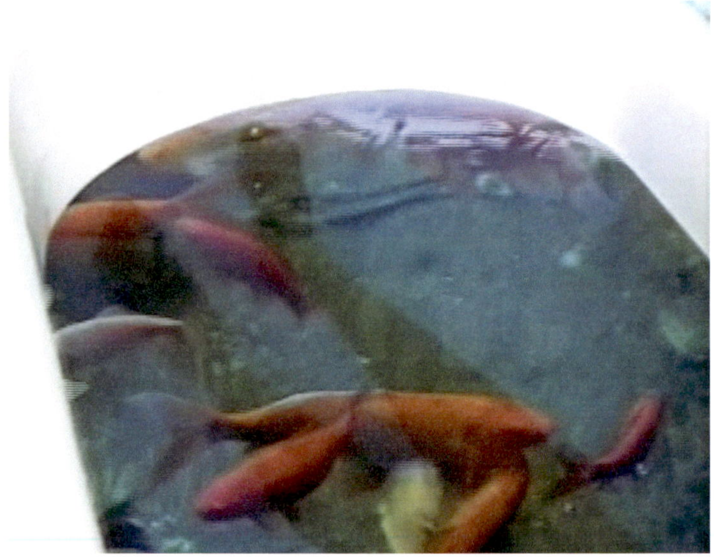

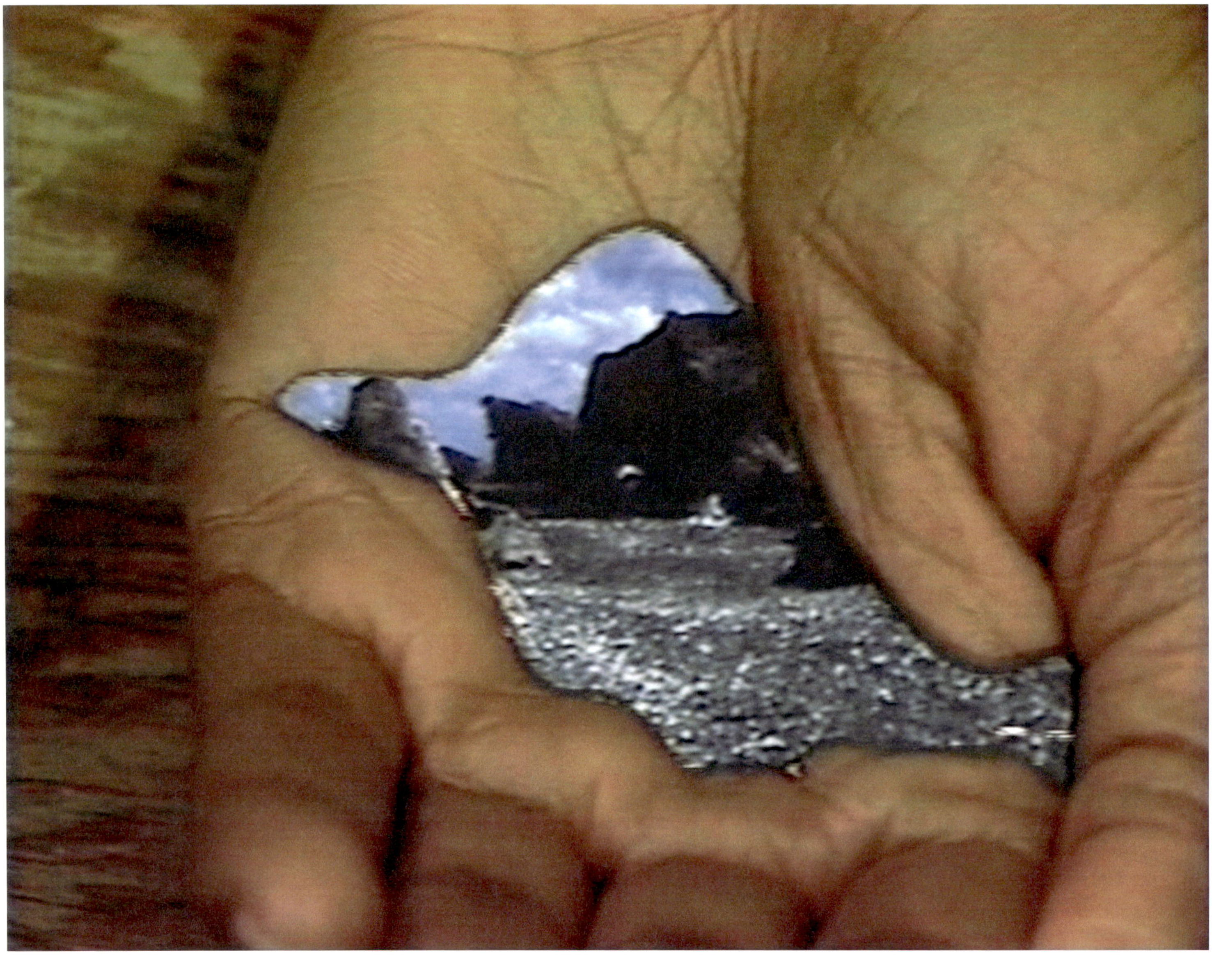

PLATE 4 Stills from video, *Baño Sagrado (Rite of Initiation, Sacred Bath)*, 1991

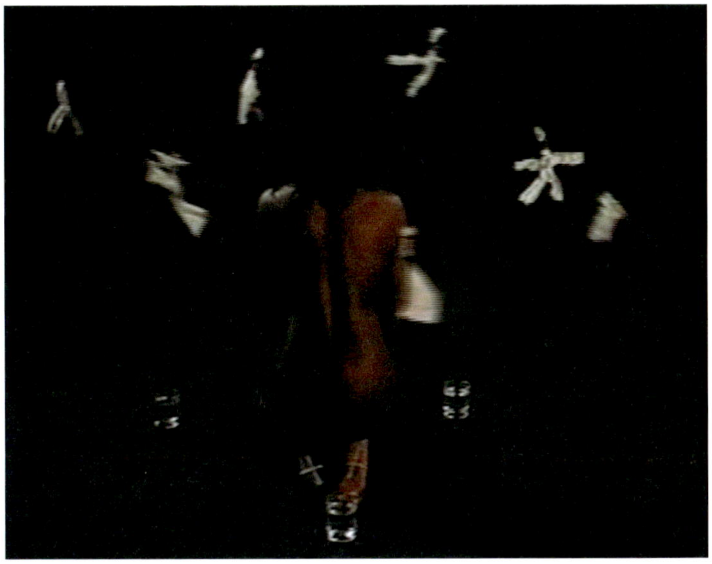

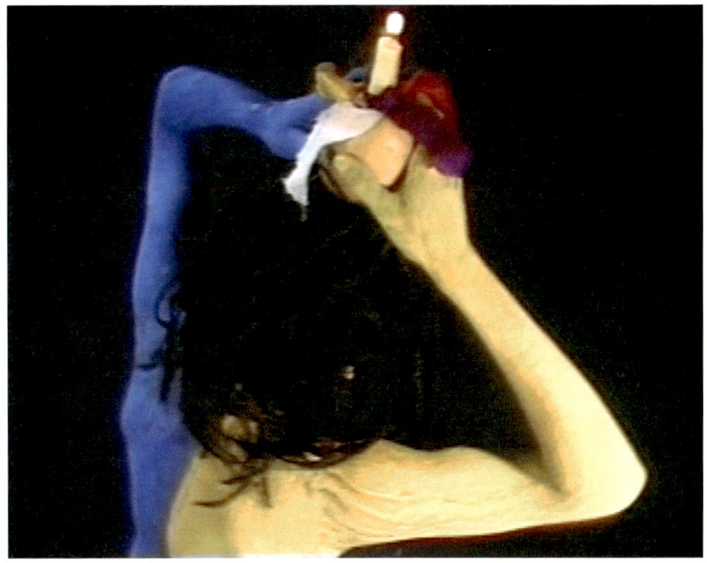

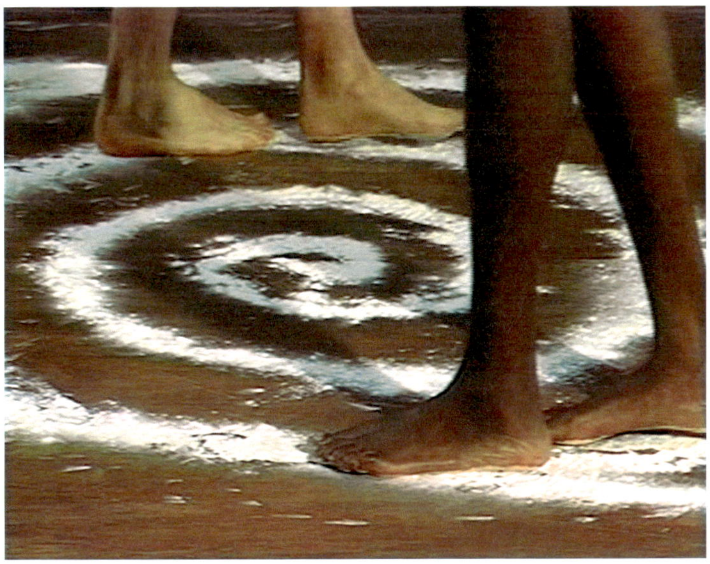

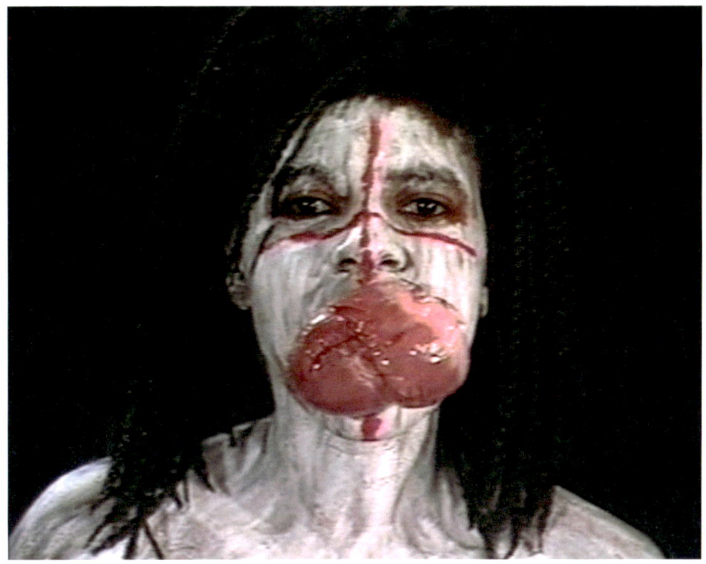

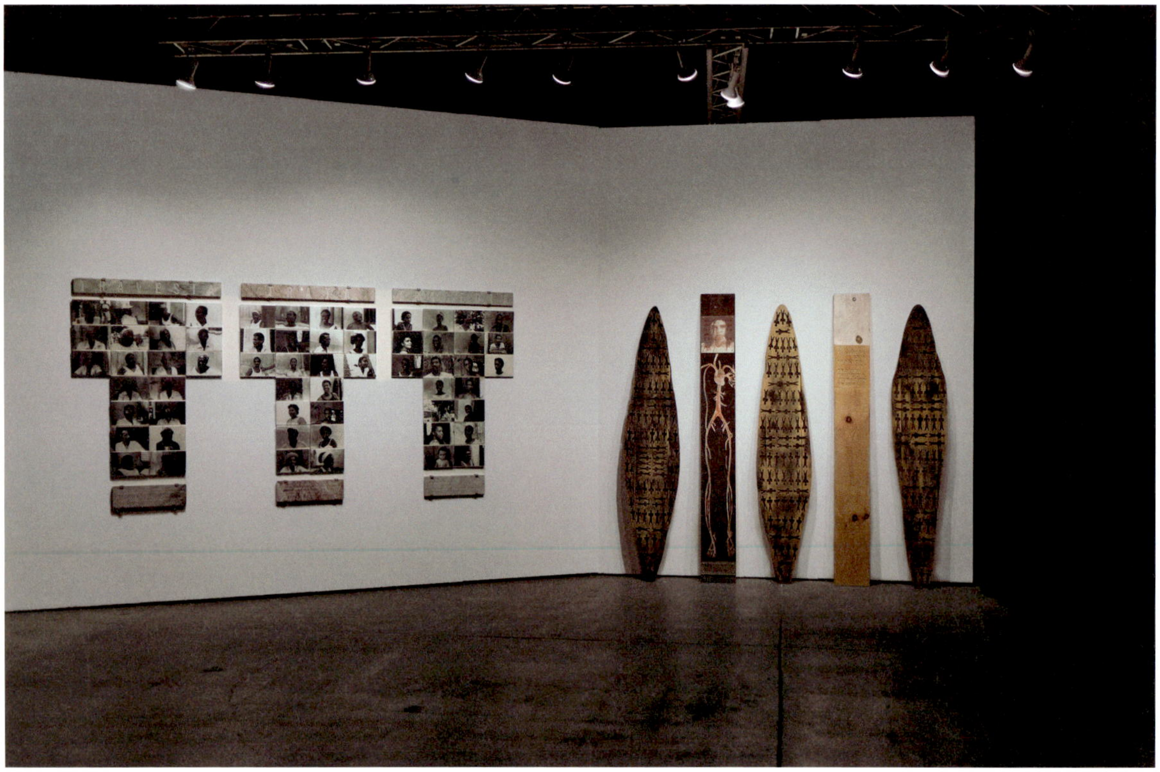

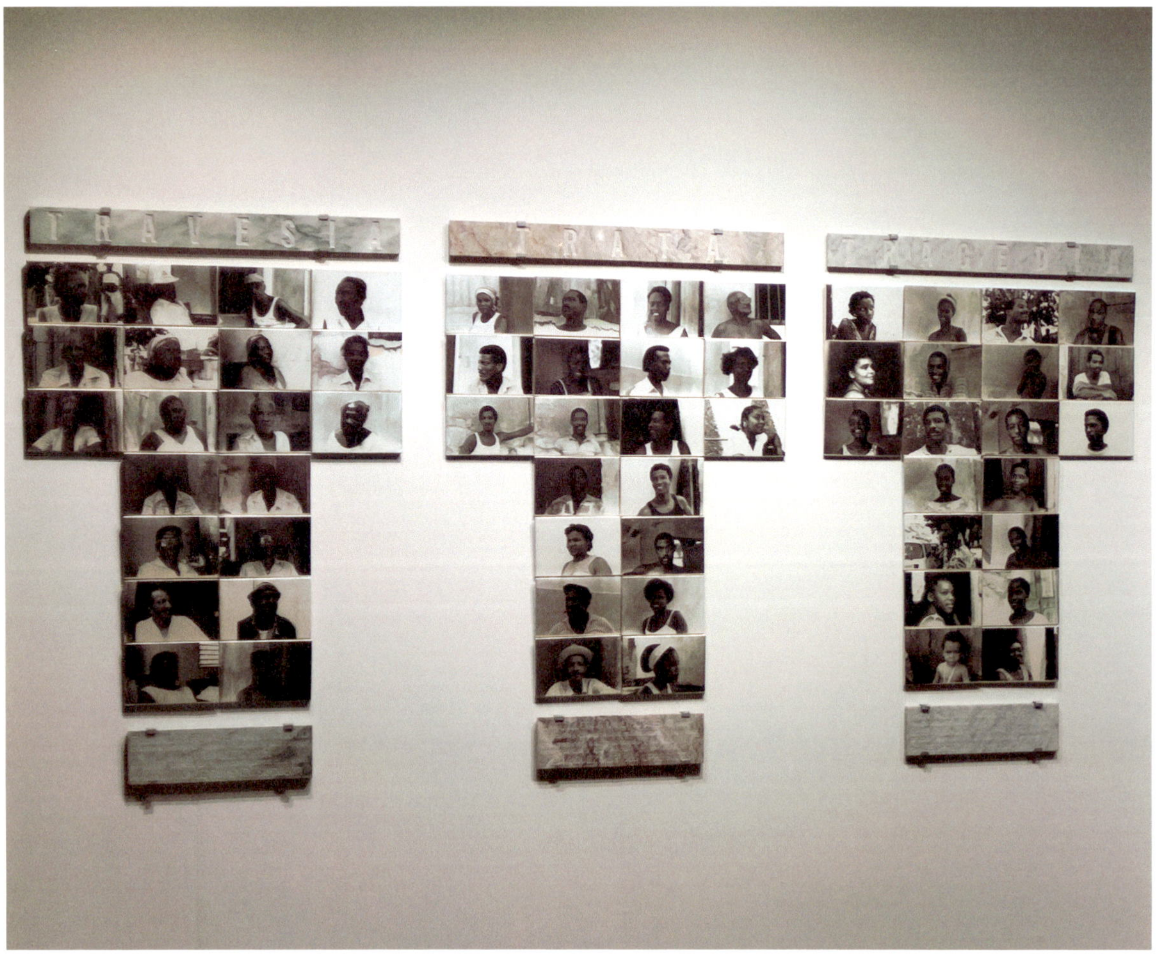

PLATE 5 *TRA* (with detail), 1991

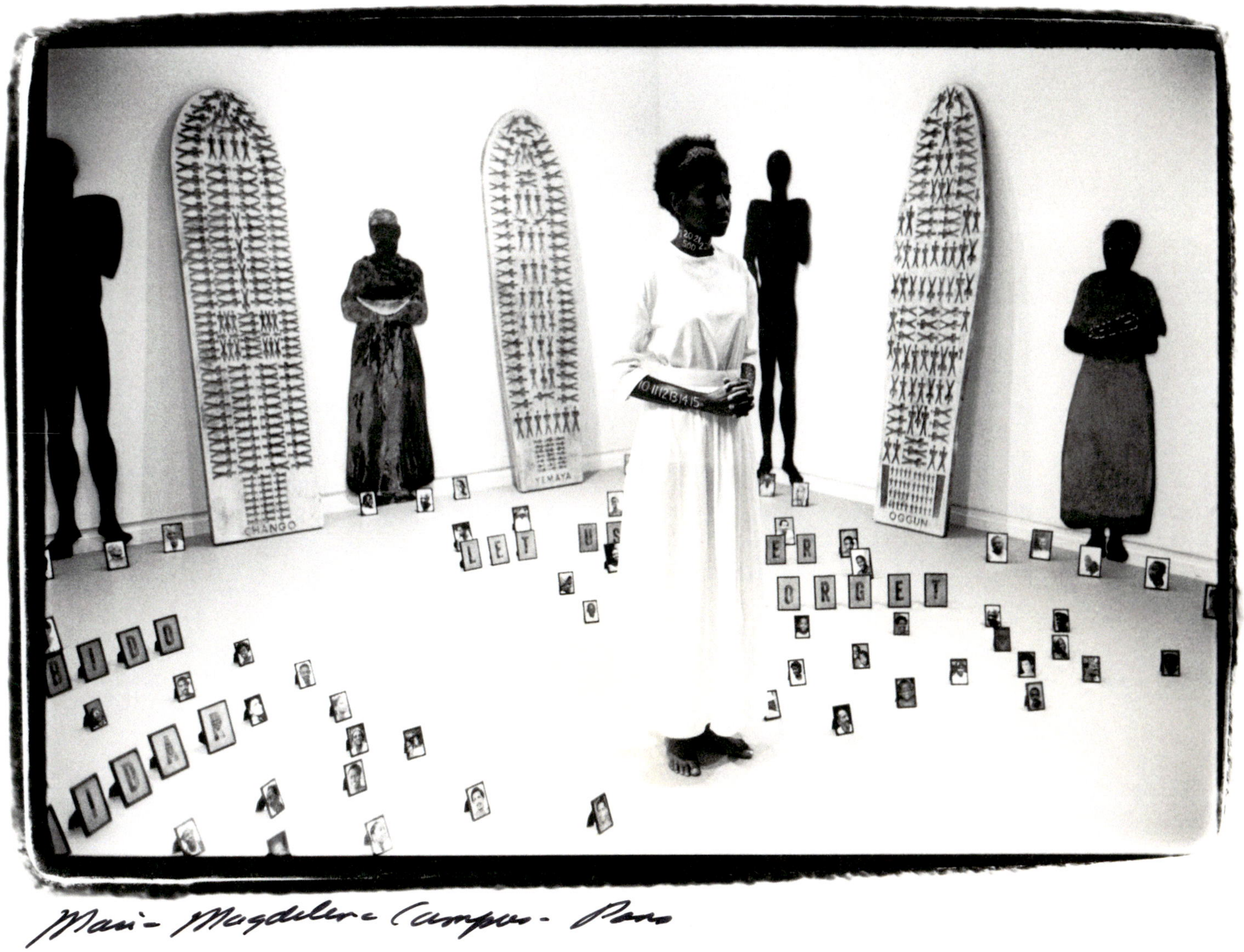

PLATE 6 Performance with *The Seven Powers Come by the Sea*, 1992

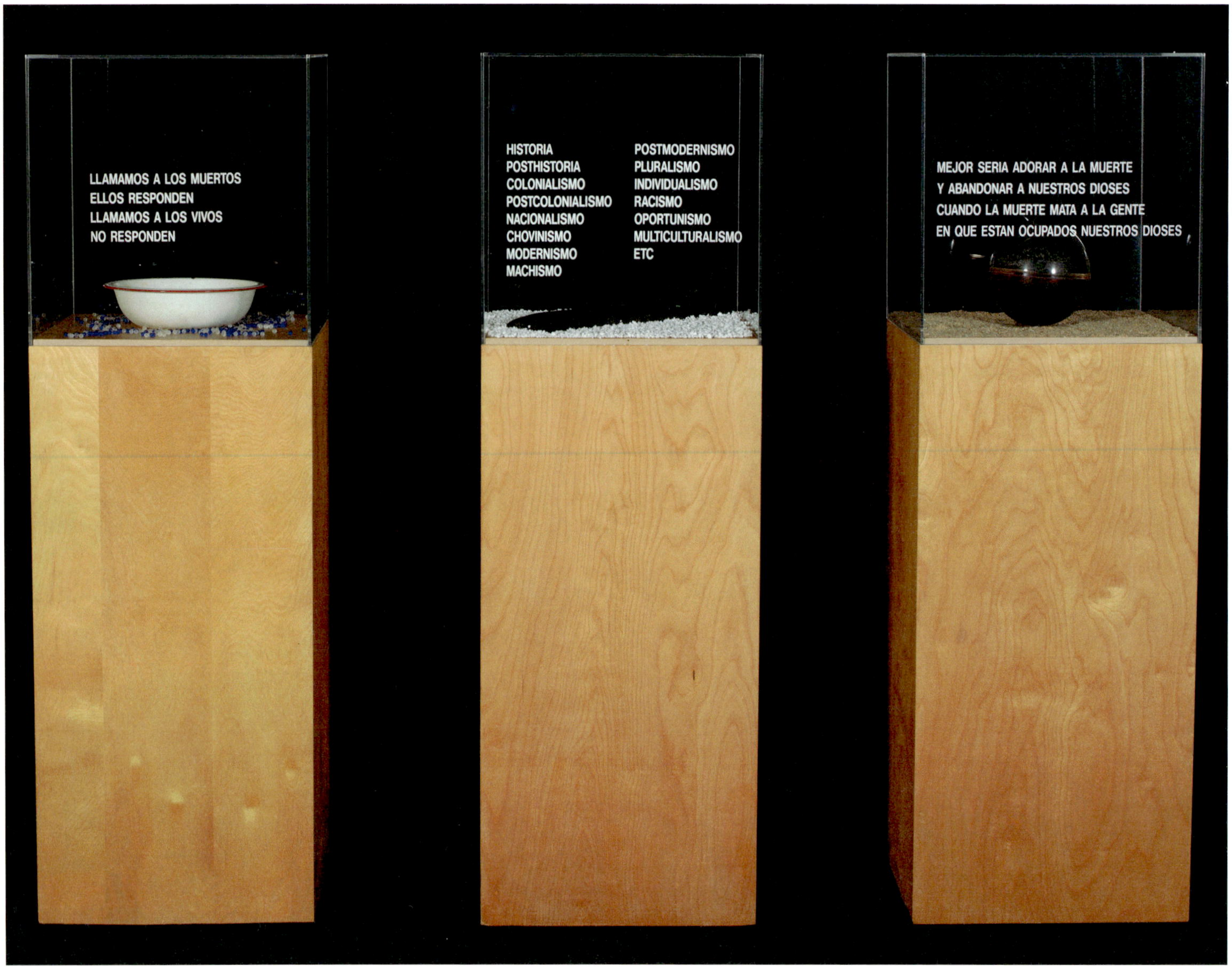

PLATE 7 *Oh... the Isms, Footprints of a Journey*, 1992

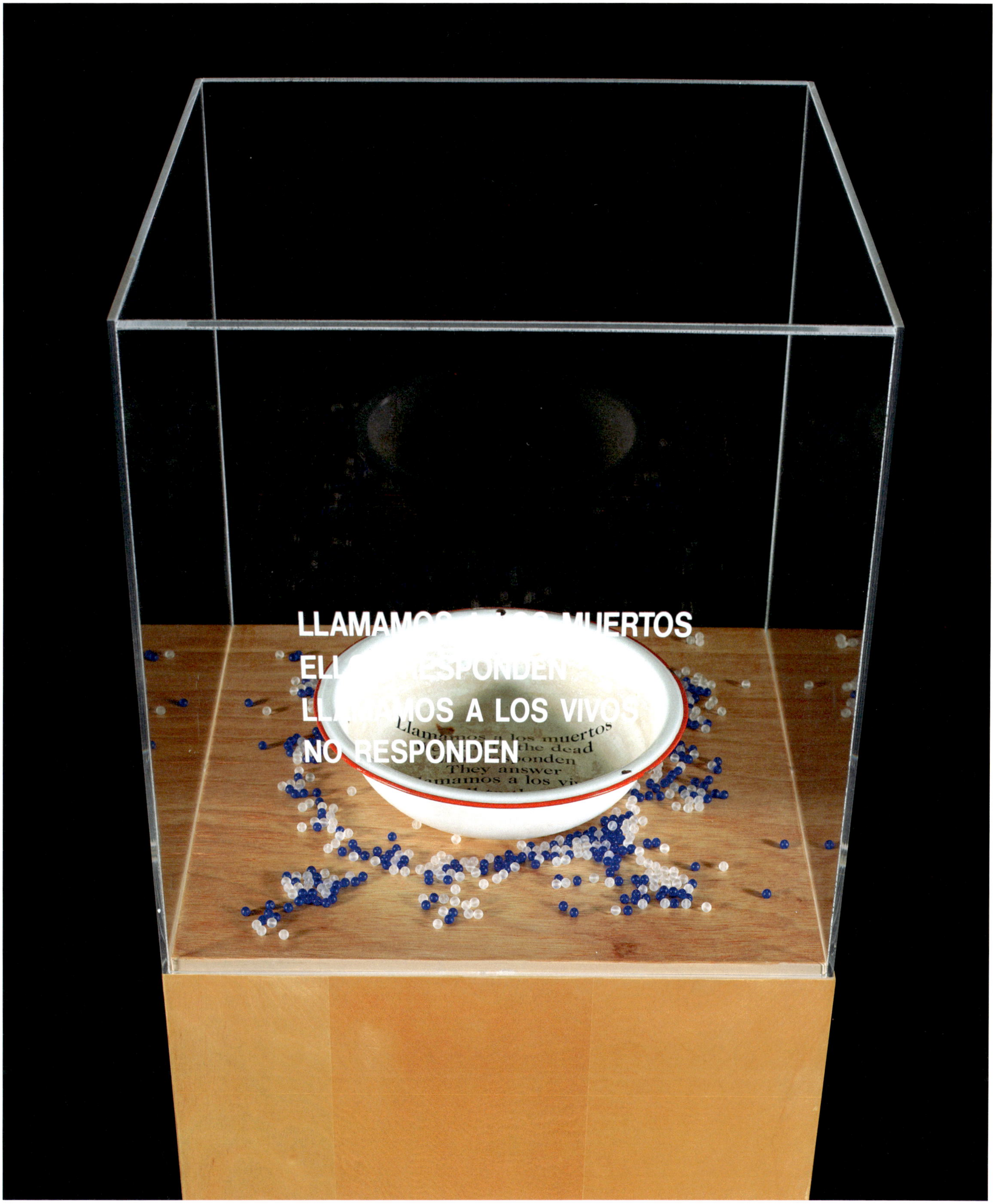
NO RESPONDEN

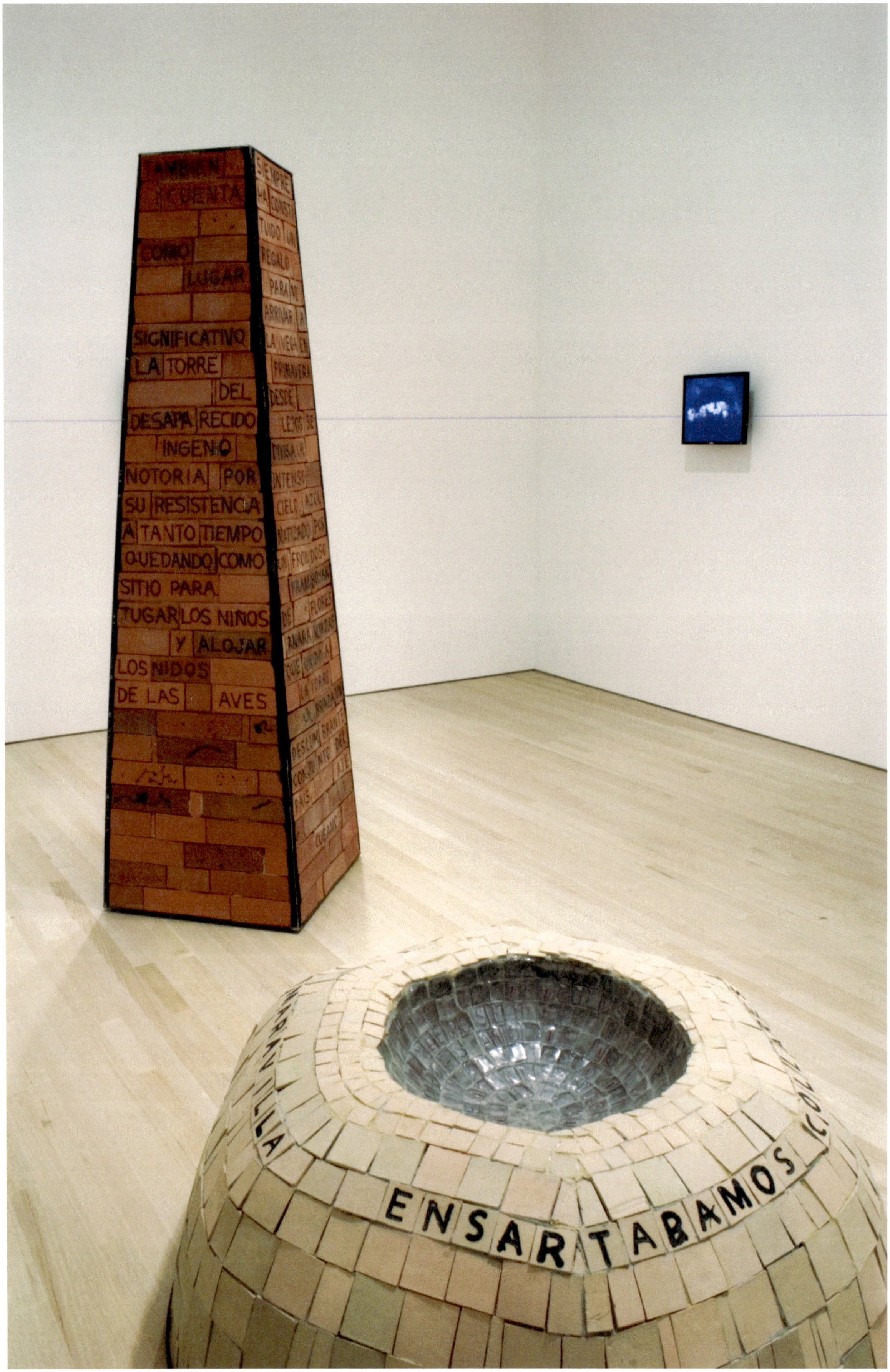

PLATE 8 *History of a People Who Were Not Heroes: A Town Portrait* (with details), 1994

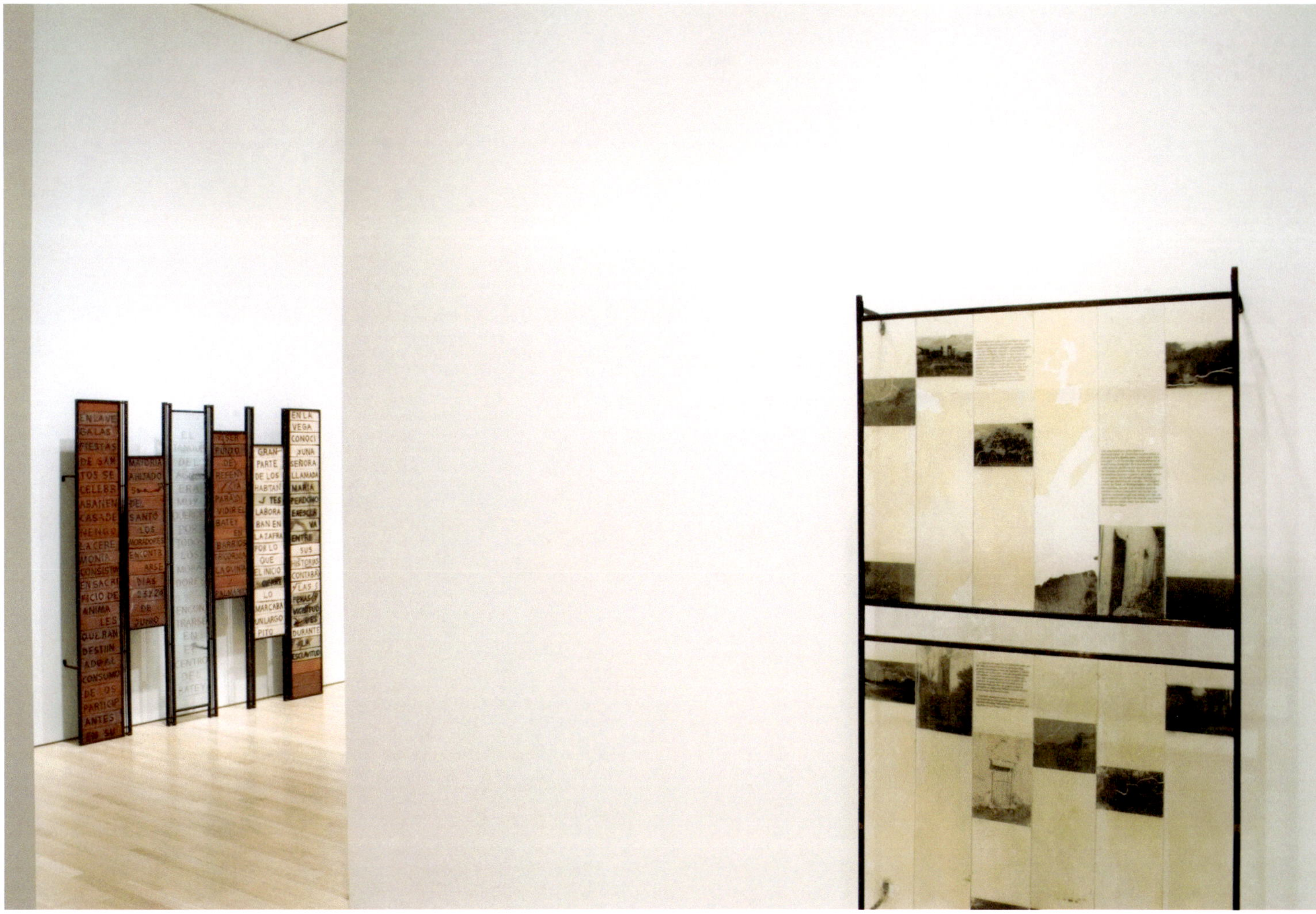

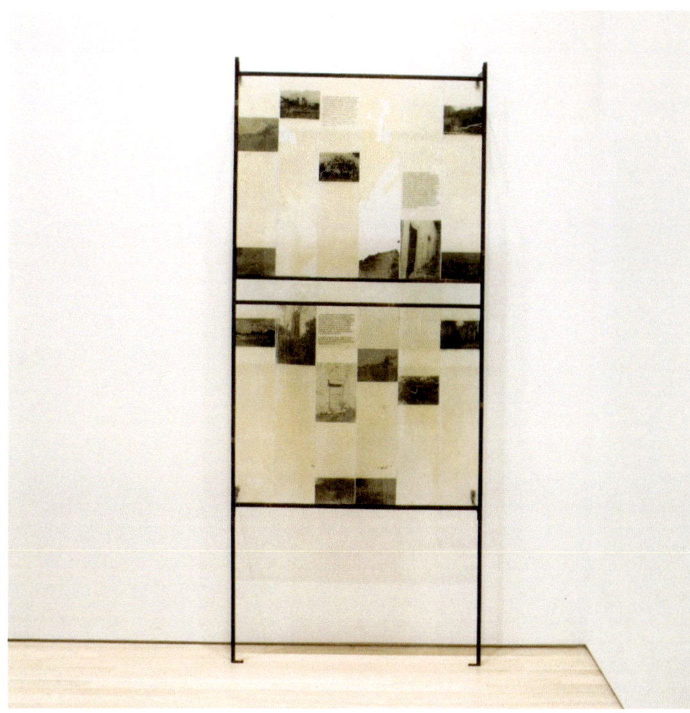

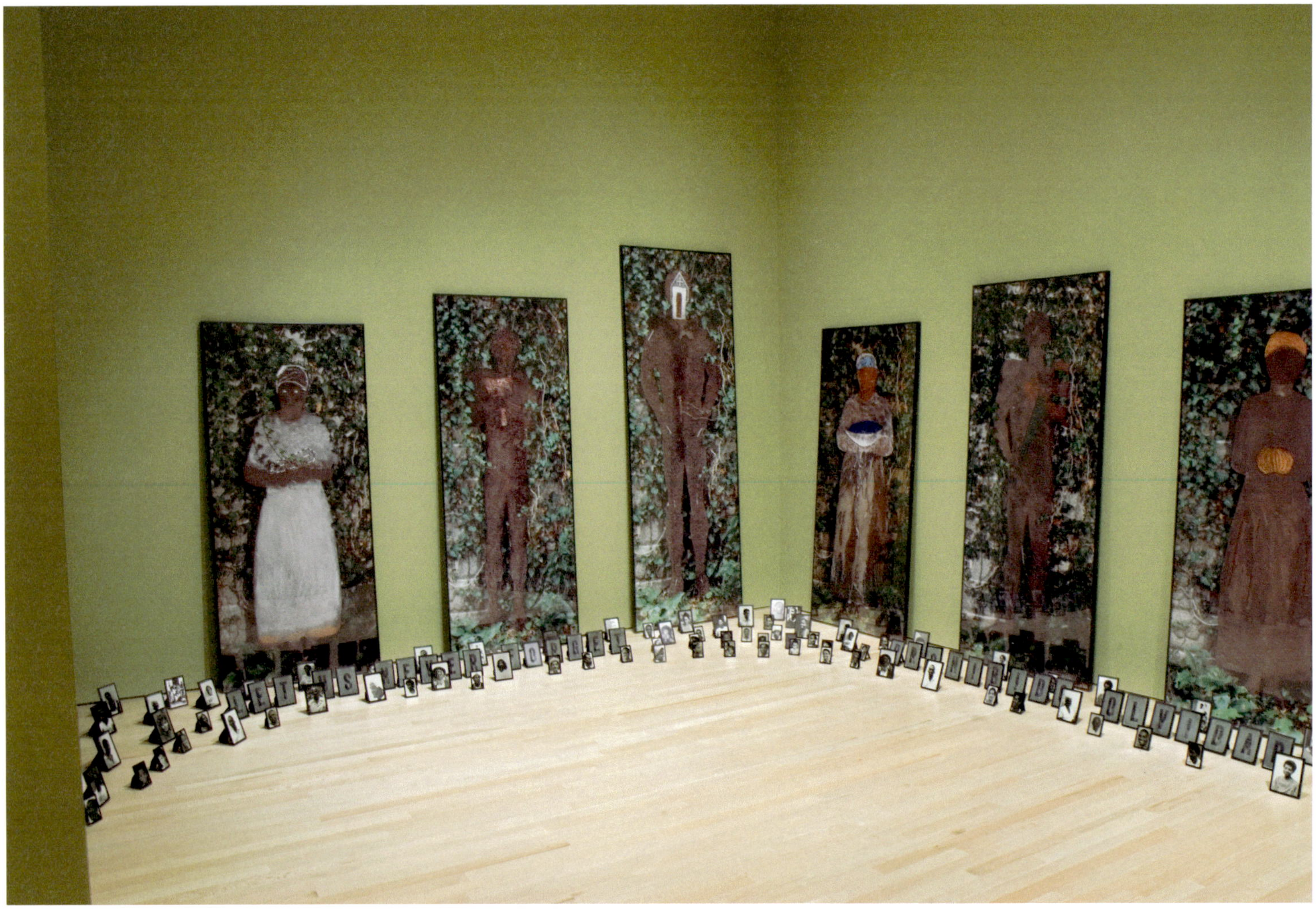

PLATE 9 *The Seven Powers*, 1994

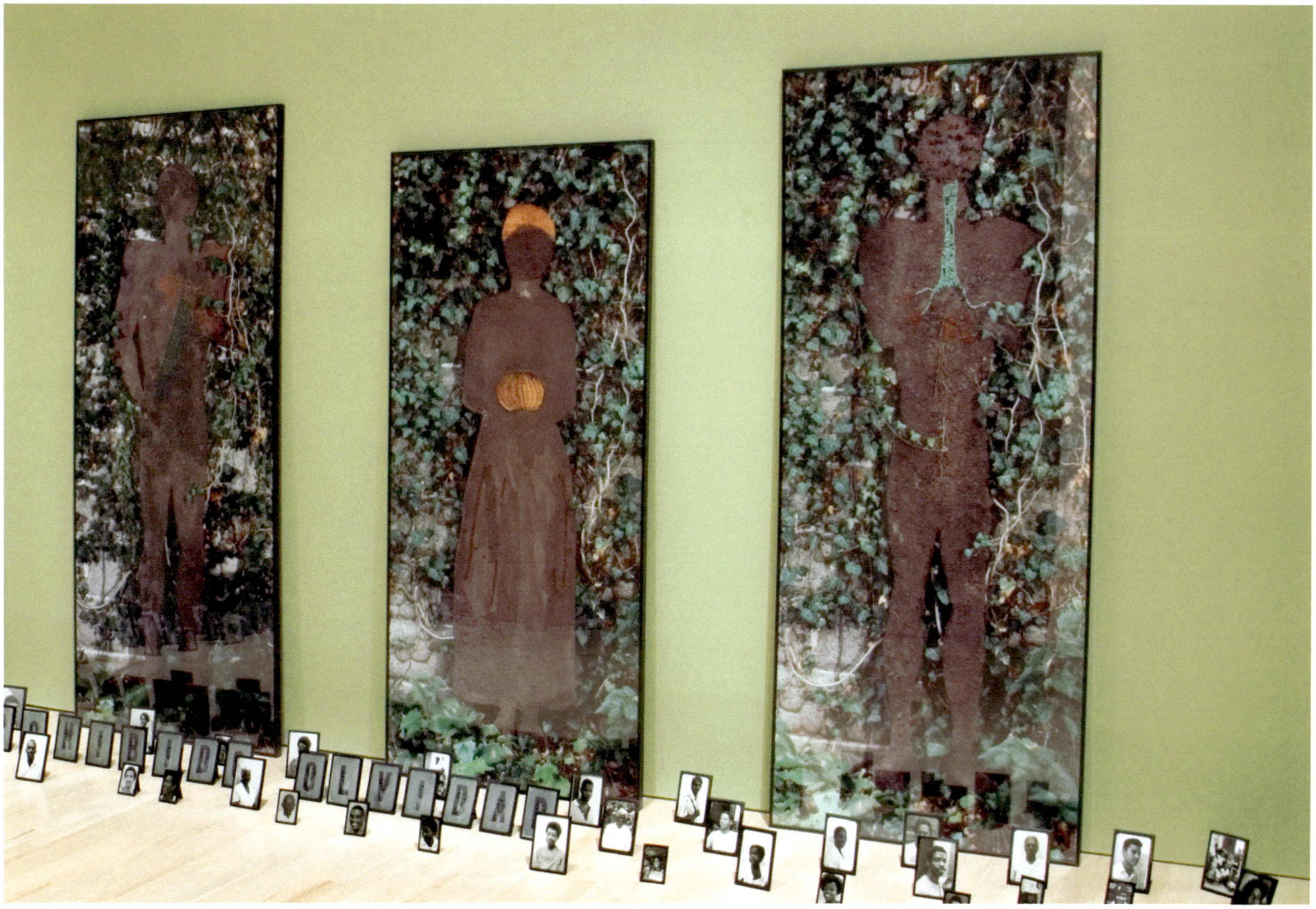

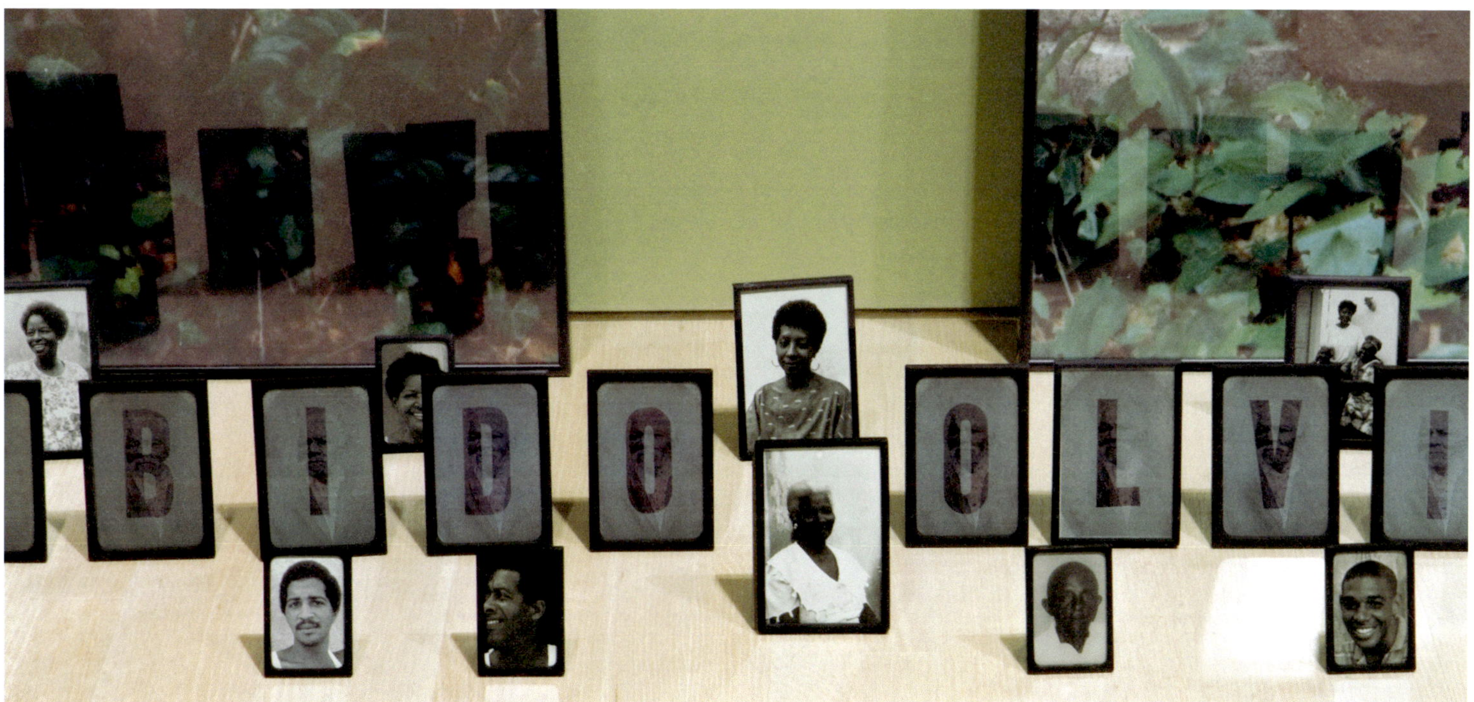
BIDO OLVI

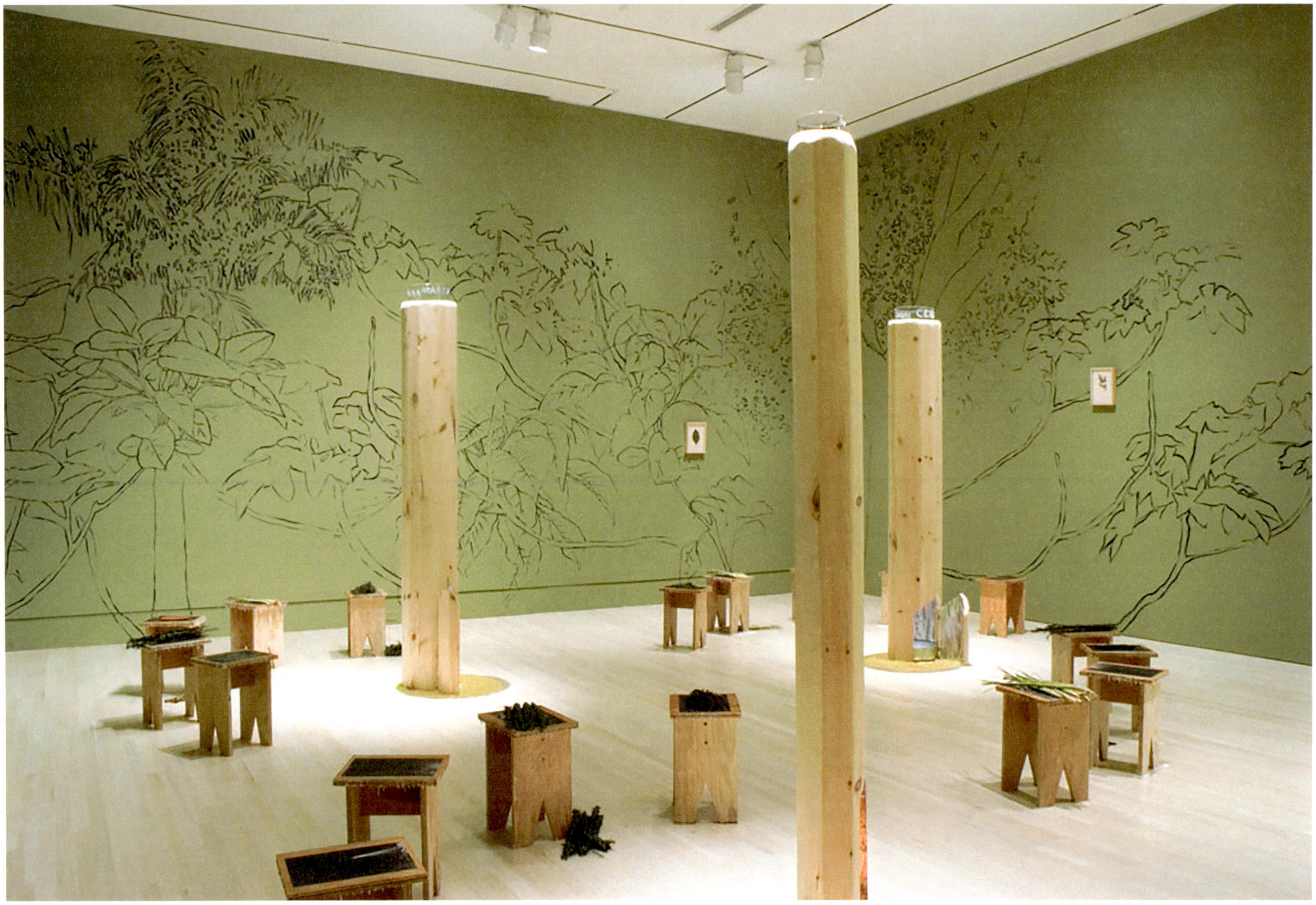

PLATE 10 *The Herbalist's Tools*, 1994

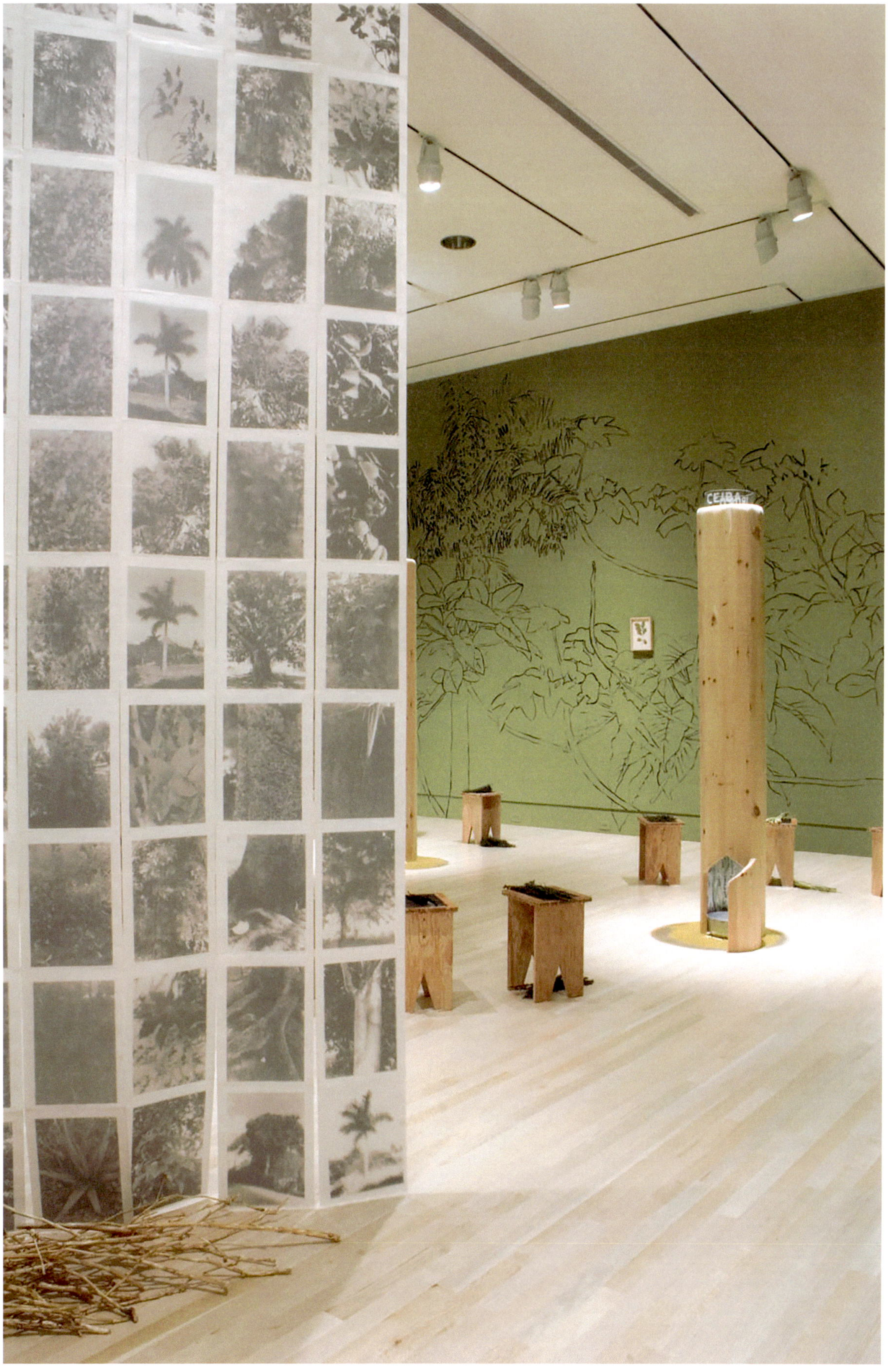

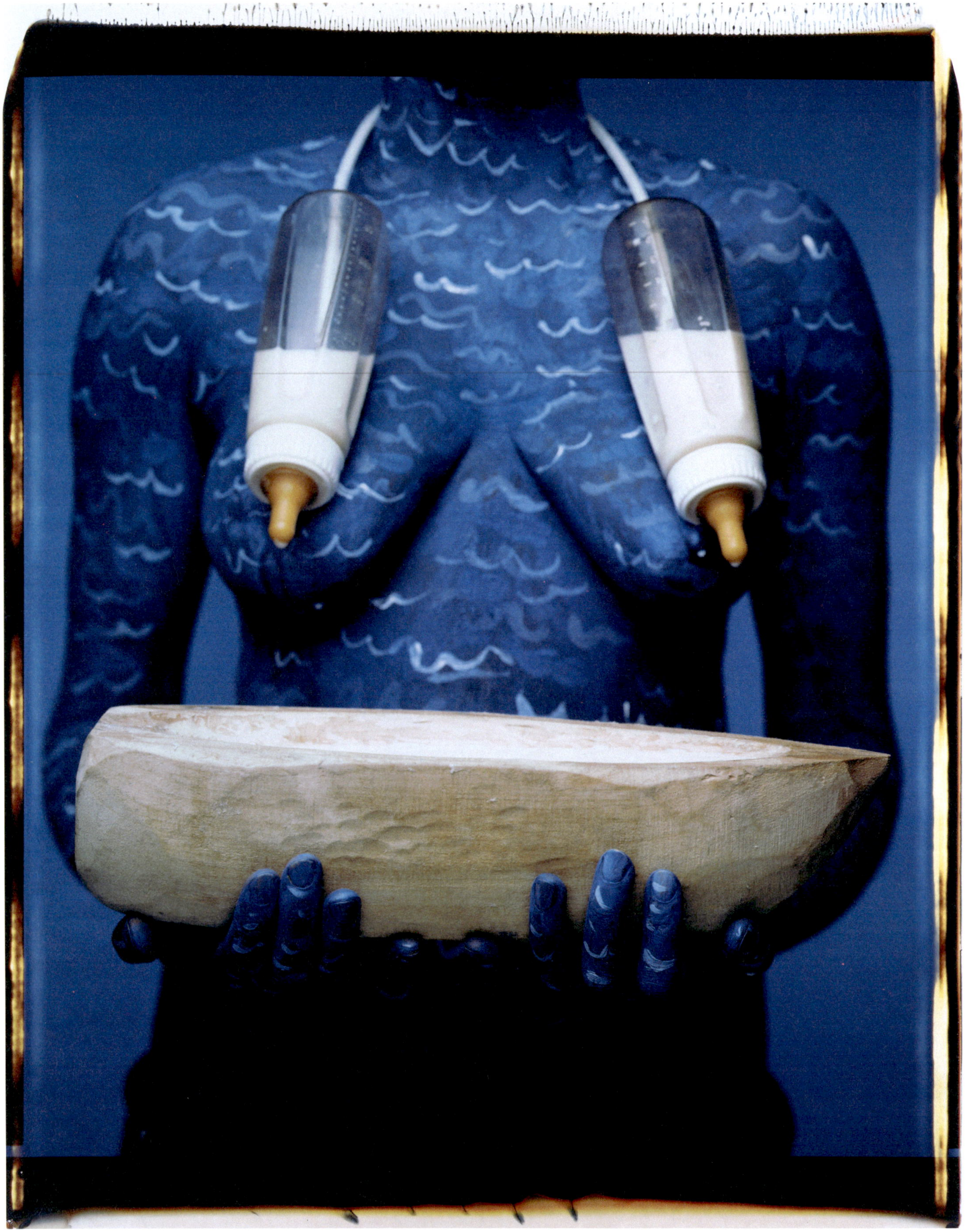

PLATE 11 *When I Am Not Here / Estoy Allá*, 1994

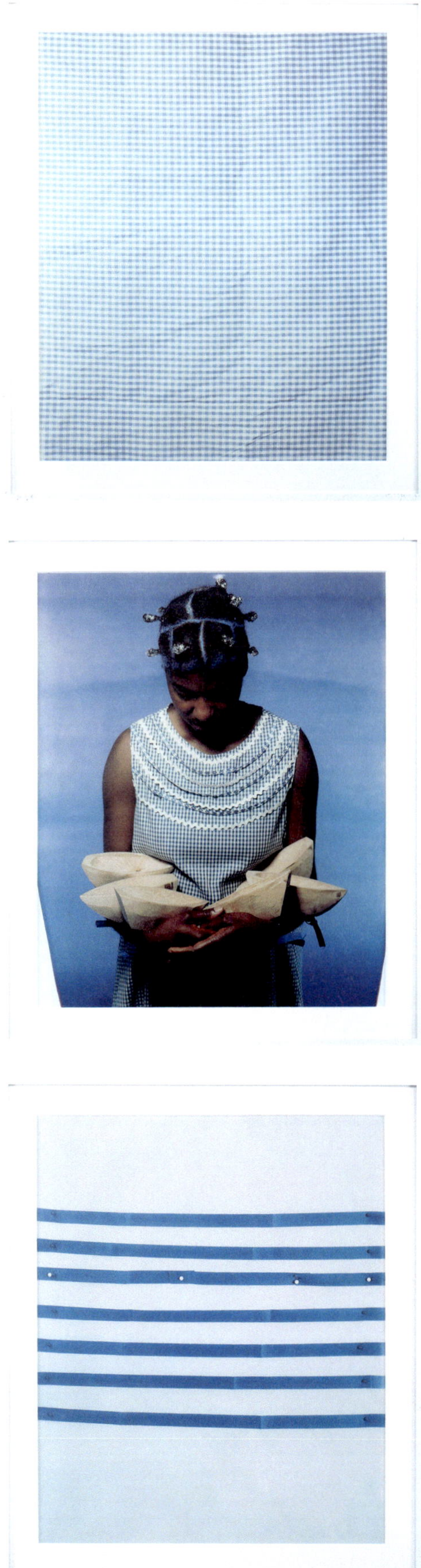

PLATE 12 *When I Am Not Here / Estoy Allá*, 1994

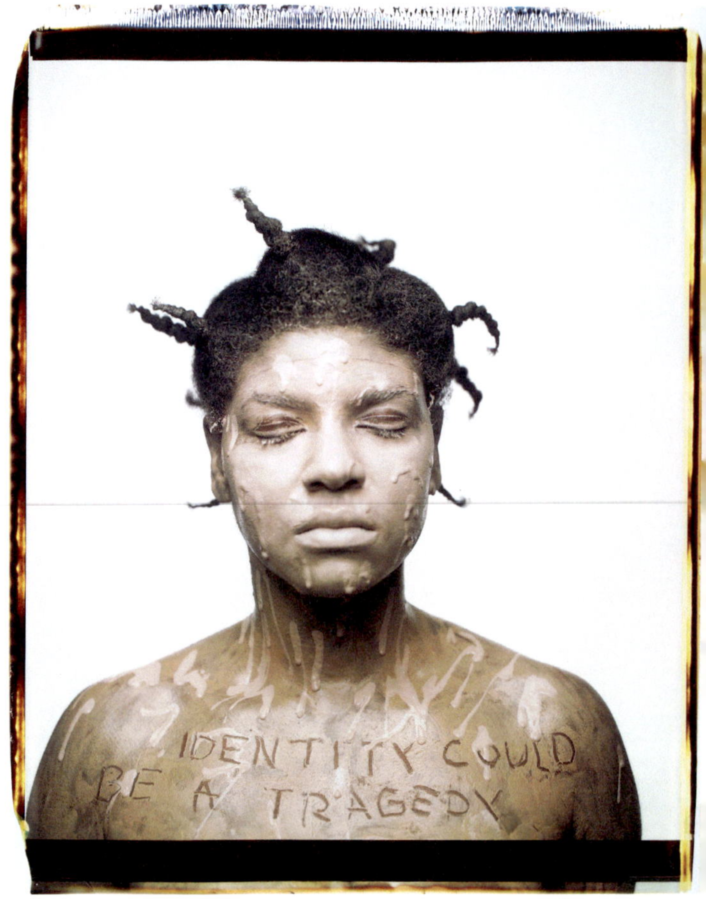

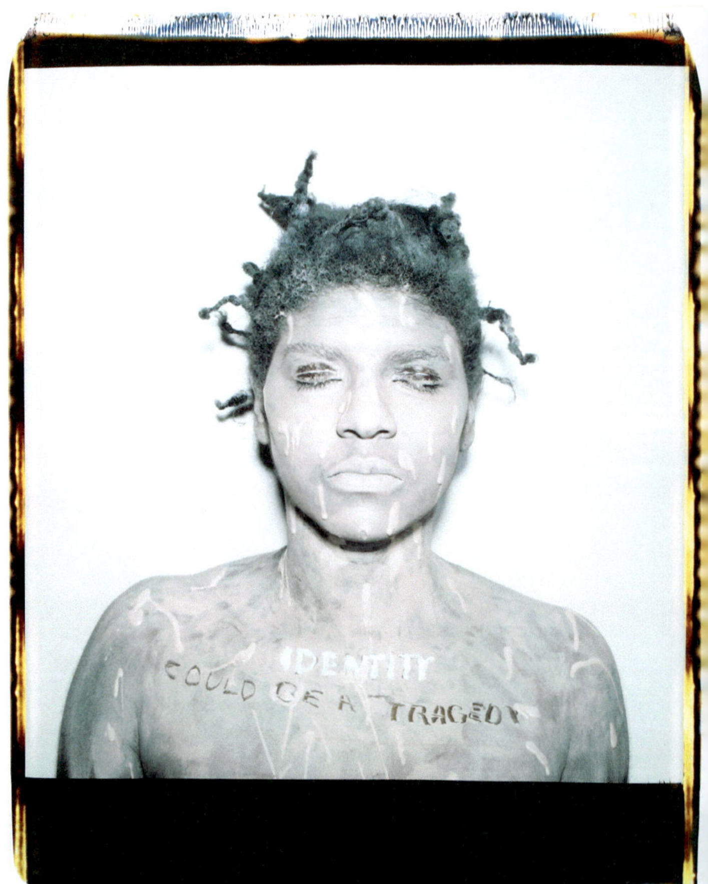

PLATE 13 *Identity Could Be a Tragedy*, from the When I Am Not Here / Estoy Allá series, 1995–96

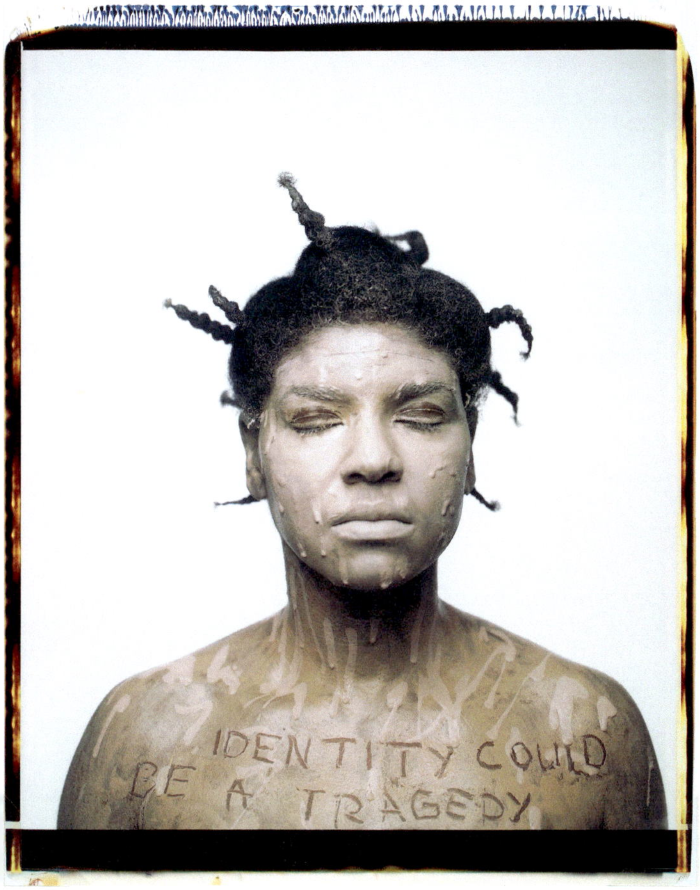
IDENTITY COULD
BE A TRAGEDY

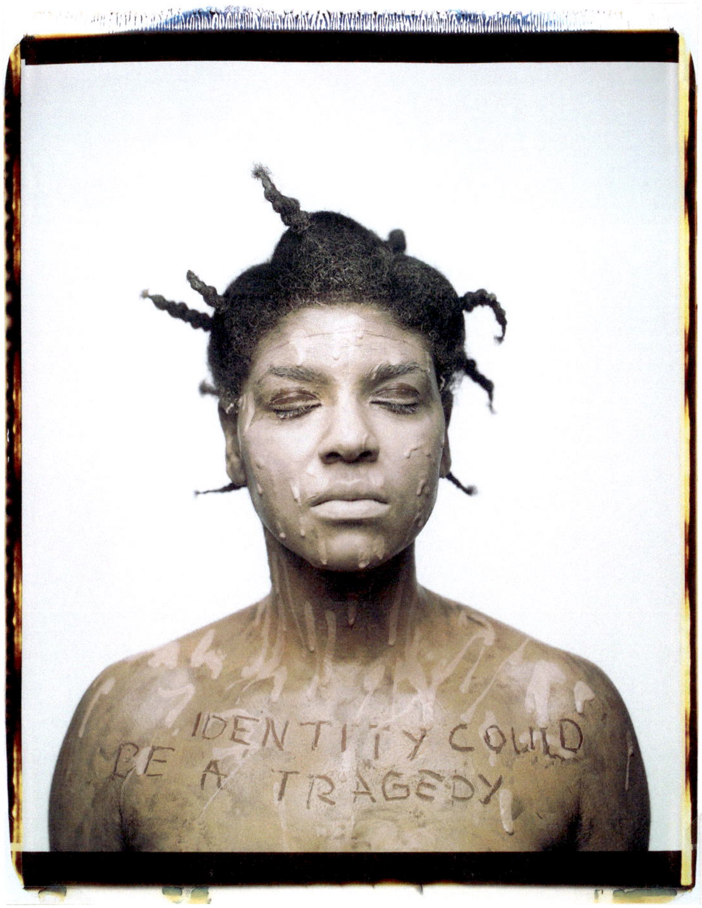
IDENTITY COULD
BE A TRAGEDY

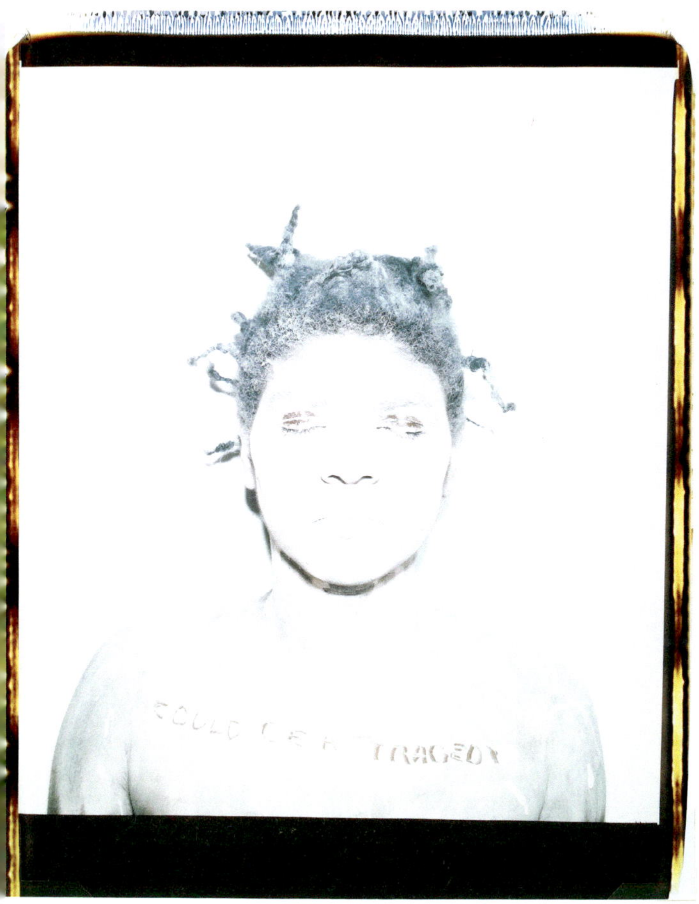
COULD BE A TRAGEDY

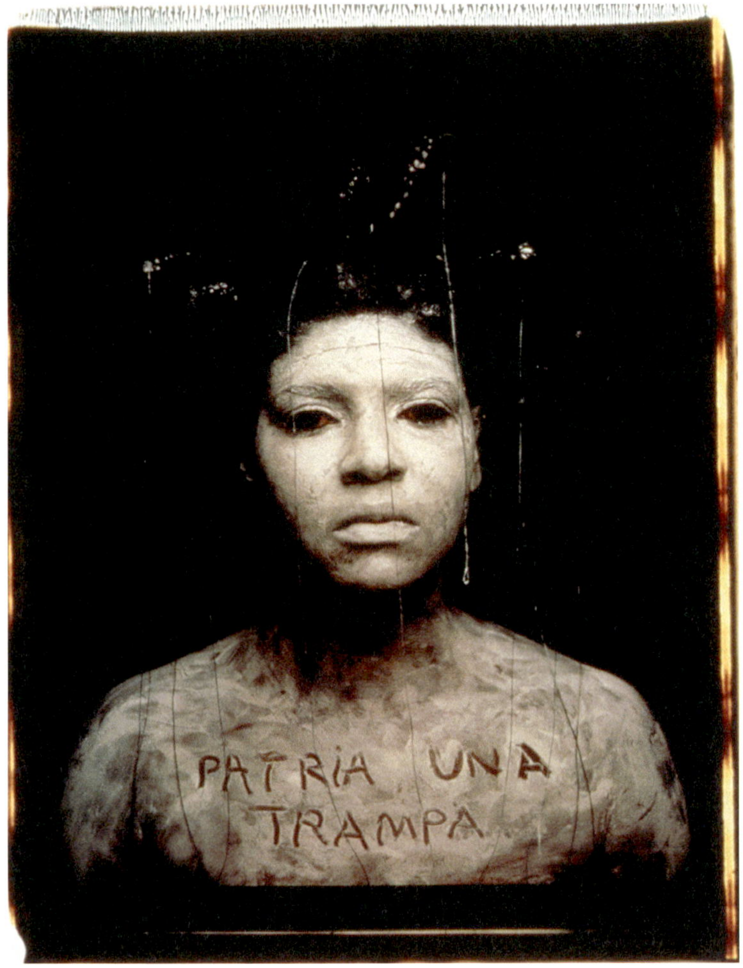

PLATE 14 *When I Am Not Here / Estoy Allá, Tríptico I*, 1996

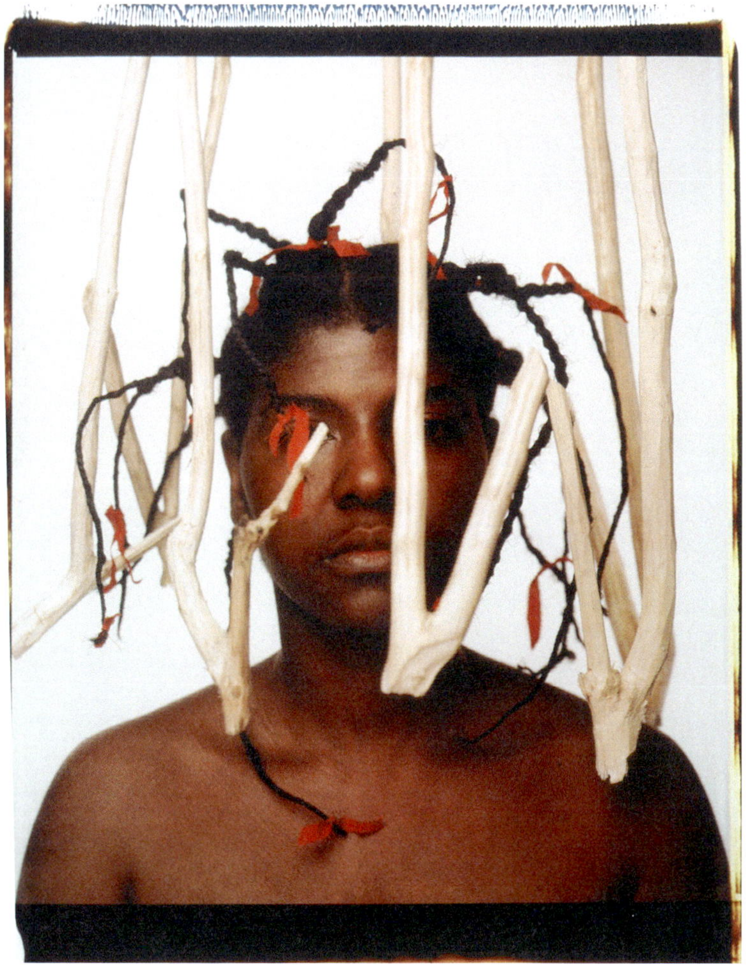

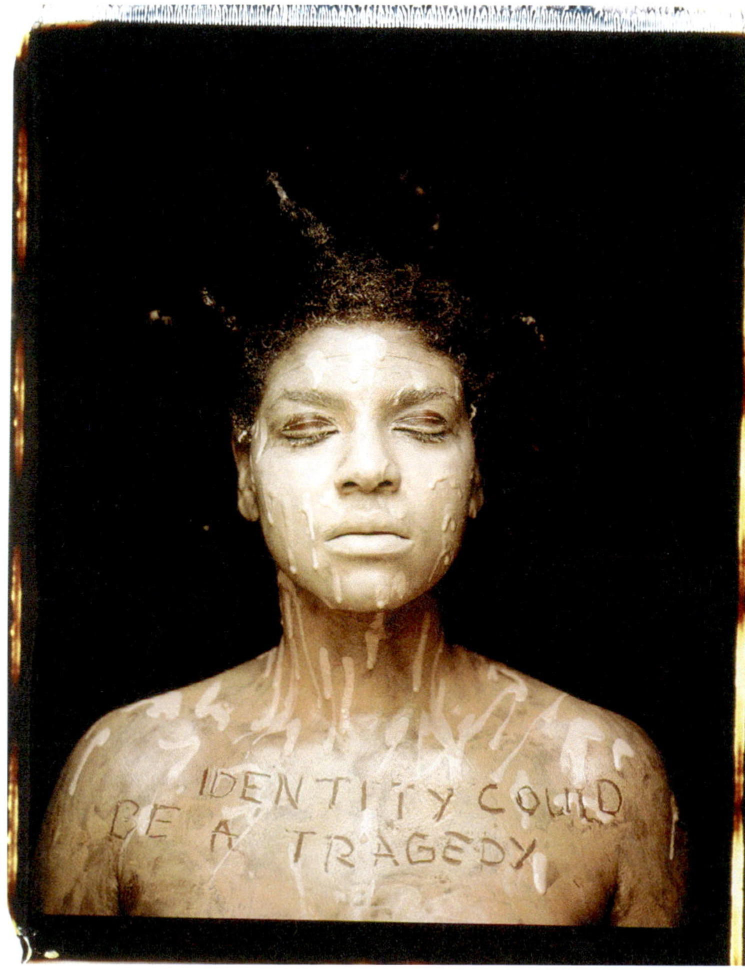
IDENTITY COULD
BE A TRAGEDY

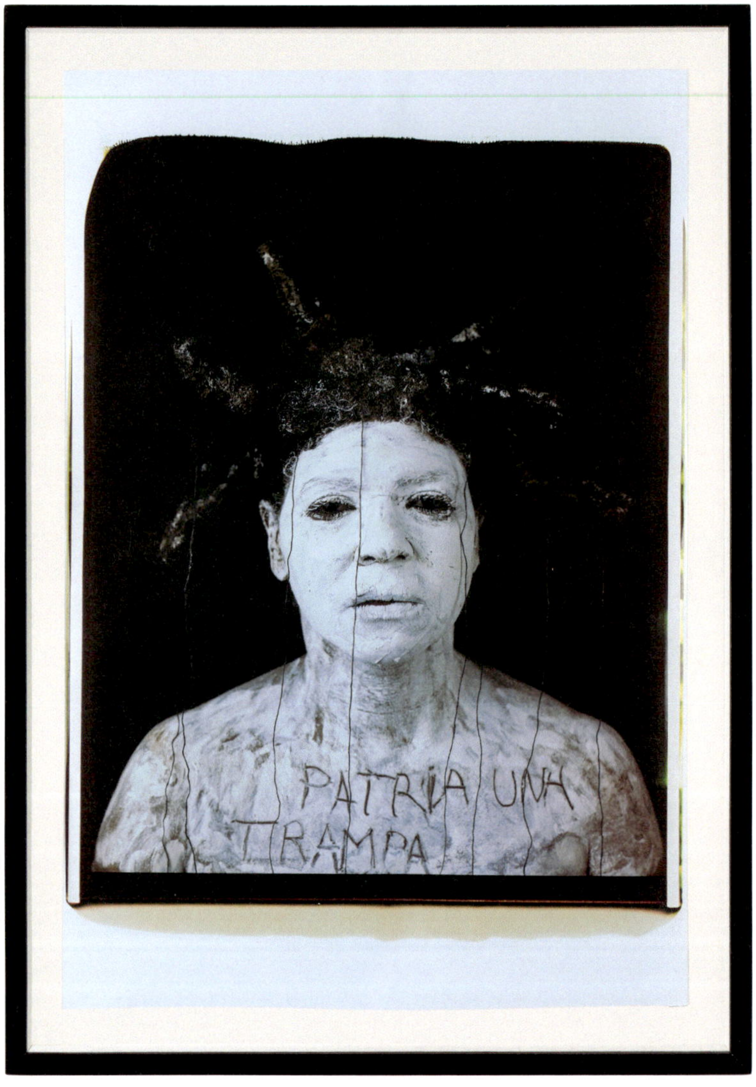

PLATE 15 *When I Am Not Here / Estoy Allá, Tríptico I (remade)*, 1996/2013

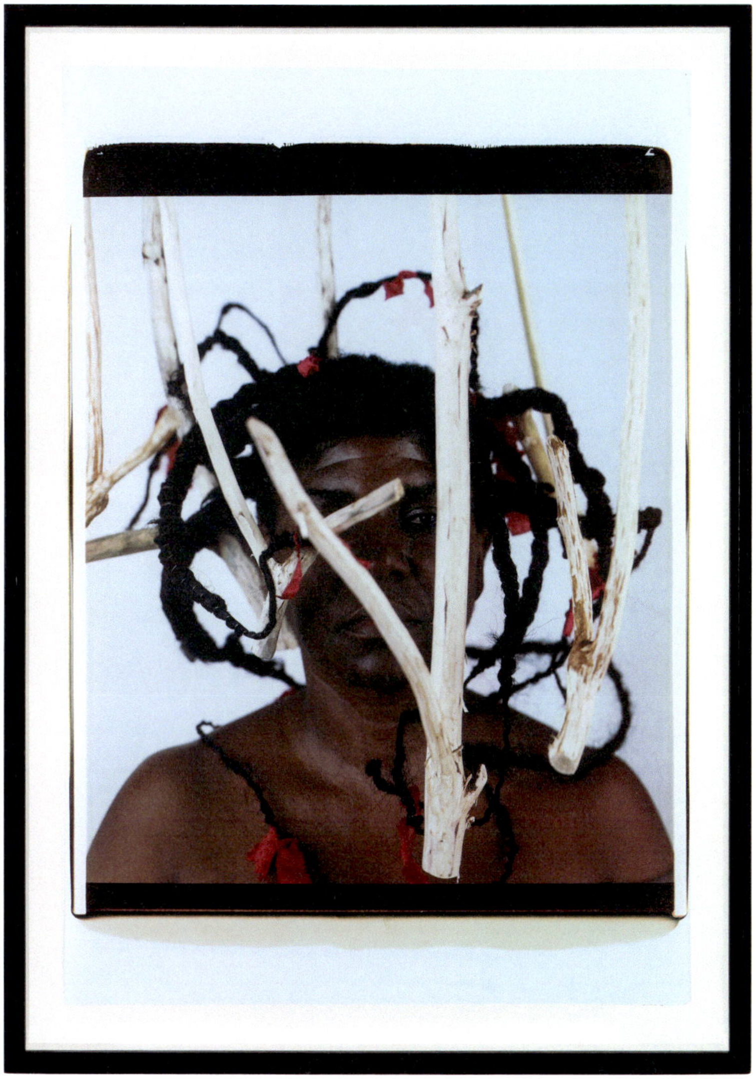

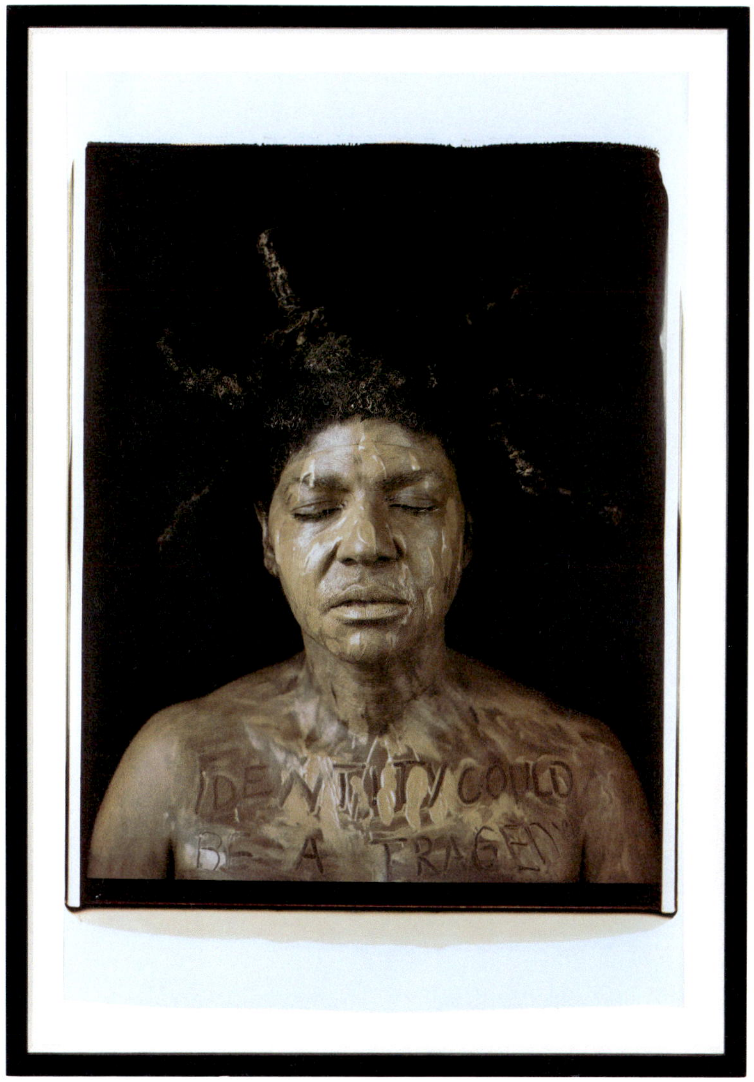

IDENTITY COULD
BE A TRAGED

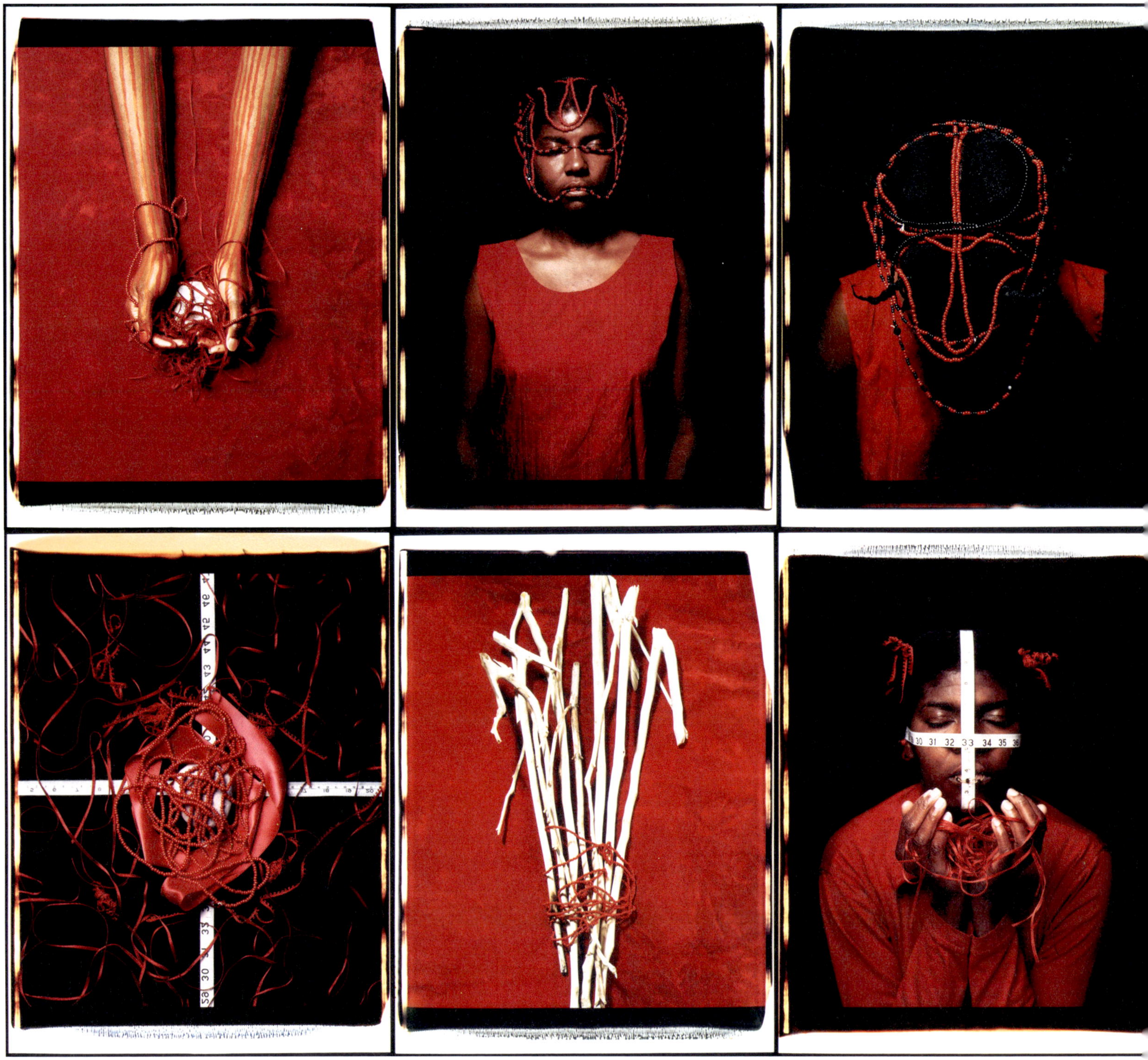

PLATE 16 *Abridor de Caminos (The One Who Opens the Path)*, 1997

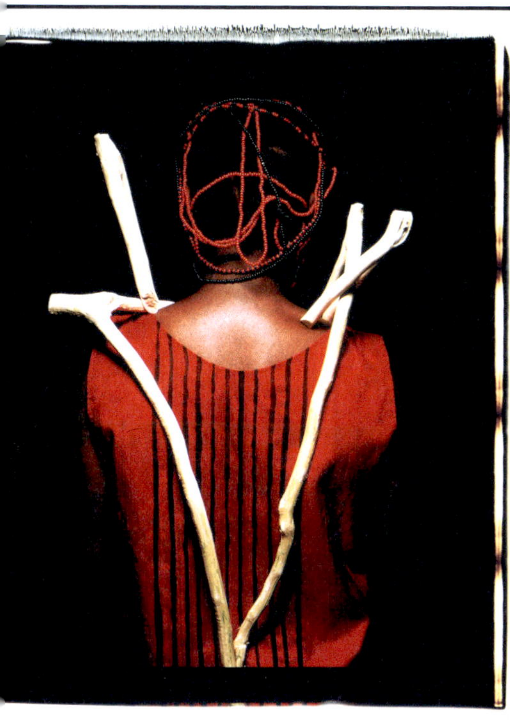

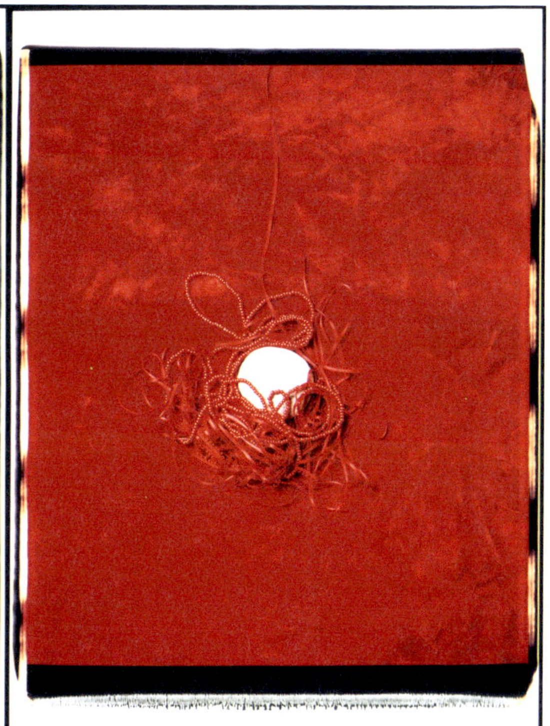

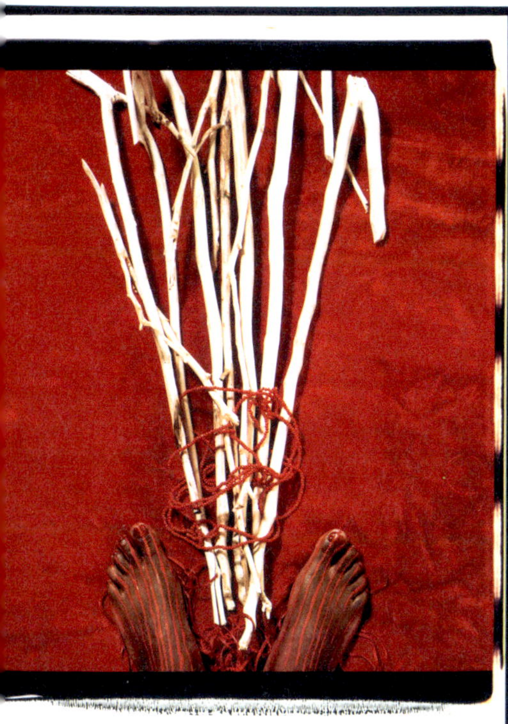

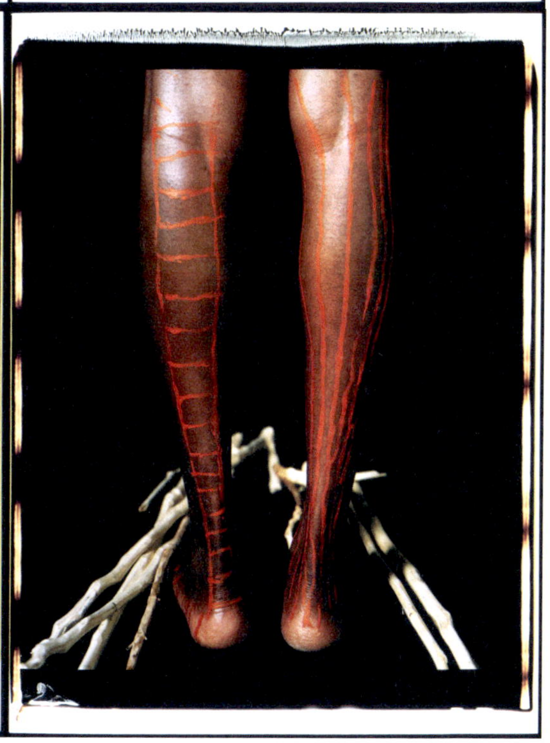

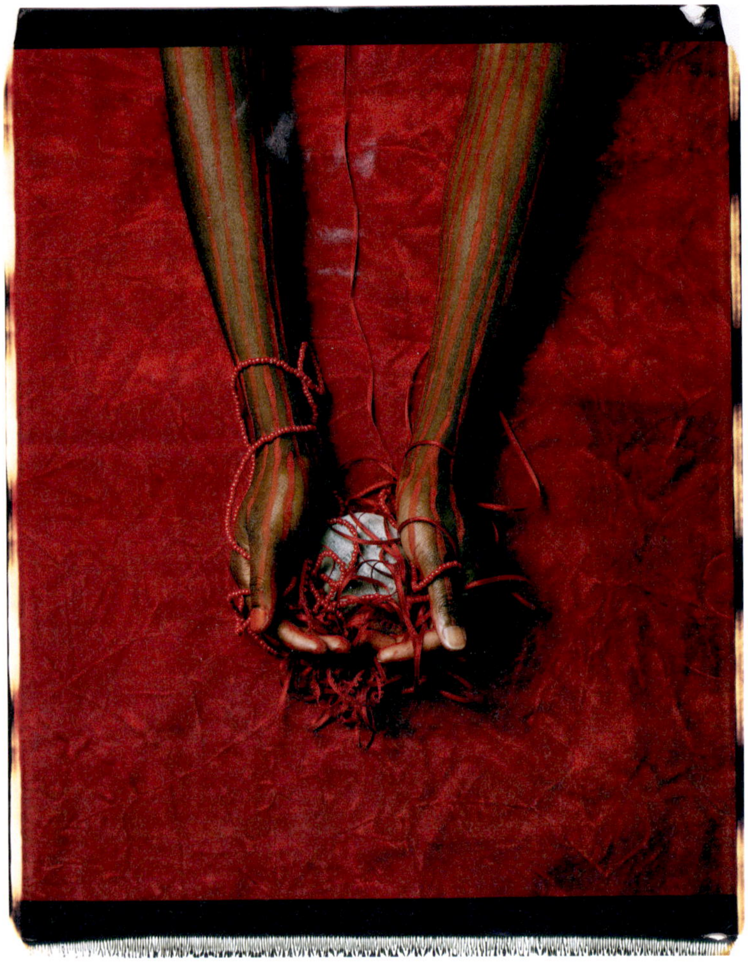

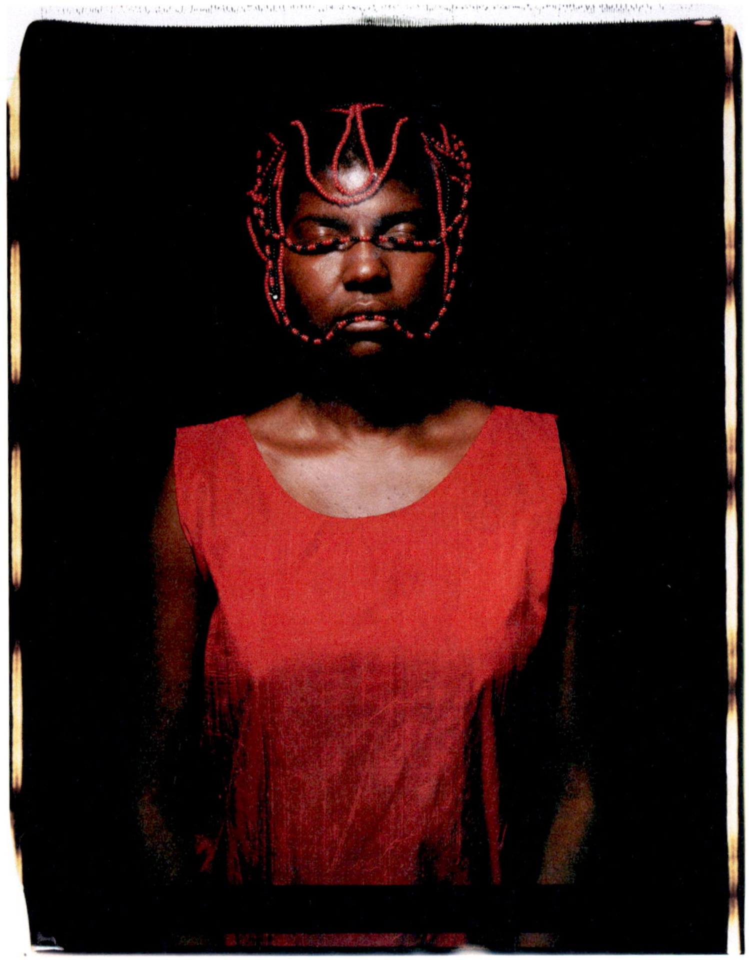

PLATE 17 *Red Composition*, from the Los Caminos (The Path) series, 1997

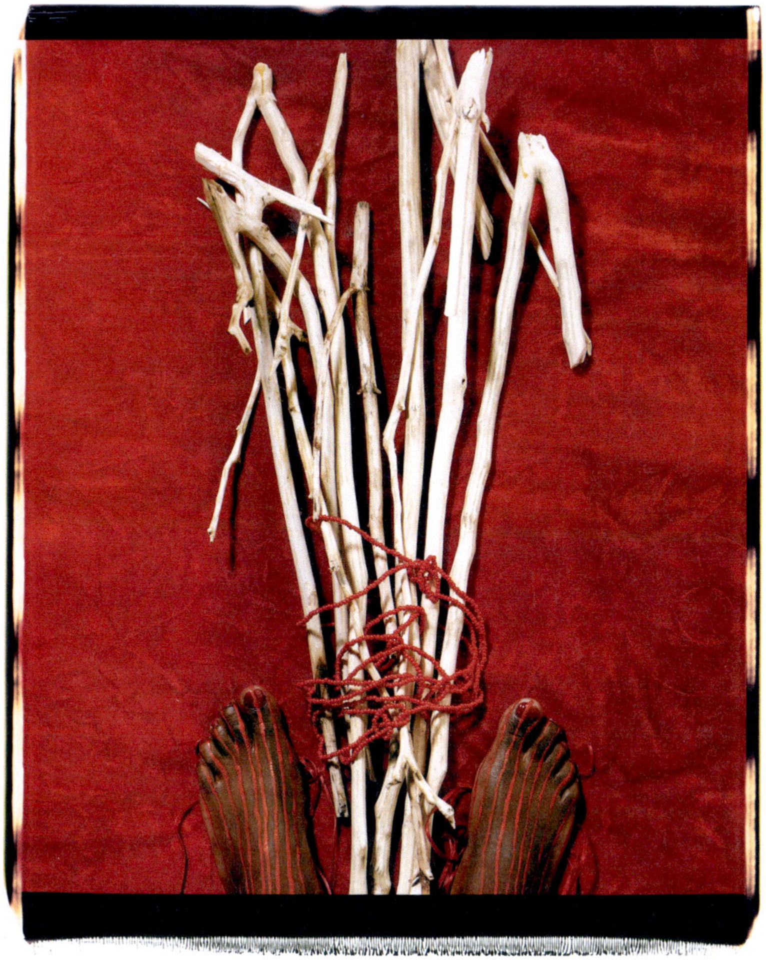

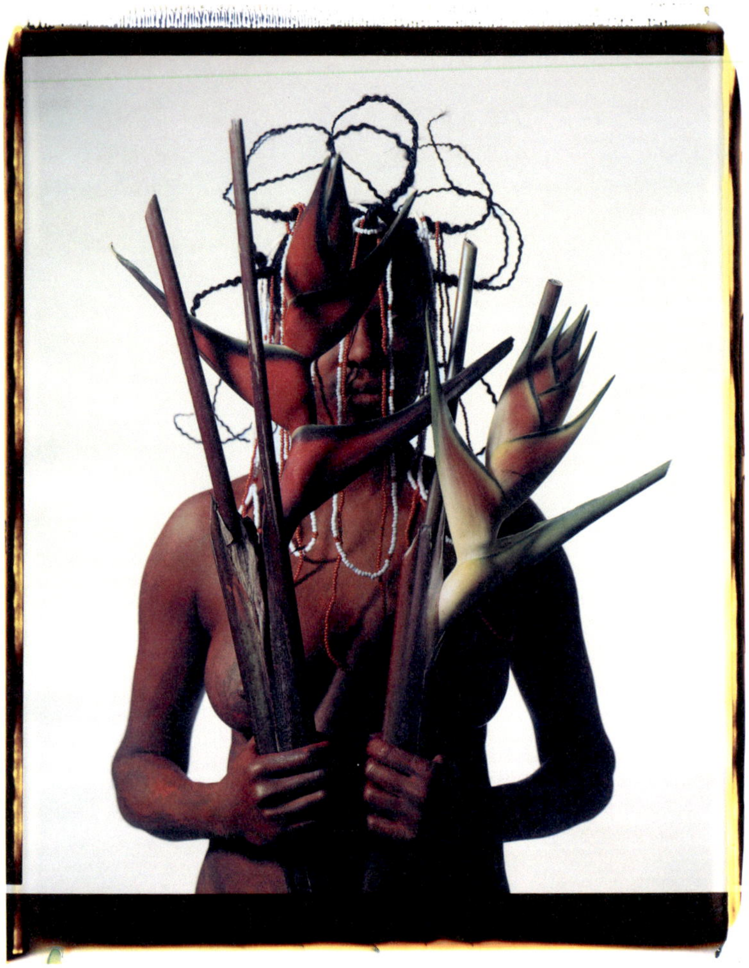

PLATE 18 *Red Composition*, from the Los Caminos (The Path) series, 1997

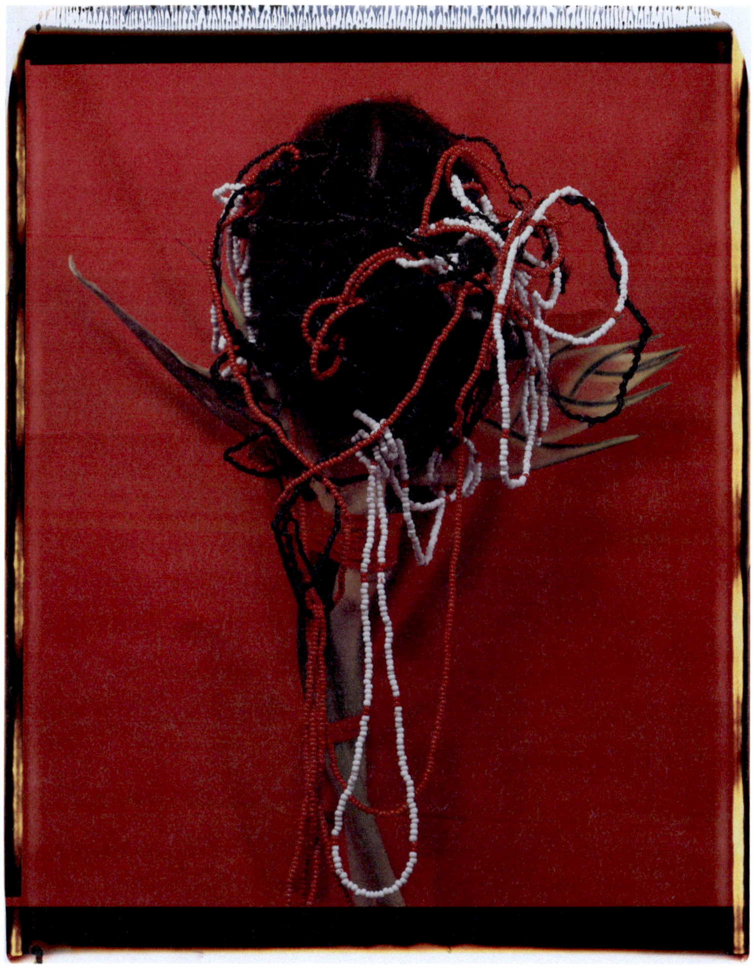

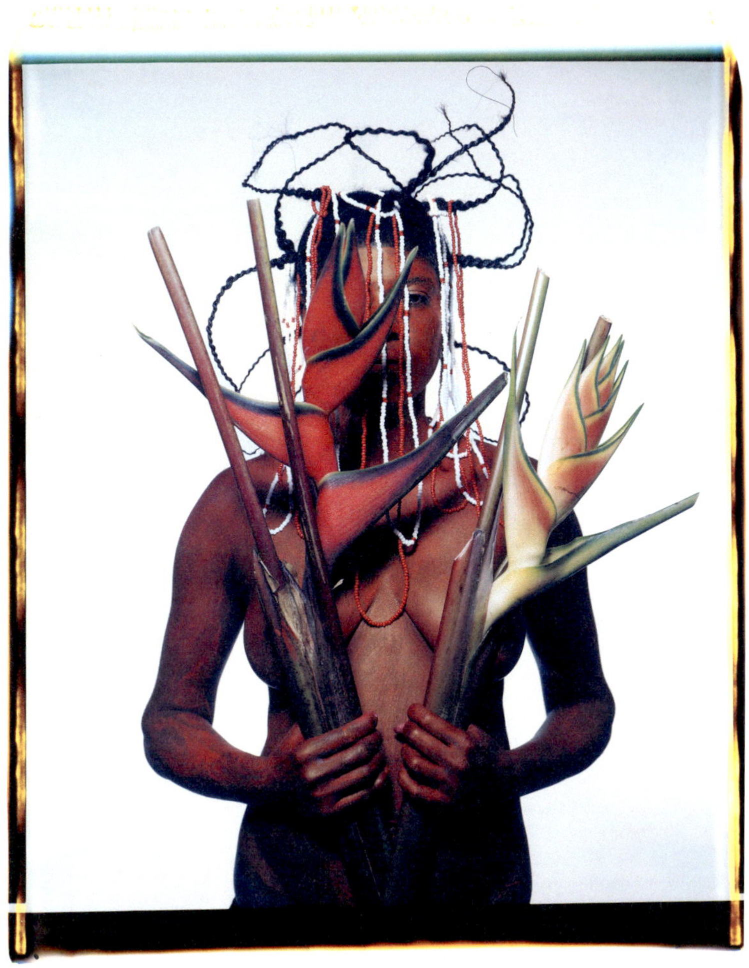

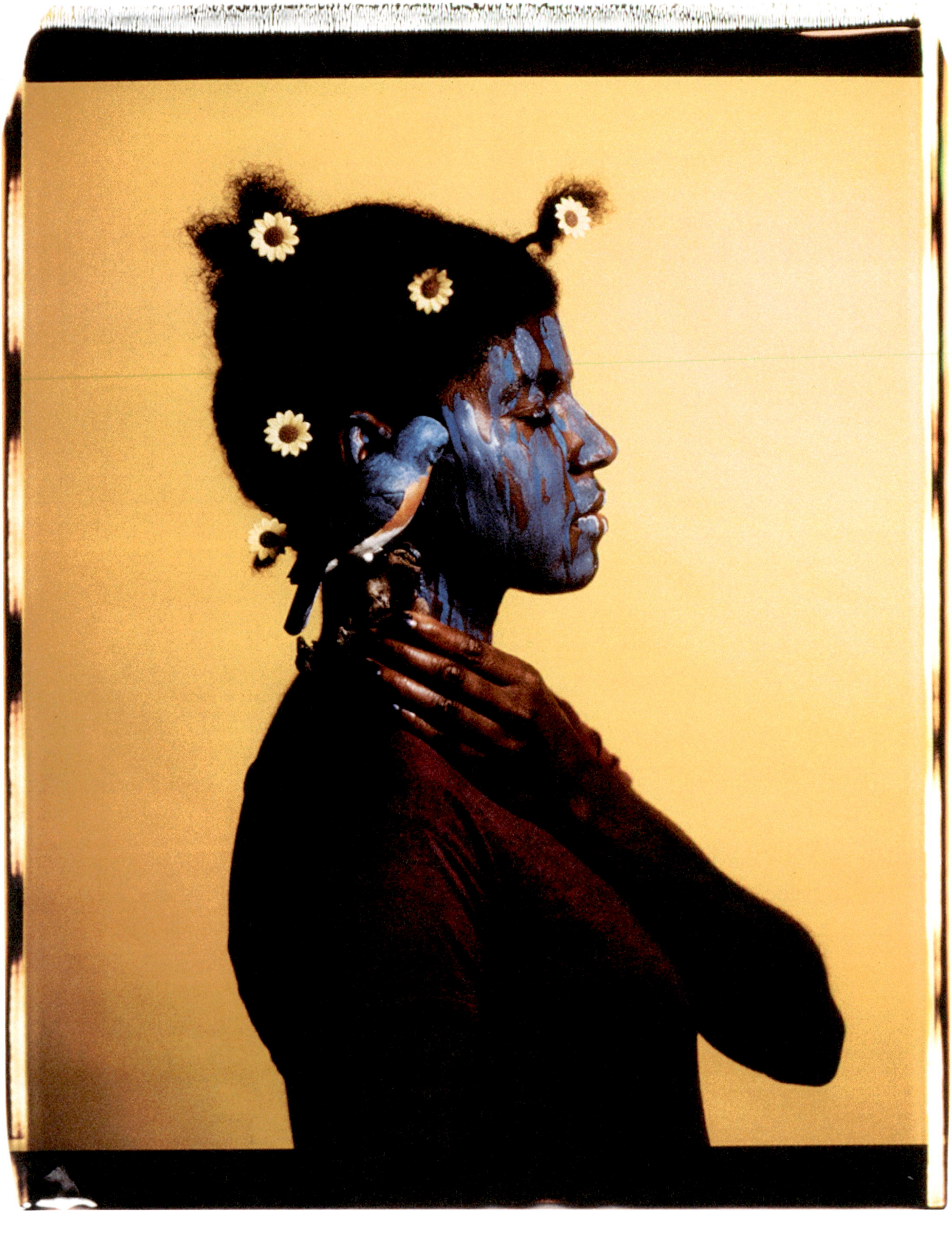

PLATE 19 *Susurro (Whispers)*, 1997

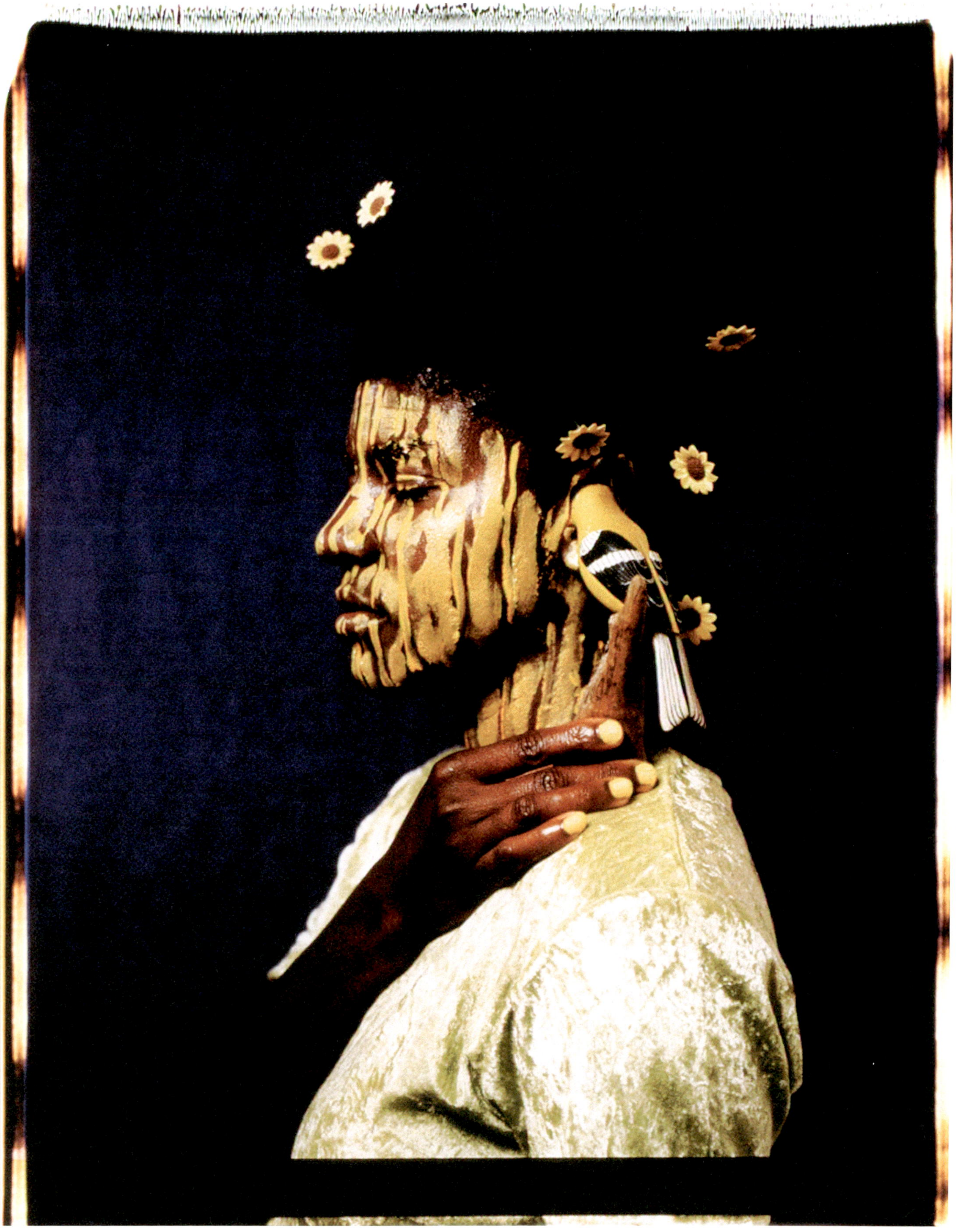

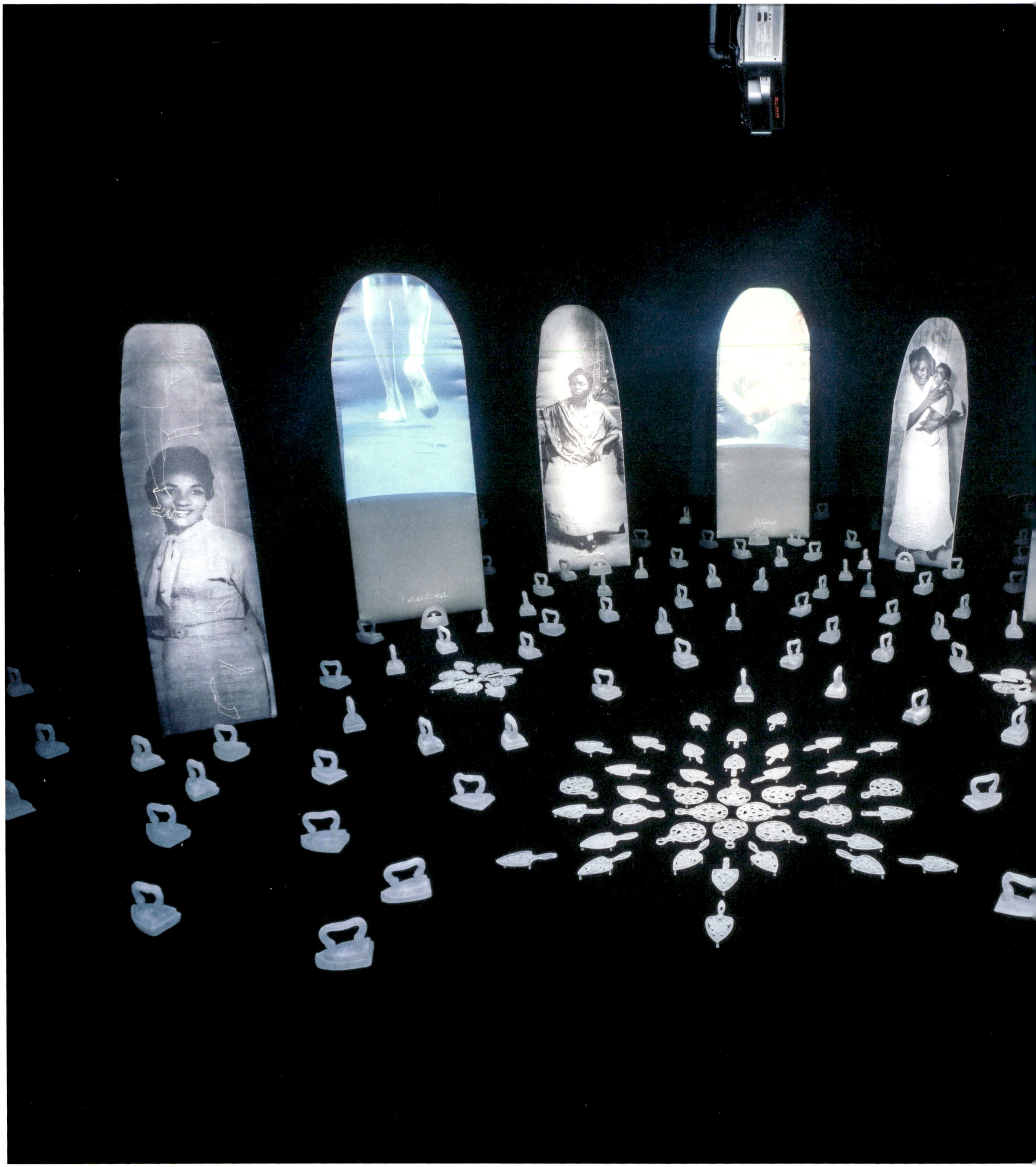

PLATE 20 *History of a People Who Were Not Heroes: Spoken Softly with Mama* (with details), 1998

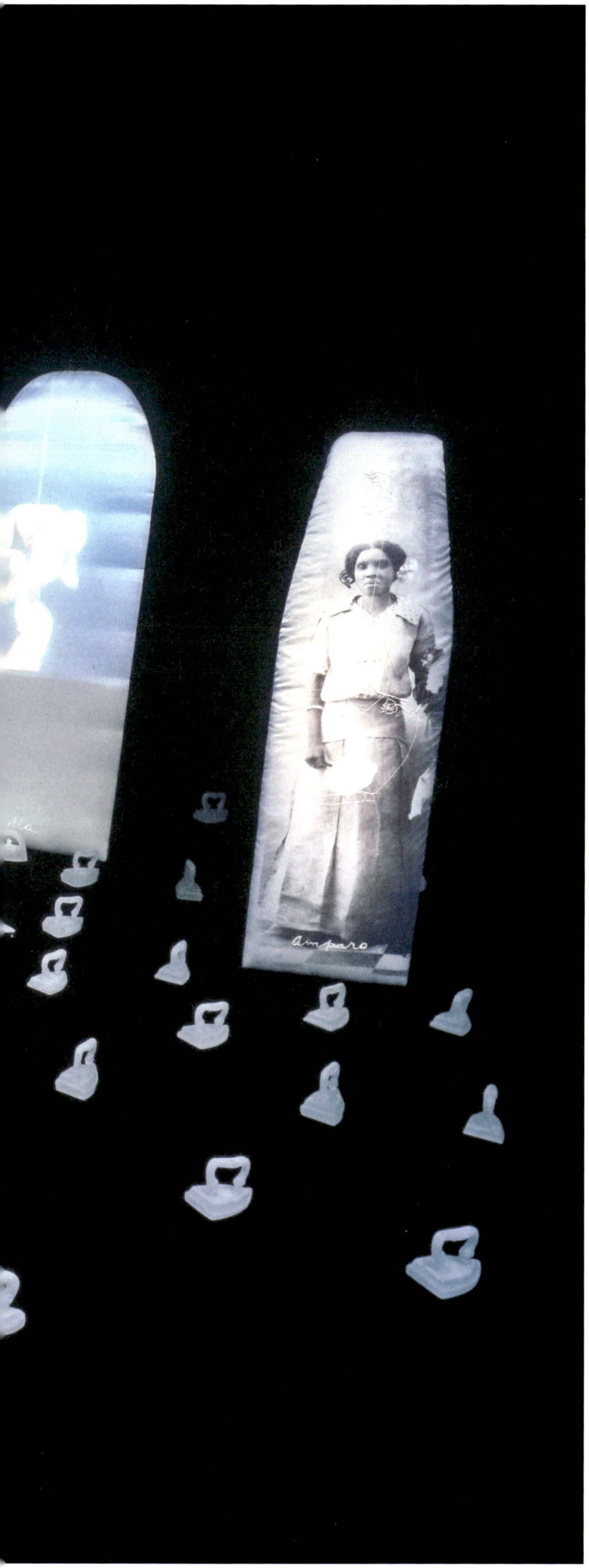
Amparo

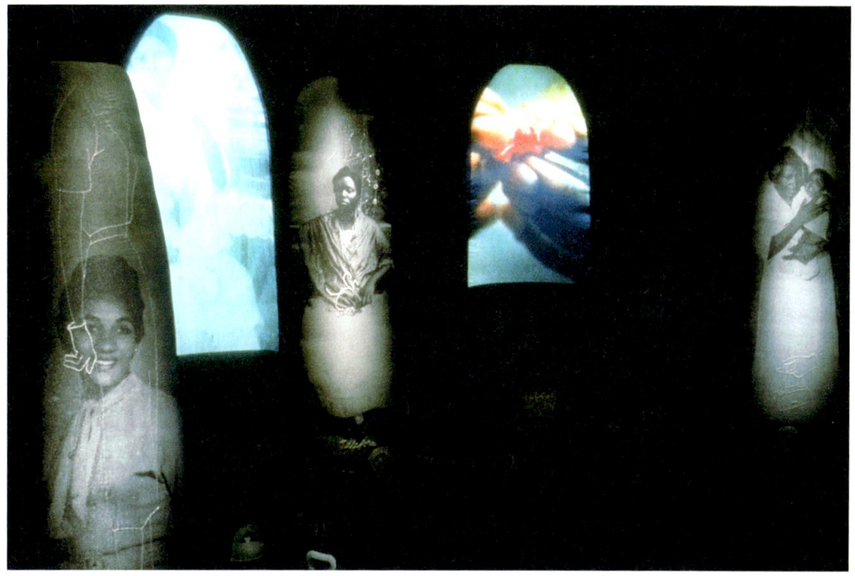

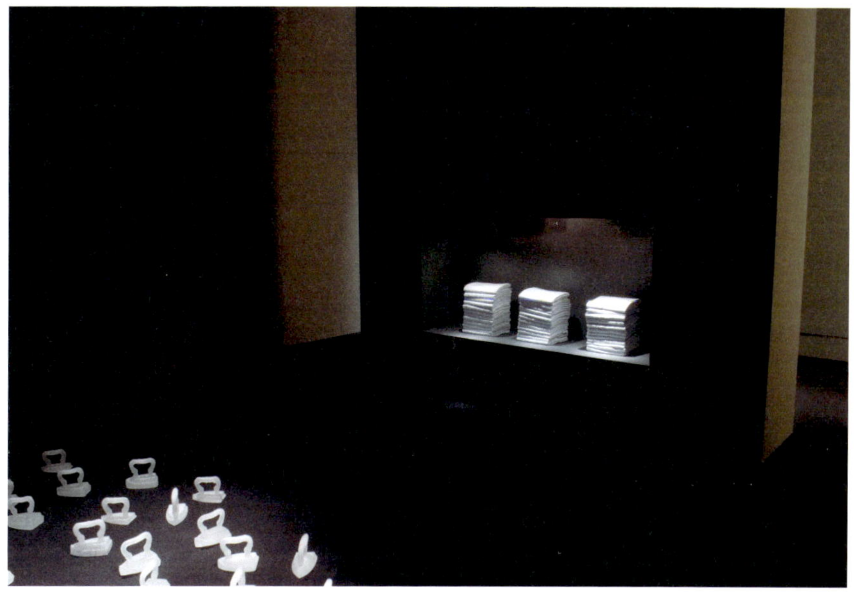

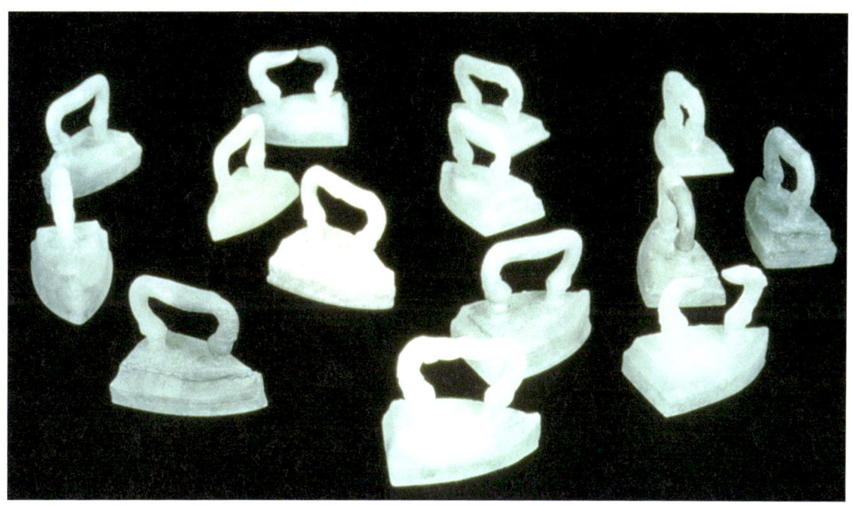

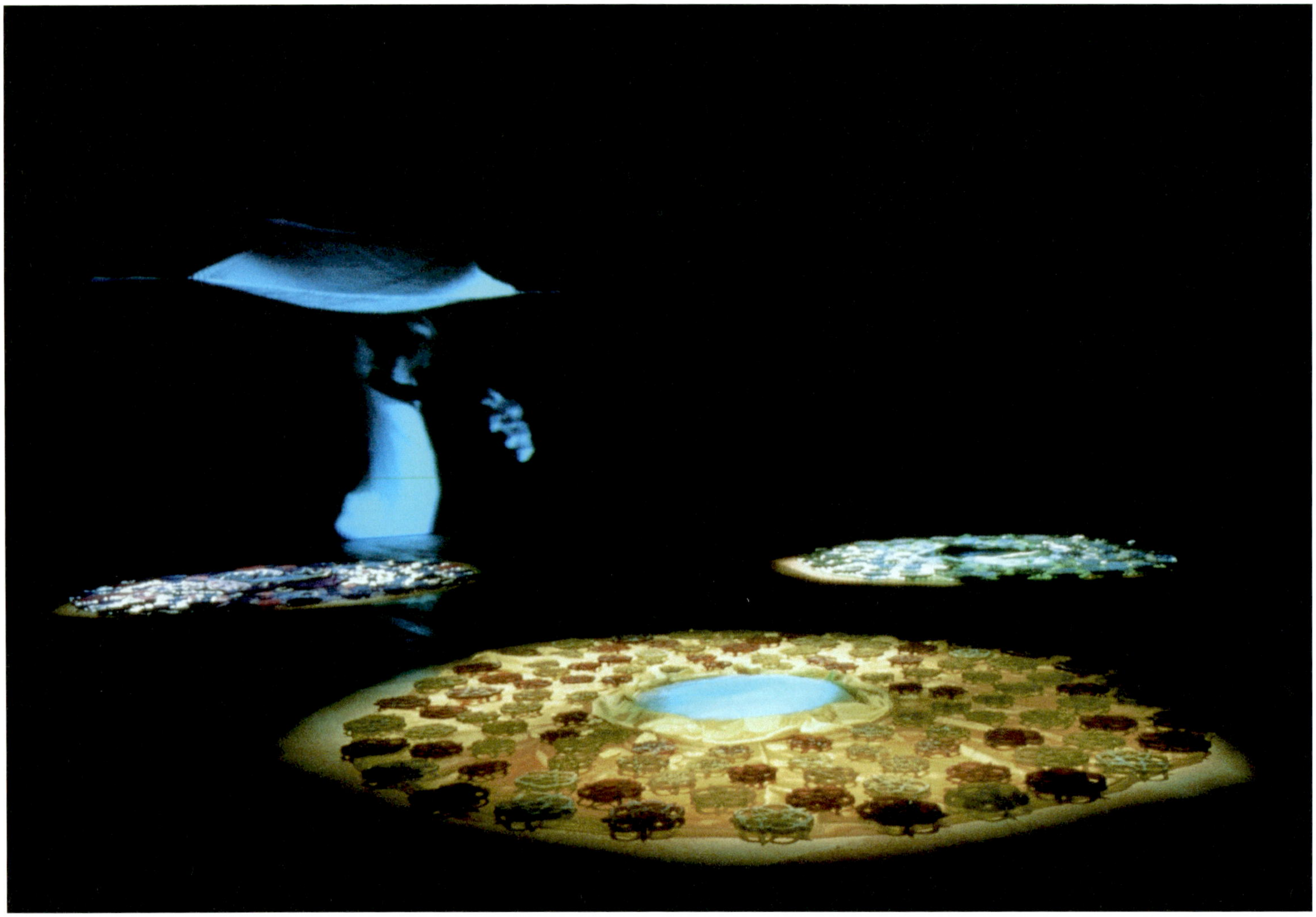

PLATE 21 Stills from video, *History of a People Who Were Not Heroes: Meanwhile the Girls Were Playing*, 1999–2000

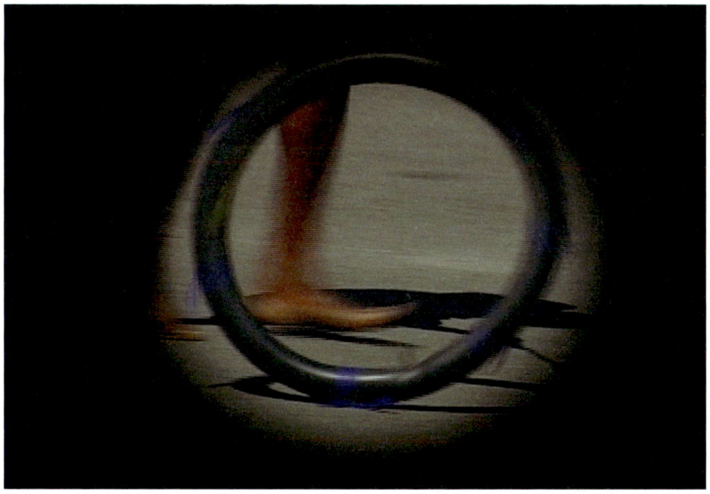
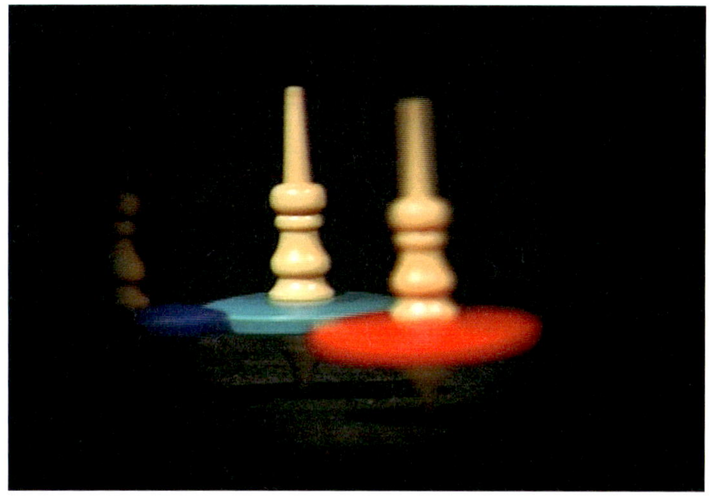
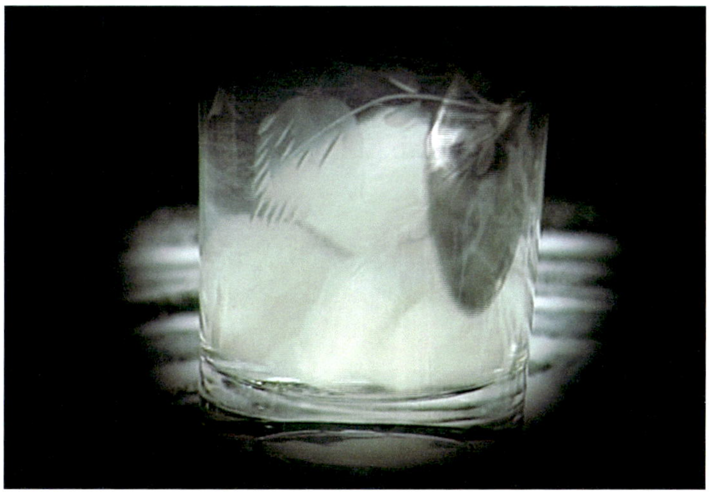
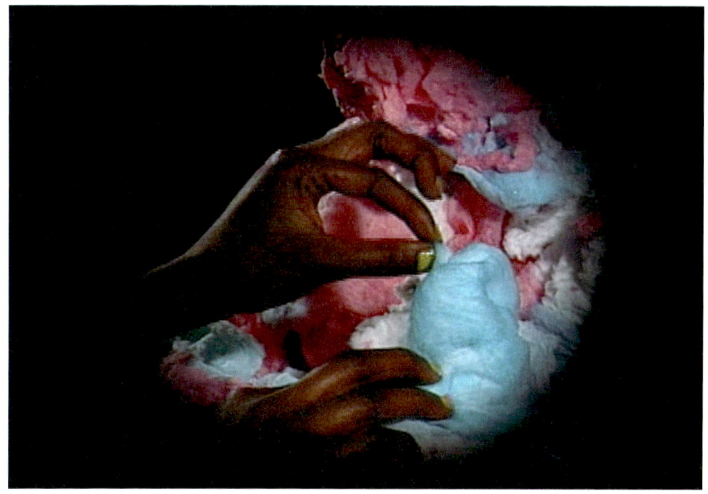
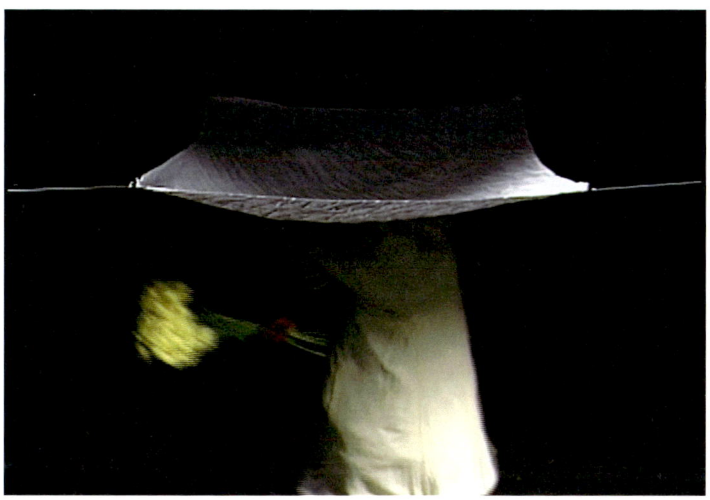
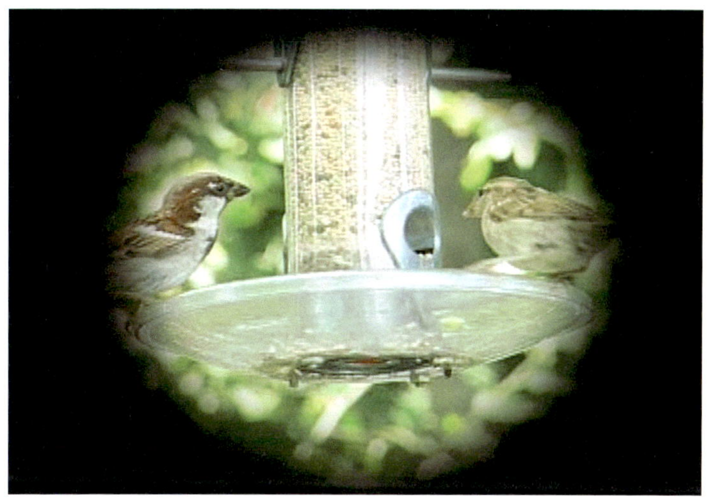

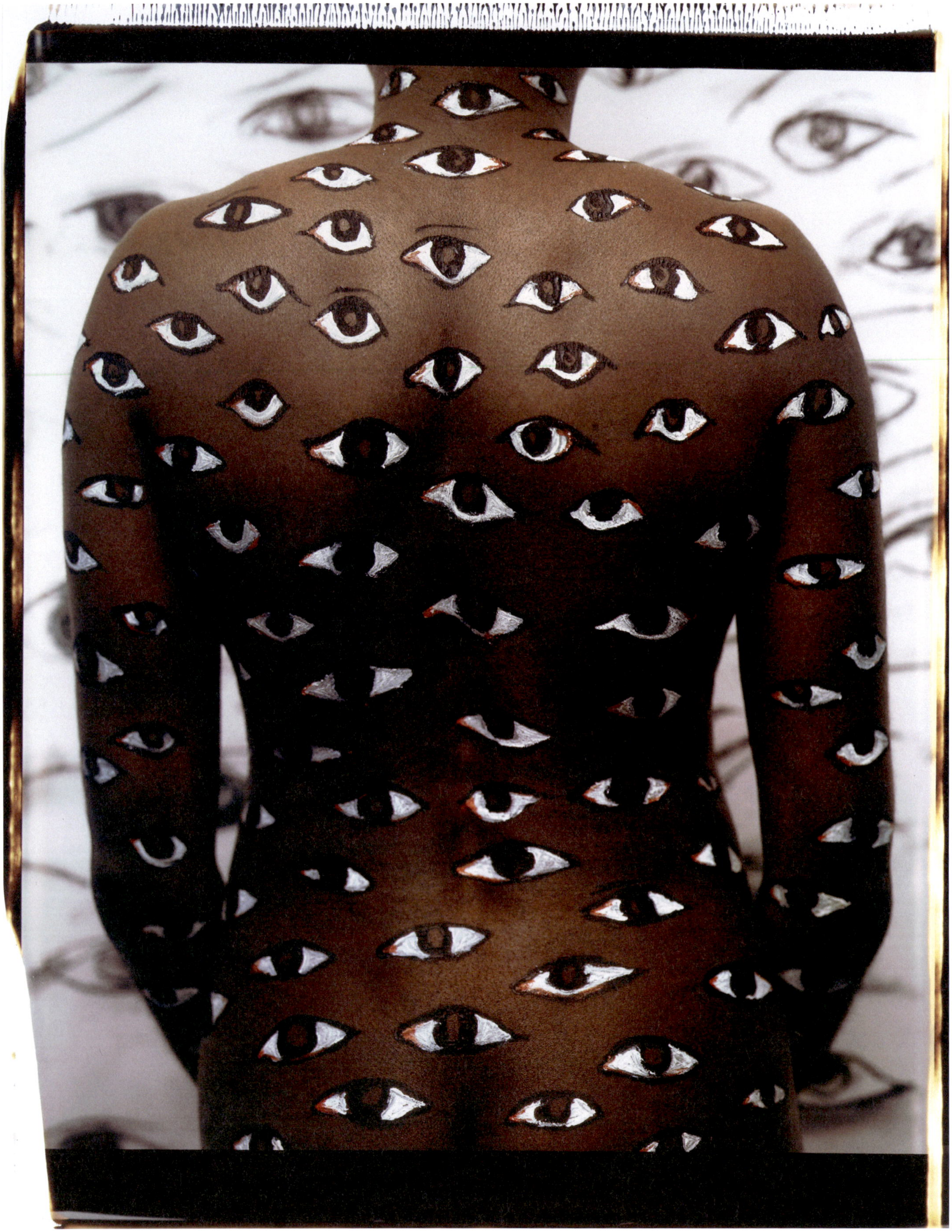

PLATE 22 *The Right Protection*, 1999

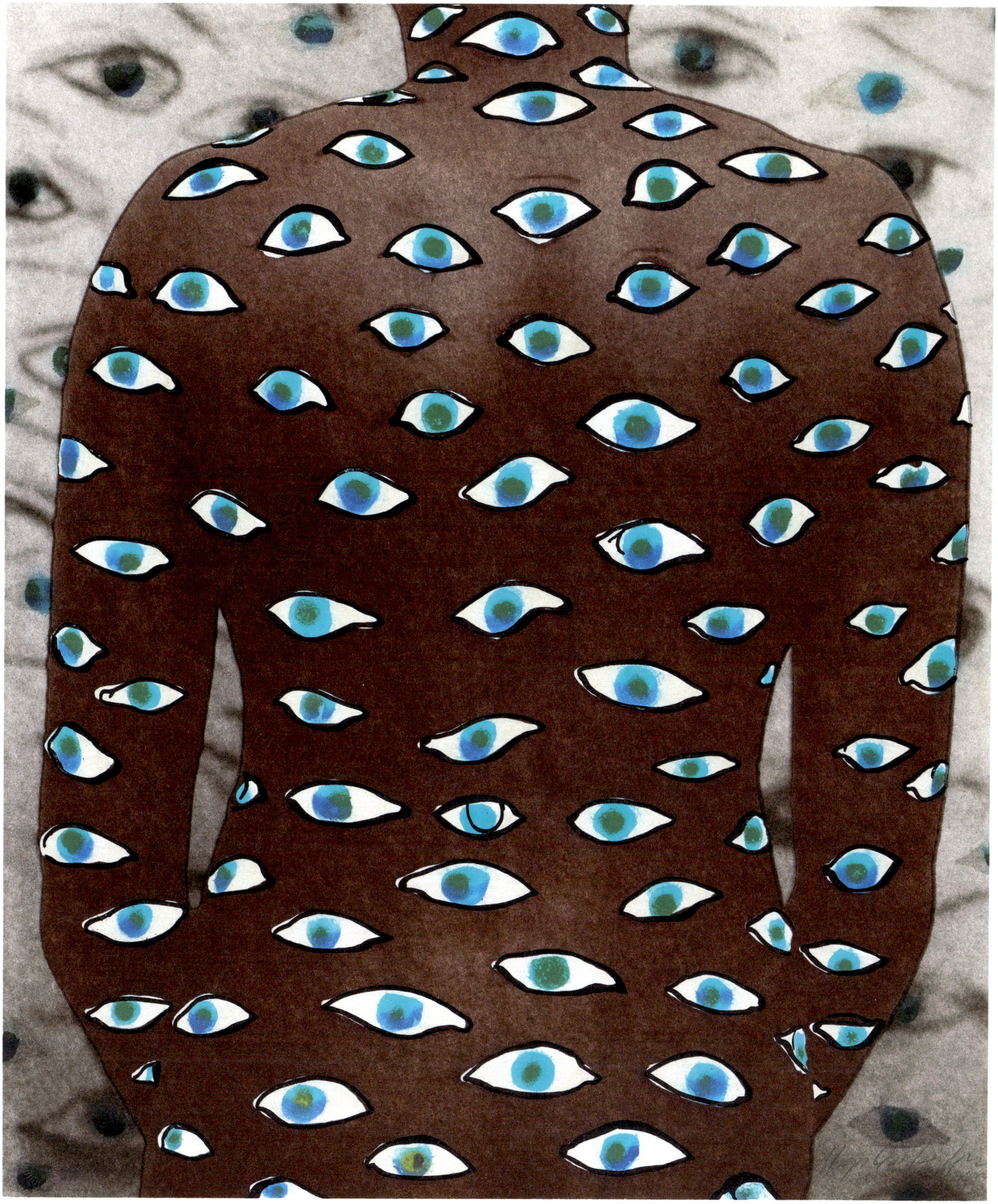

PLATE 23 *Untitled (The Right Protection)*, 1999

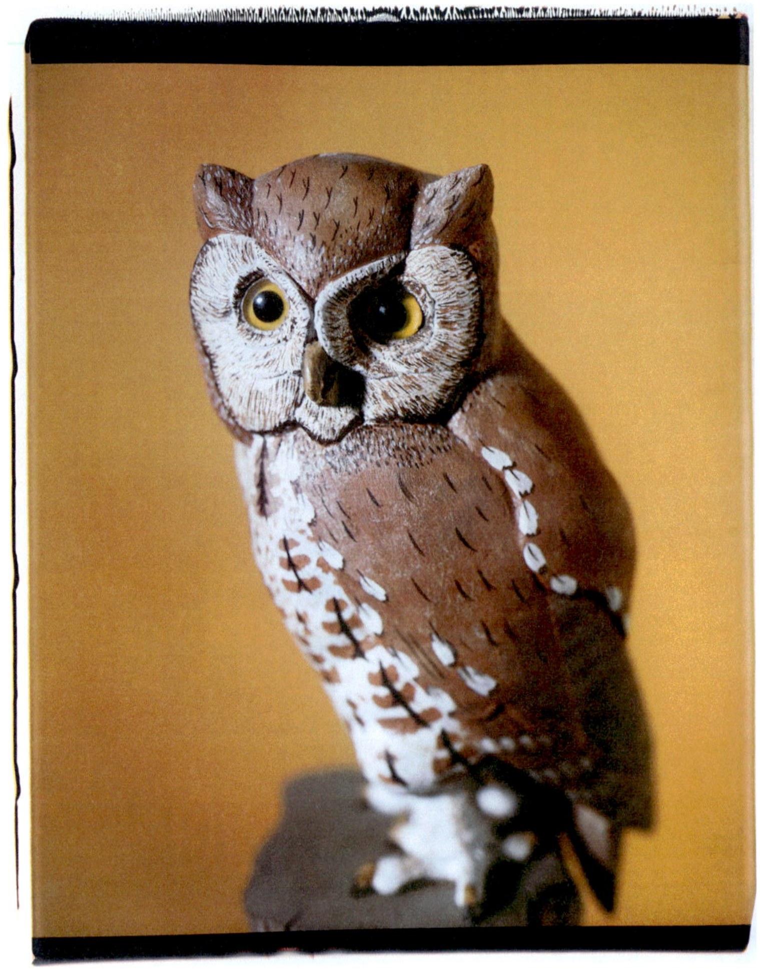

PLATE 24 *Nesting II*, 2000

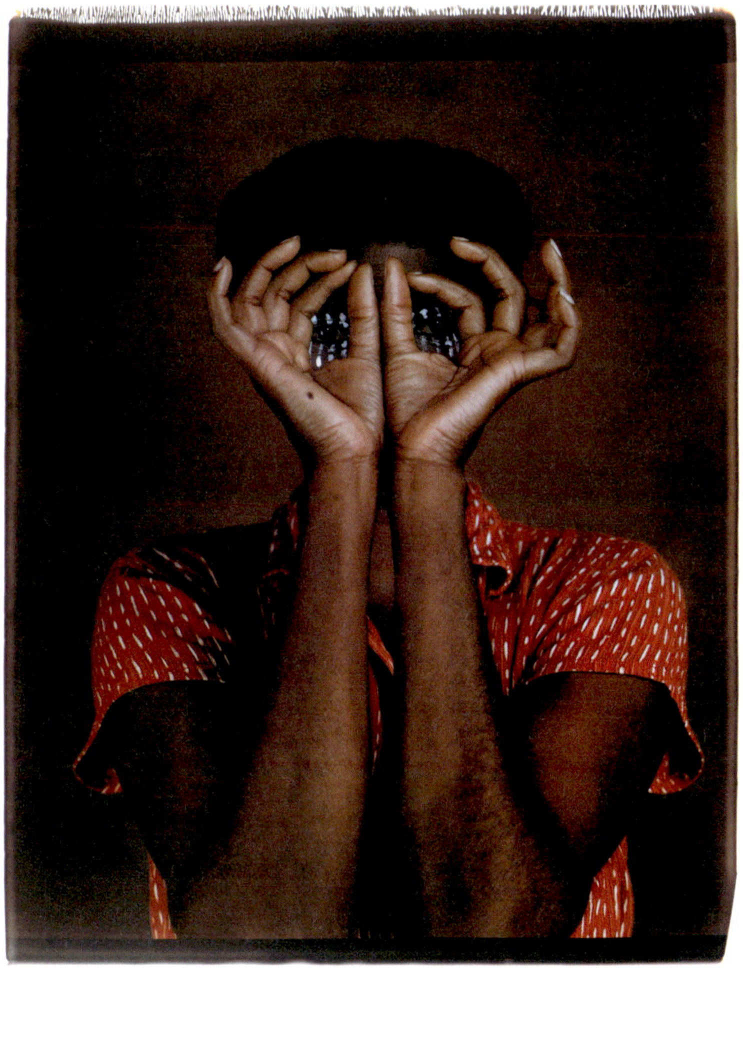
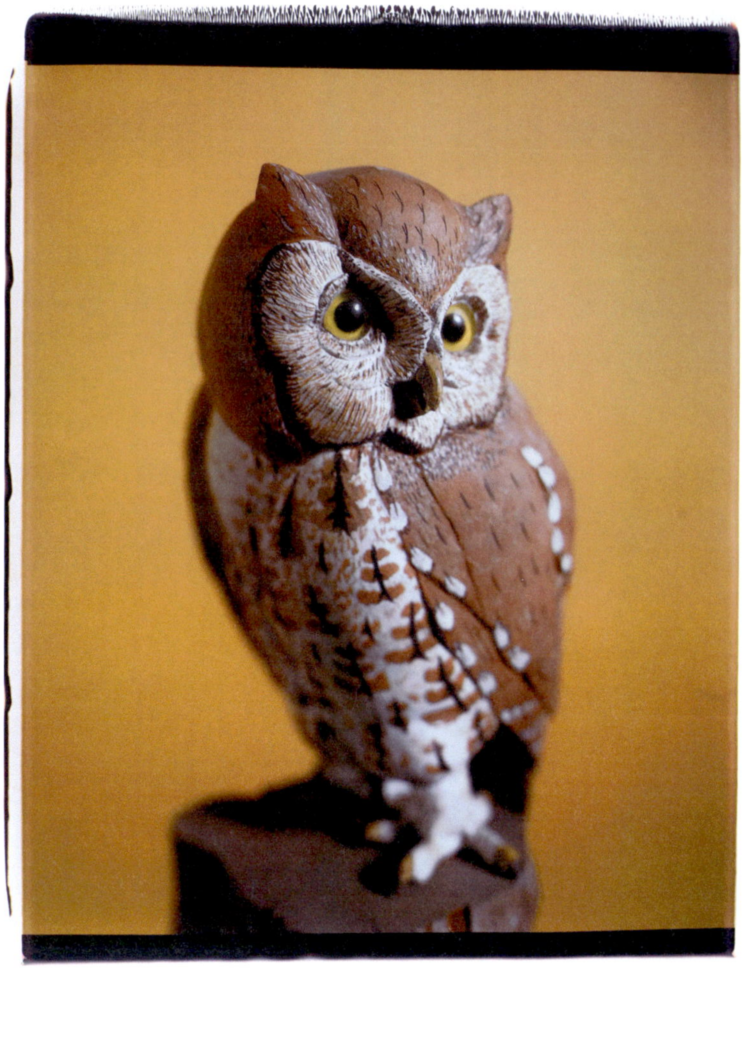

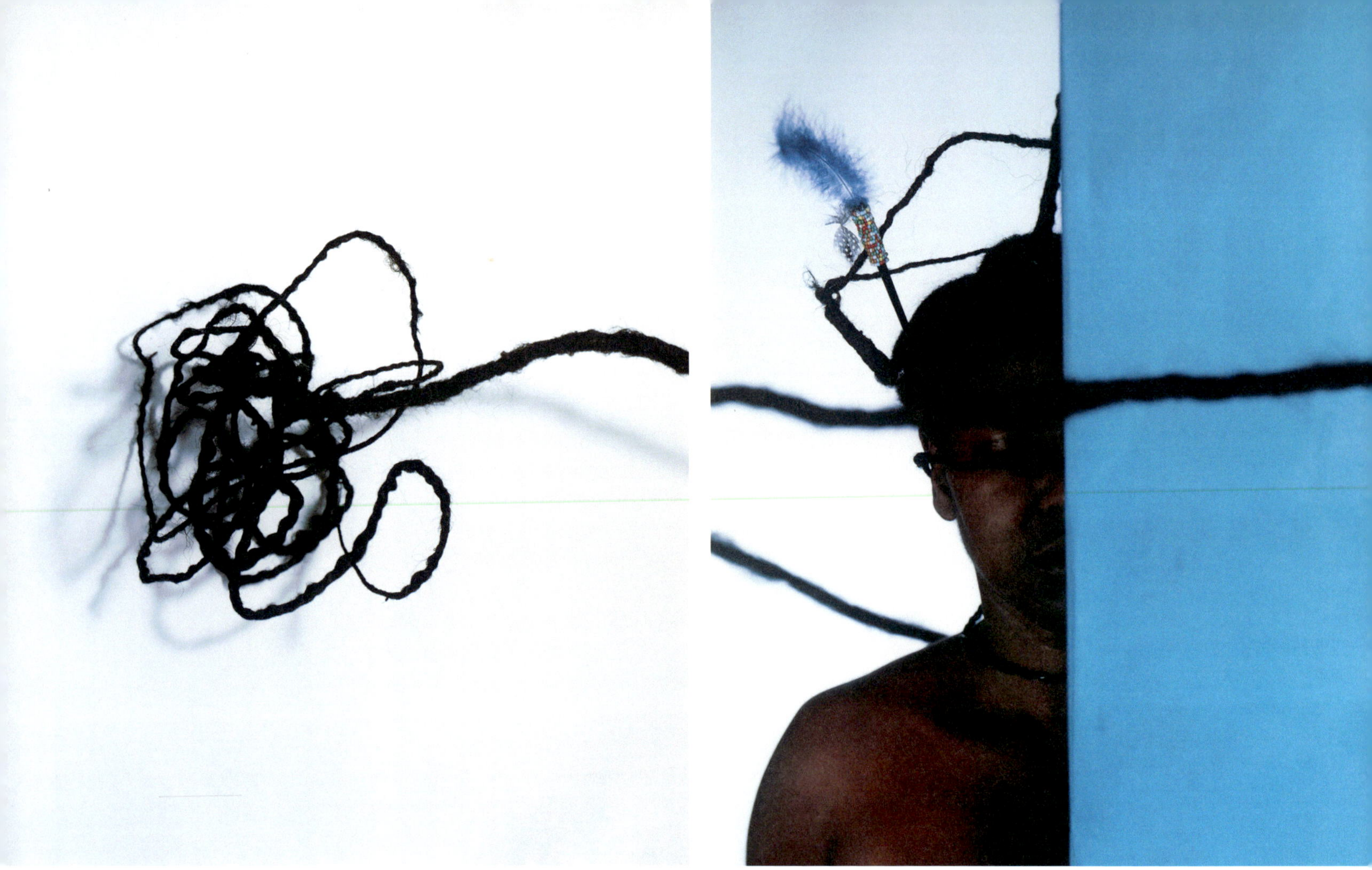

PLATE 25 *Nesting IV*, 2000

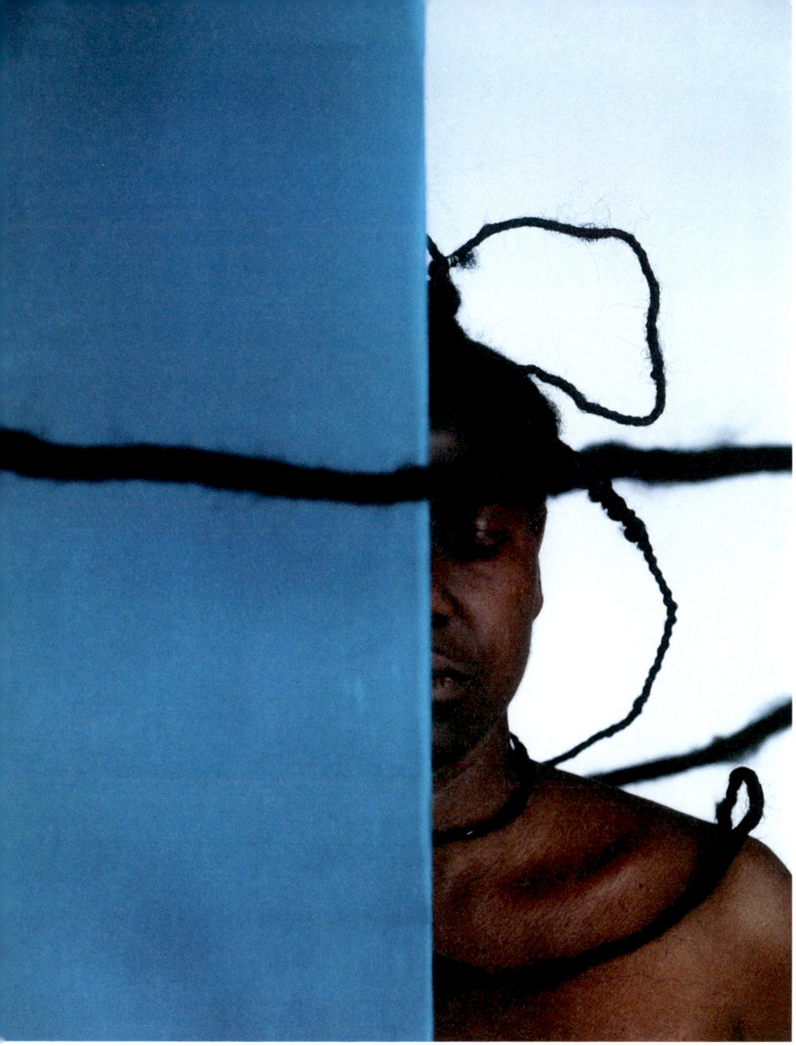

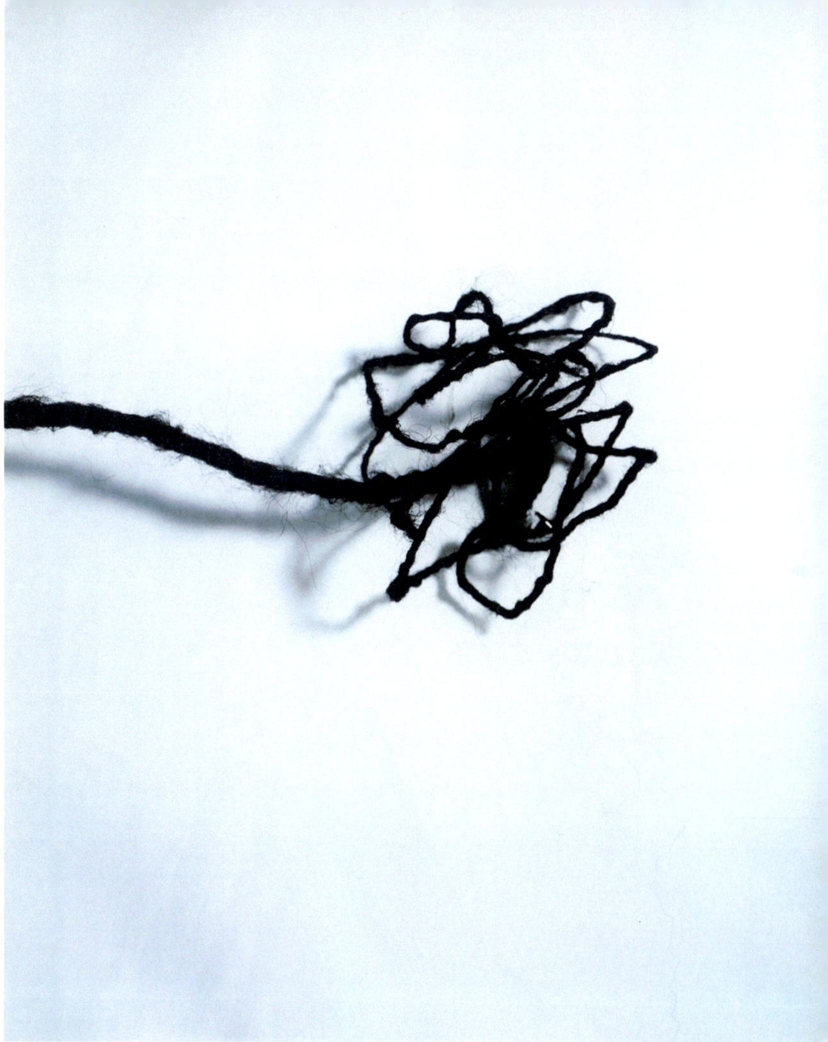

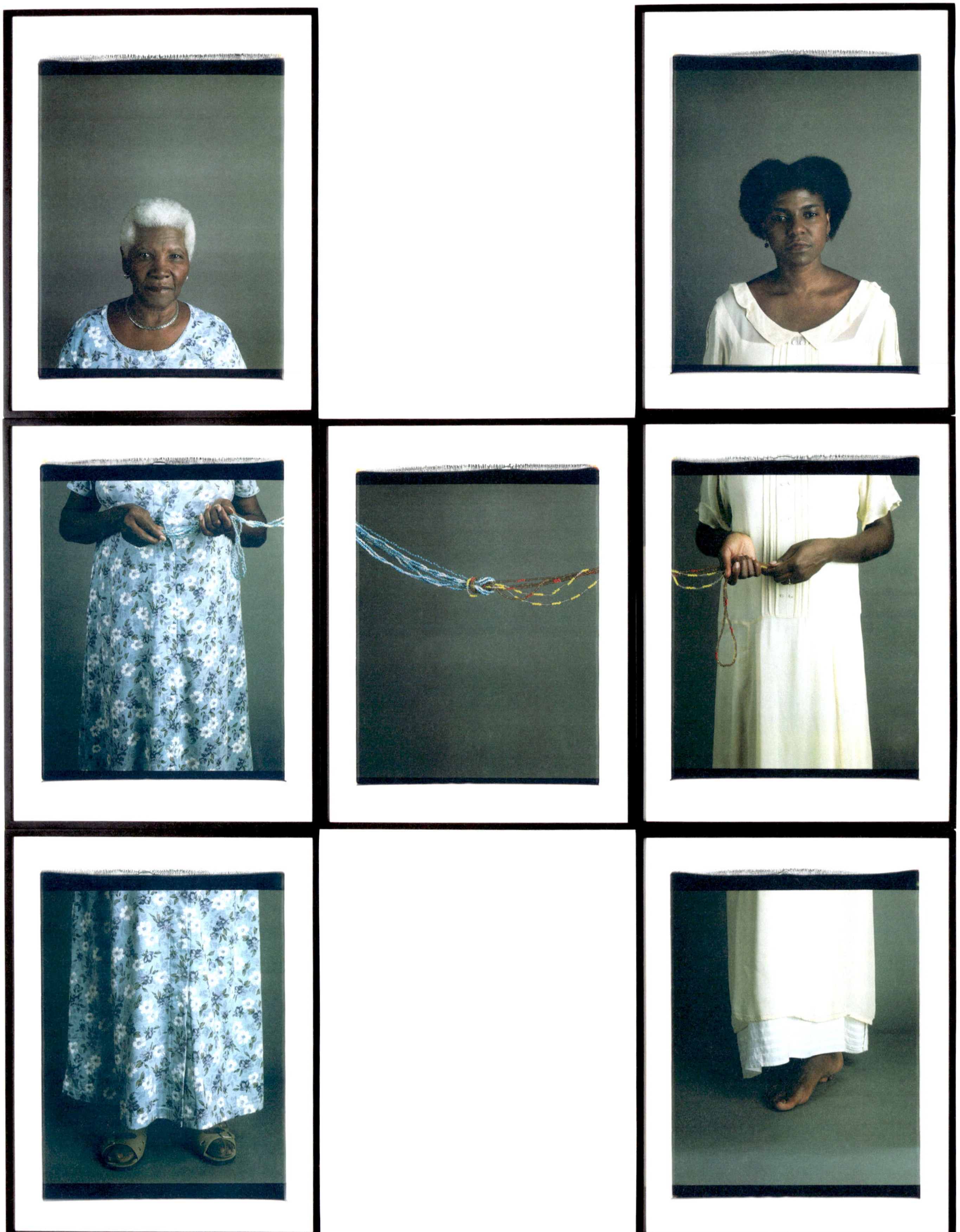

PLATE 26 *Replenishing*, 2001

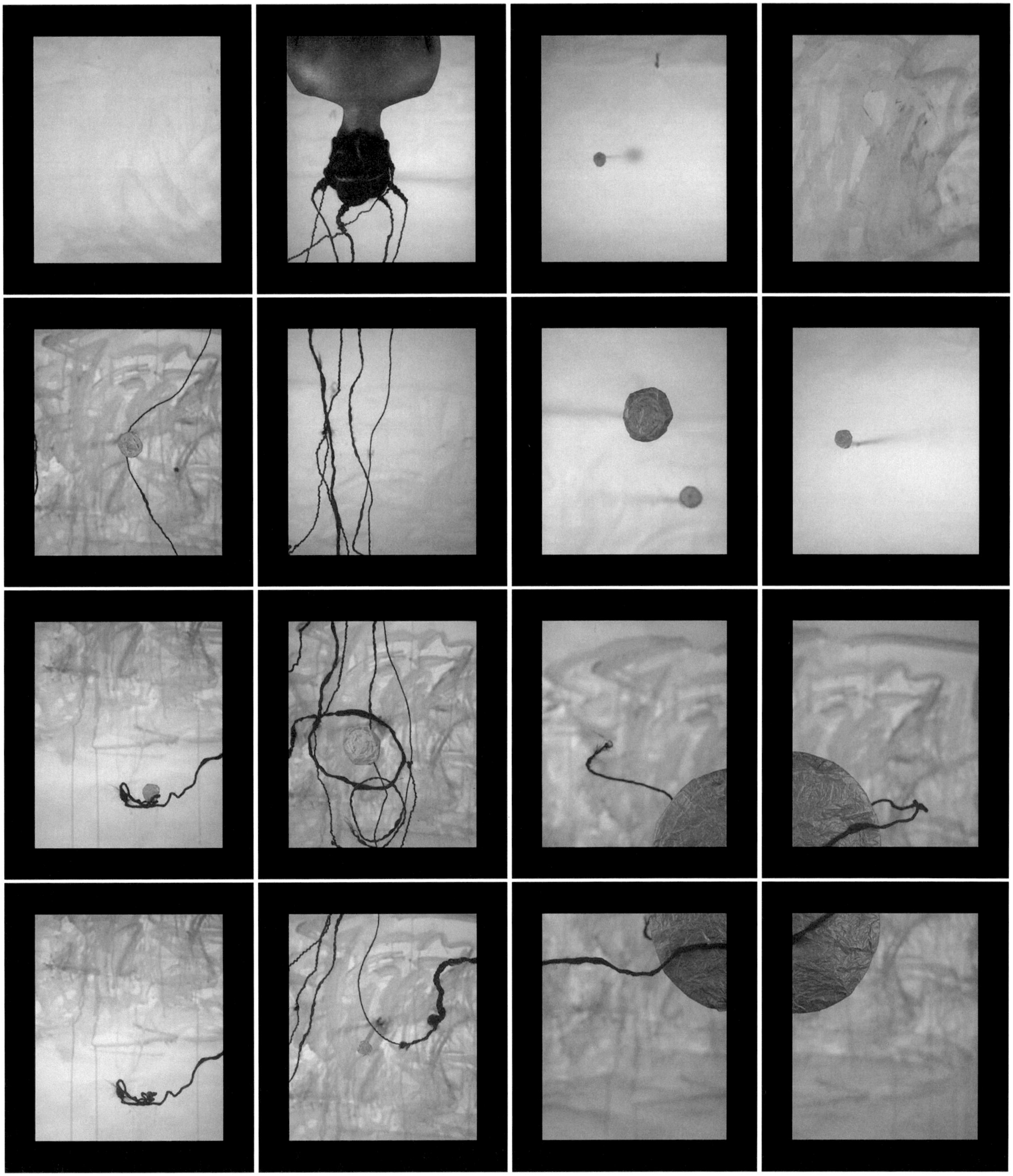

PLATE 27 *Elevata*, 2002

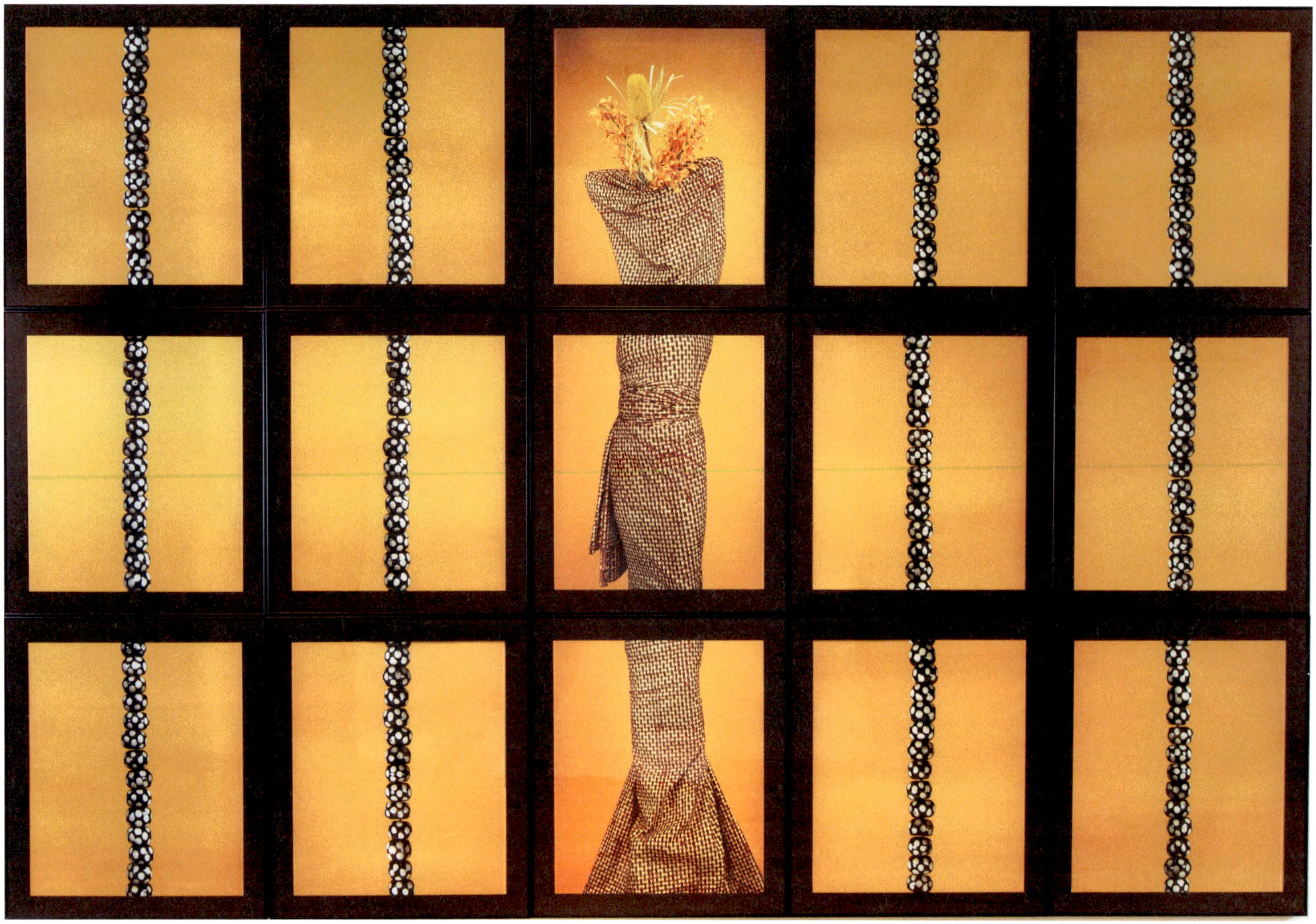

PLATE 28 *Classic Creole*, 2003

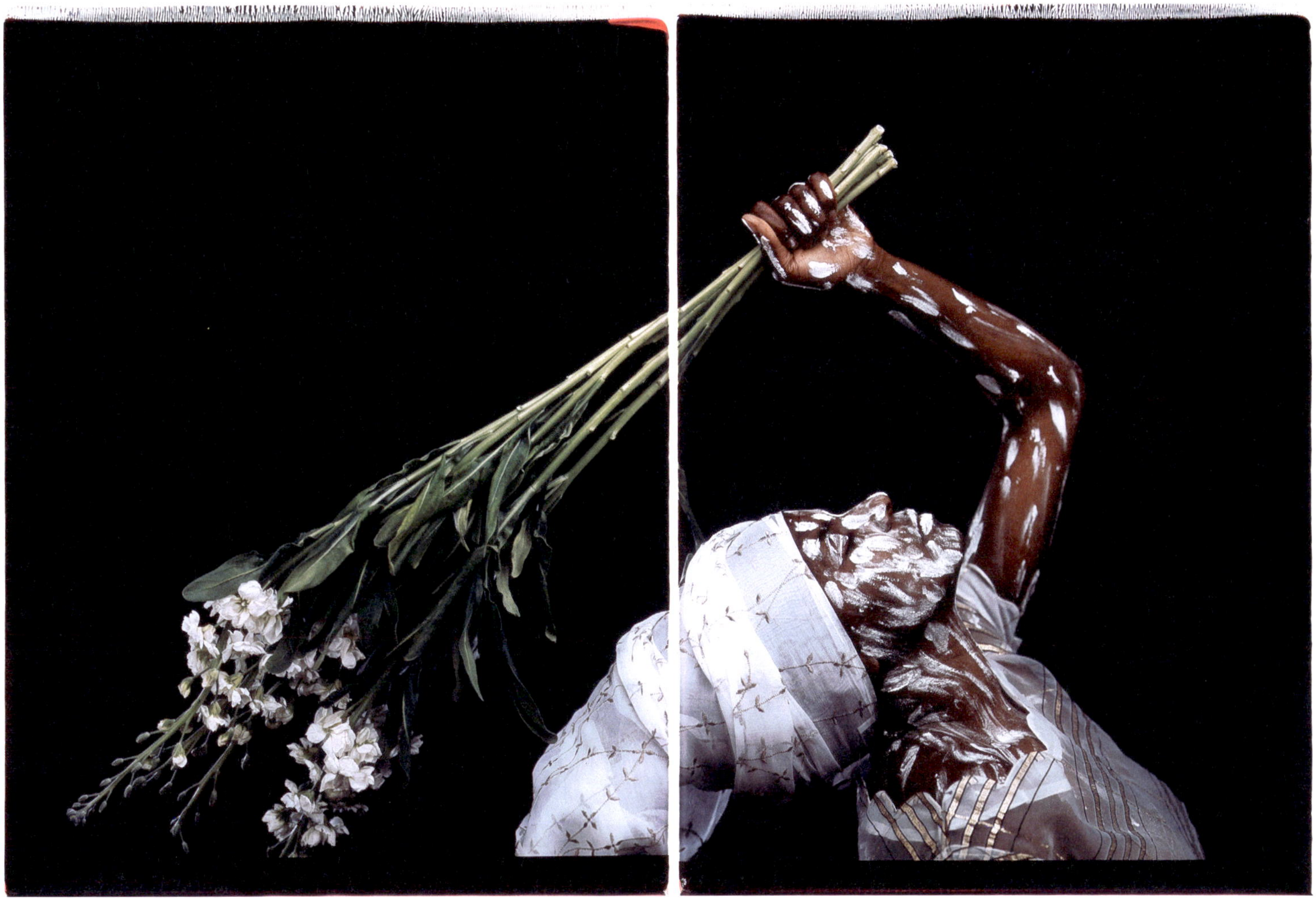

PLATE 29 *The Calling*, 2003

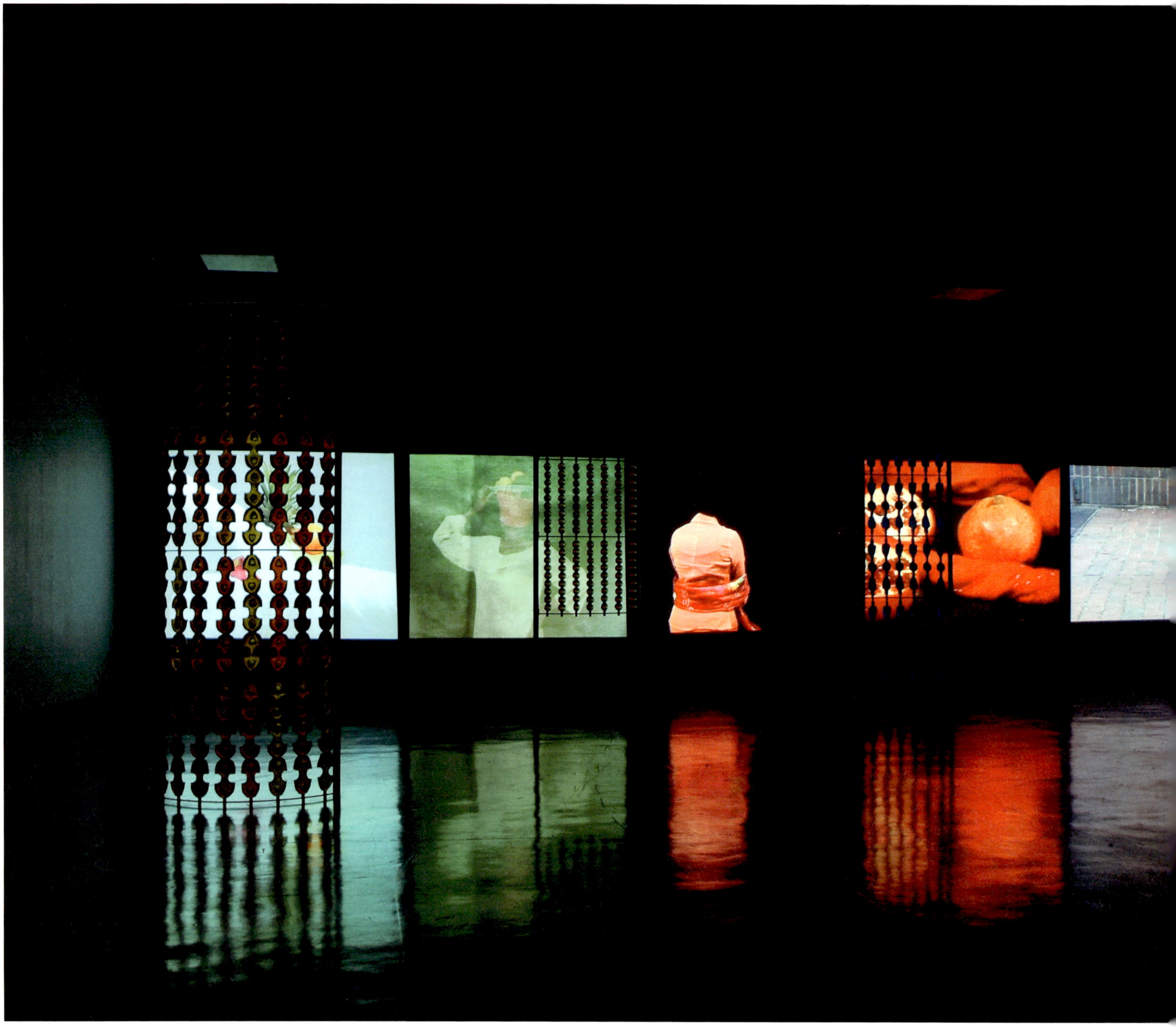

PLATE 30 *One Thousand Ways to Say Goodbye / Mil maneras para decir adiós / Threads of Memory*, 2003

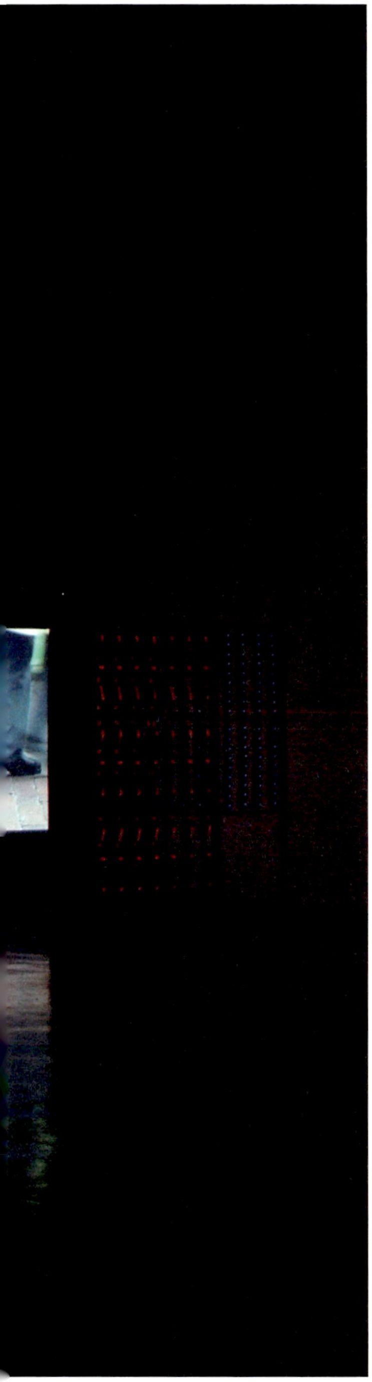

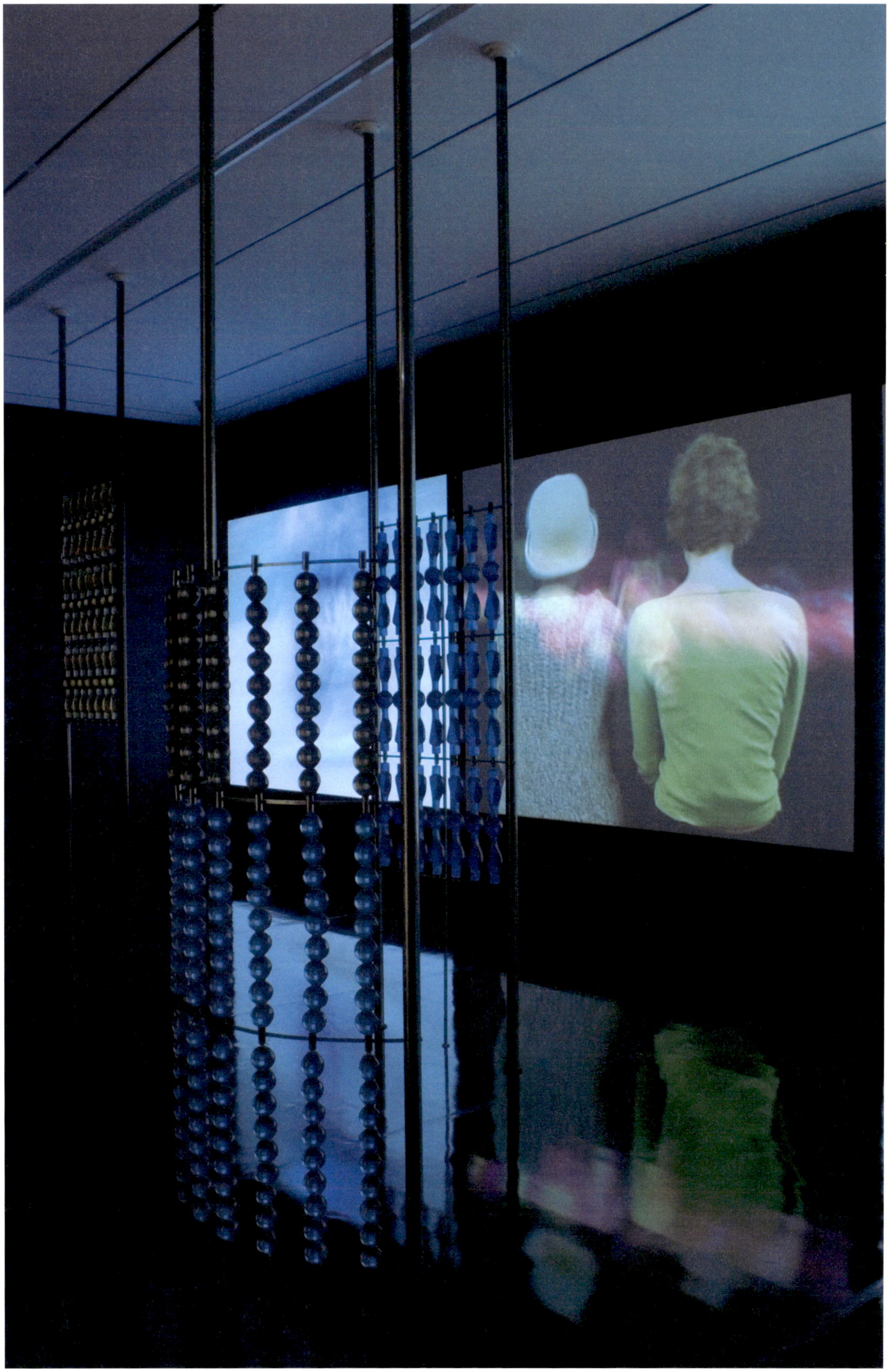

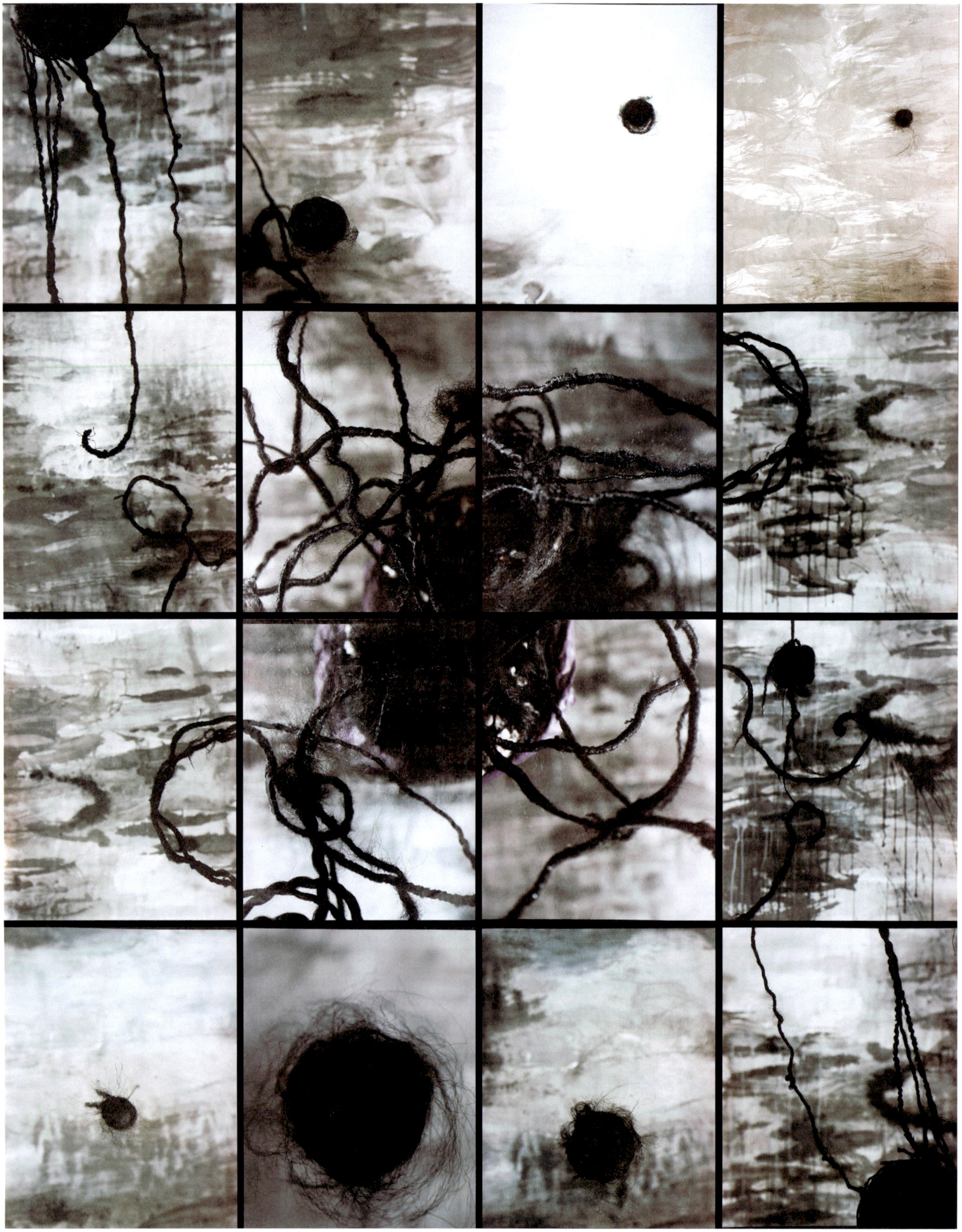

PLATE 31 *Constellation*, 2004

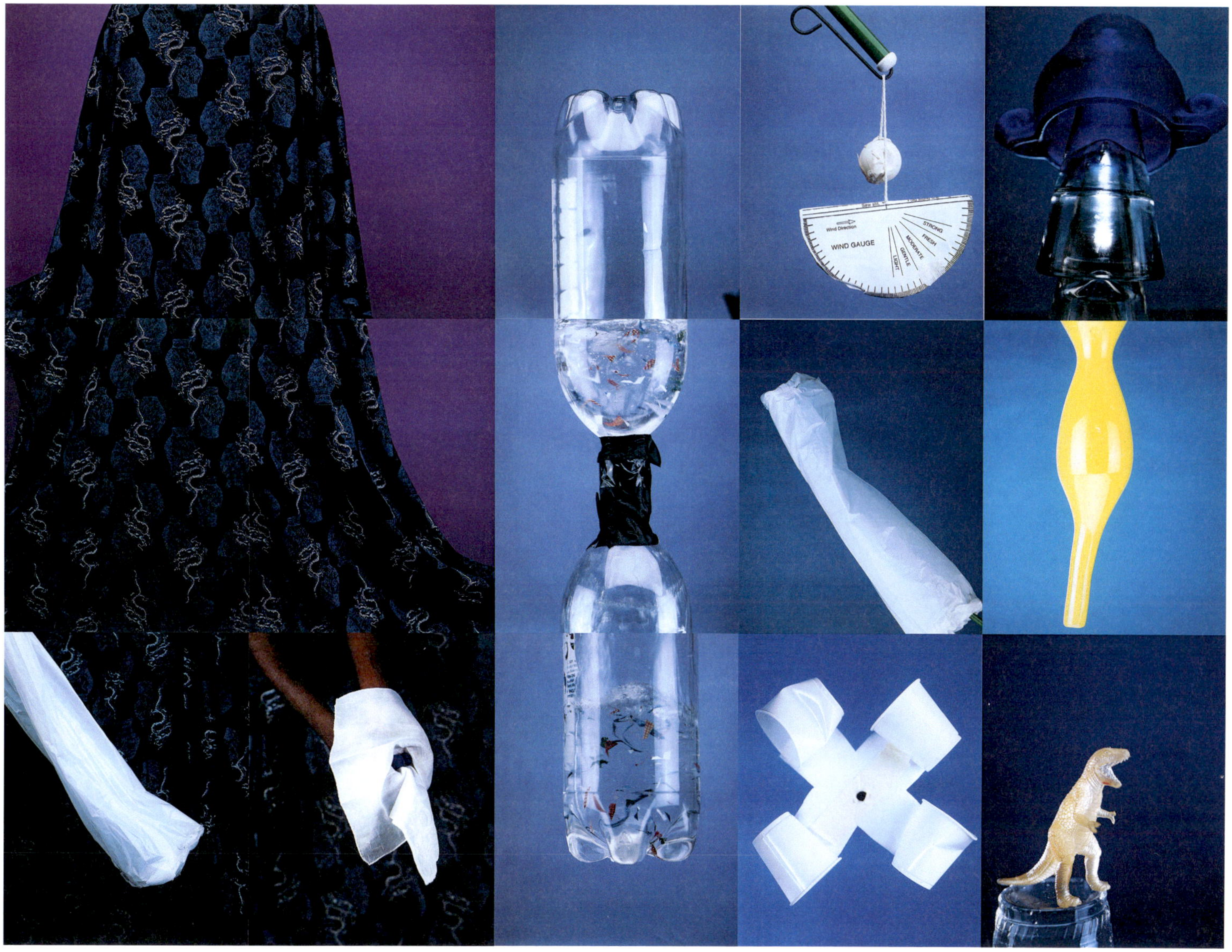

PLATE 32 *The Magician's Tools*, 2004

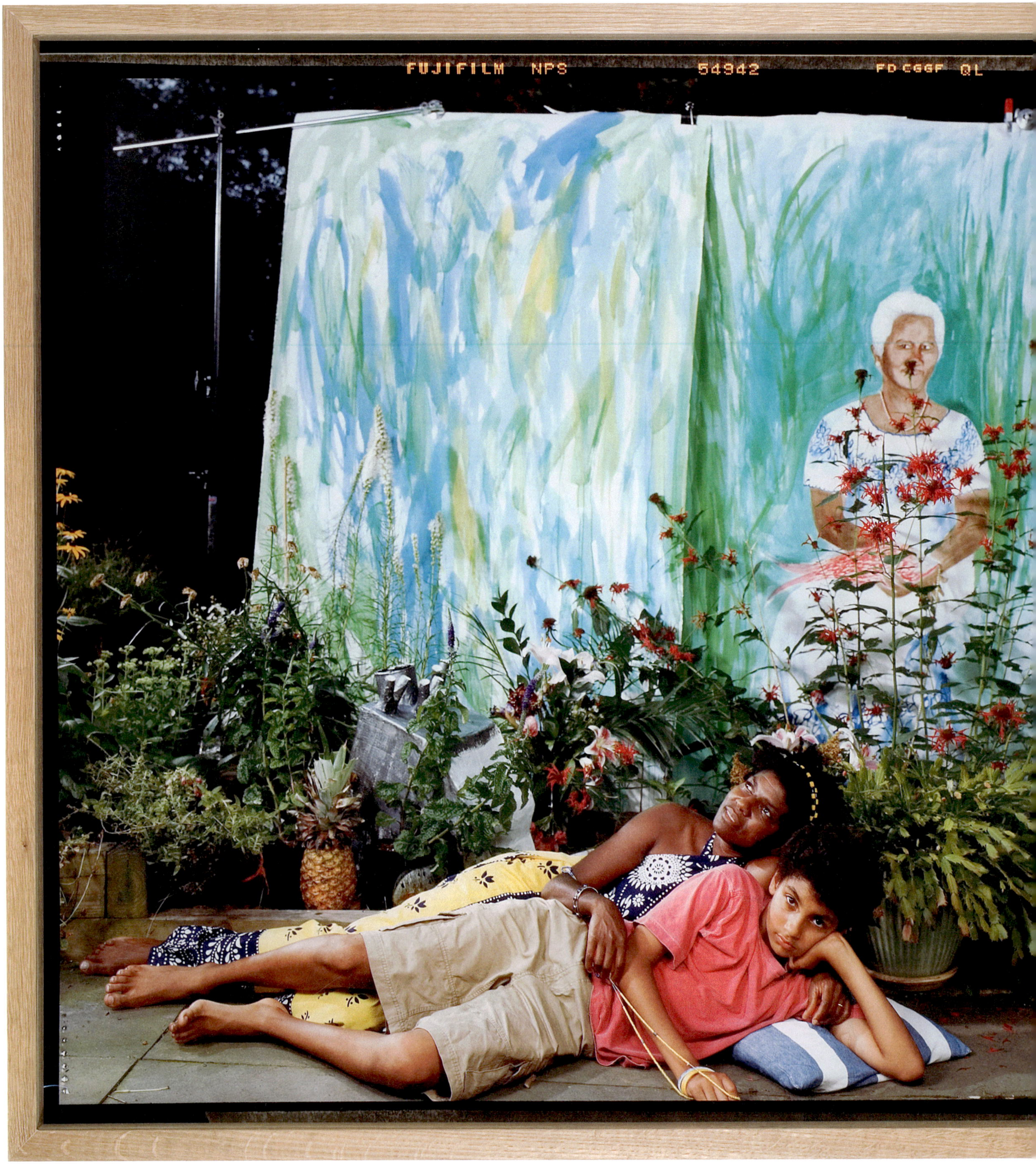

PLATE 33 *Backyard Dreams #8*, 2005

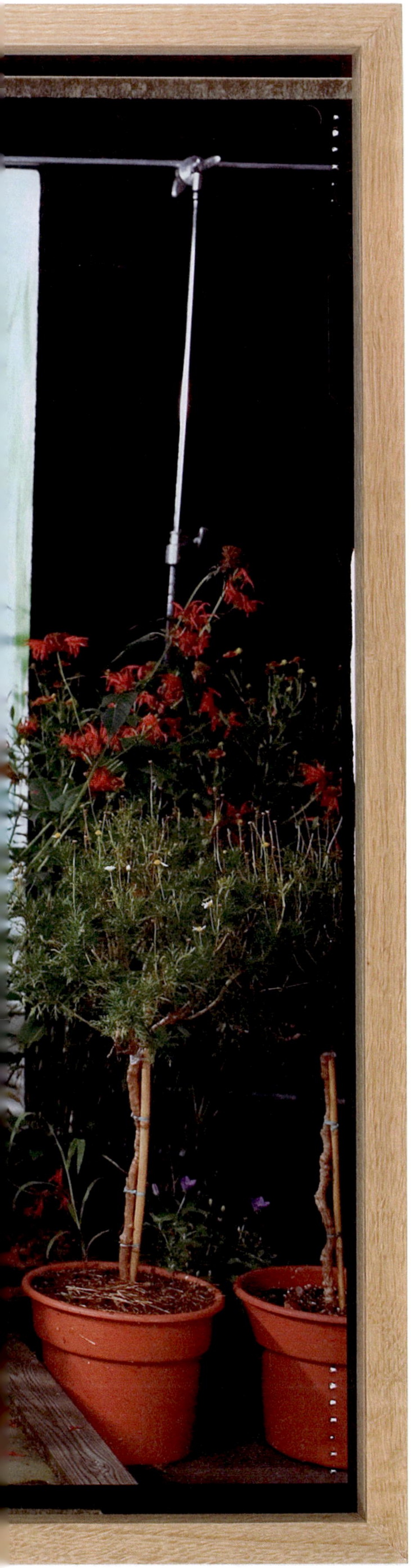

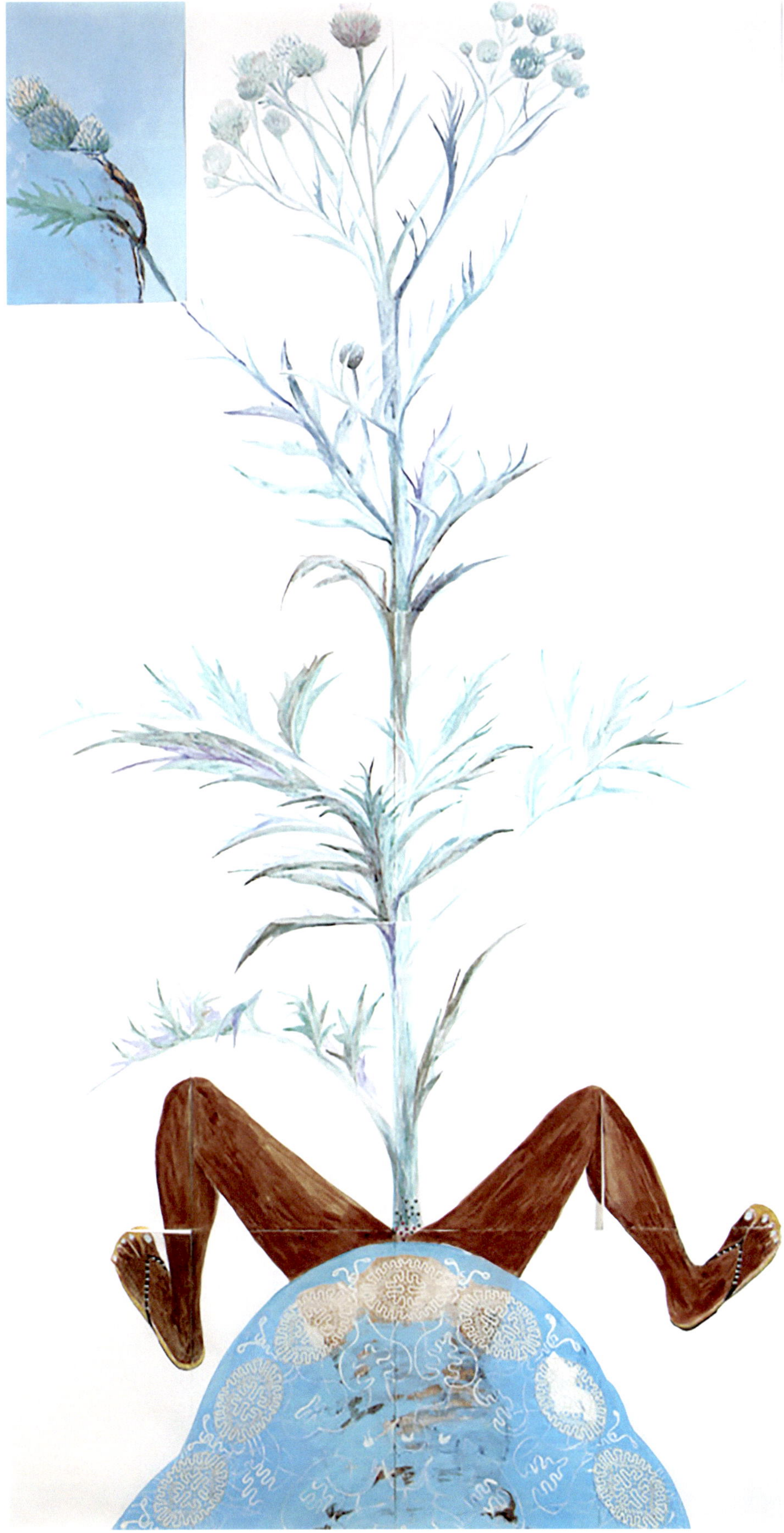

PLATE 34 *El Nacimiento de la Flor de Cardi,* 2006

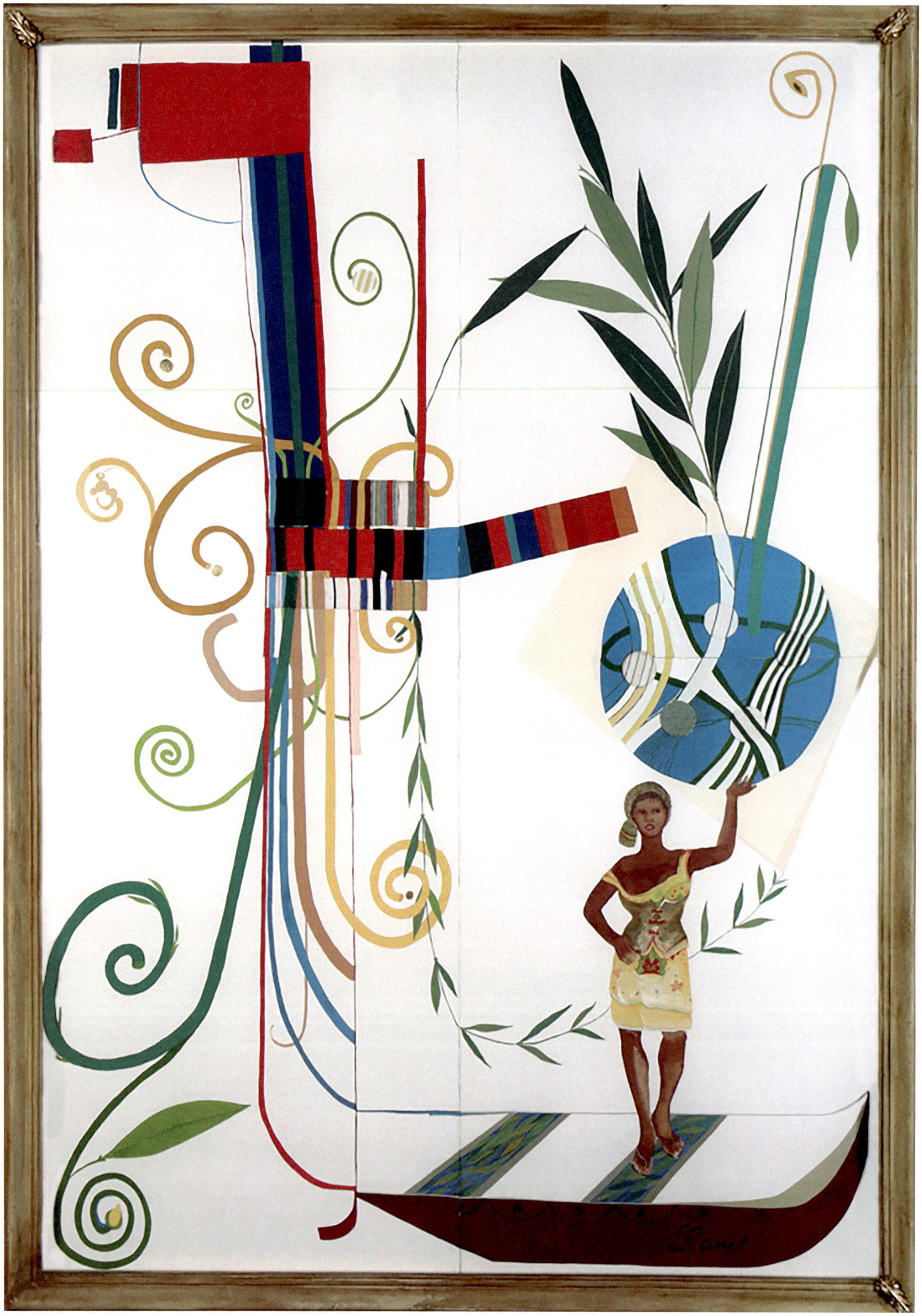

PLATE 35 *A Reason Why Janet Jackson Should Move to the Veneto Region: A Wardrobe Malfunction Early on Goes Unnoticed*, 2006

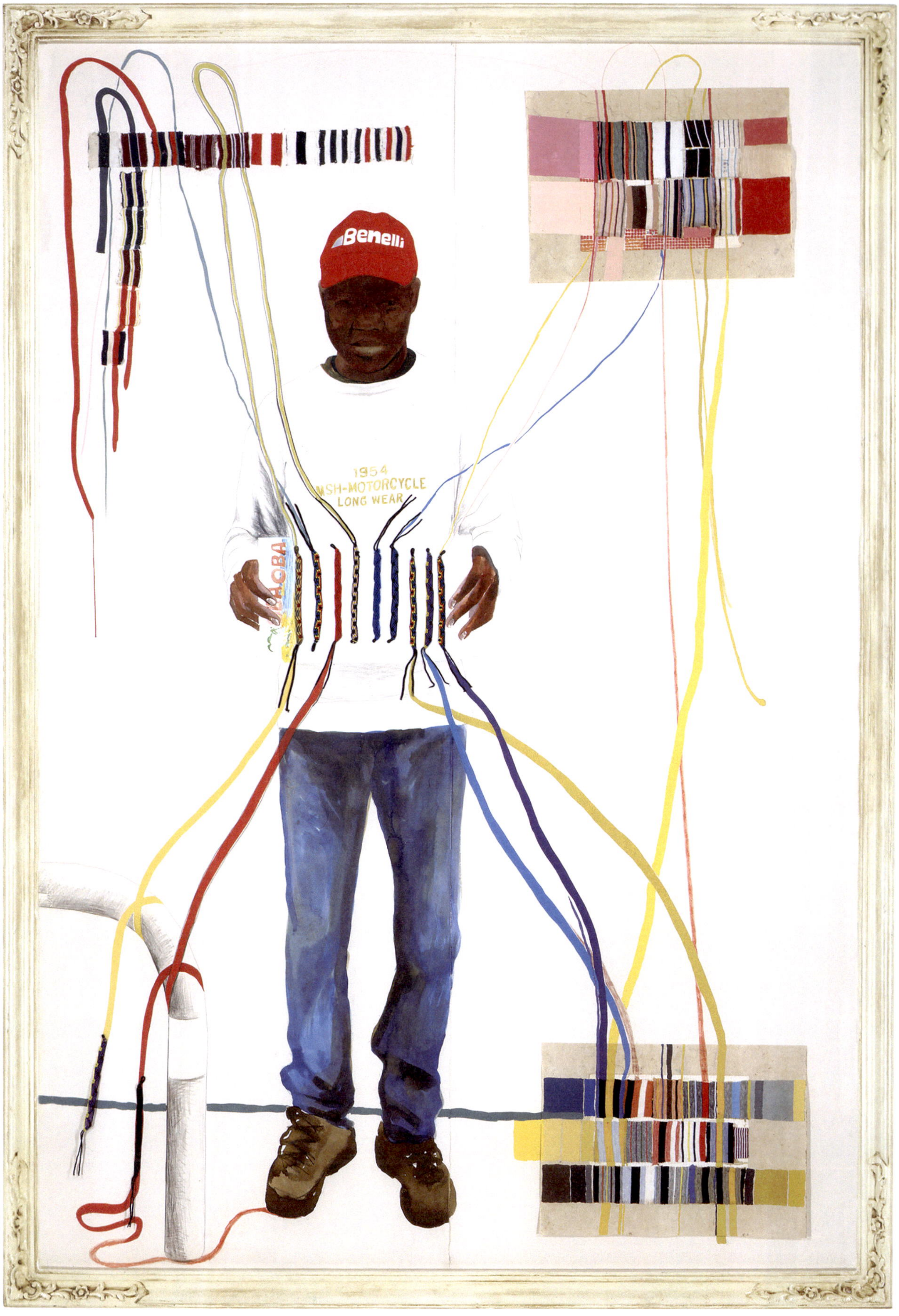

PLATE 36 *Pied-à-terre, Everyone Needs His Oba Oba*, 2006

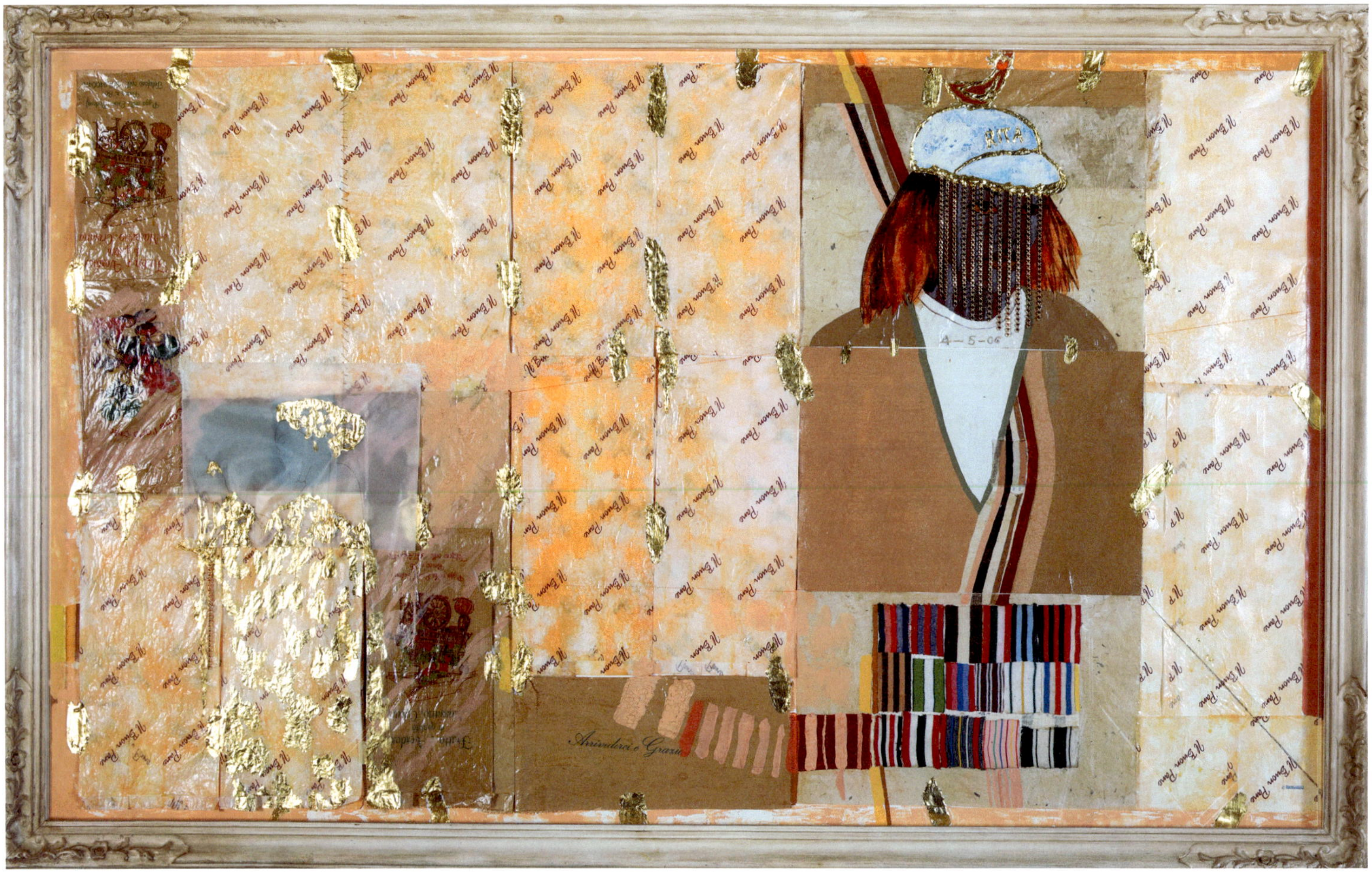

PLATE 37 *Invocazione alla Questura - Rita of Nigeria*, 2006

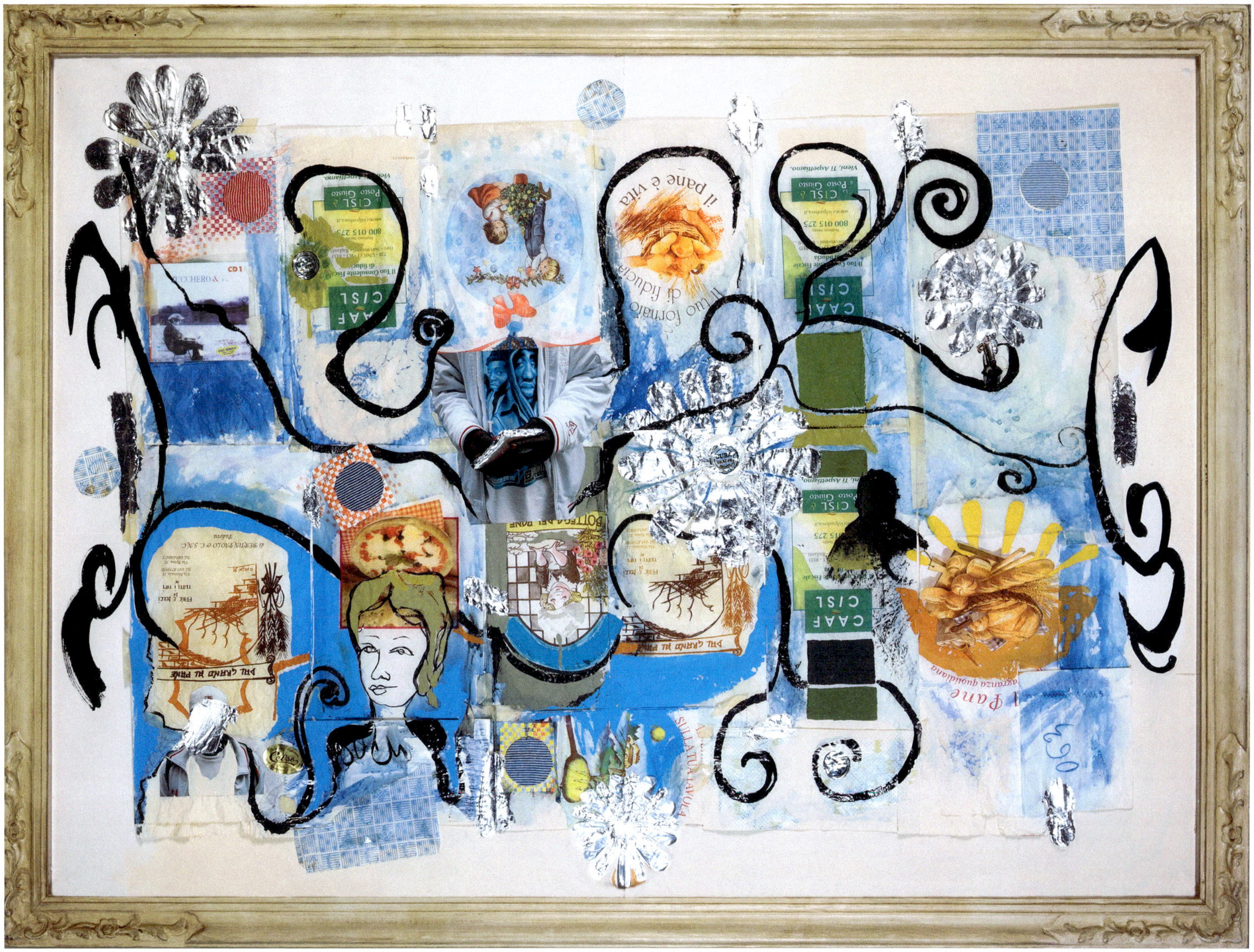

PLATE 38 *Il pane è vita. Zucchero and company are good*, 2006

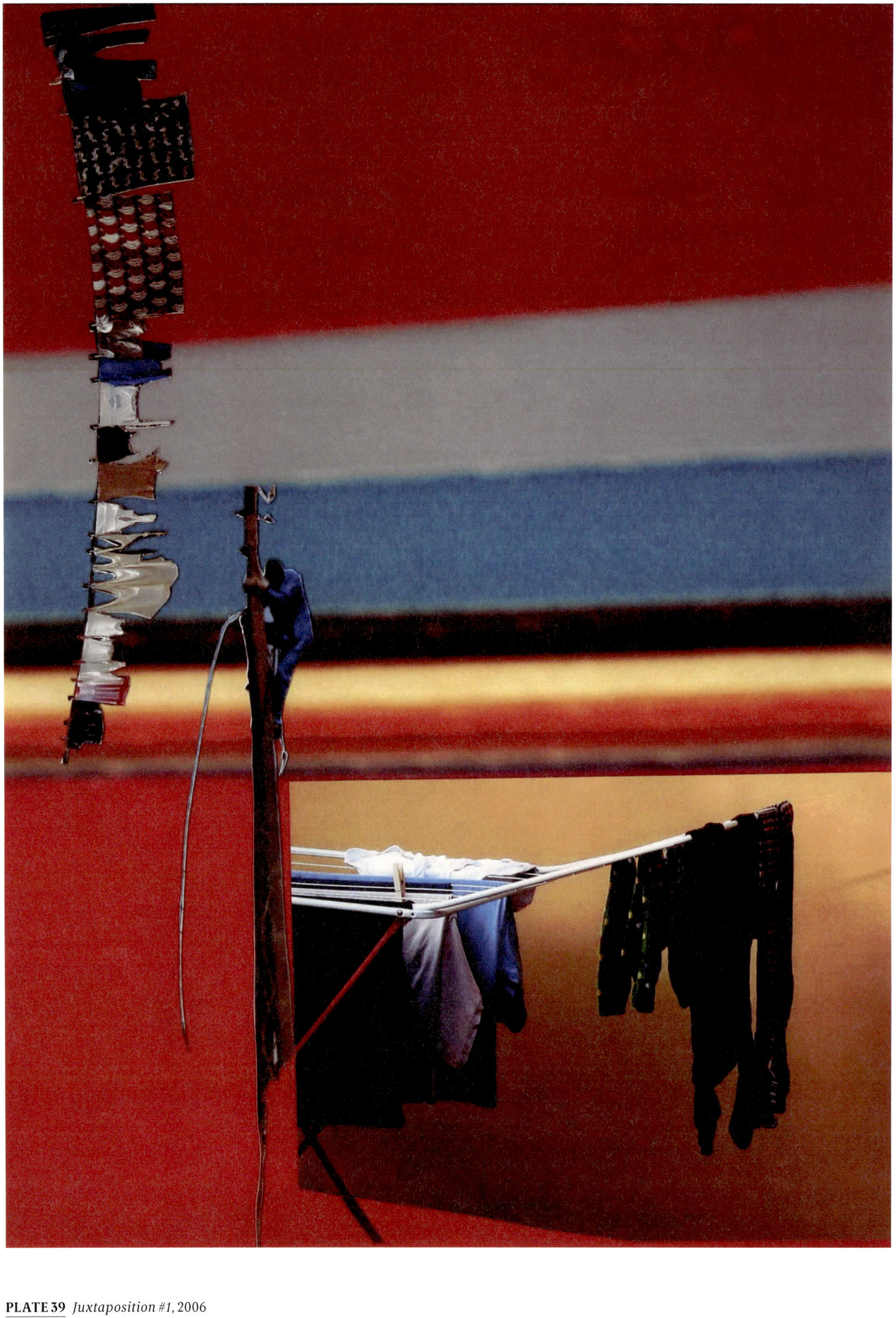

PLATE 39 *Juxtaposition #1*, 2006

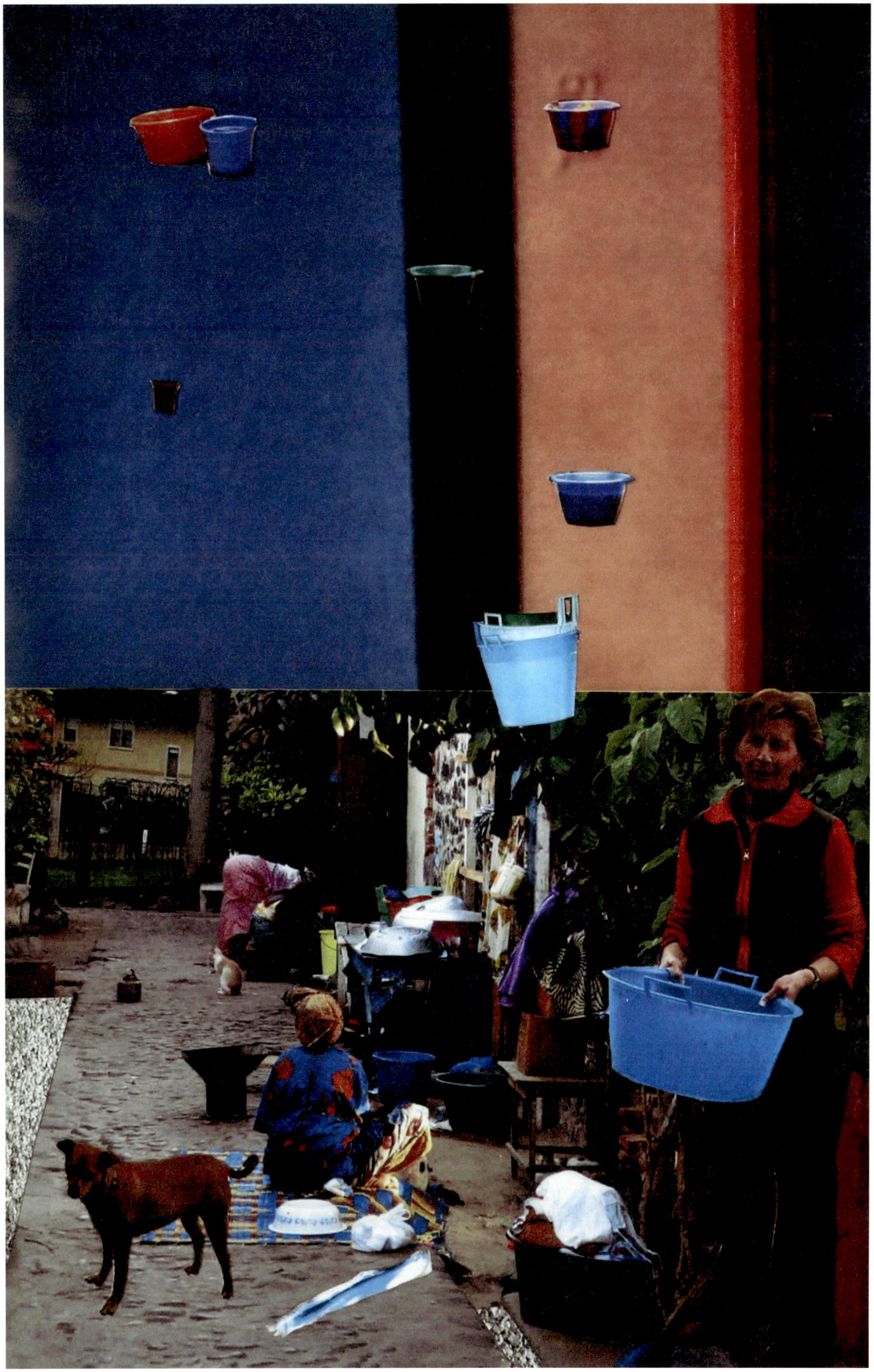

PLATE 40 *Juxtaposition #3*, 2006

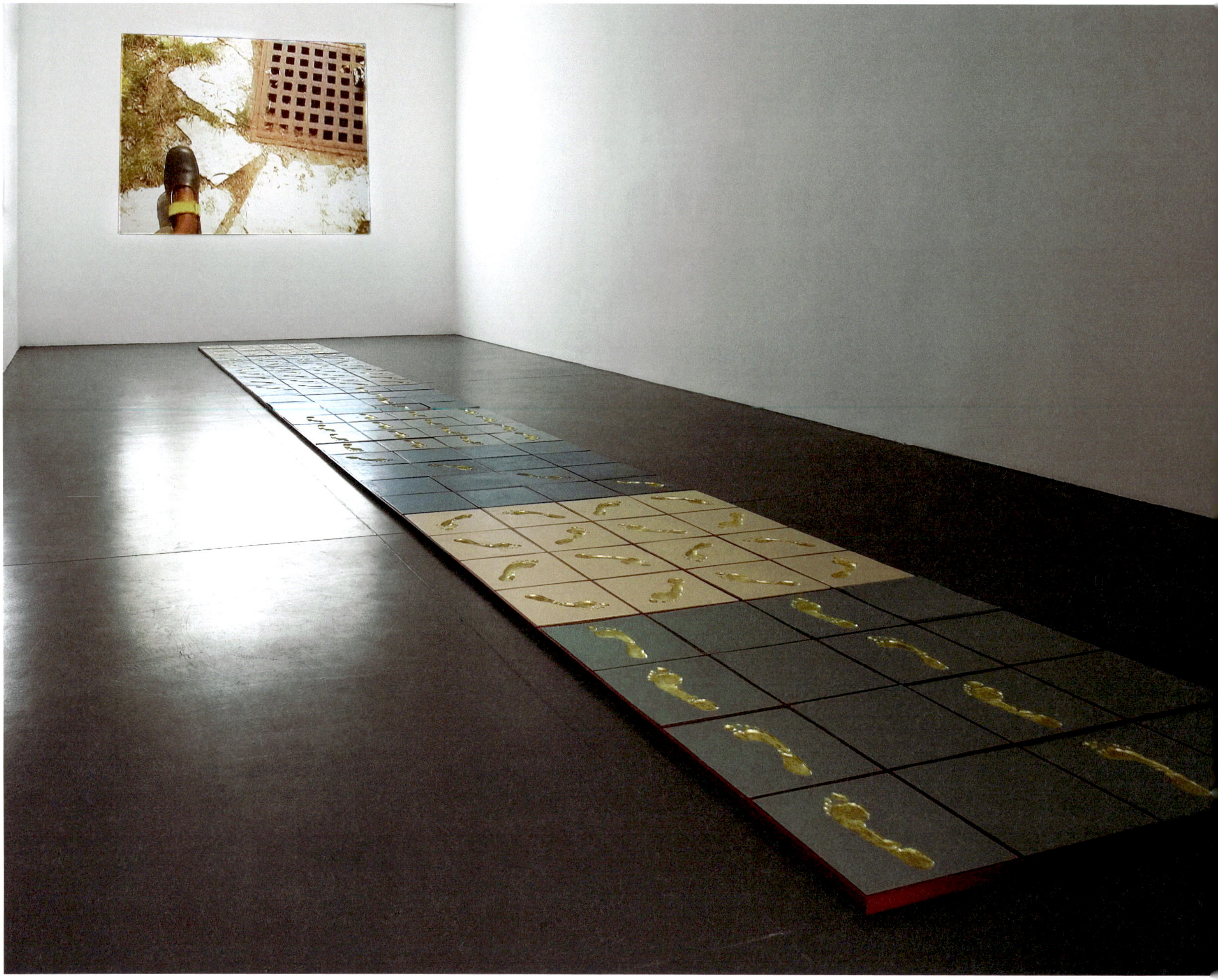

PLATE 41 *Madonna Pellegrina - La Viajera*, 2006

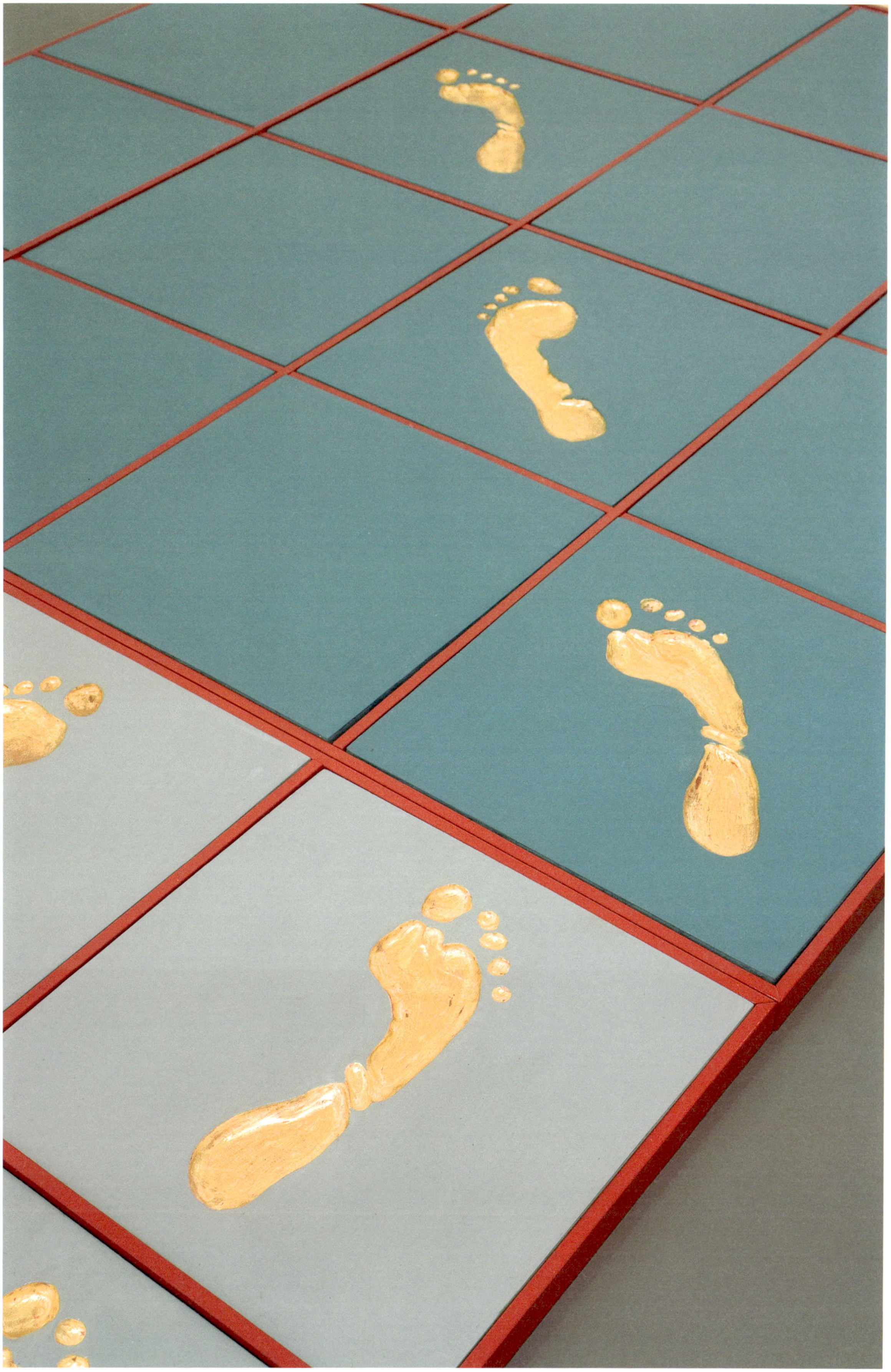

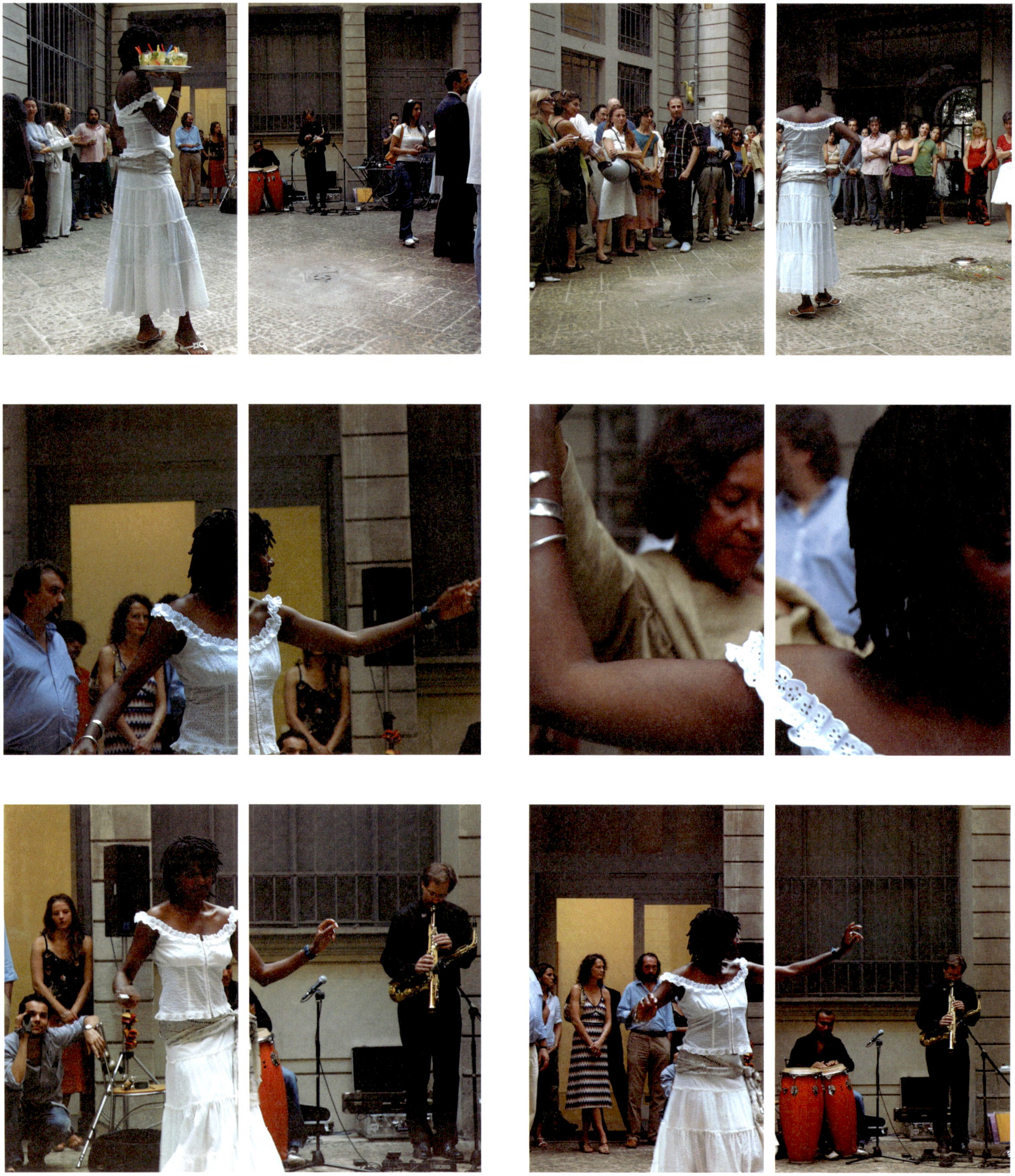

PLATE 42 *Habilitation, Mojitos, and Crocodile's Tears*, performance, 2006

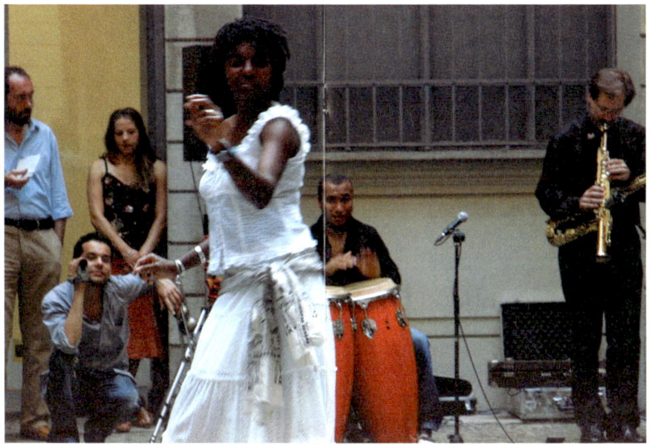
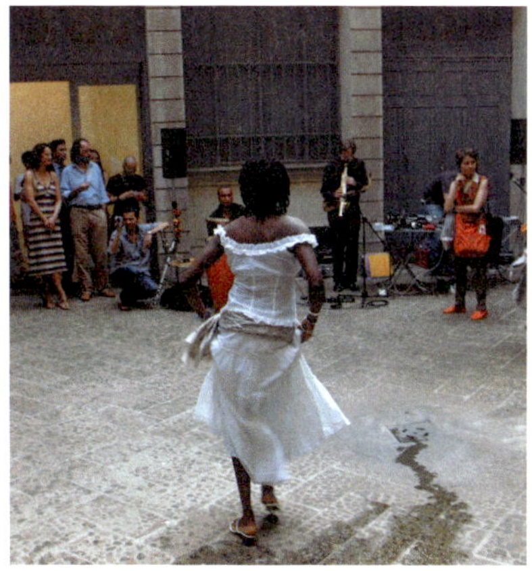
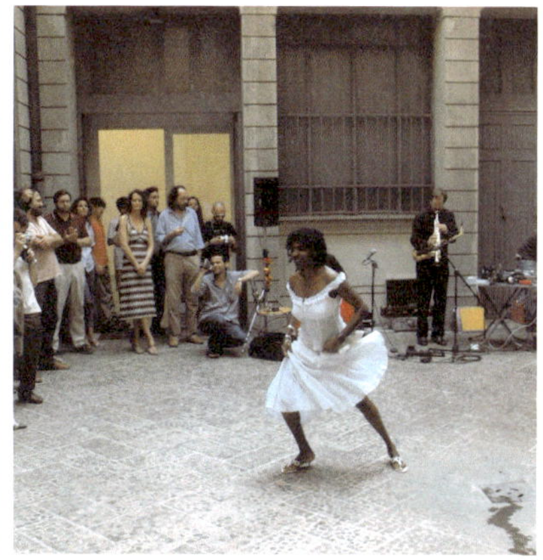
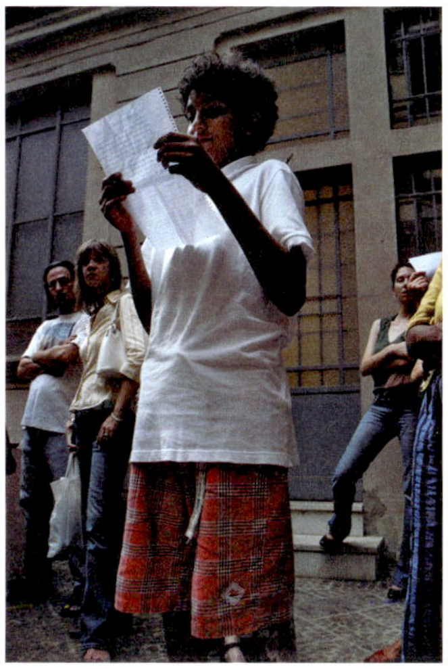
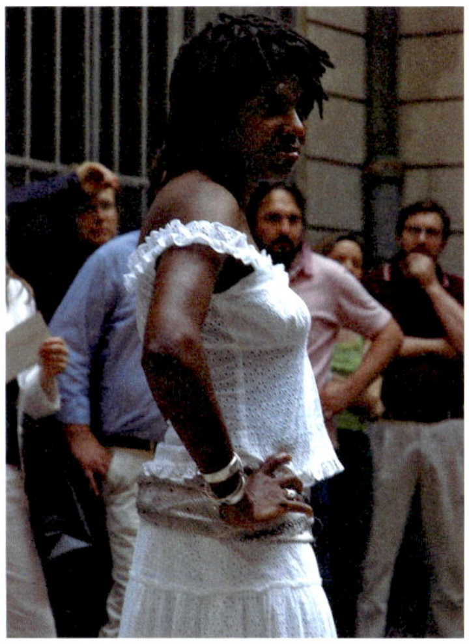
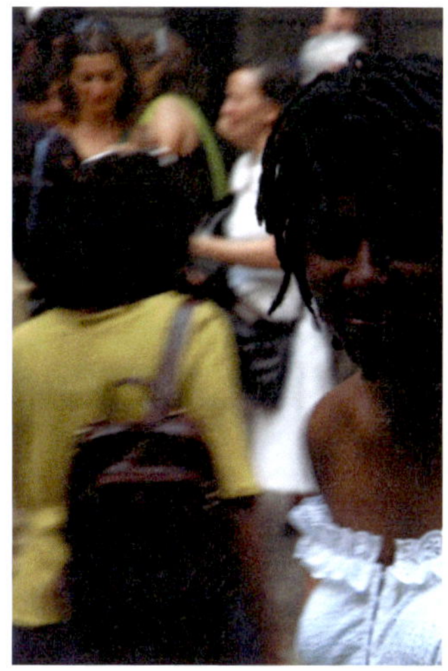
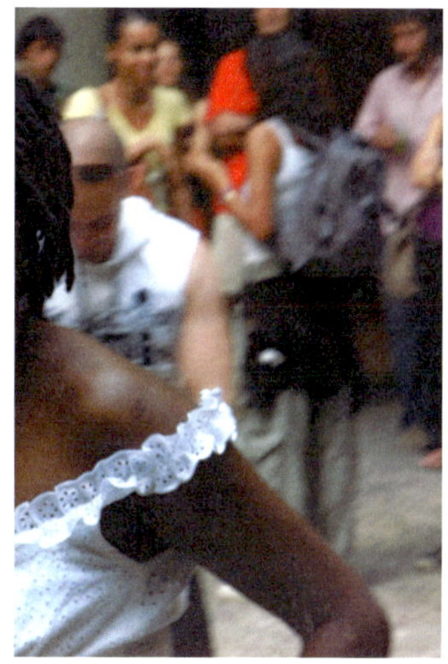
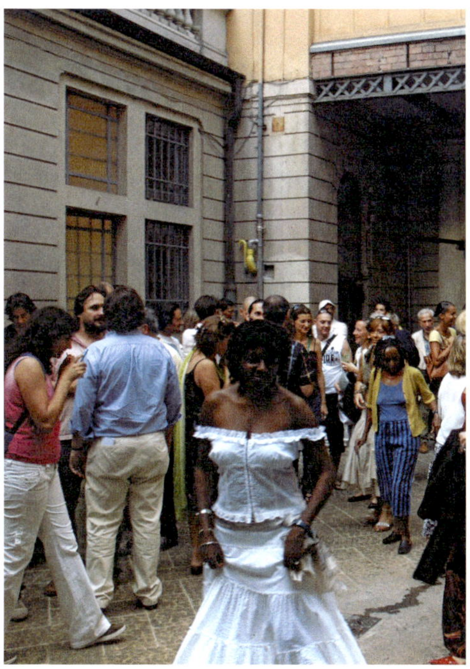
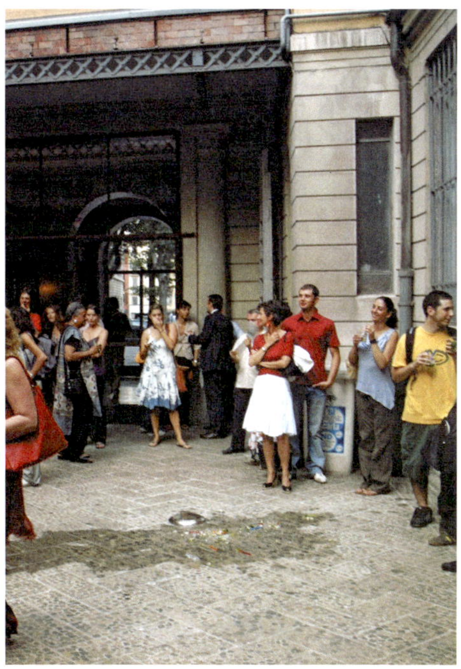
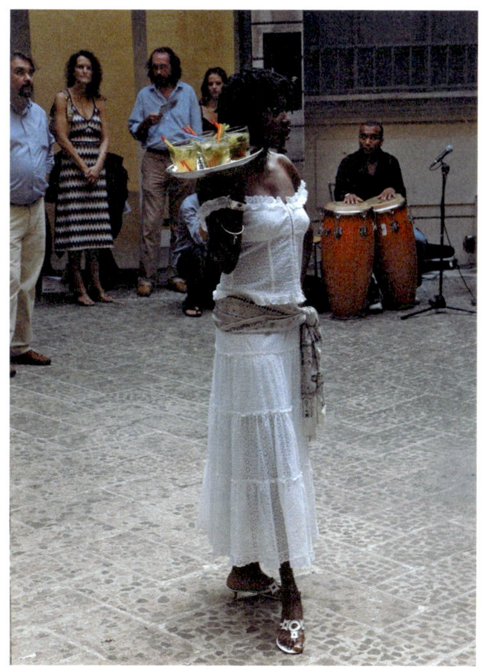

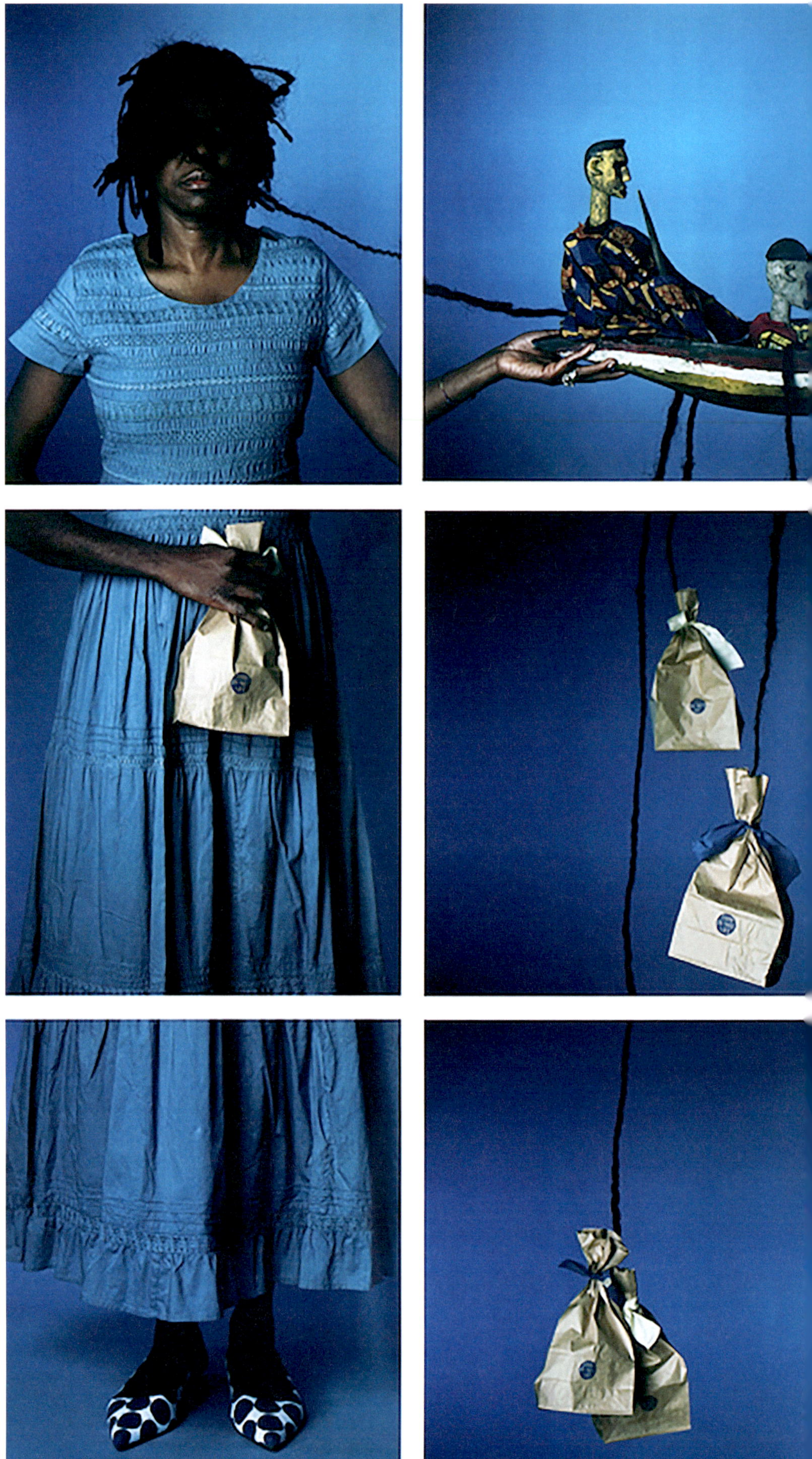

PLATE 43 *De Las Dos Aguas (Of the Two Waters)*, 2007

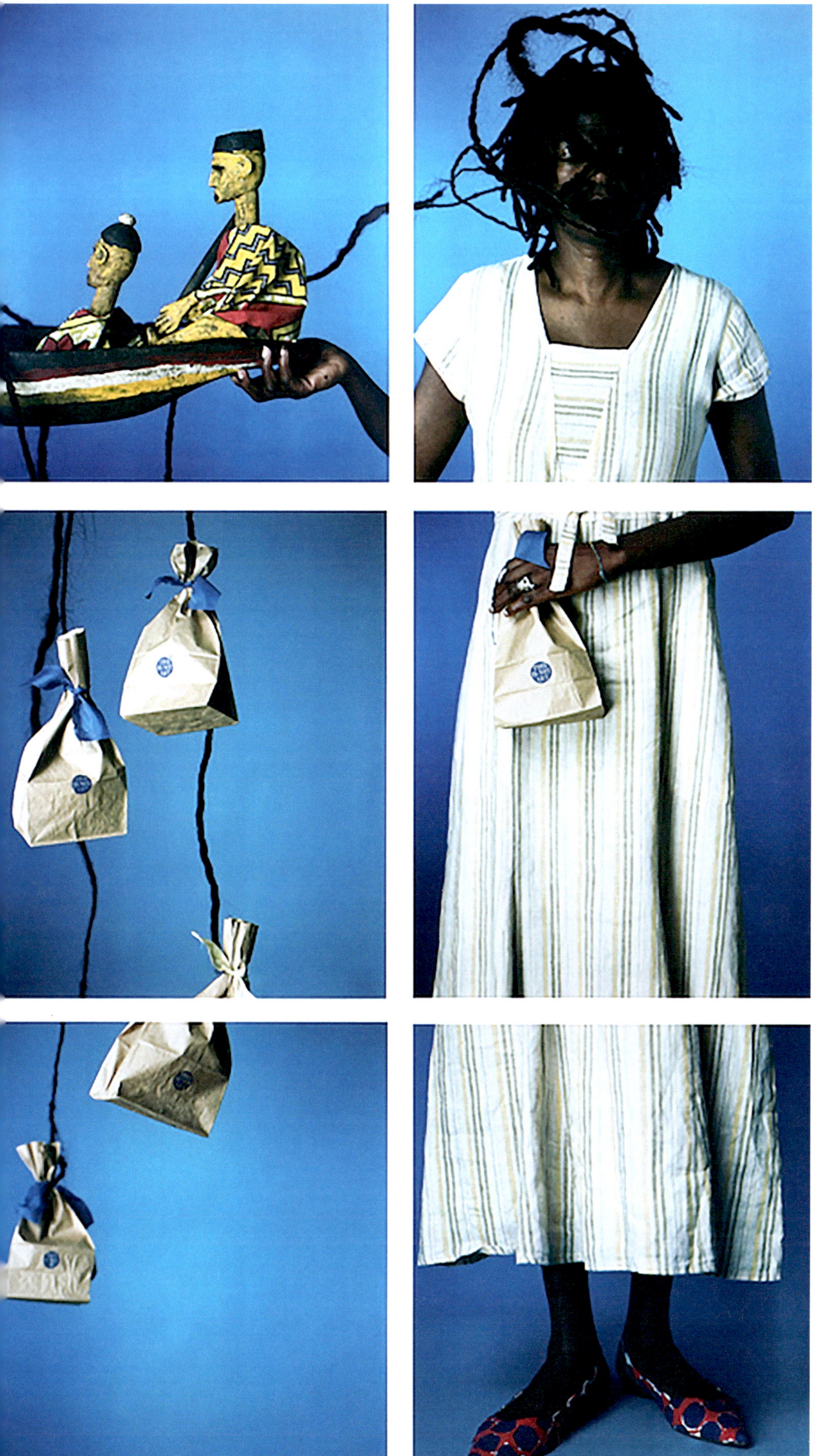

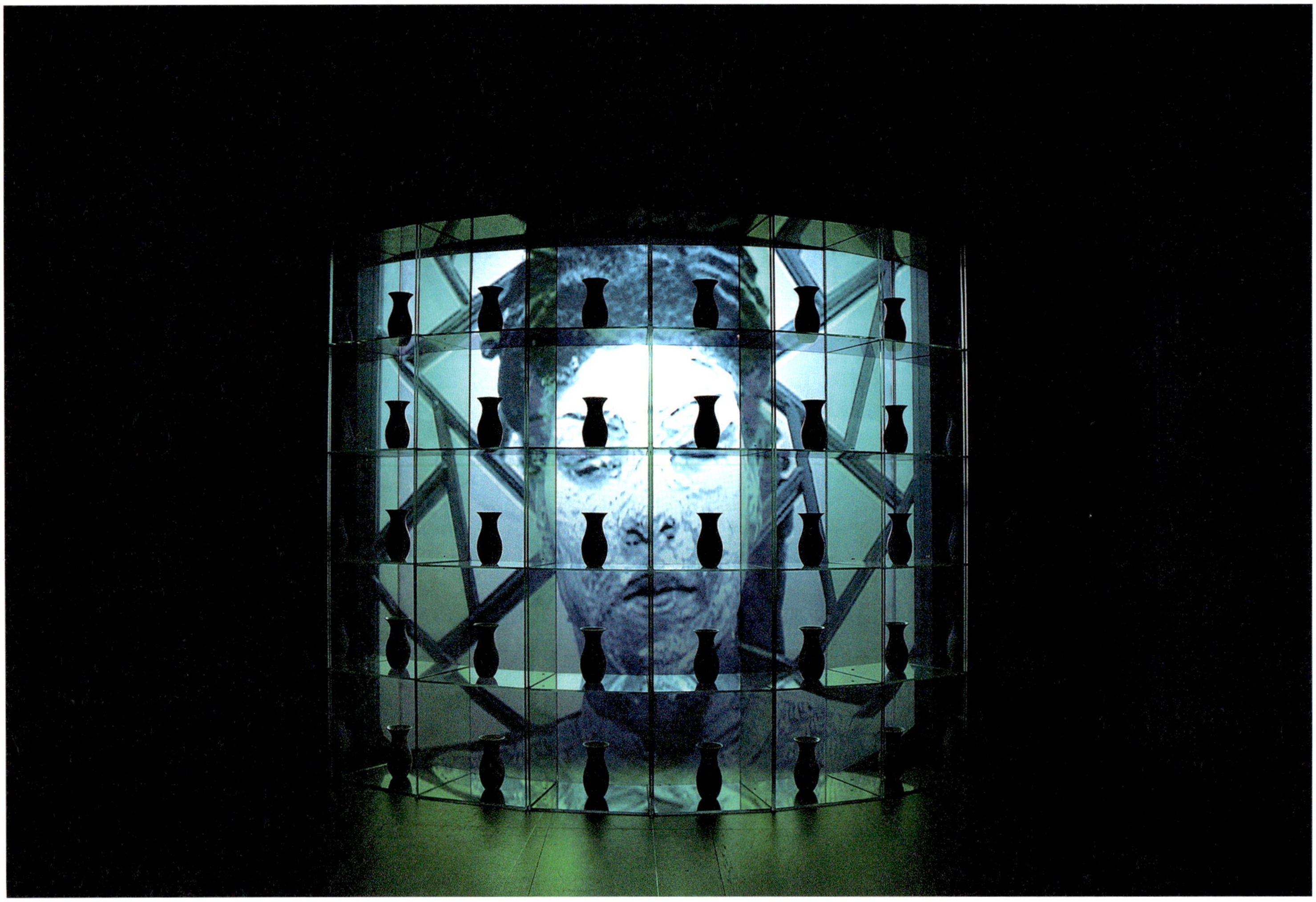

PLATE 44 *My Mother Told Me I Am Chinese: China Porcelain,* installation and preparatory sketches for the vases, 2008

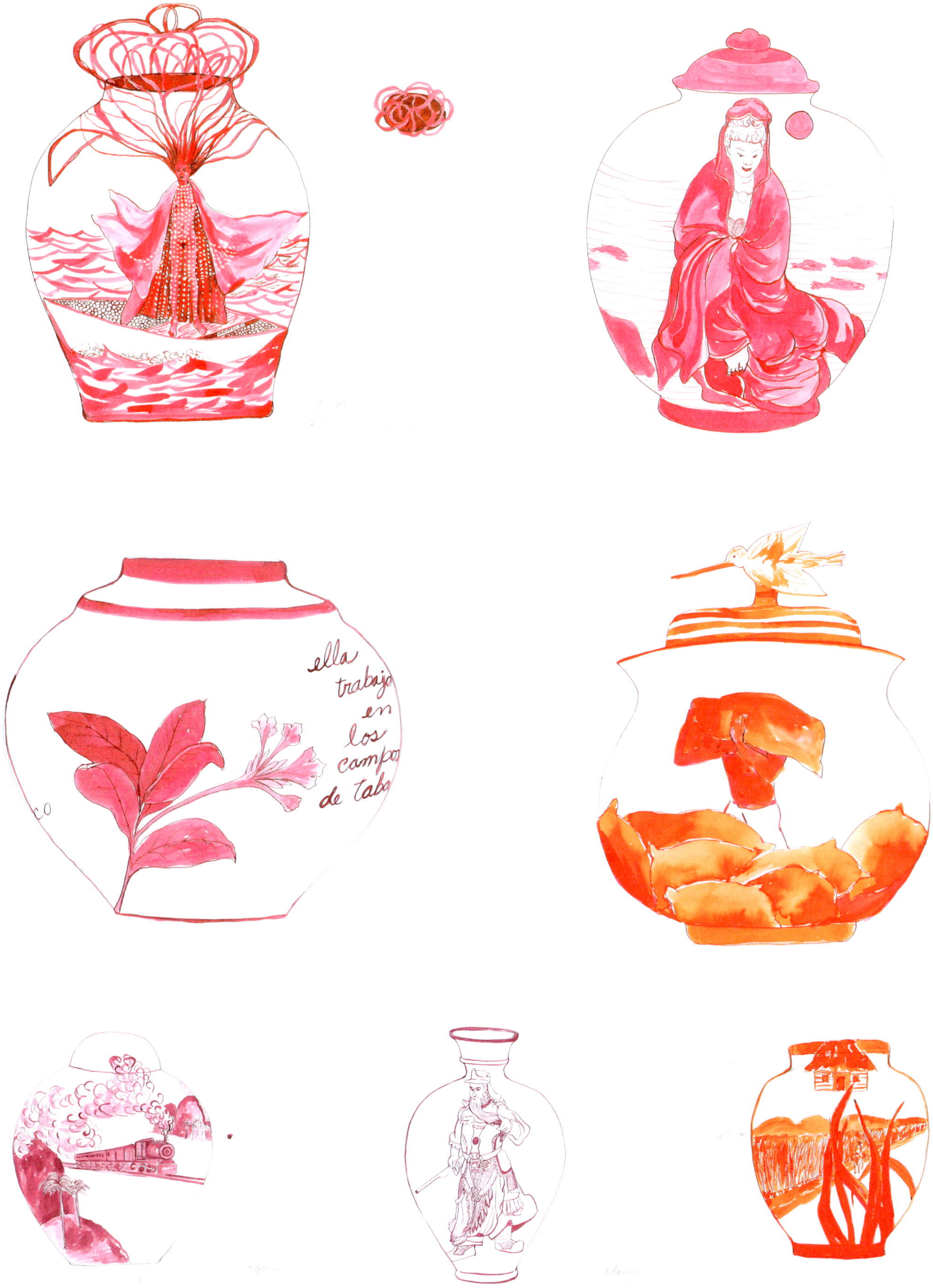
ella
trabaja
en
los
campo
de taba

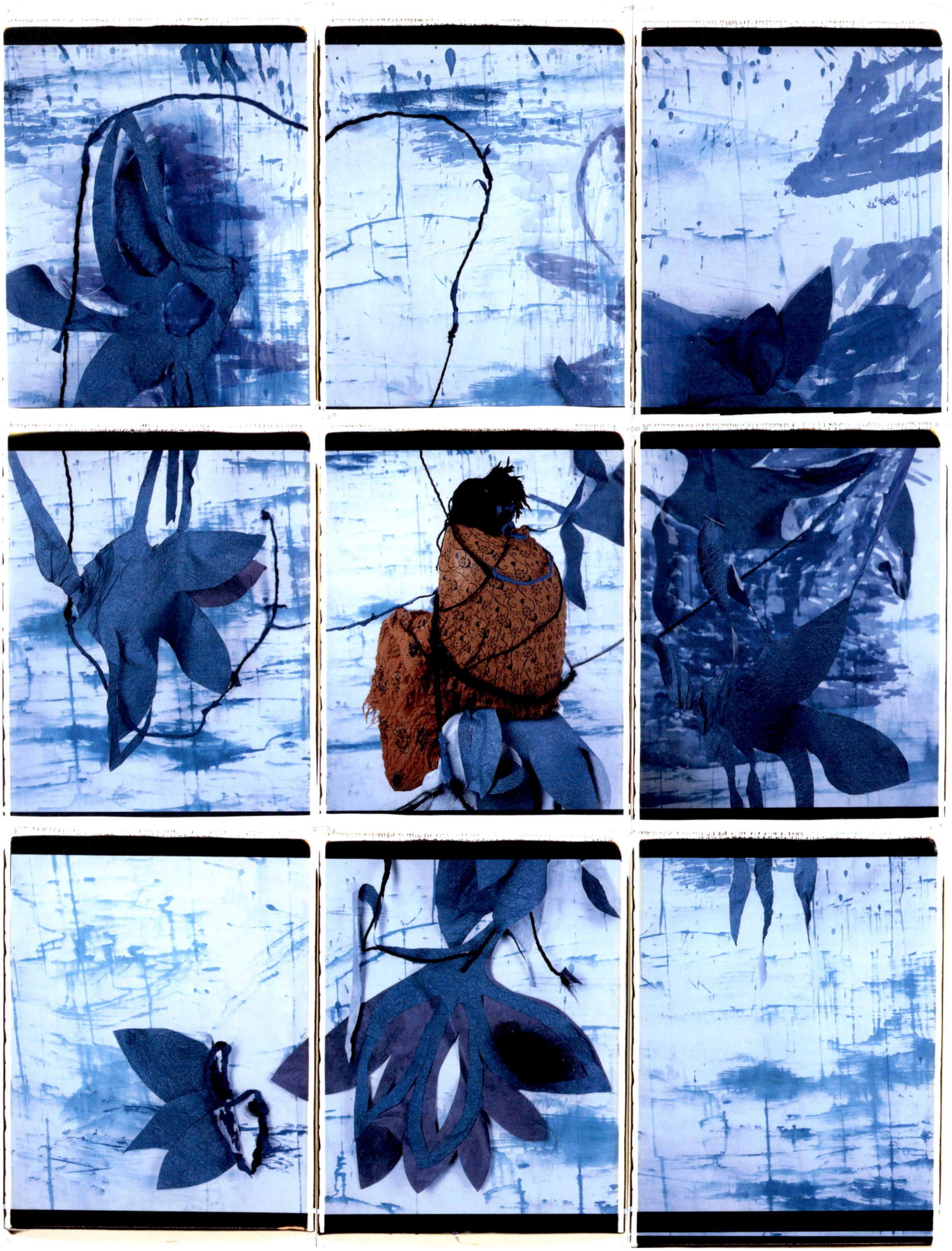

PLATE 45 *Blue Refuge*, 2008

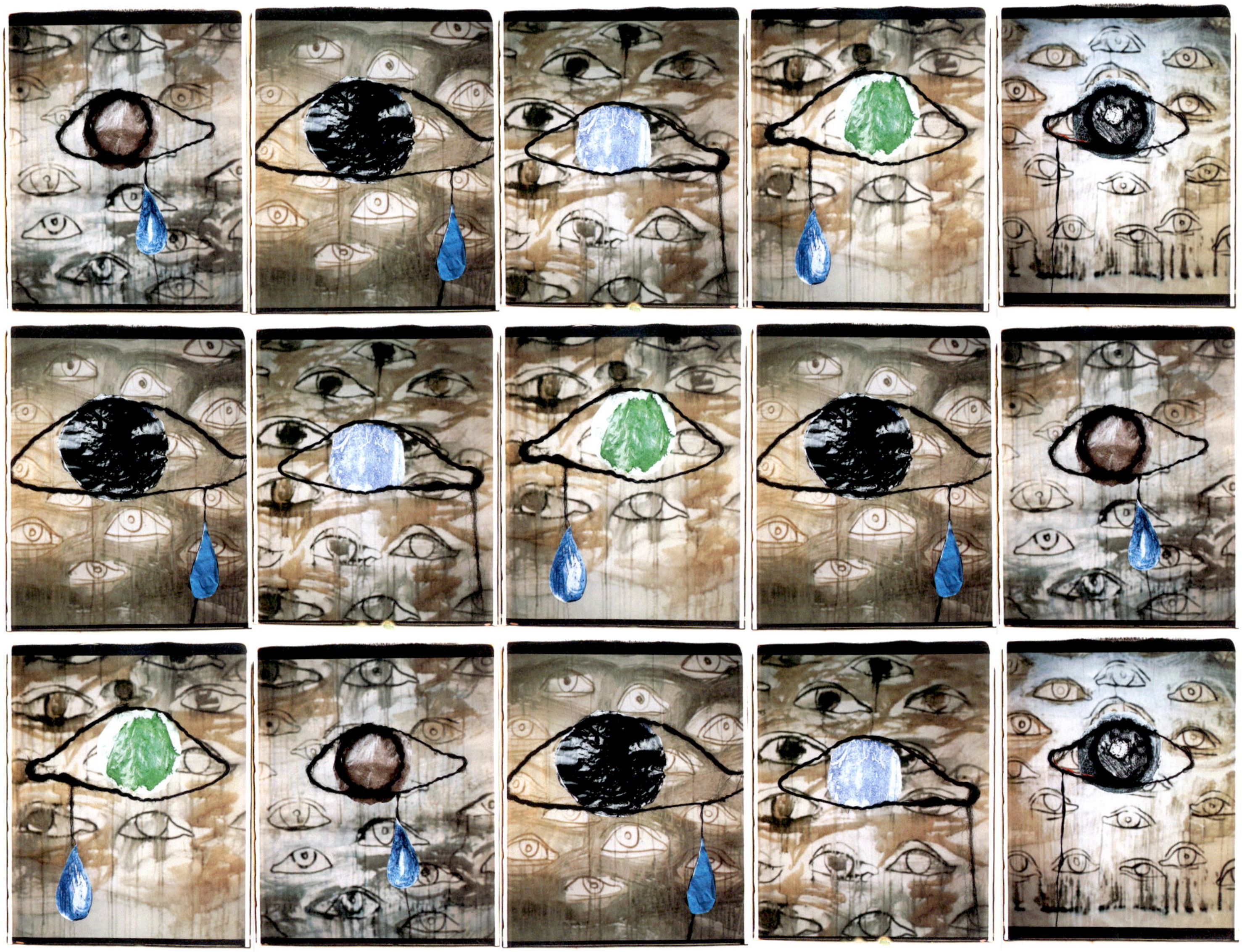

PLATE 46 *Voyeurs and Beholders of . . .*, 2008/2015

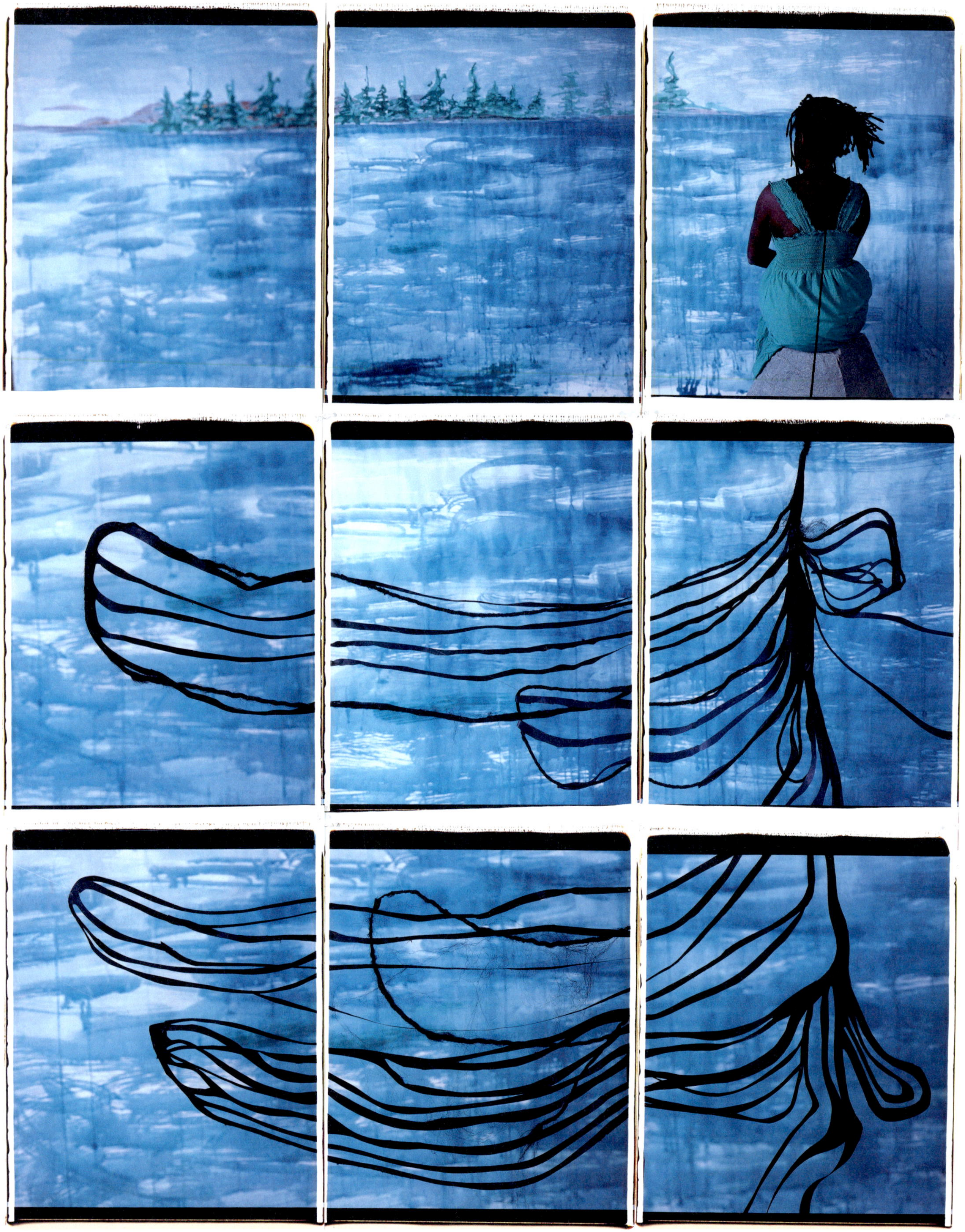

PLATE 47 *Dreaming of an Island*, 2008

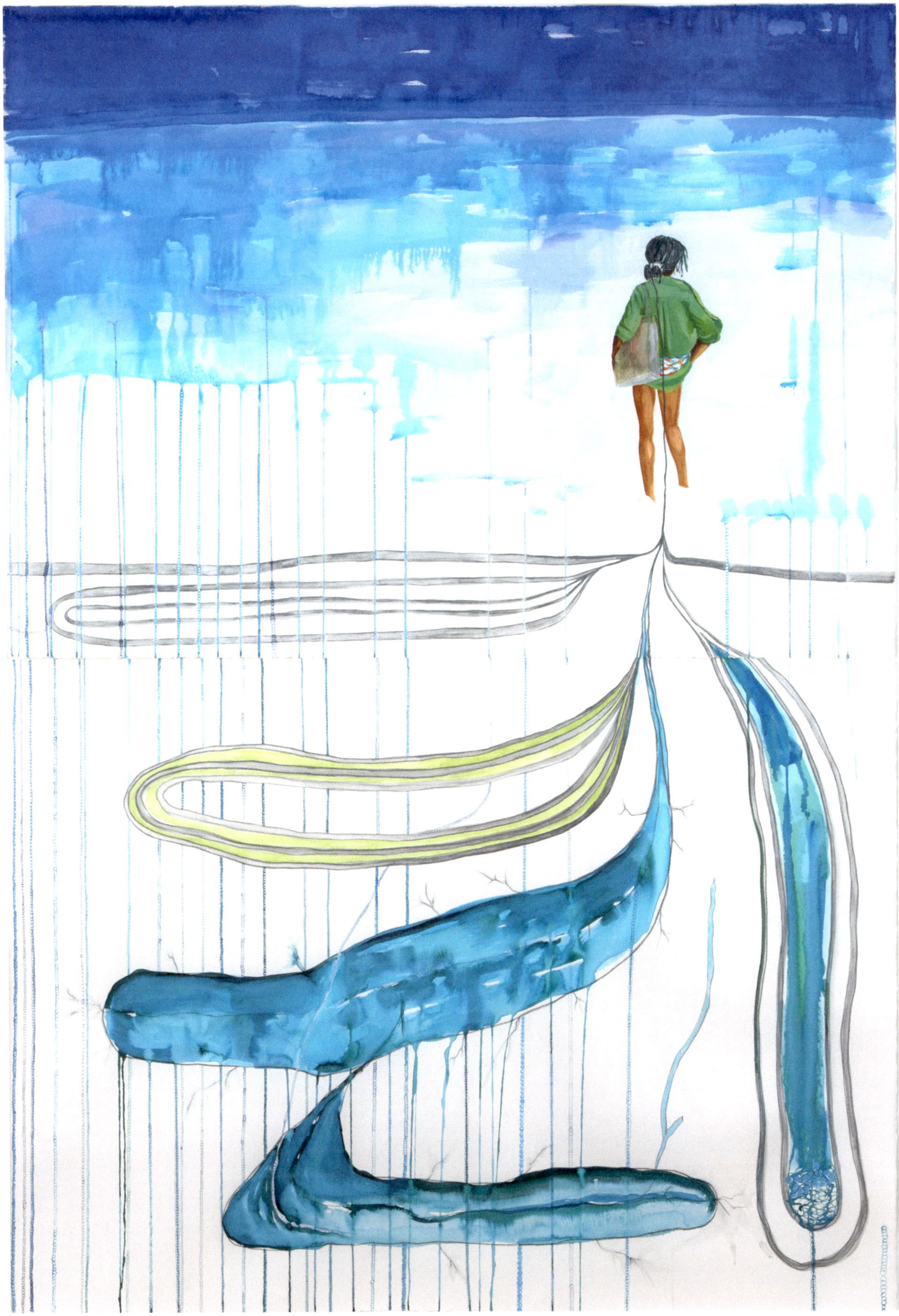

PLATE 48 *Thinking of It,* 2008

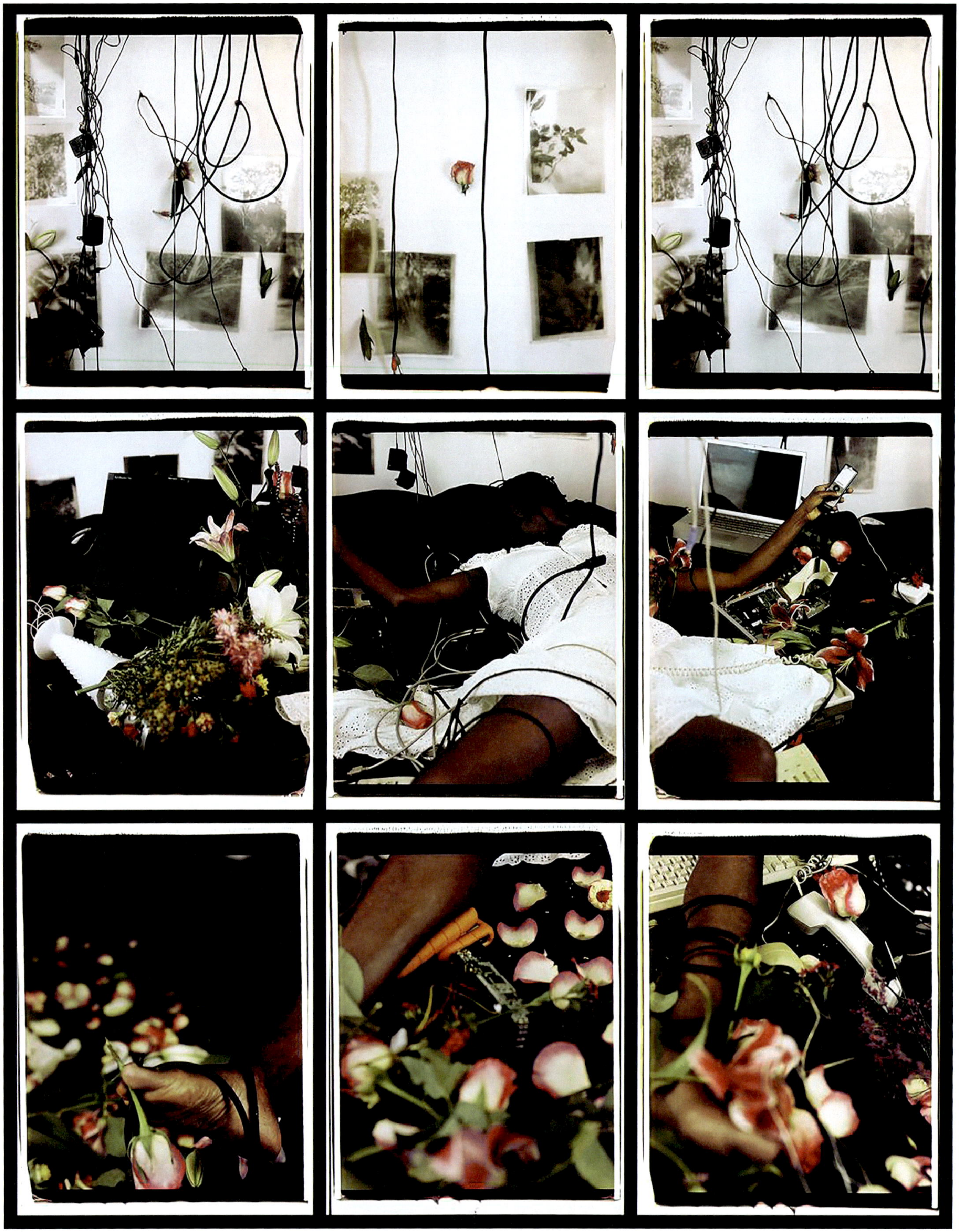

PLATE 49 *After Duchamp*, 2010

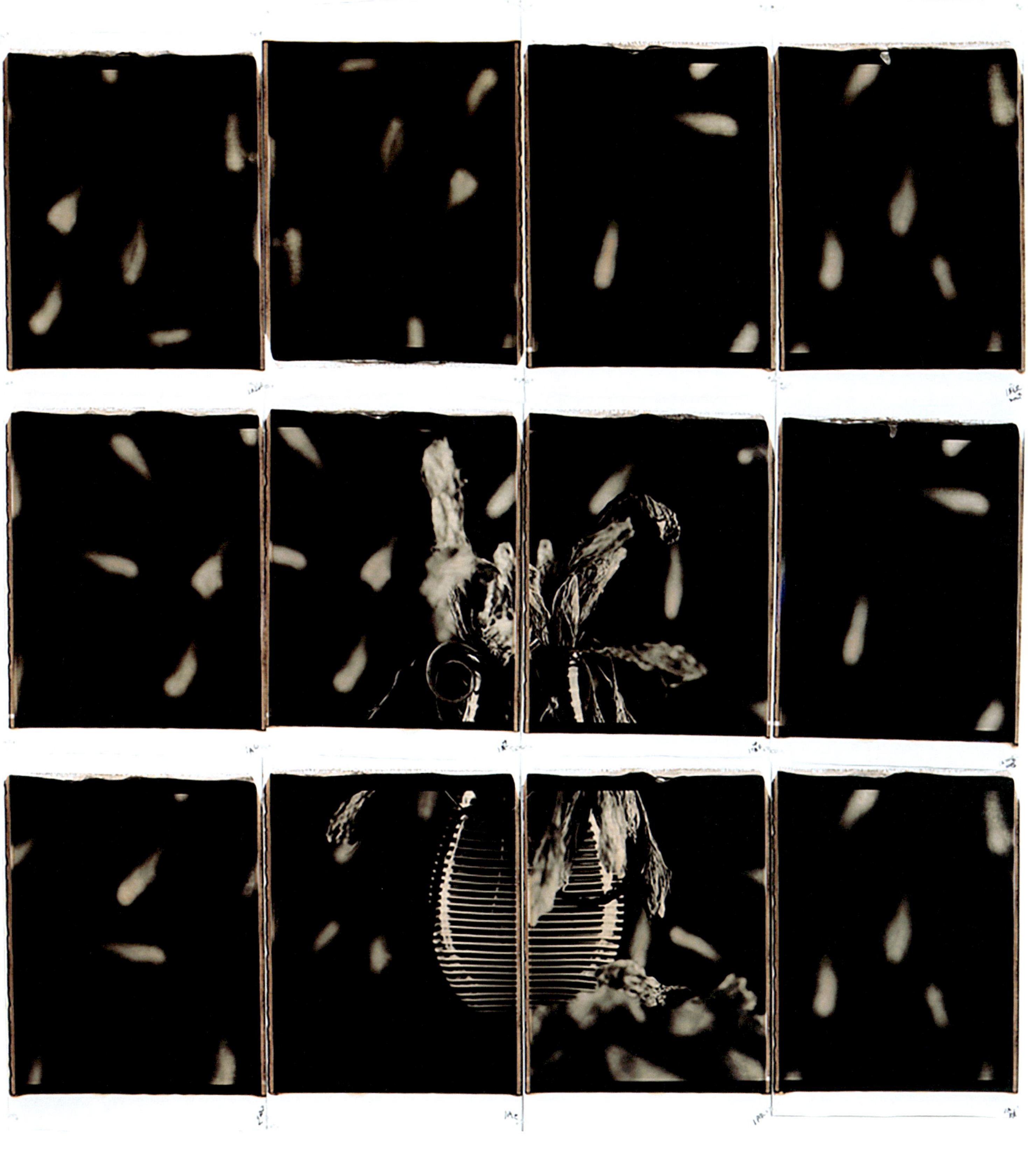

PLATE 50 *Shooting Stars for Fallen Soldiers*, 2010

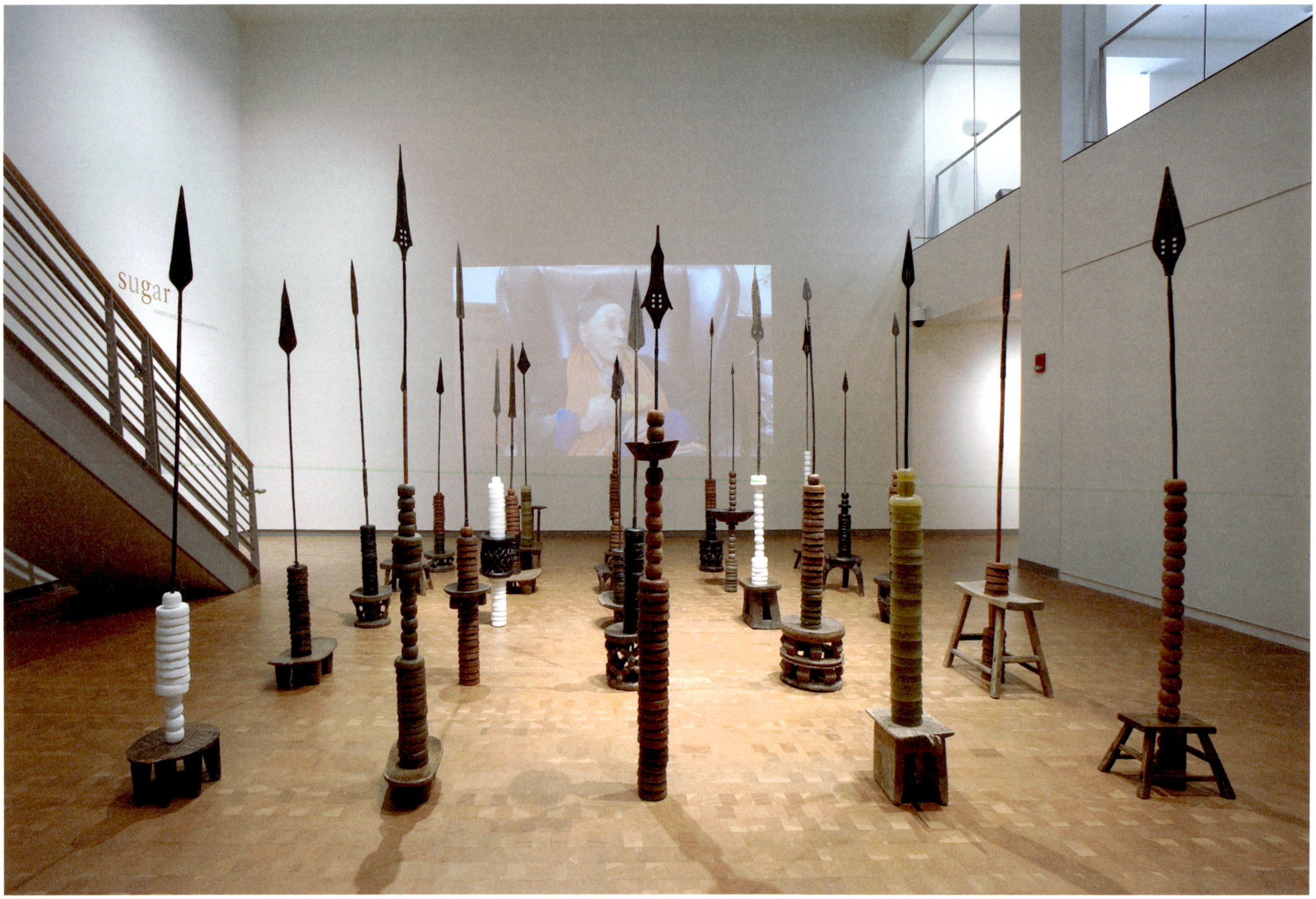

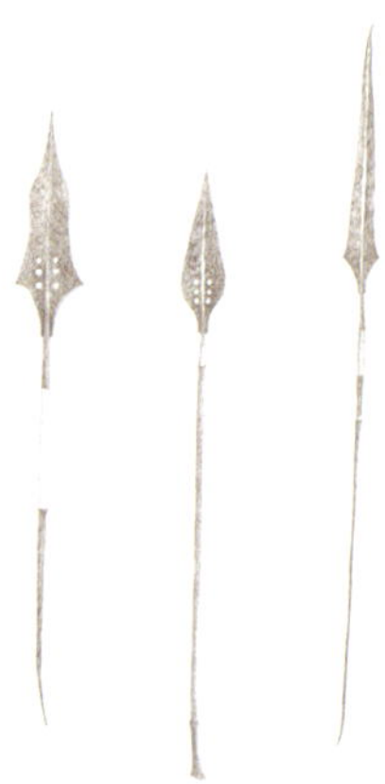

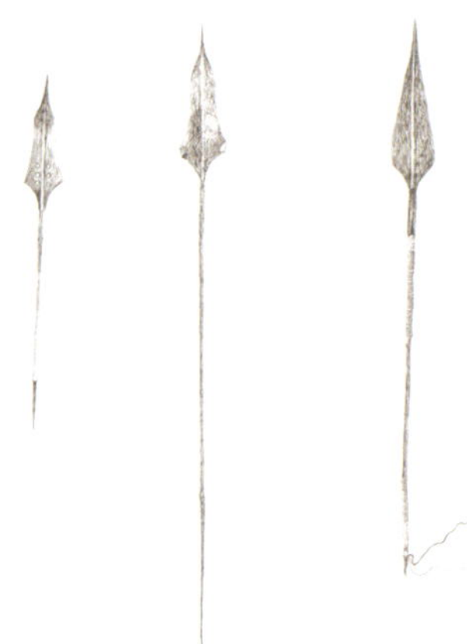

PLATE 51 *Sugar/Bittersweet*, installation and drawings, 2010

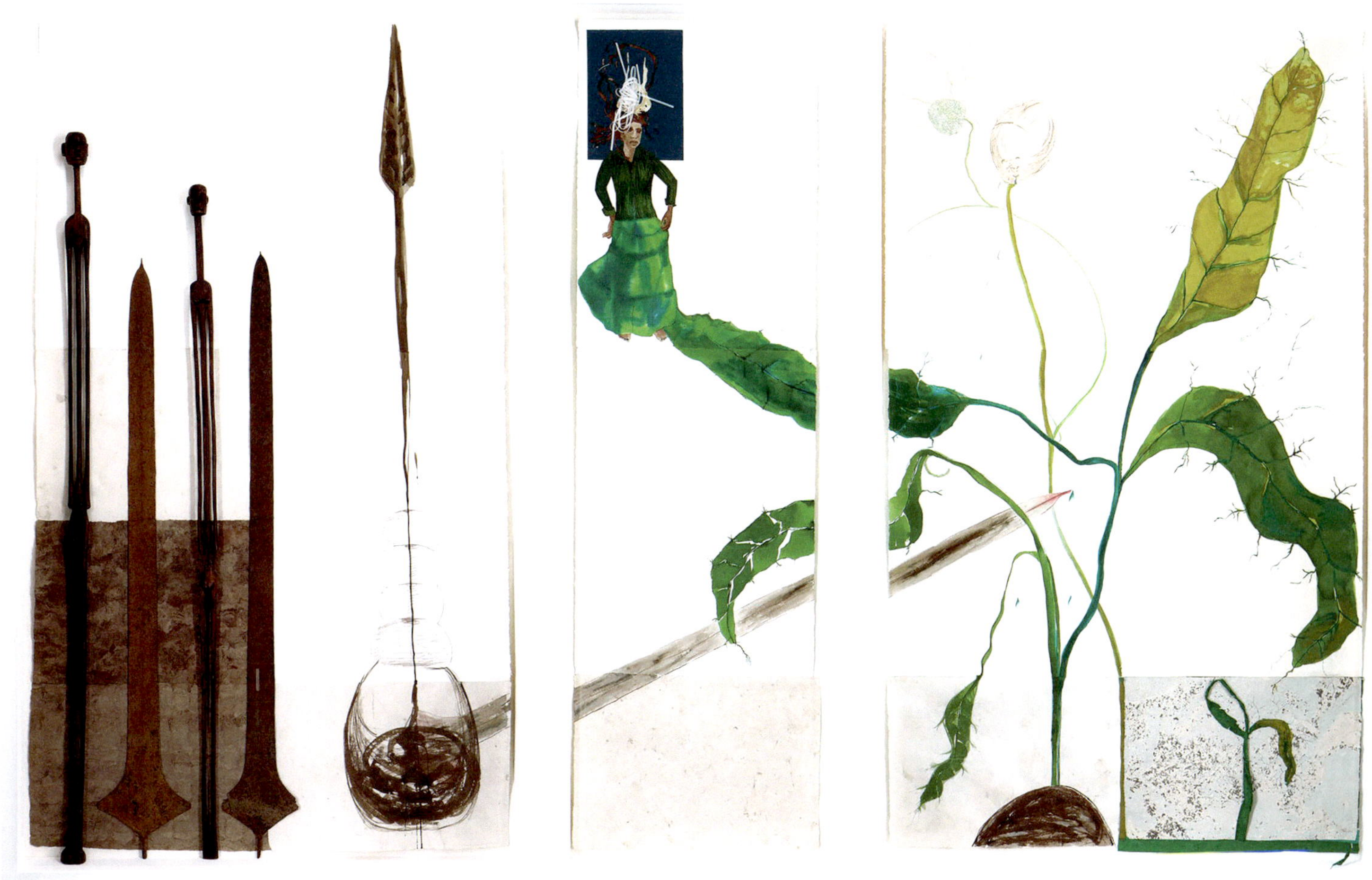

PLATE 52 *The Warrior Reservoir*, 2010–11

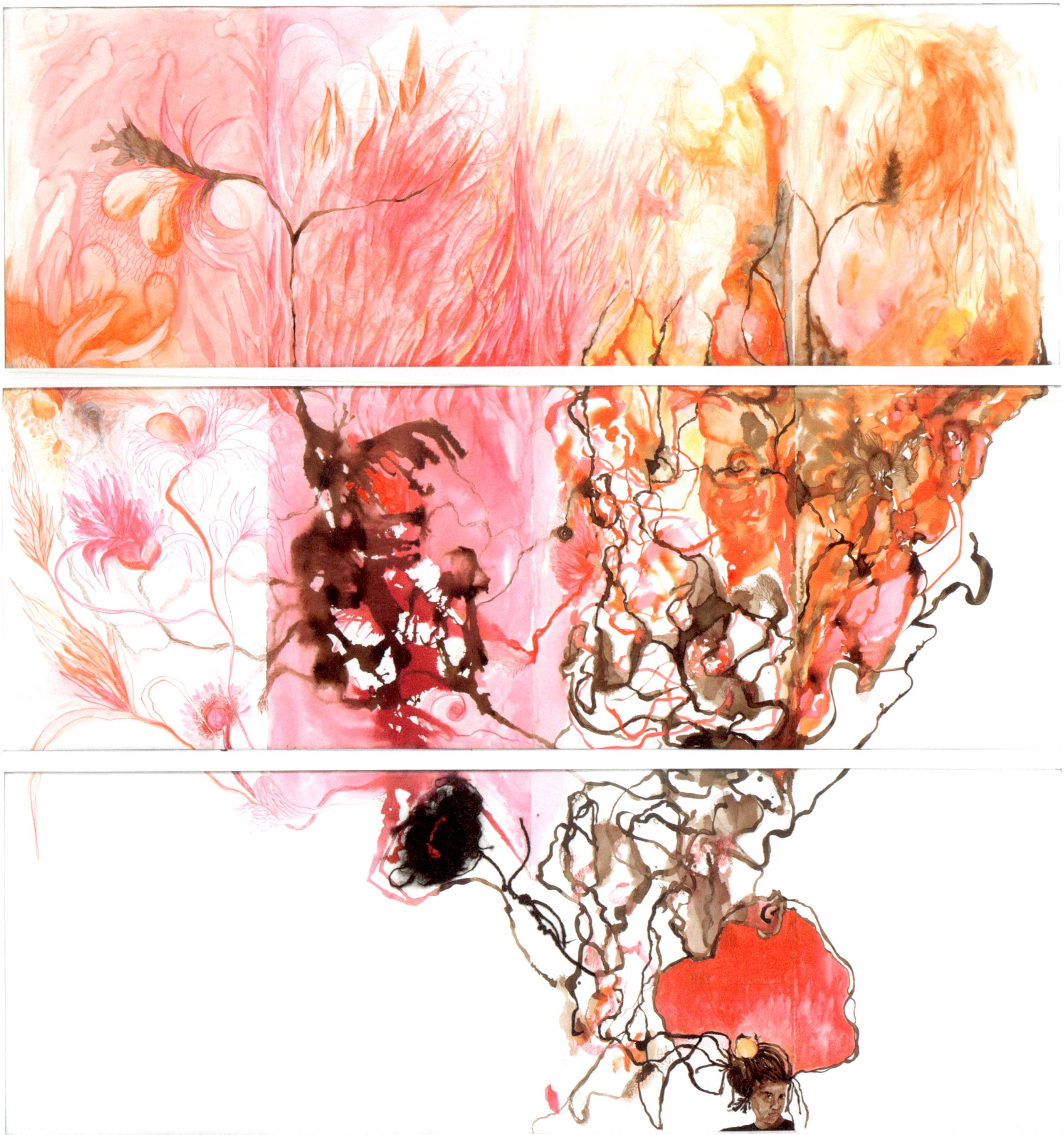

PLATE 53 *The One That Carried the Fire*, 2011

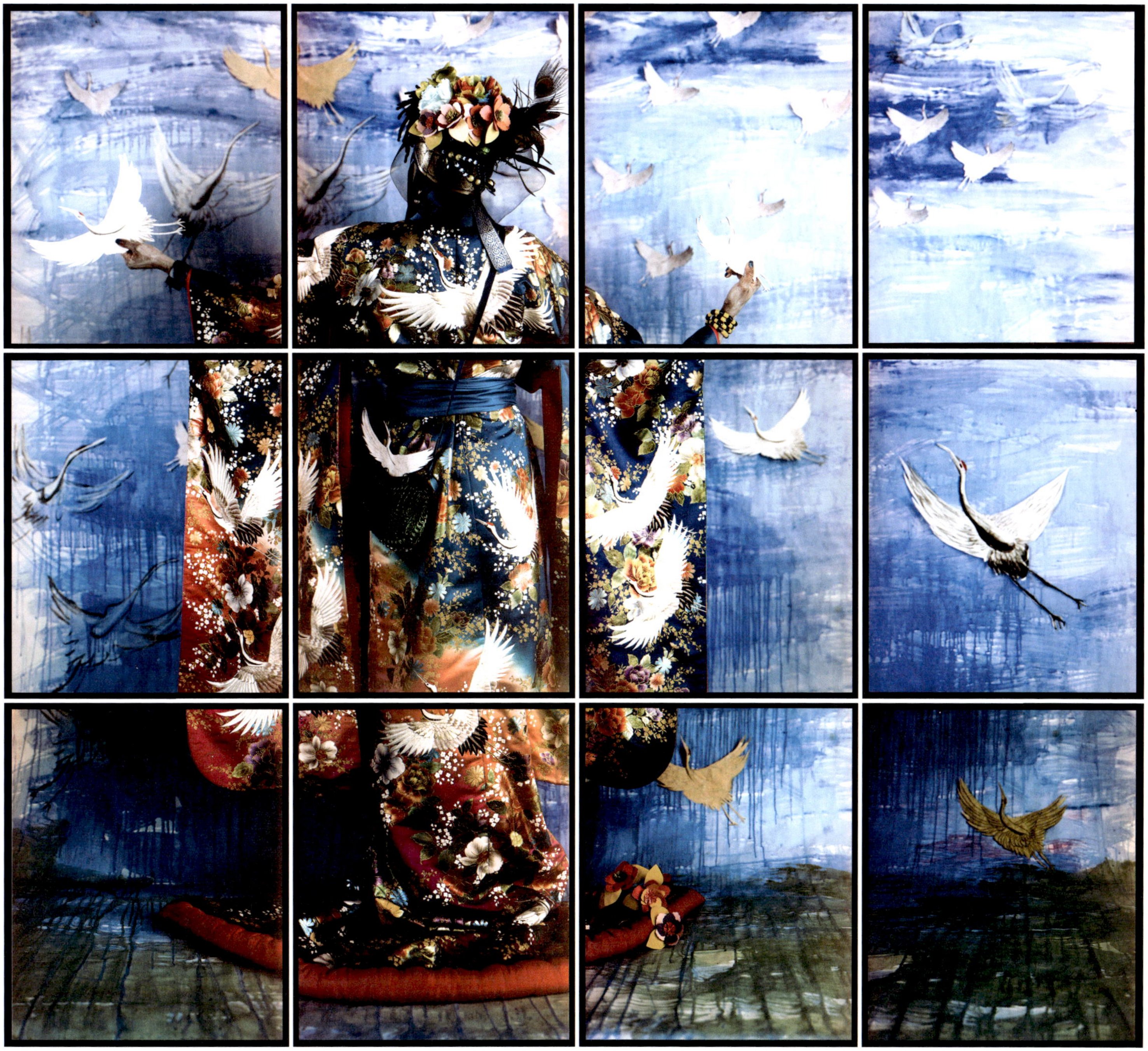

PLATE 54 *El Mensajero*, 2011

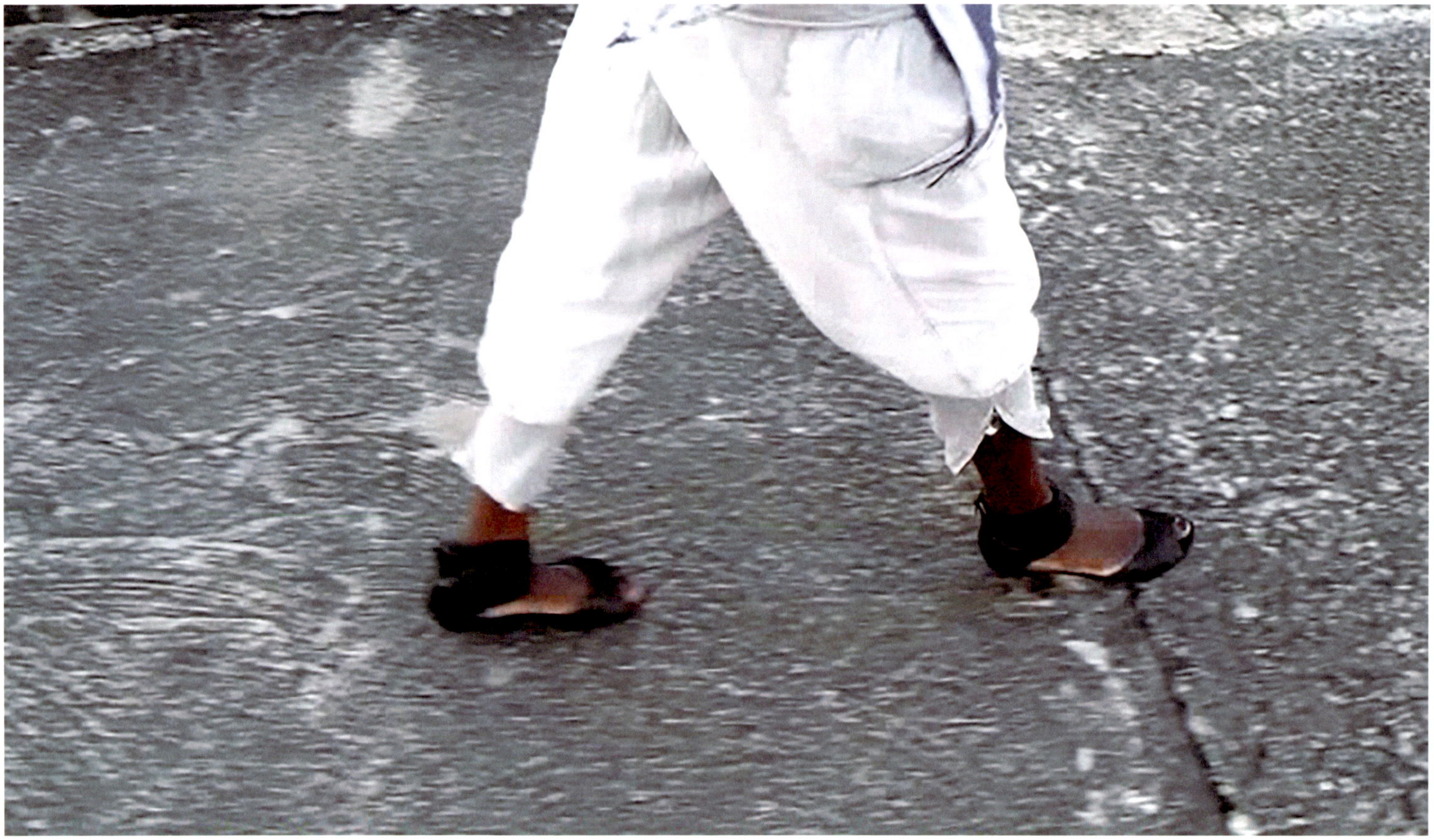

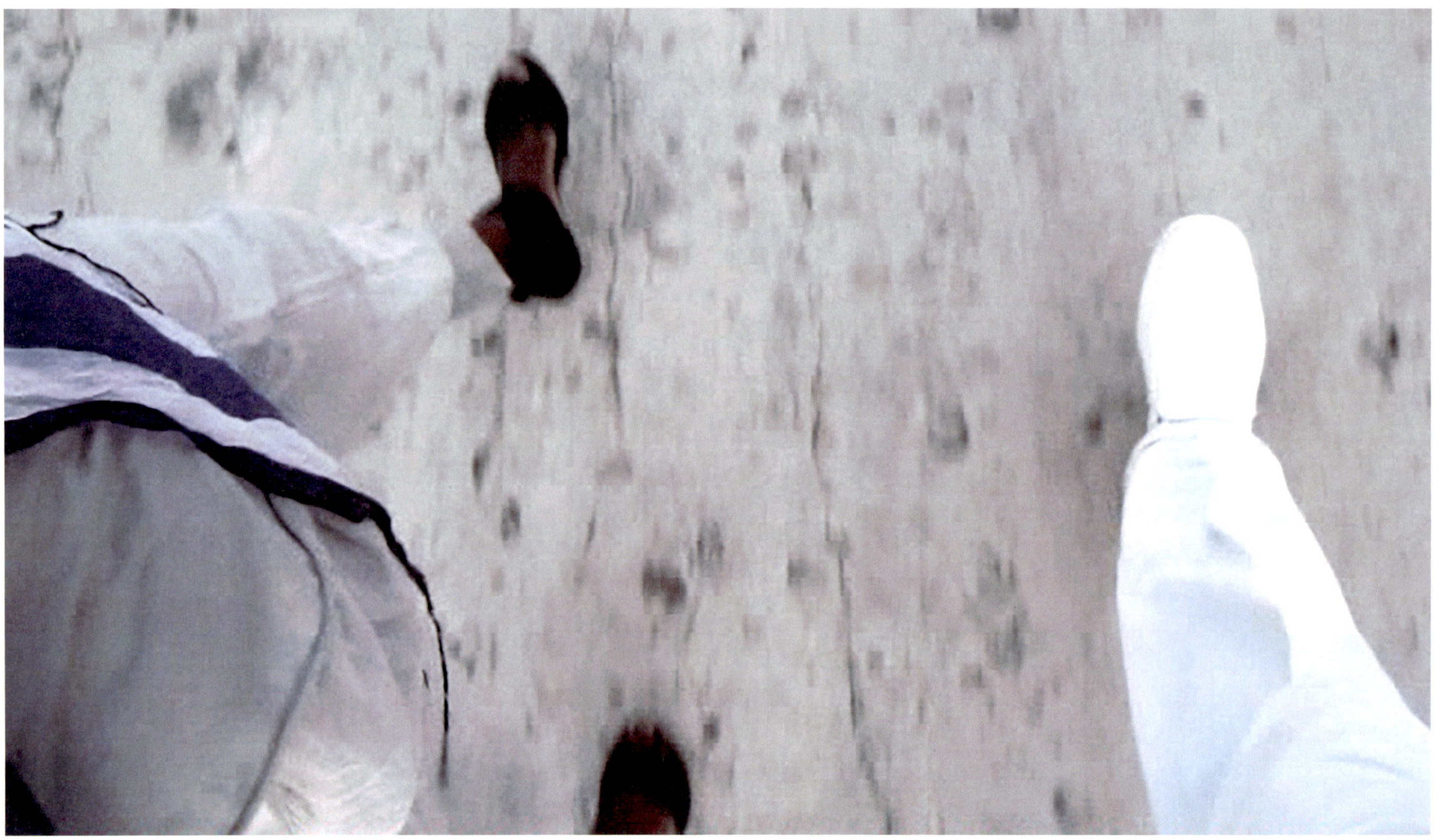

PLATE 55 *Cuba Walk*, 2012

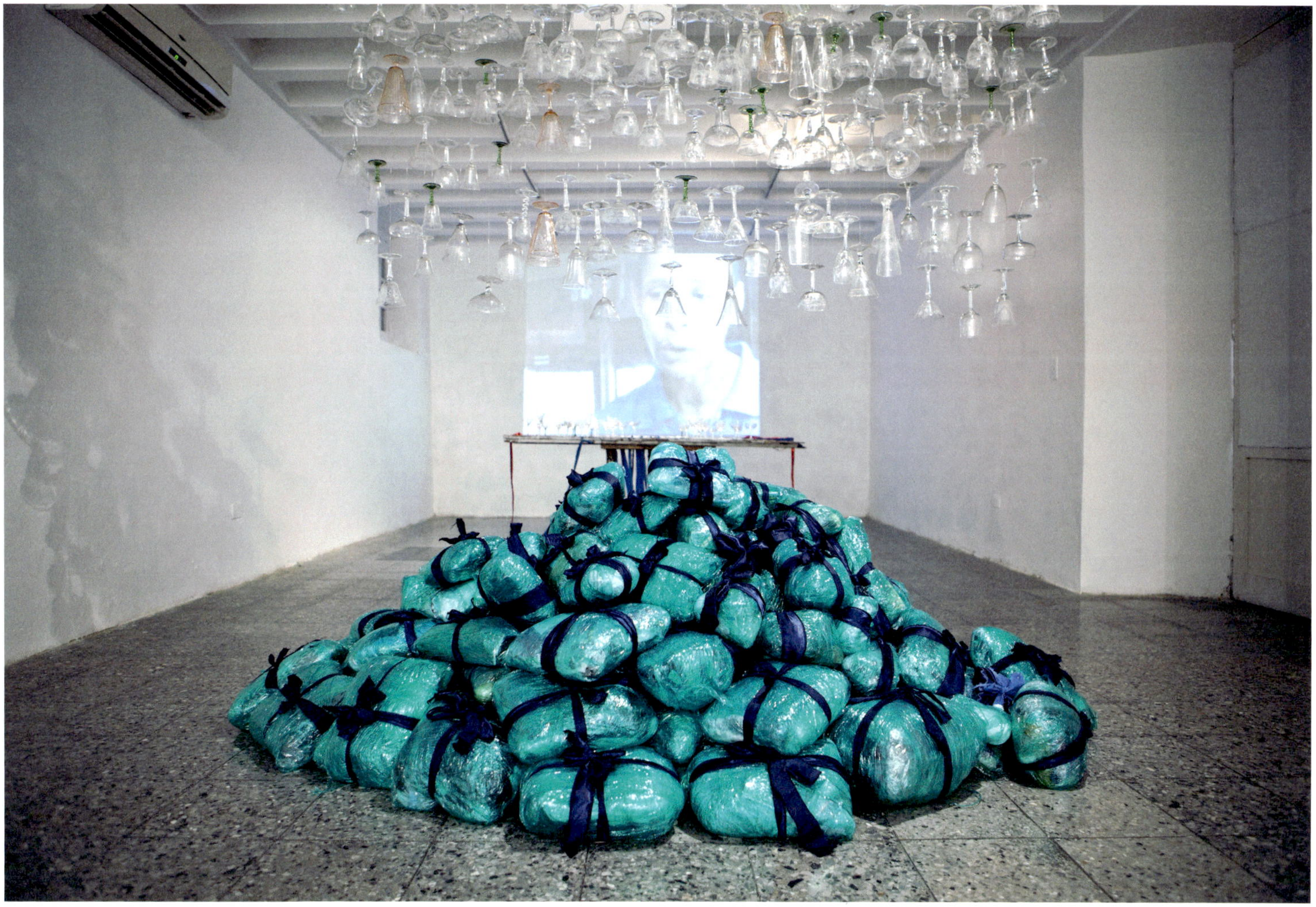

PLATE 56 *Llegooo! FeFa!*, 2012

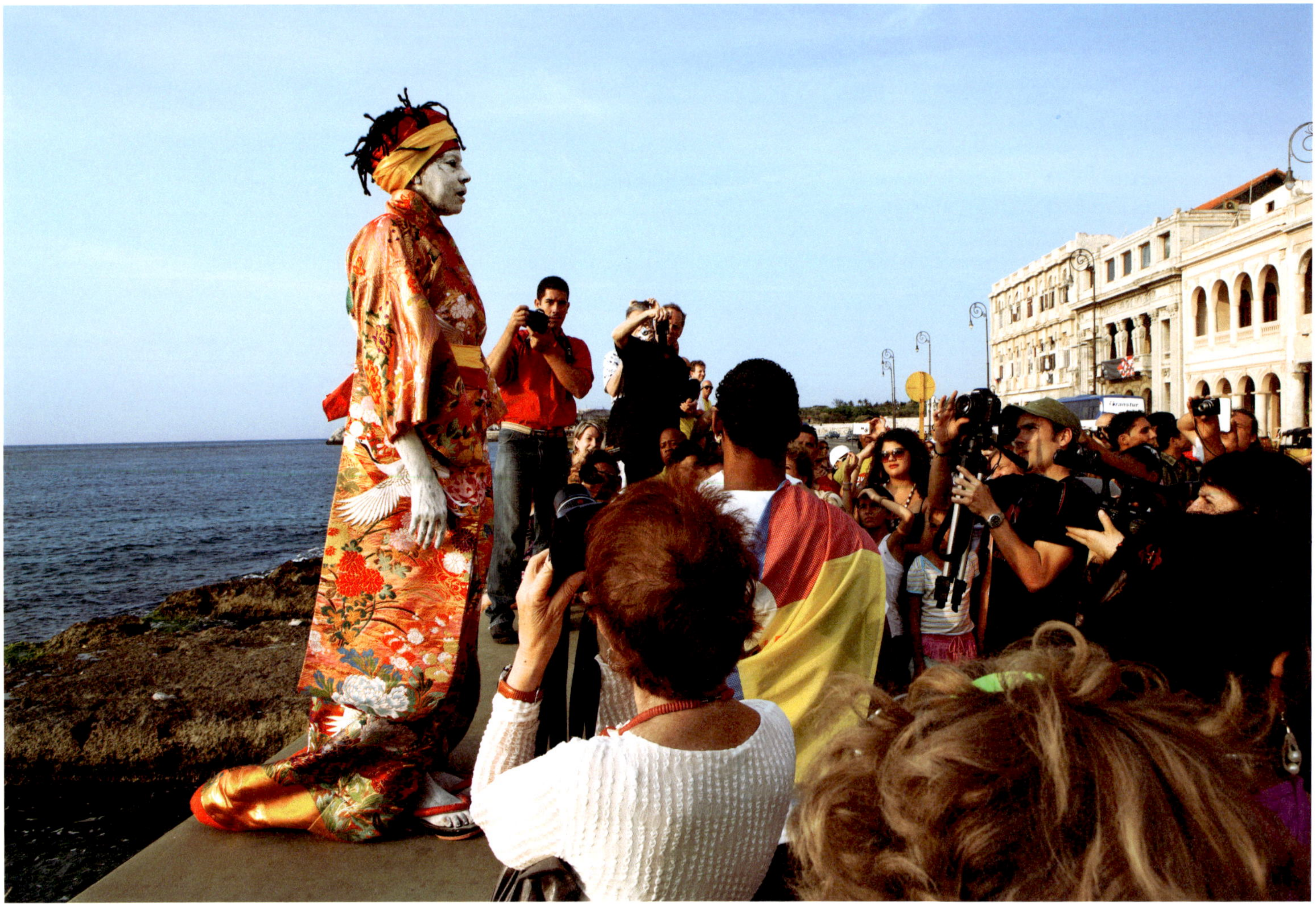

PLATE 57 *Llegooo! FeFa!*, performance, 2012

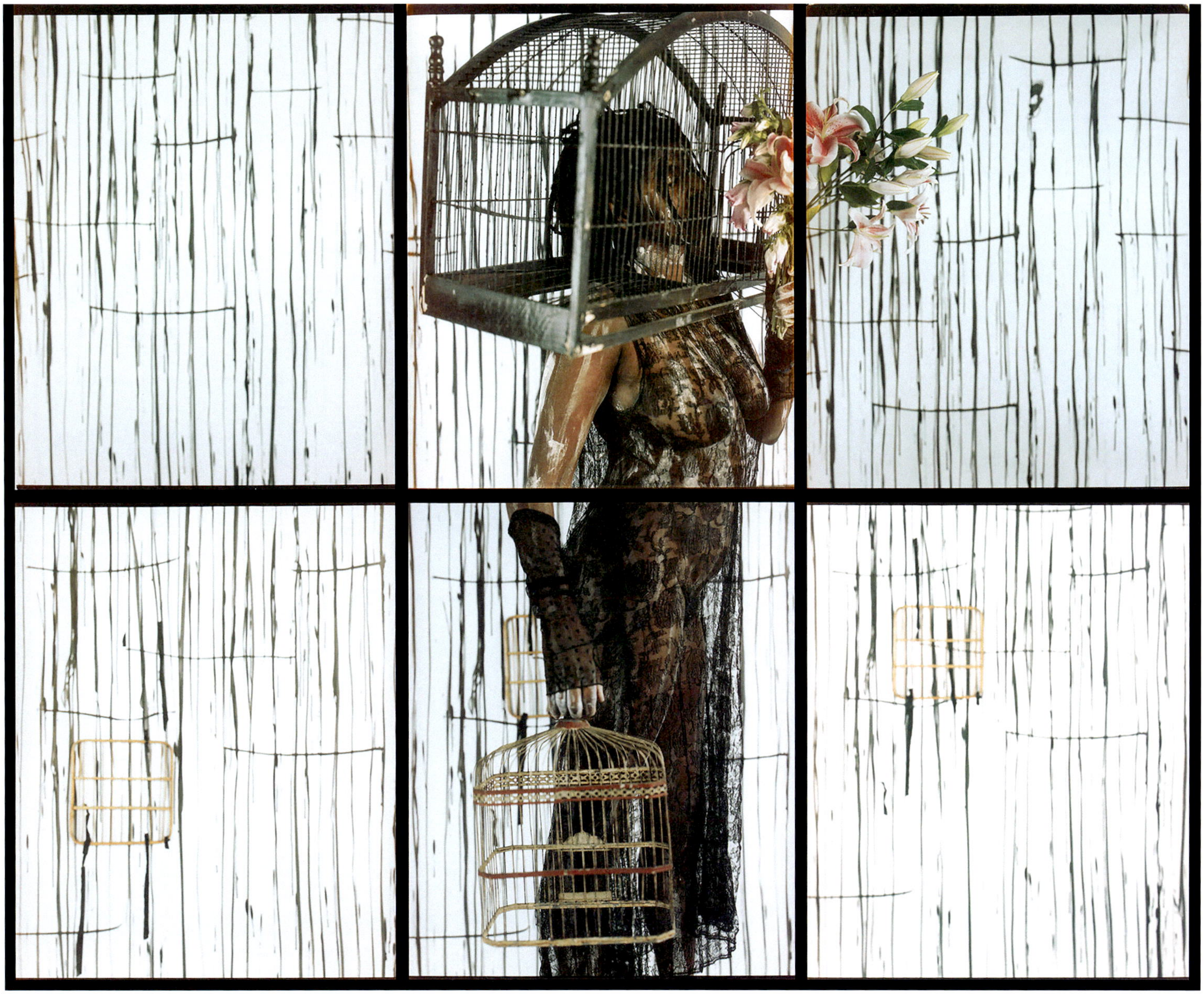

PLATE 58 *Songs of Freedom*, 2013

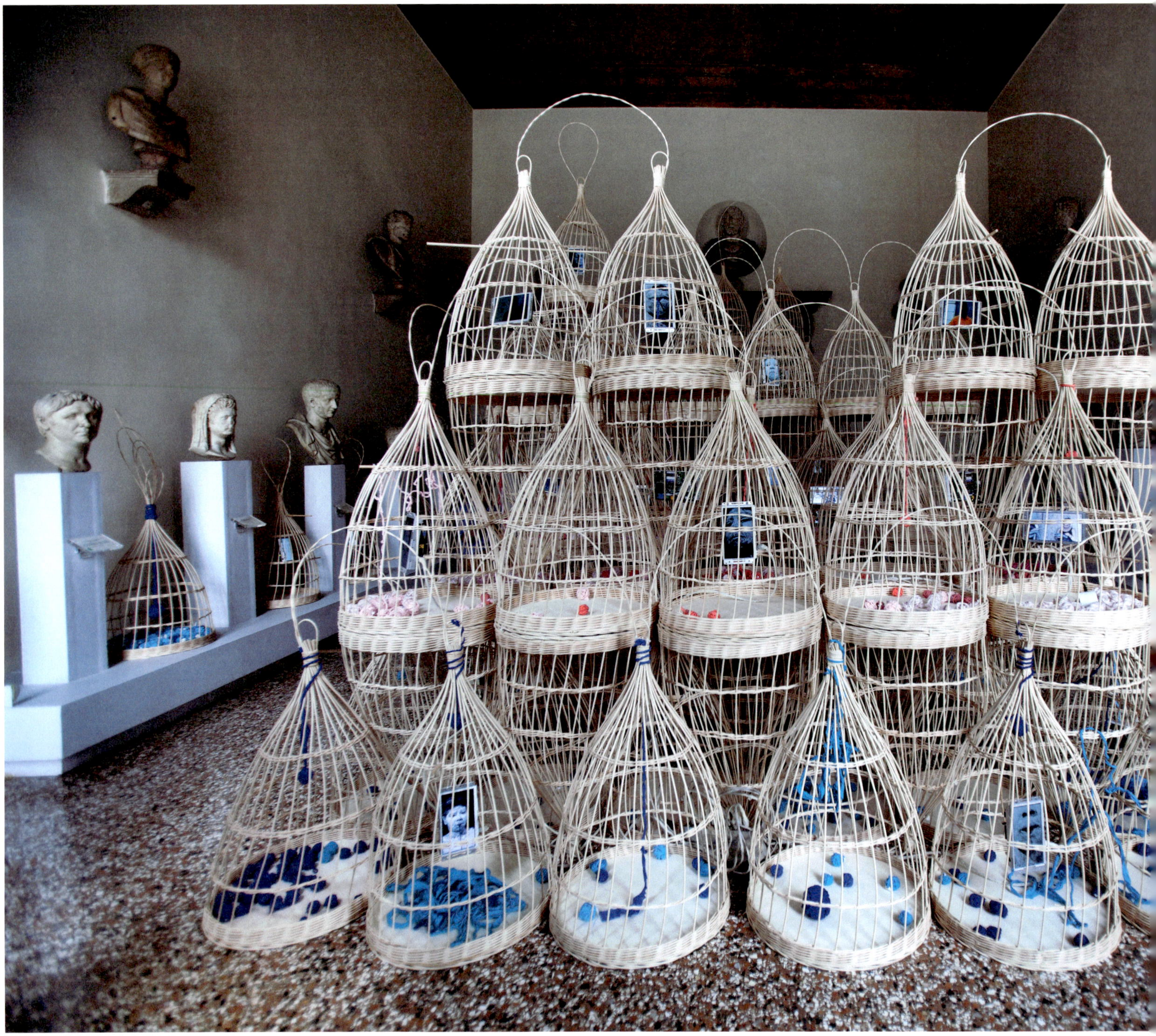

PLATE 59 *53+1=54+1=55 / Letter of the Year*, 2013

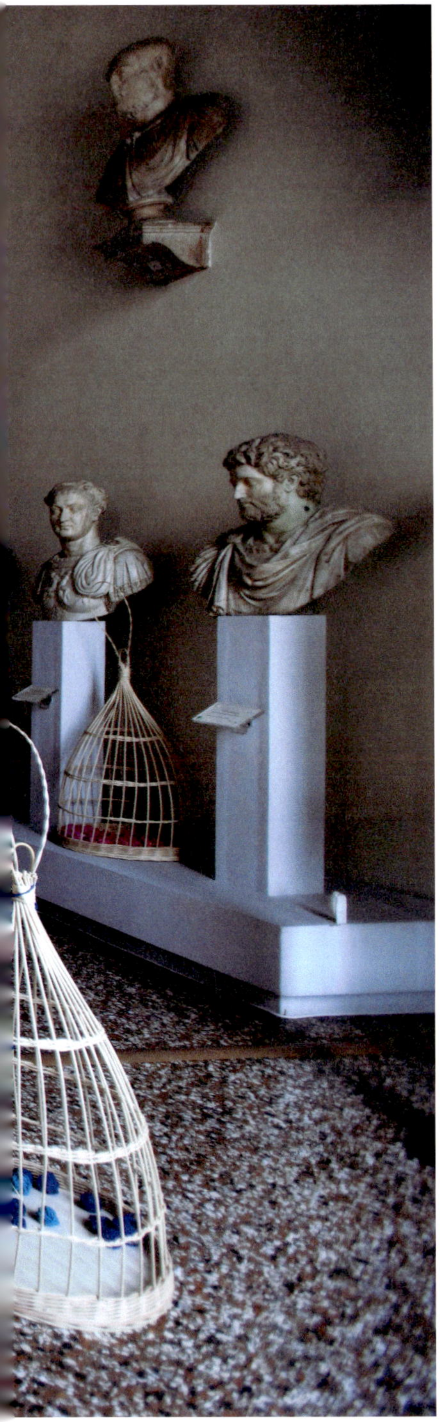

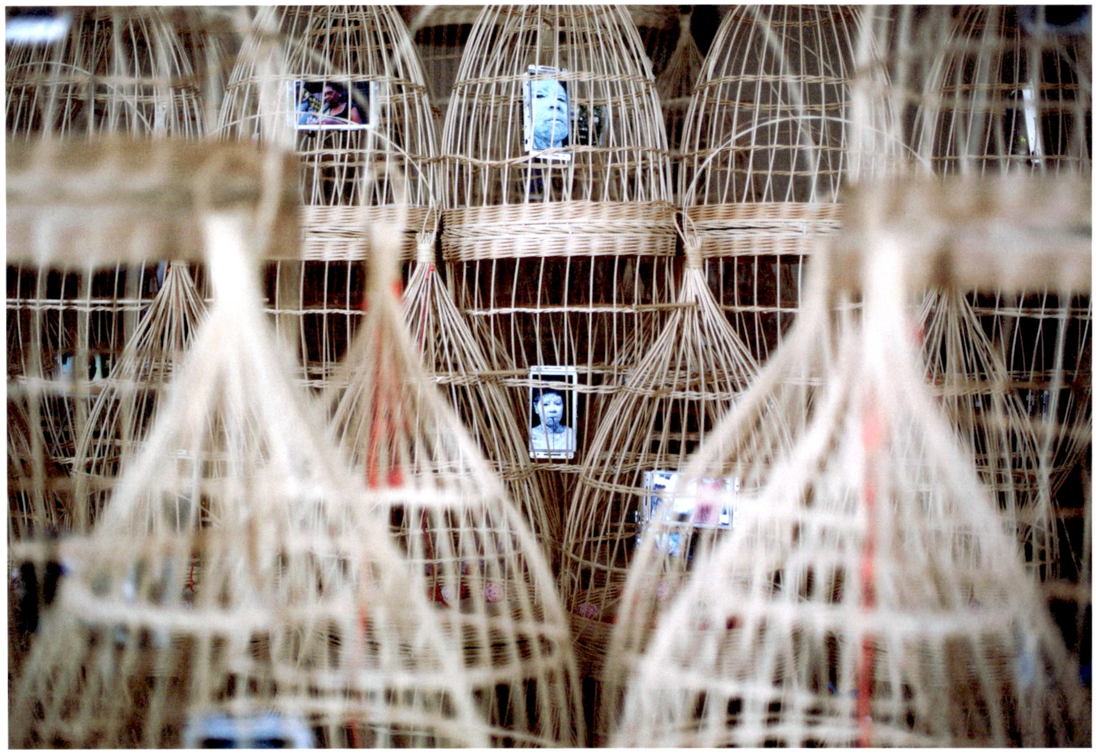

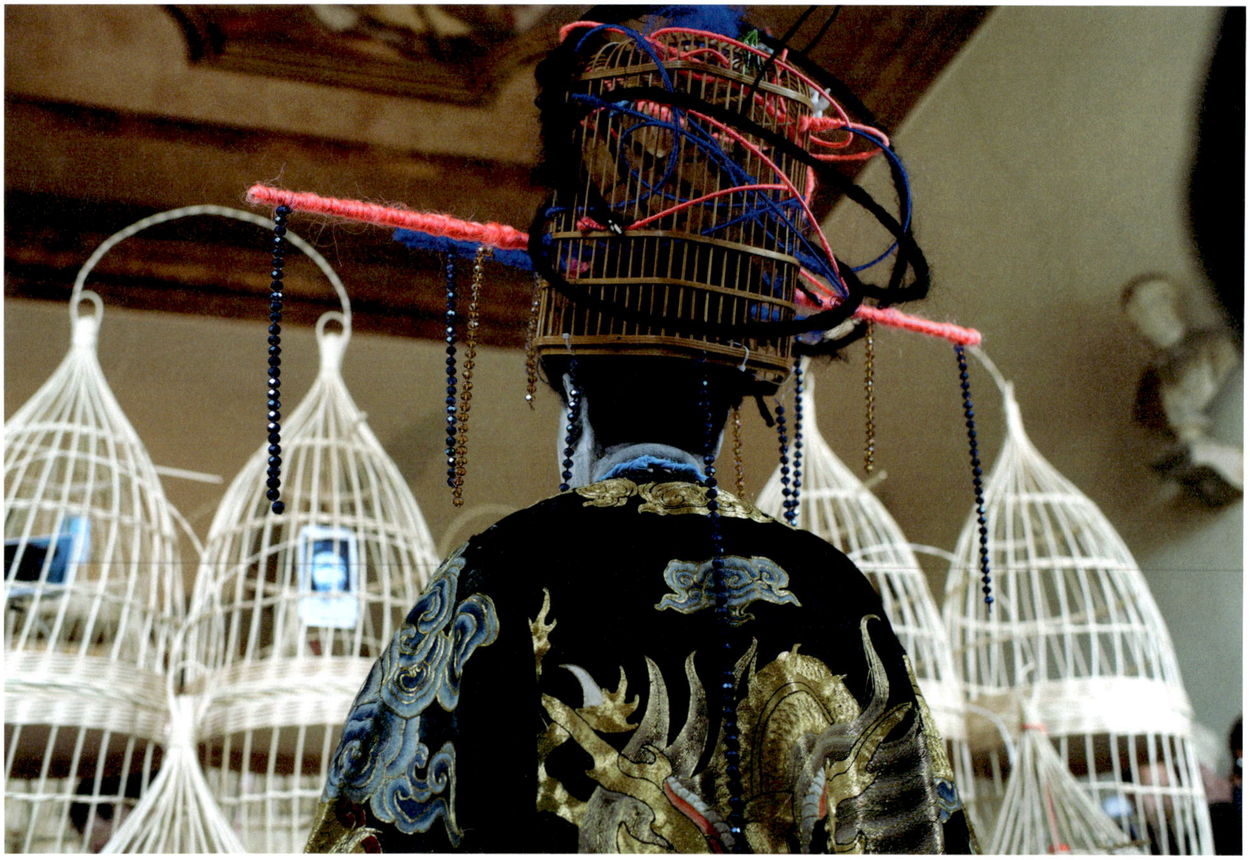

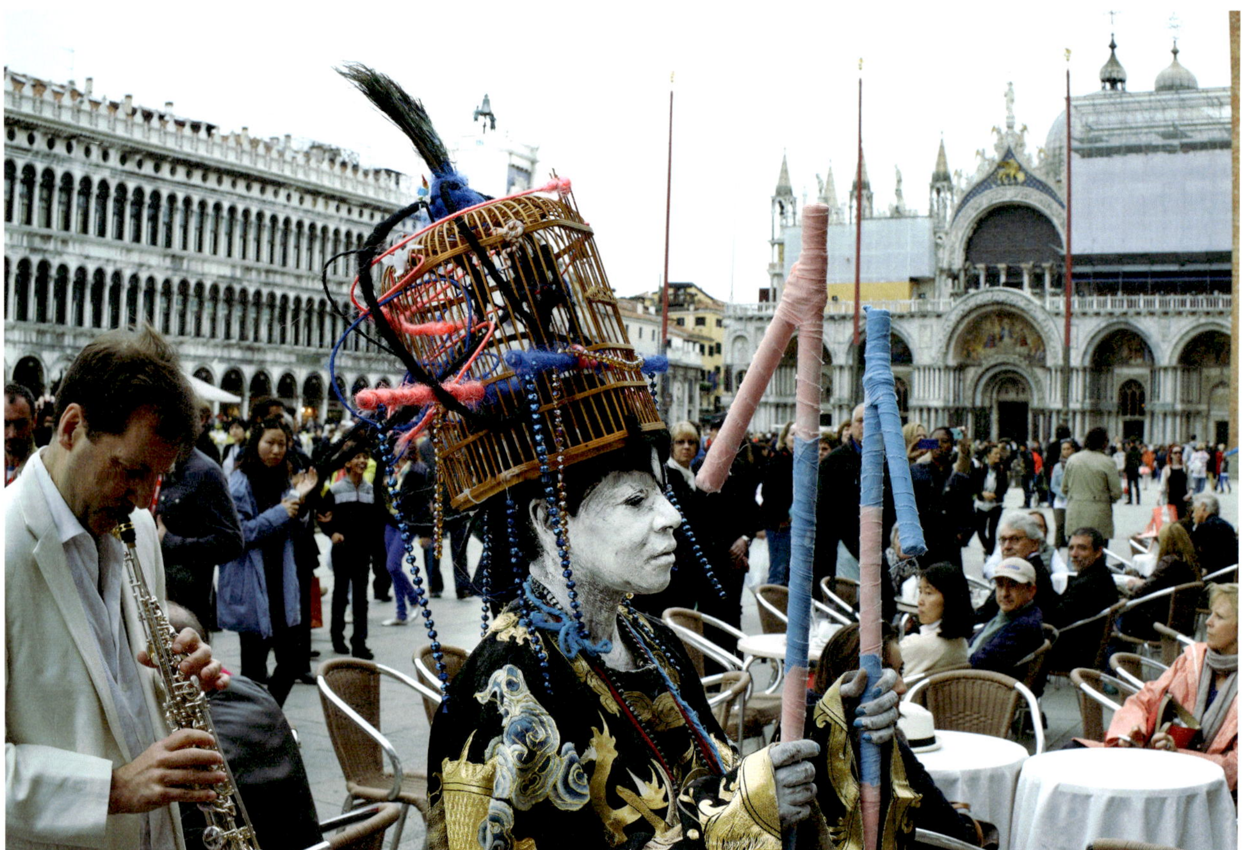

PLATE 60 *FeFa*, performance, Piazza San Marco, Venice, 2013

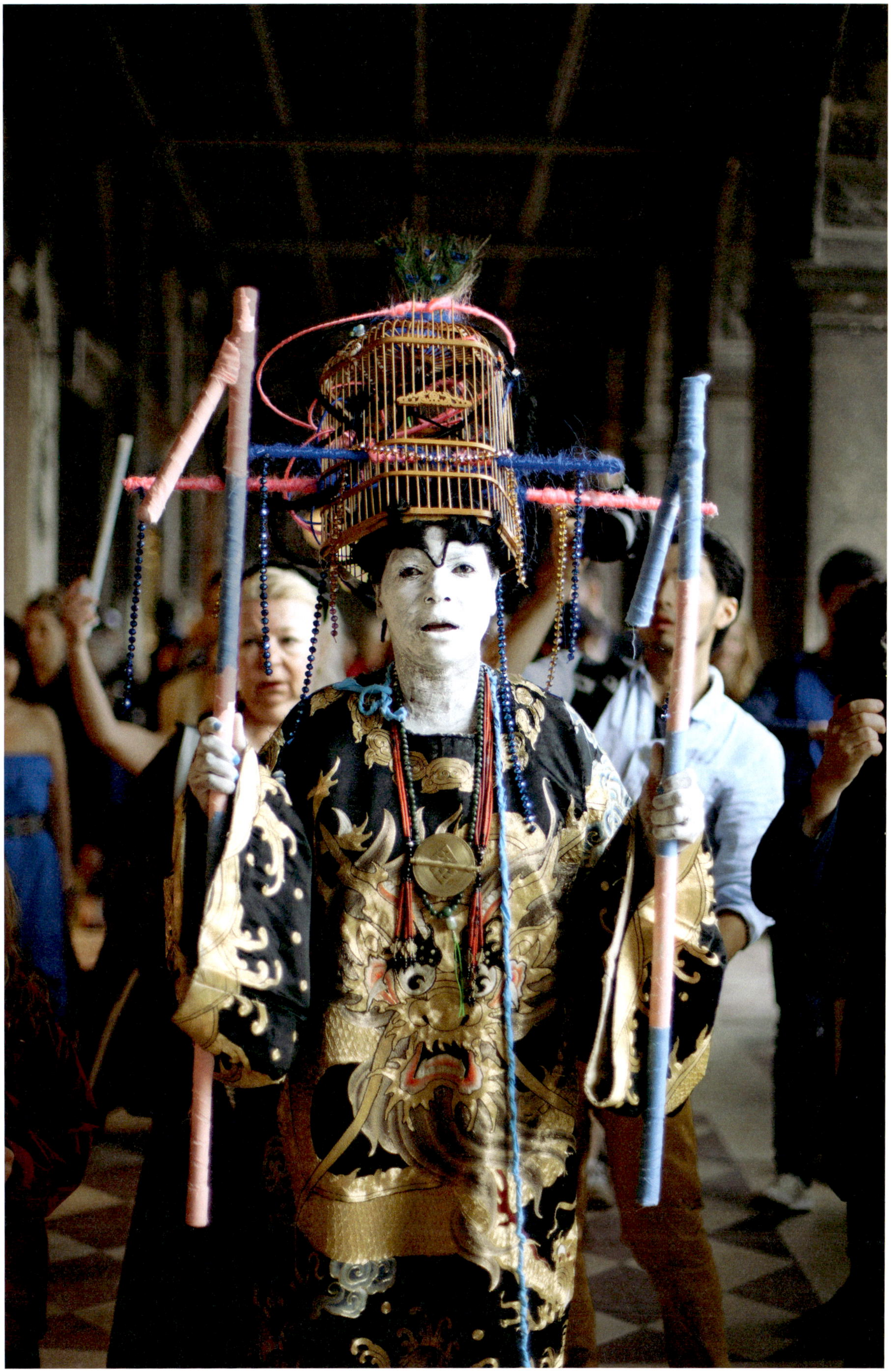

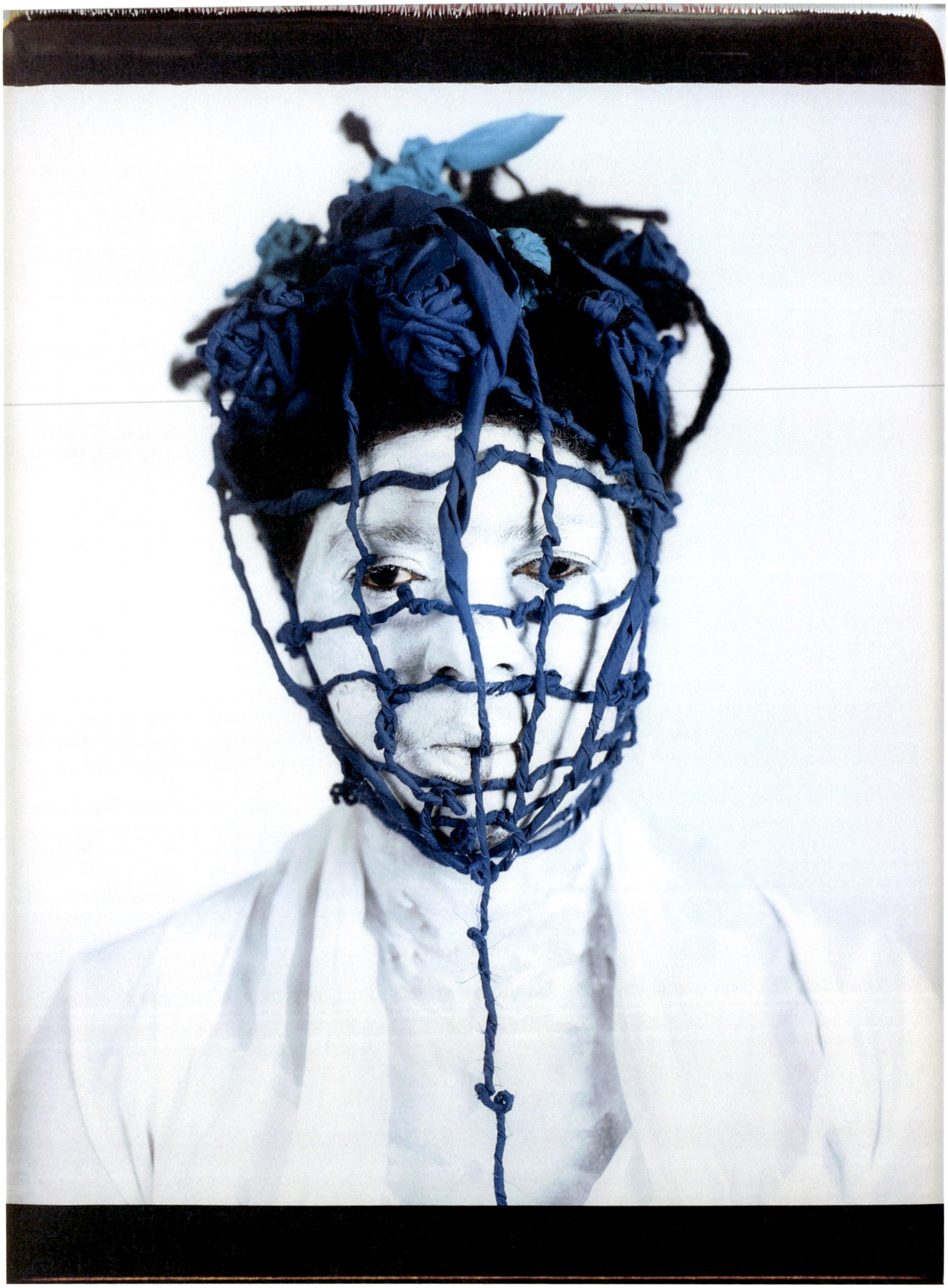

PLATE 61 *Freedom Trap*, 2013

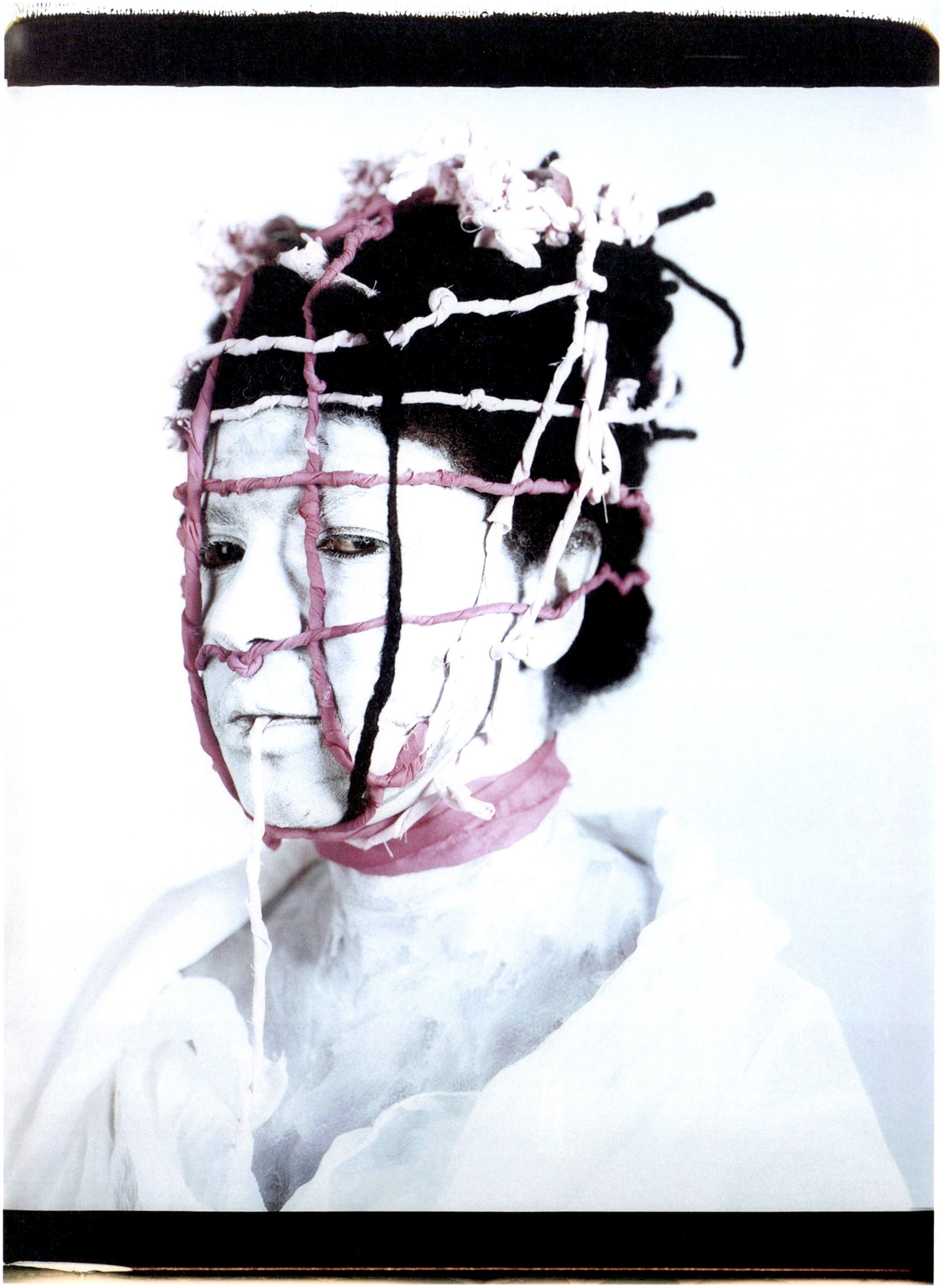

PLATE 62 *Freedom Trap*, 2013

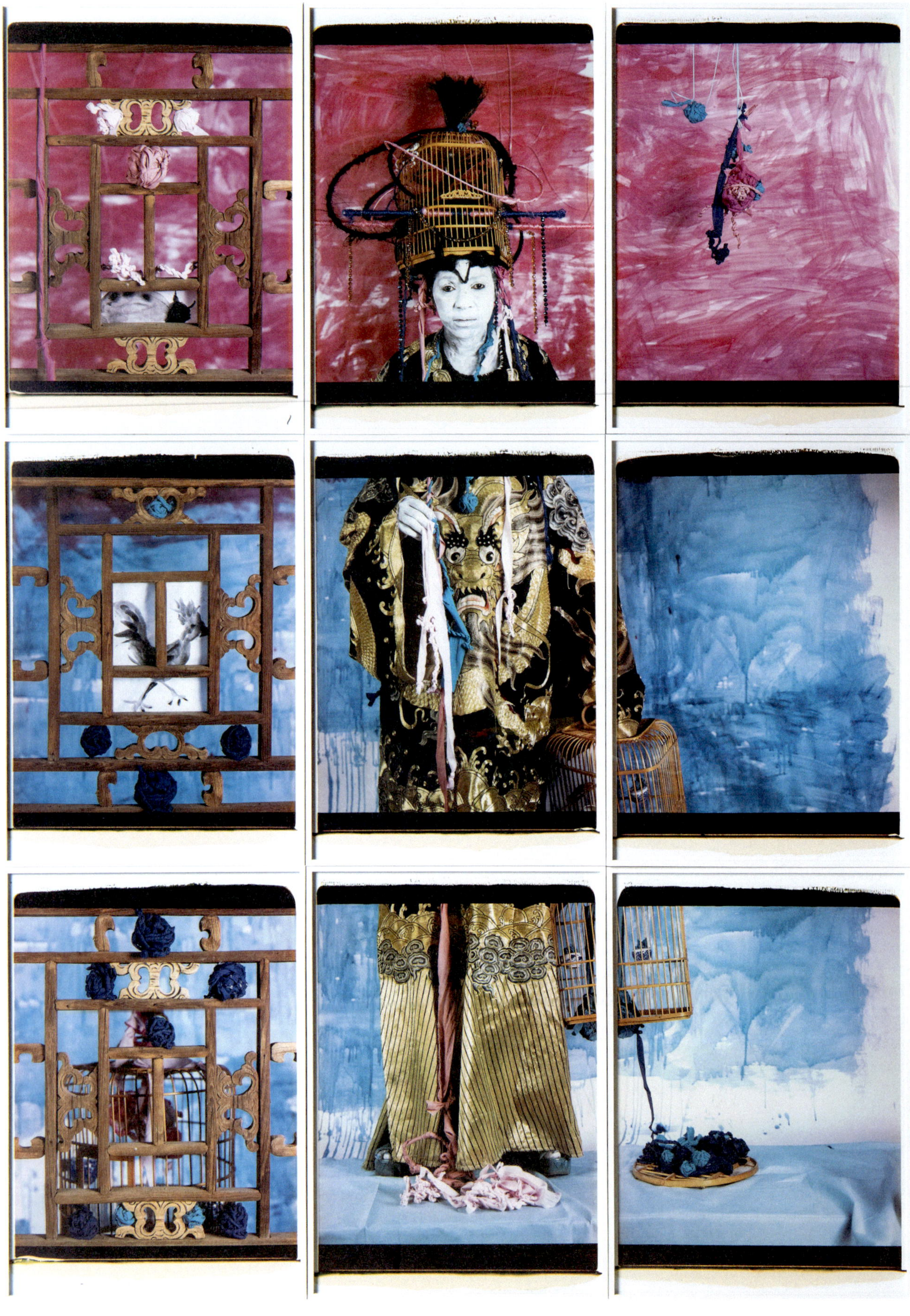

PLATE 63 *The Flag Year 13. Color Code Venice*, 2013

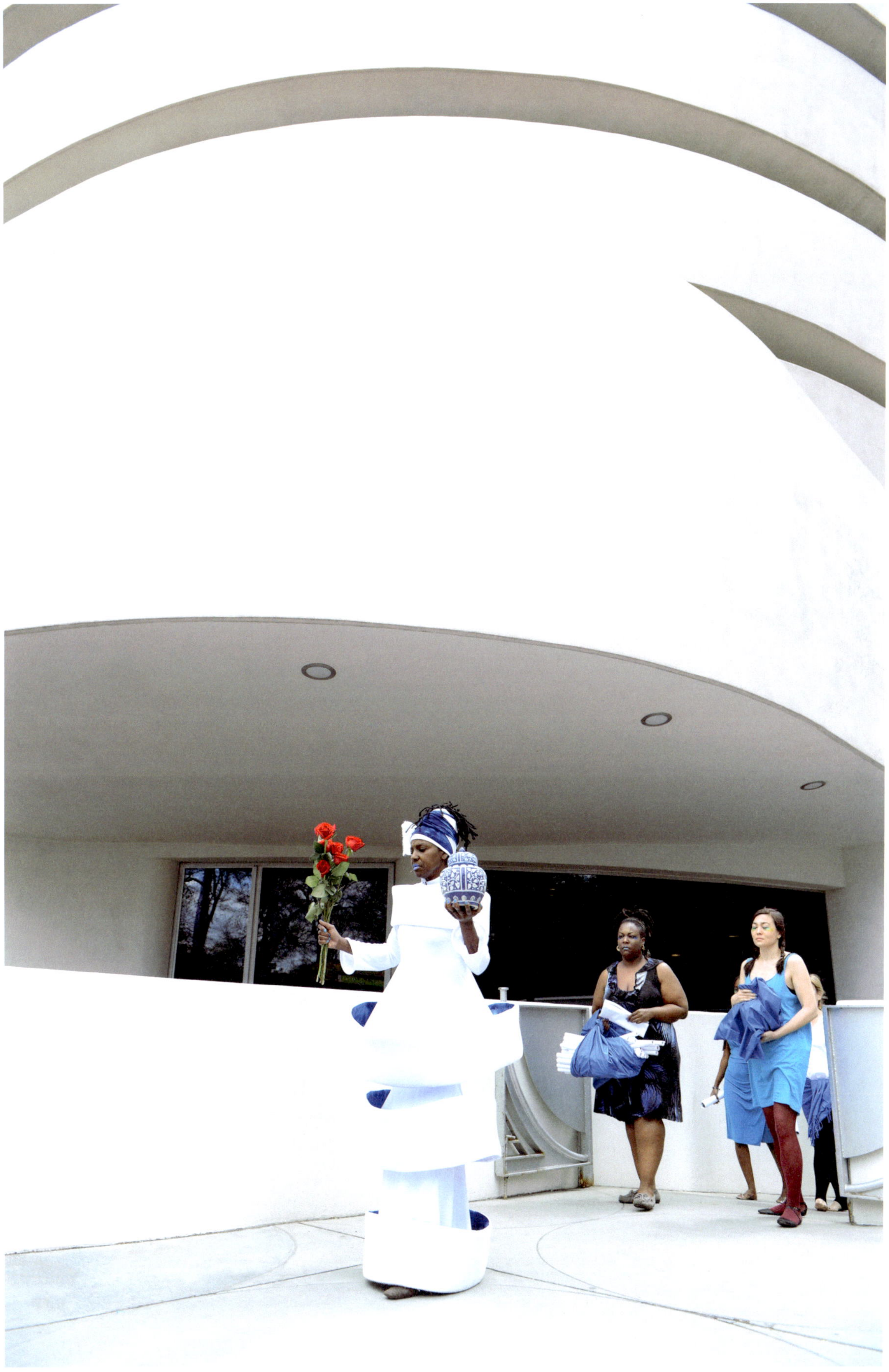

PLATE 64 *Habla La Madre*, performance, 2014

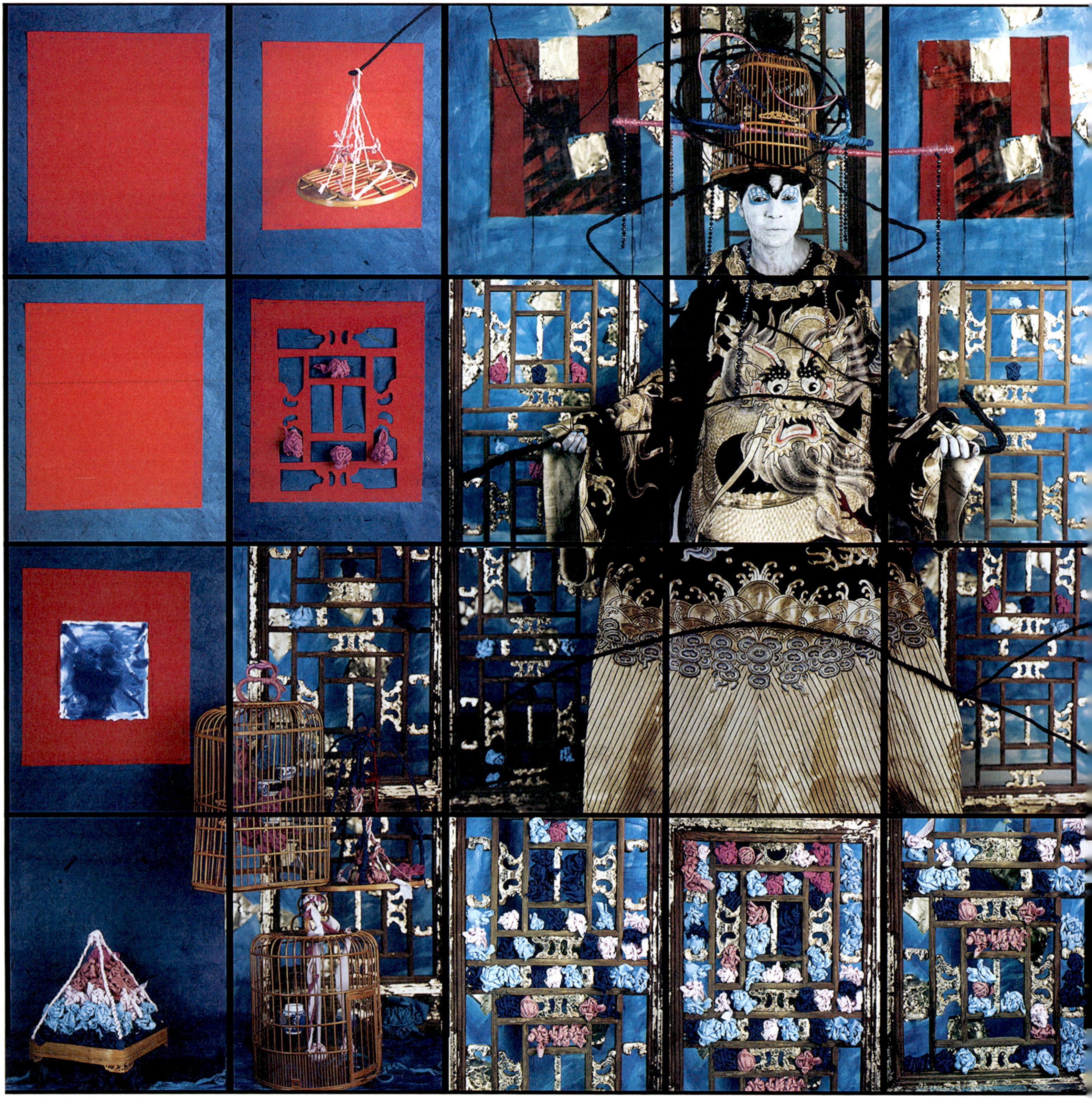

PLATE 65 *Finding Balance*, 2015

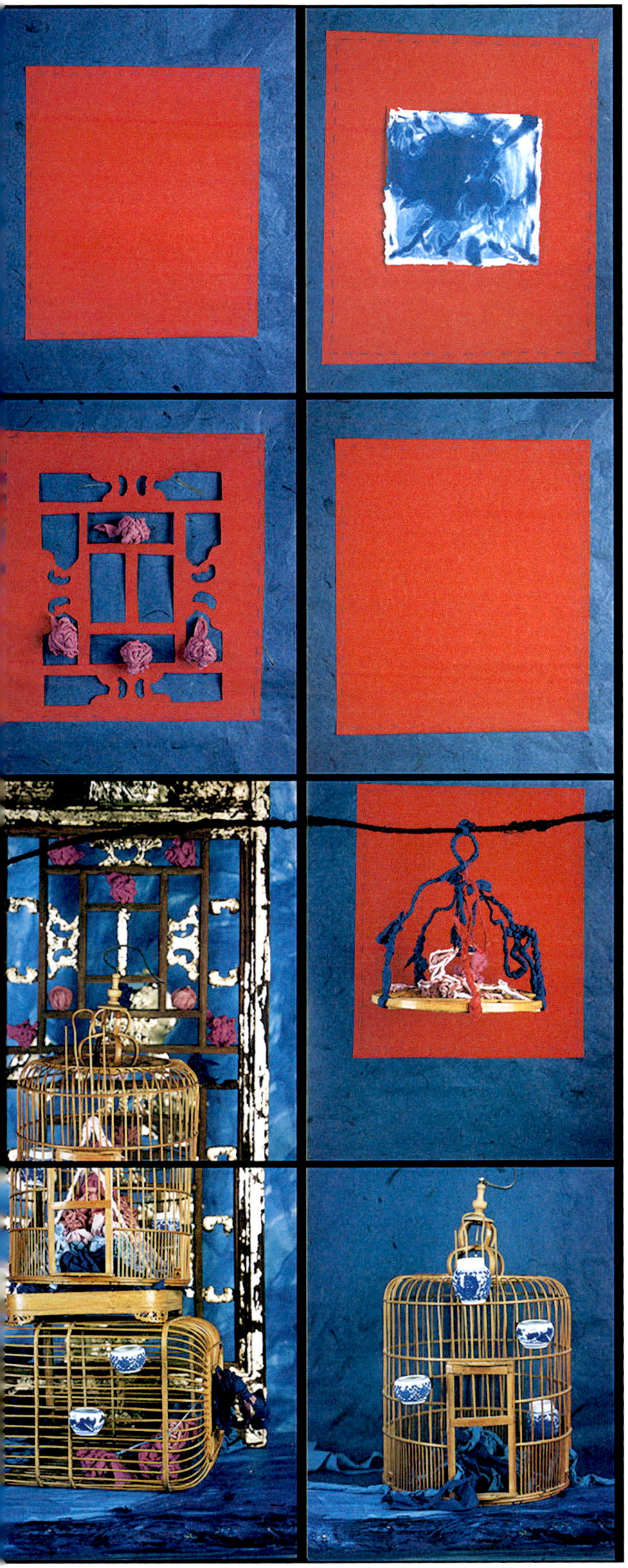

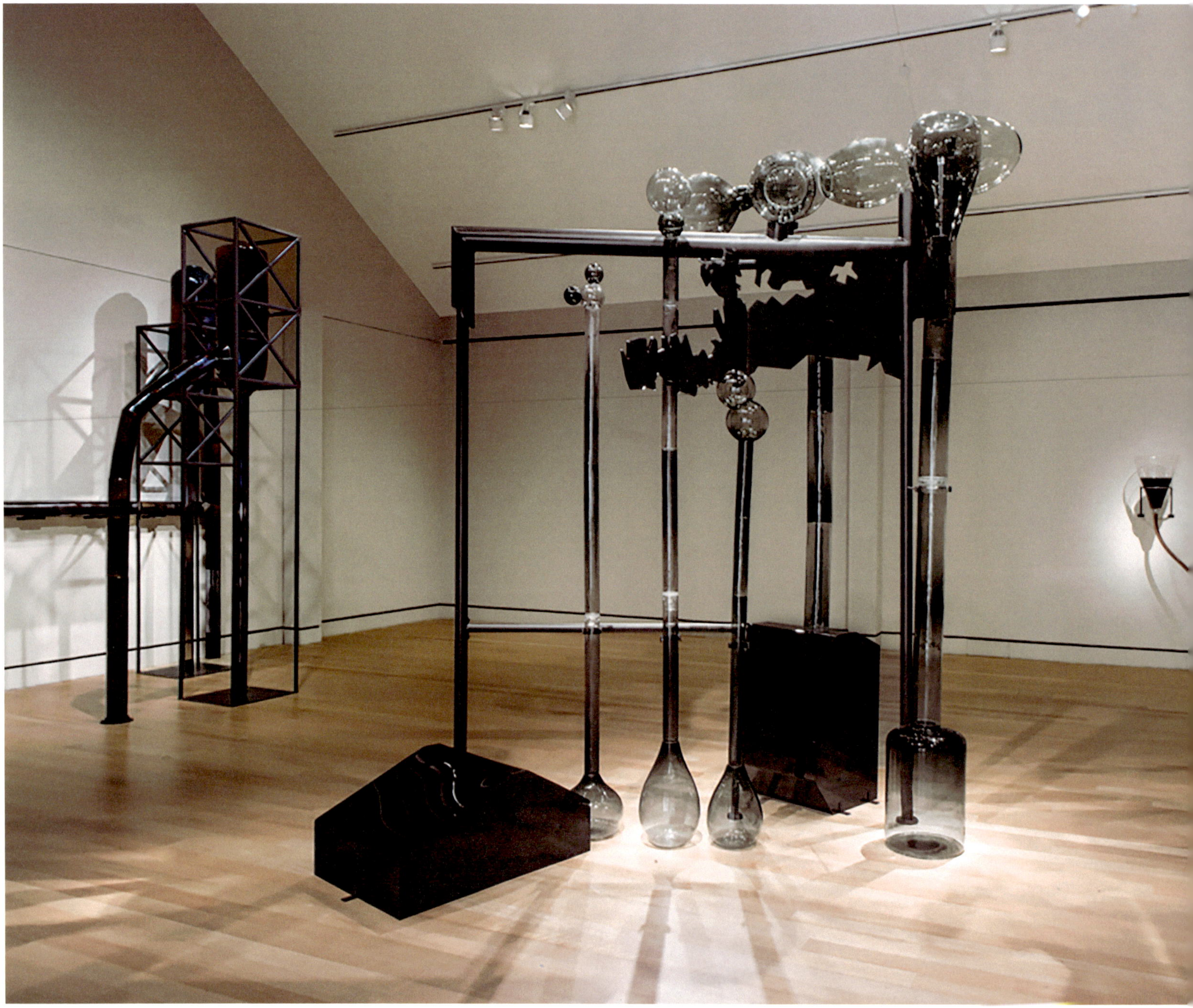

PLATE 66 *Alchemy of the Soul, Elixir for the Spirits*, 2015

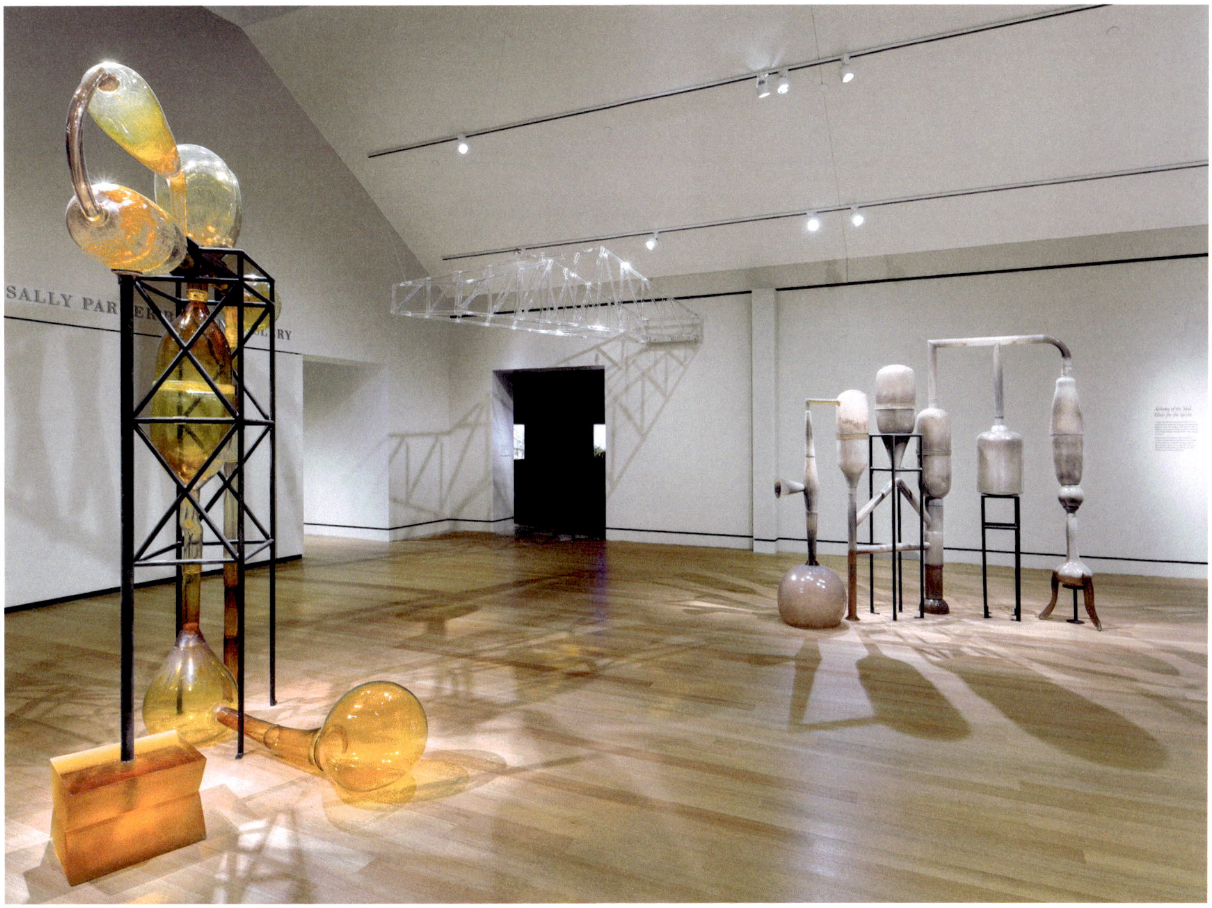

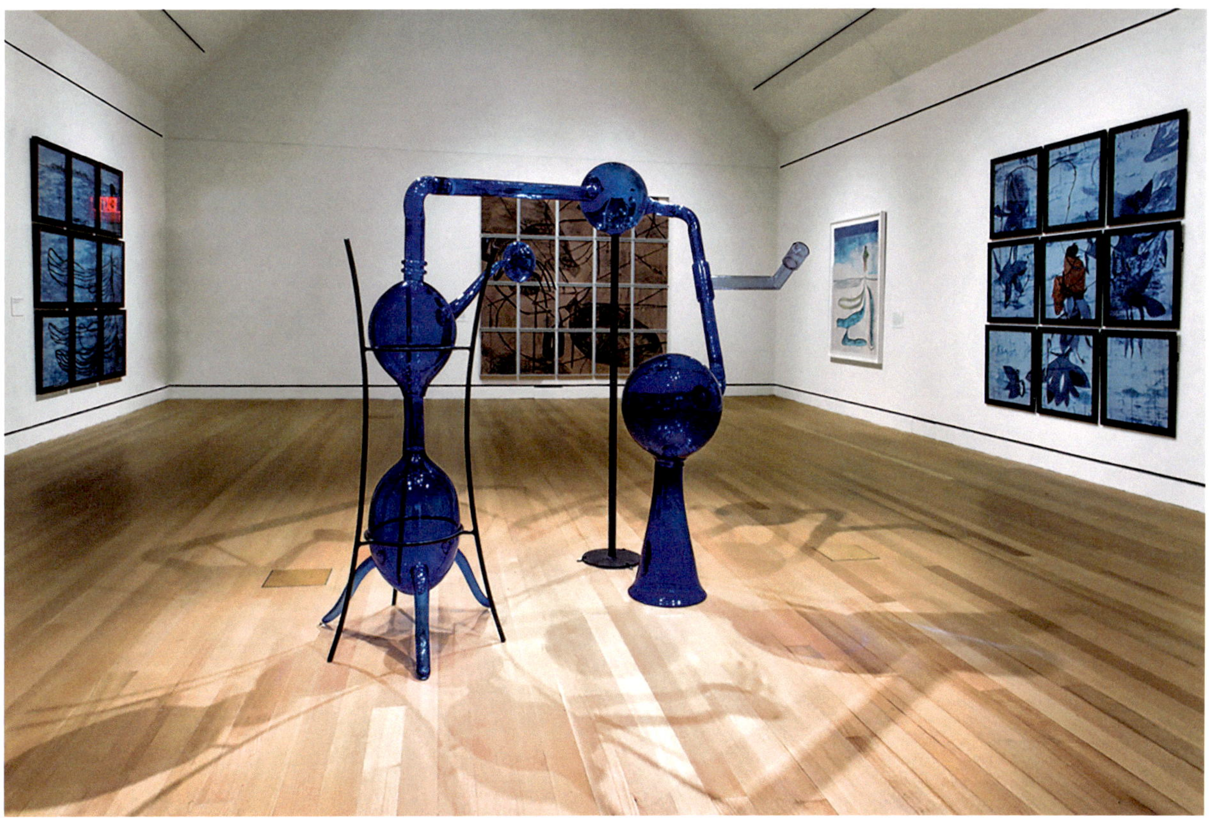

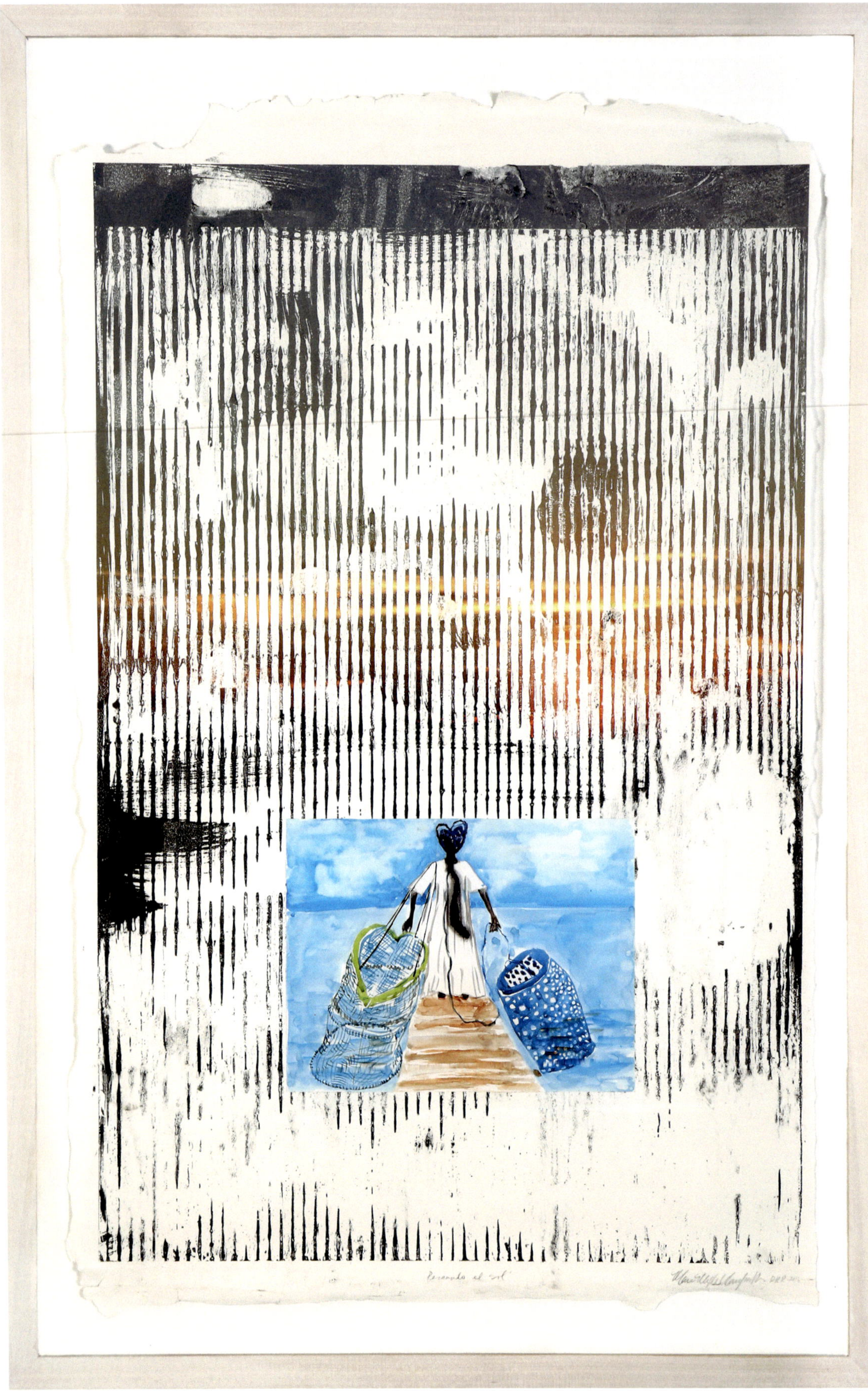

PLATE 67 *Catch of the Day #1*, from the Extreme Weather, Captiva series, 2016

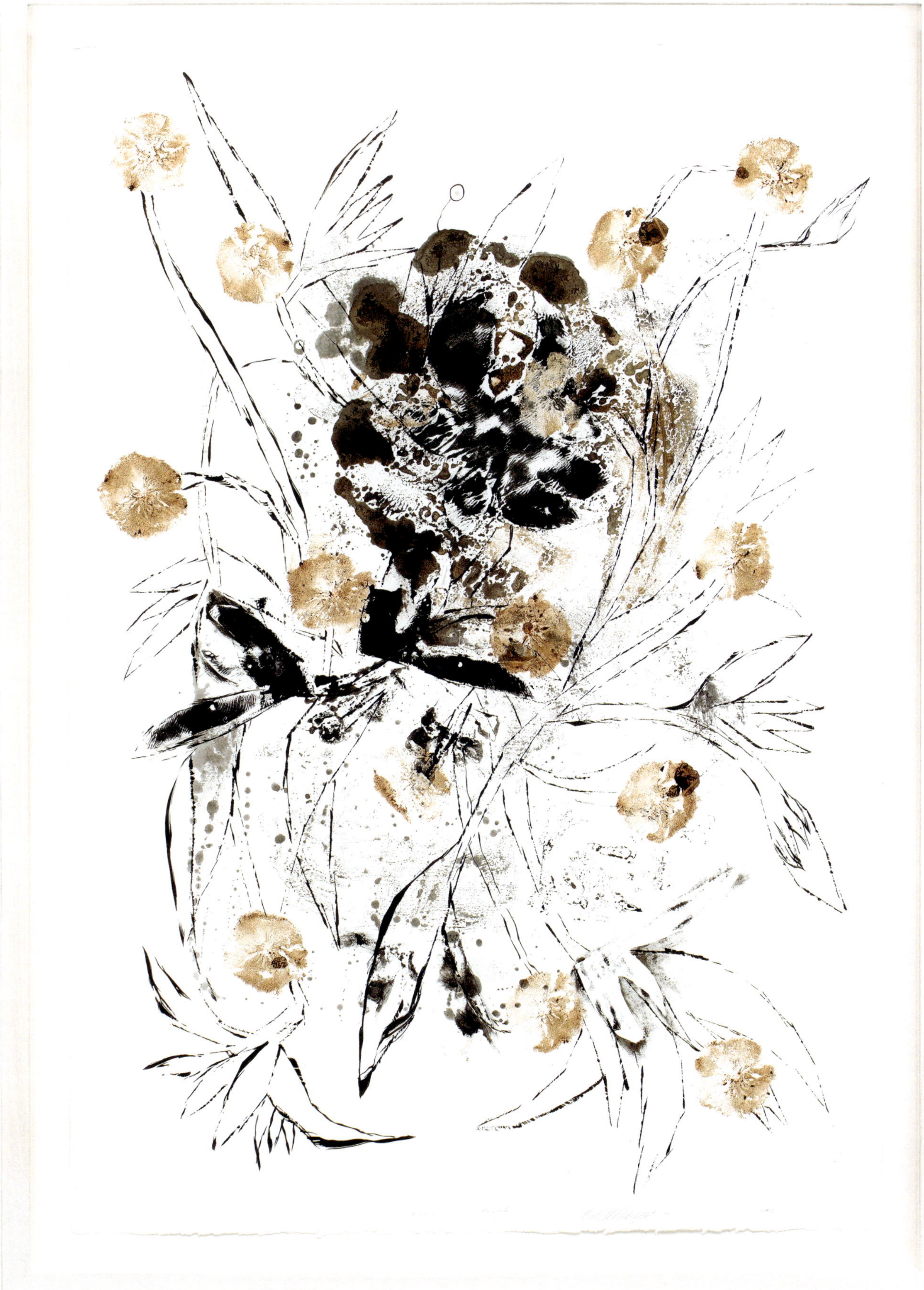

PLATE 68 *Jungle*, from the Extreme Weather, Captiva series, 2016

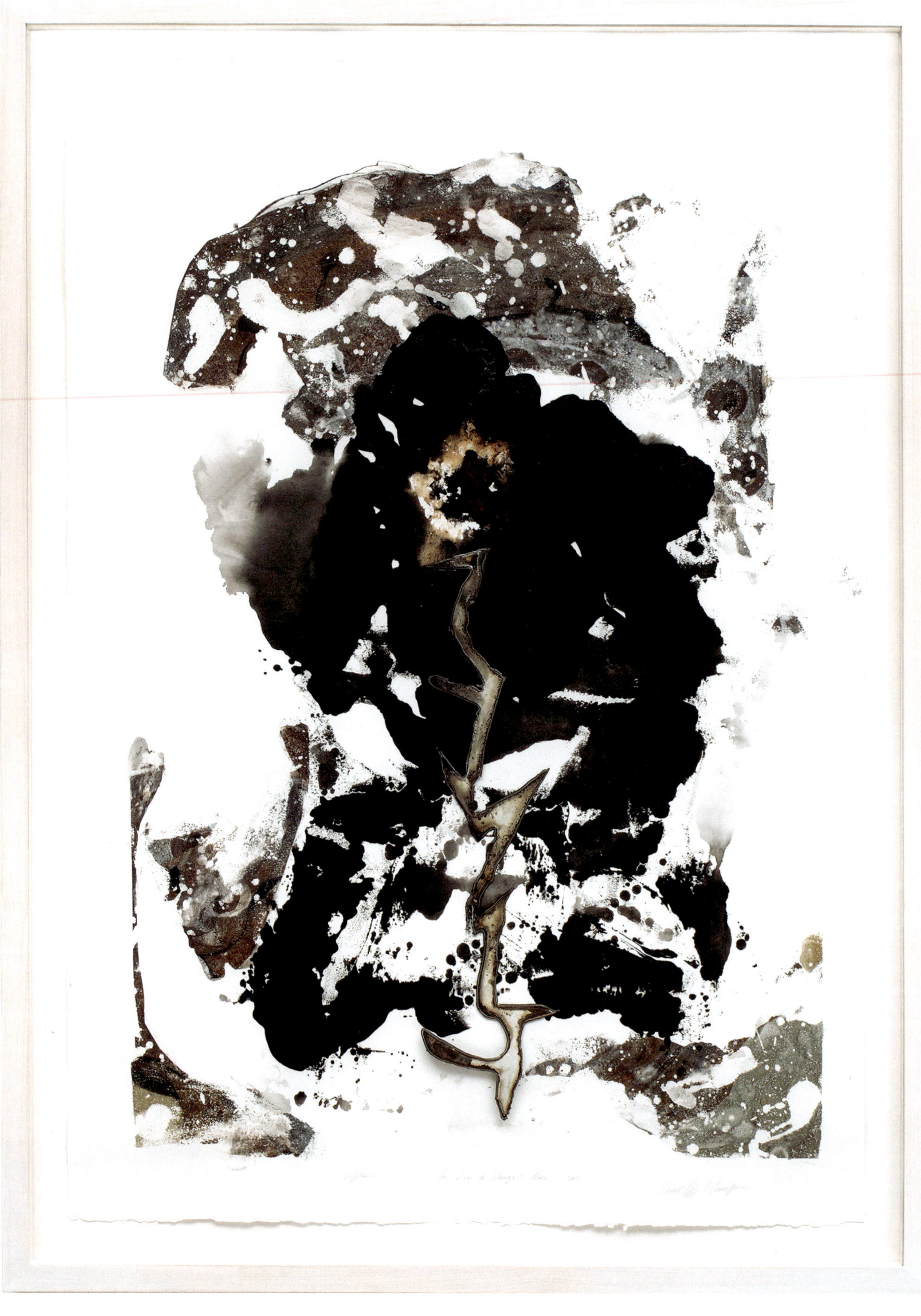

PLATE 69 *La Ira de Chango & Zeus*, from the Extreme Weather, Captiva series, 2016

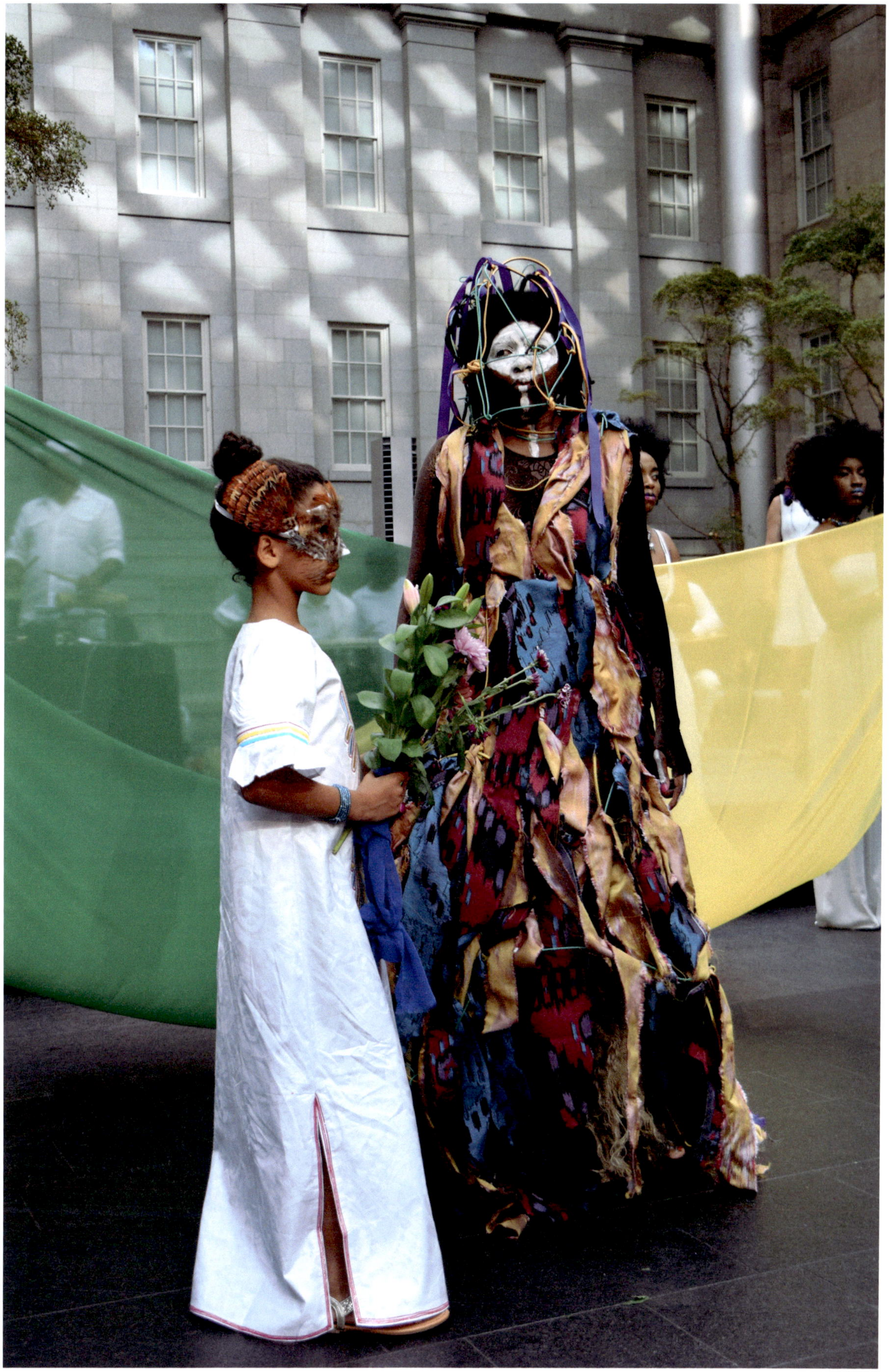

PLATE 70 *Identified*, 2016

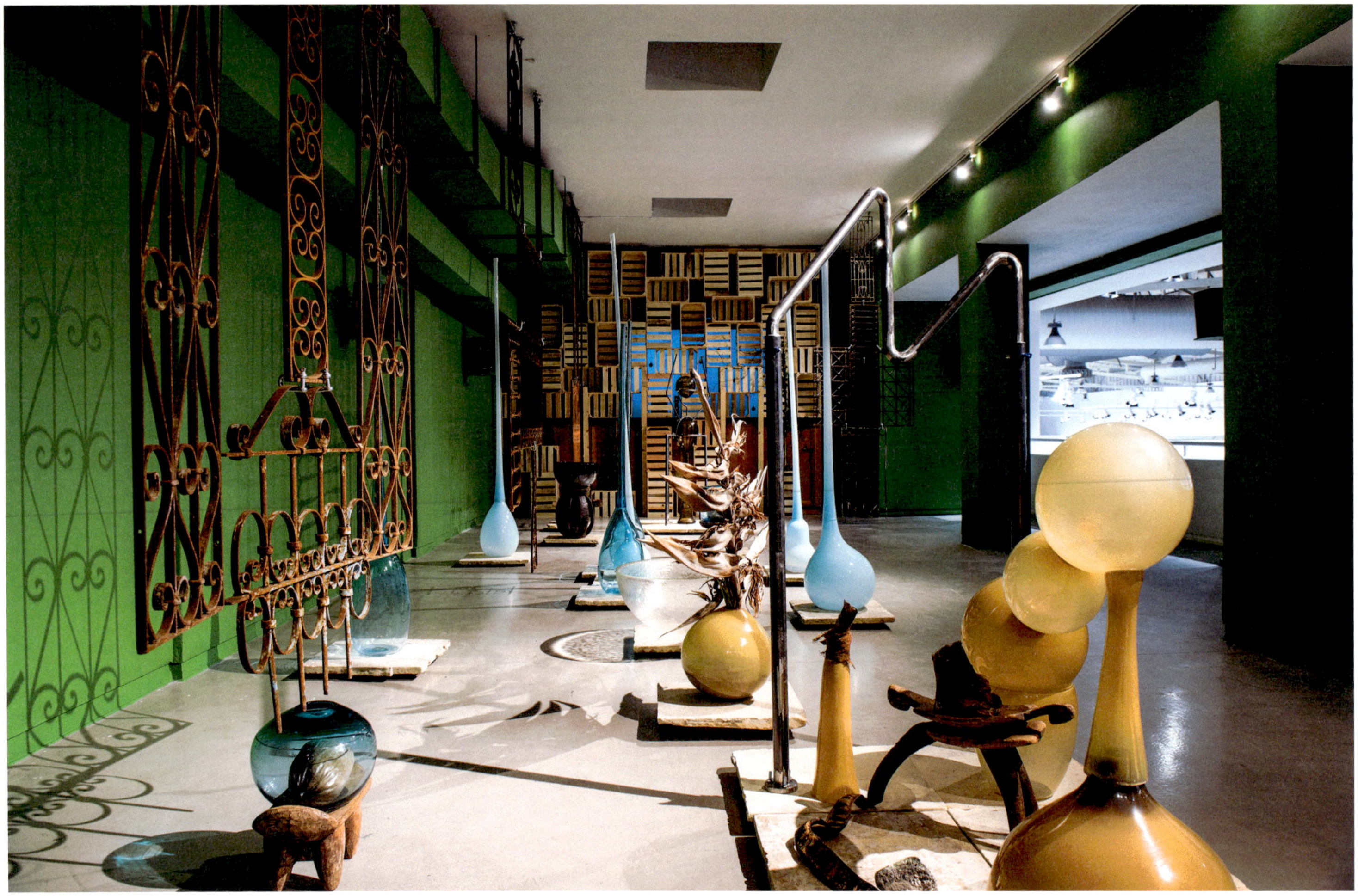

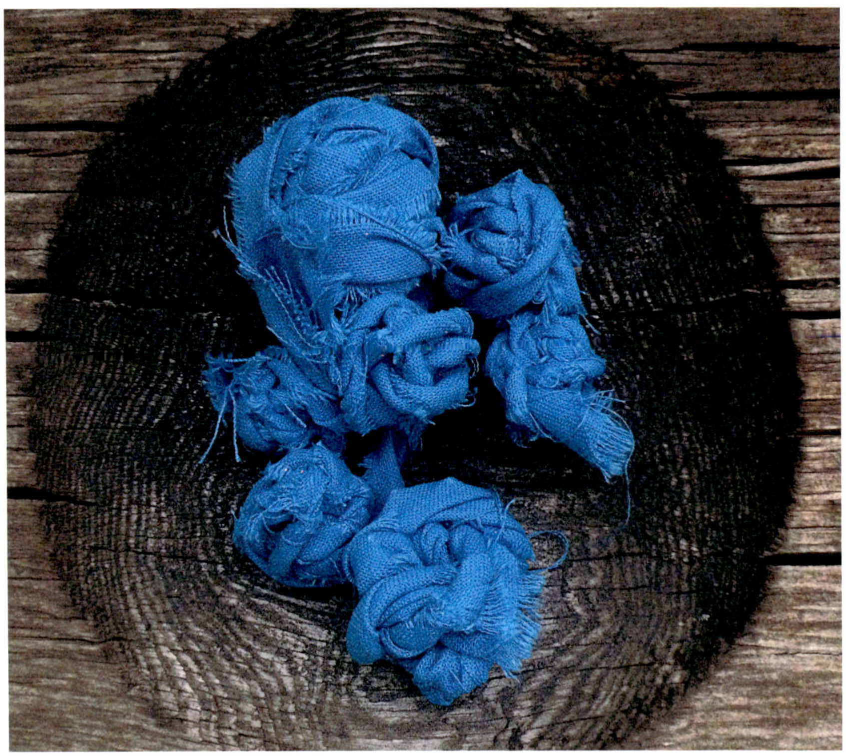

PLATE 71 *Matanzas Sound Map*, installation and stills from video, 2017

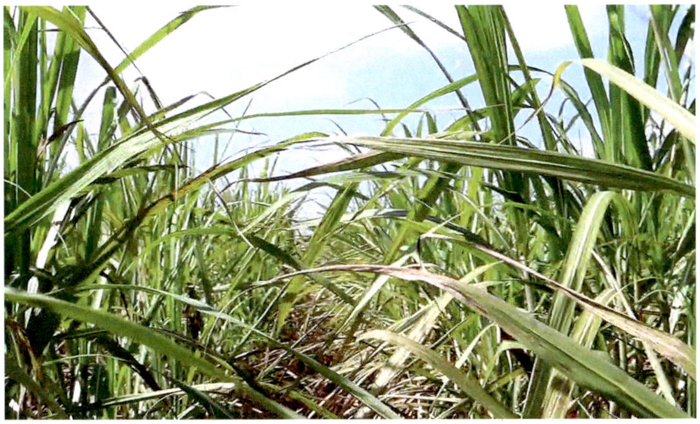

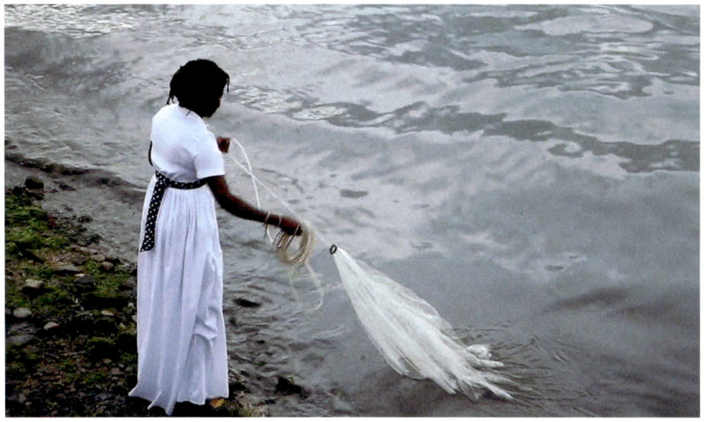

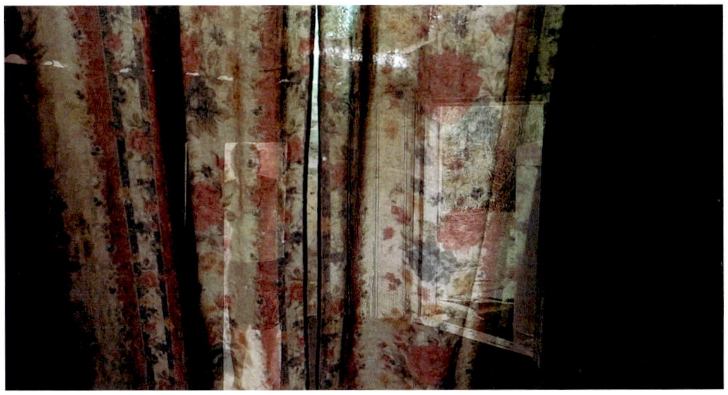

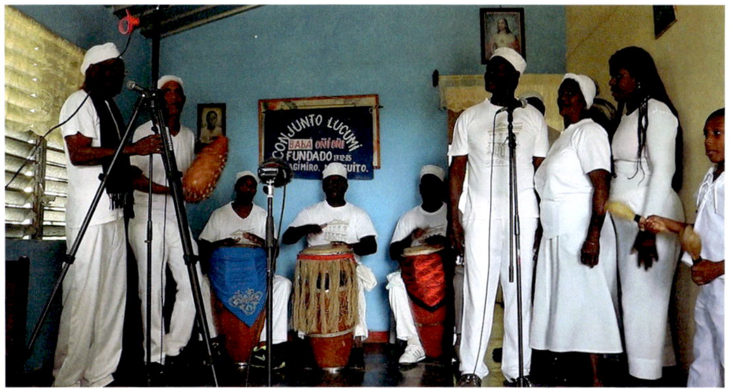
CONJUNTO LUCUMI
BABA OÑI OÑI
FUNDADO 17-12-15

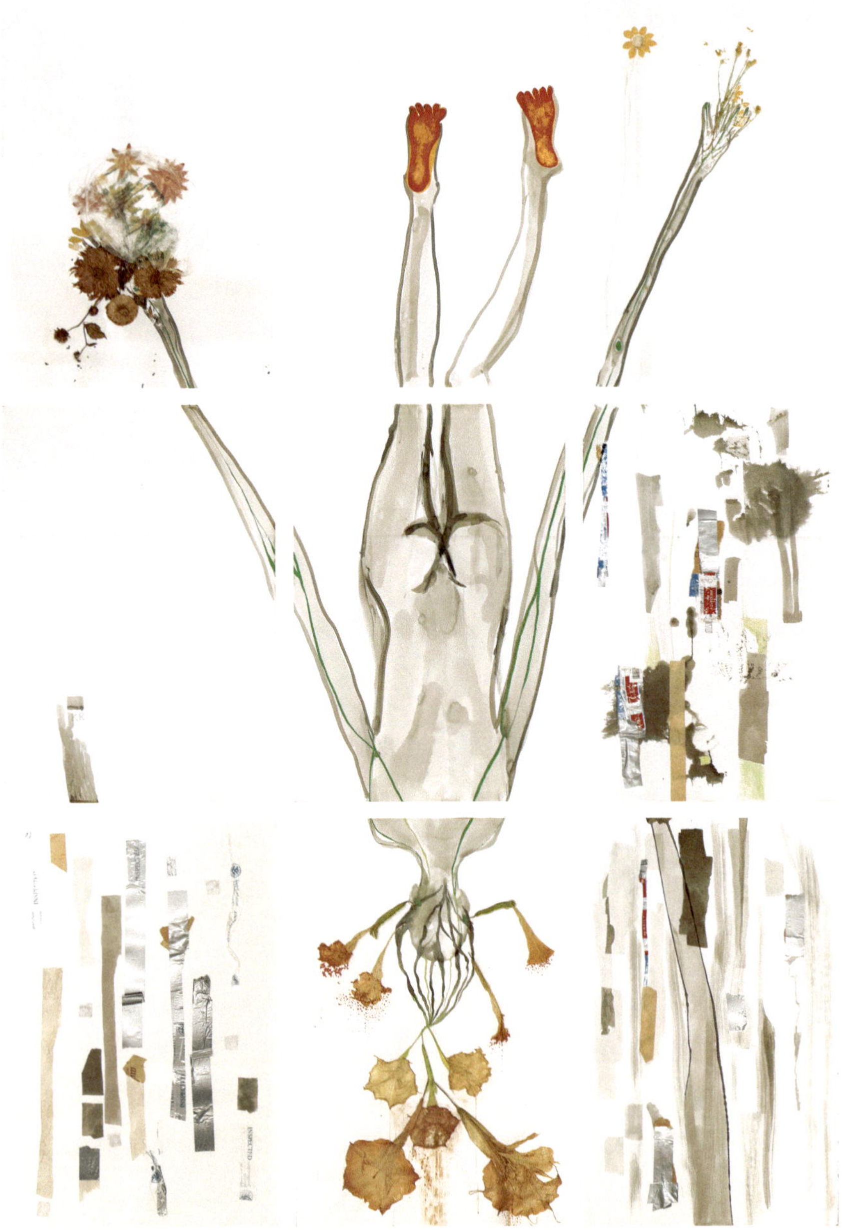

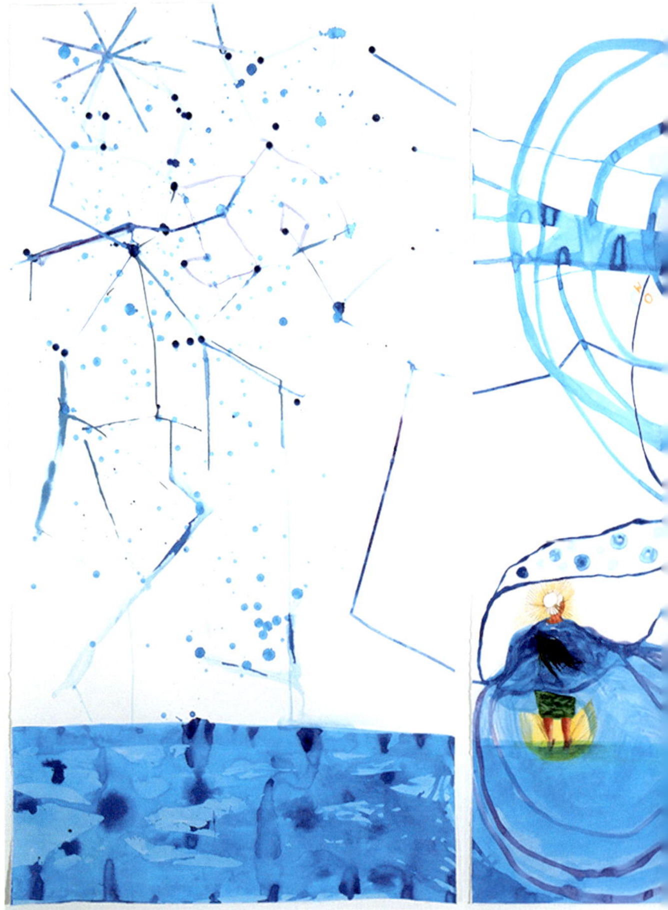

PLATE 72 *Angels' Trumpets, Devils' Bells*, 2019

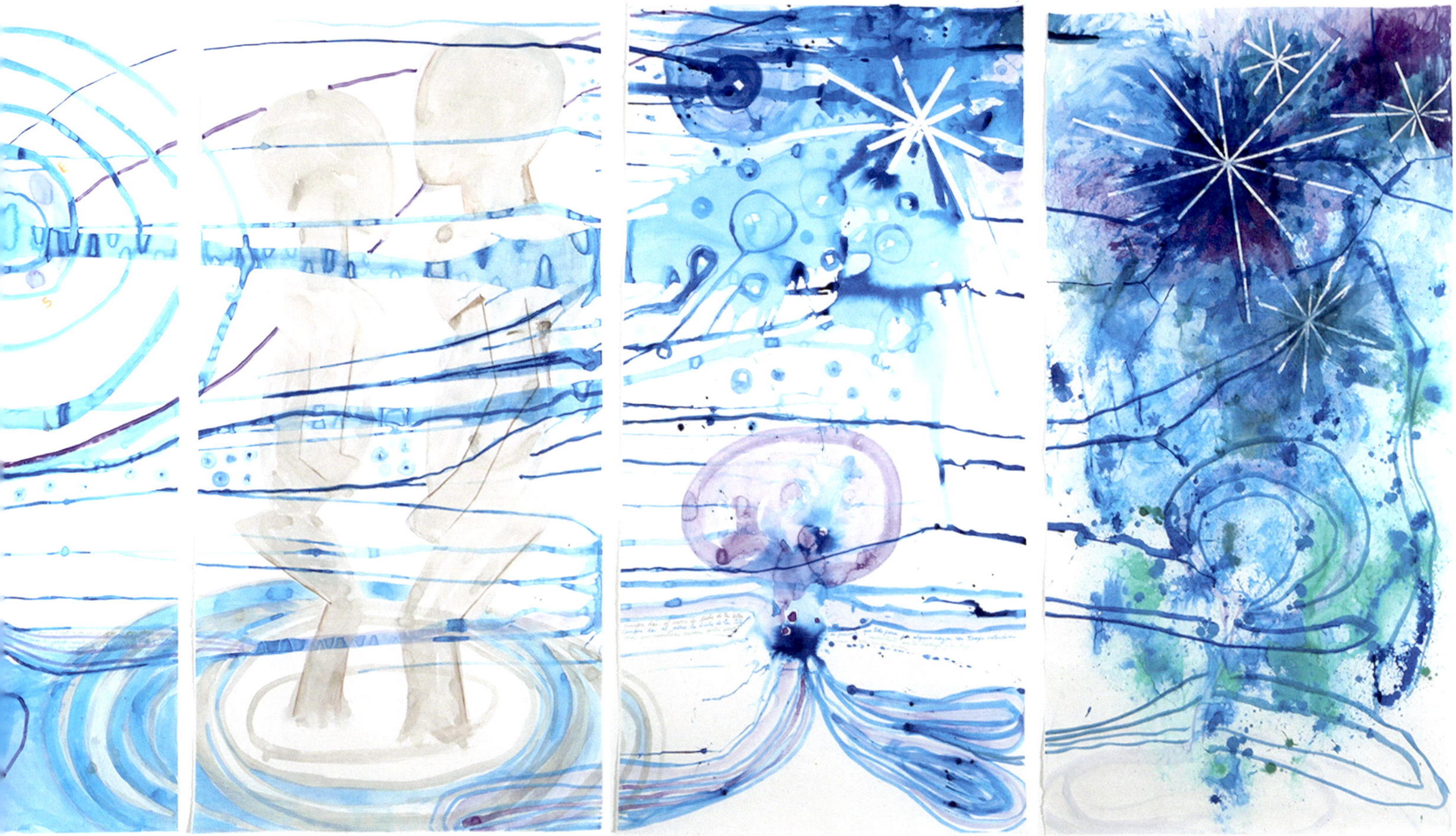

PLATE 73 *She Always Knew of the Space in Between*, 2019

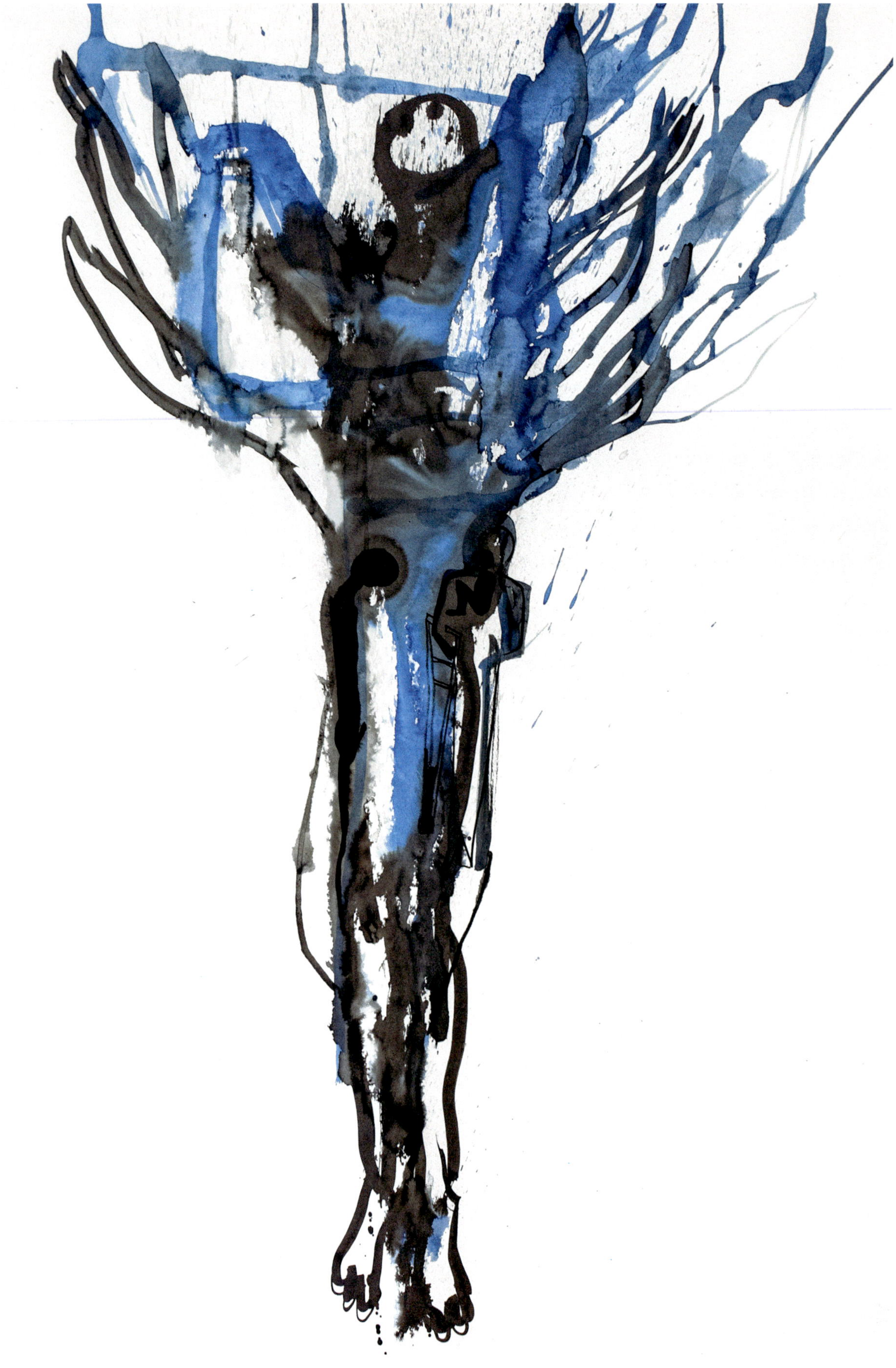

PLATE 74 *Wet All Day*, from the Un Pedazo de Mar series, 2019

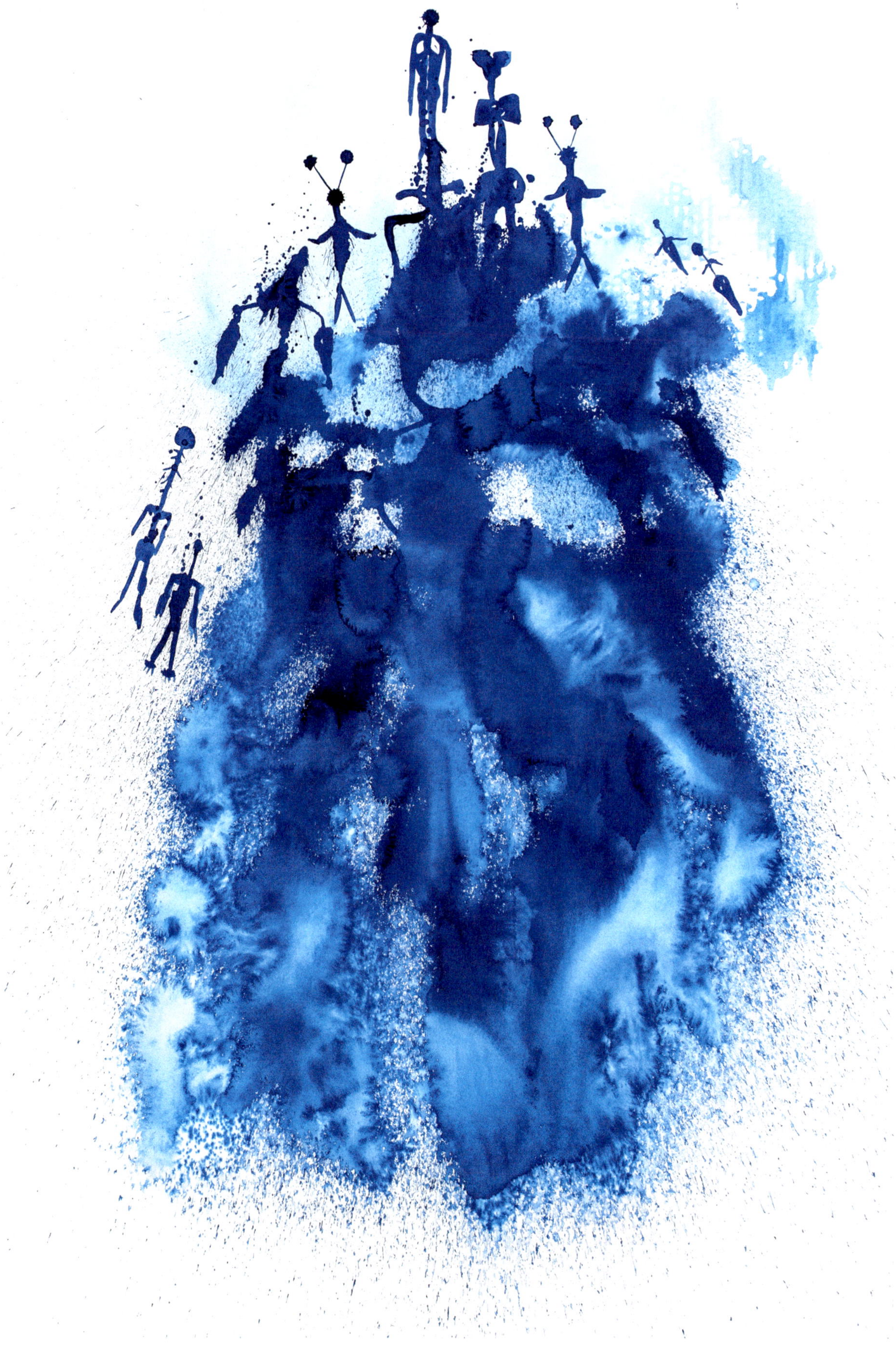

PLATE 75 *An Army of Angels*, from the Un Pedazo de Mar series, 2019

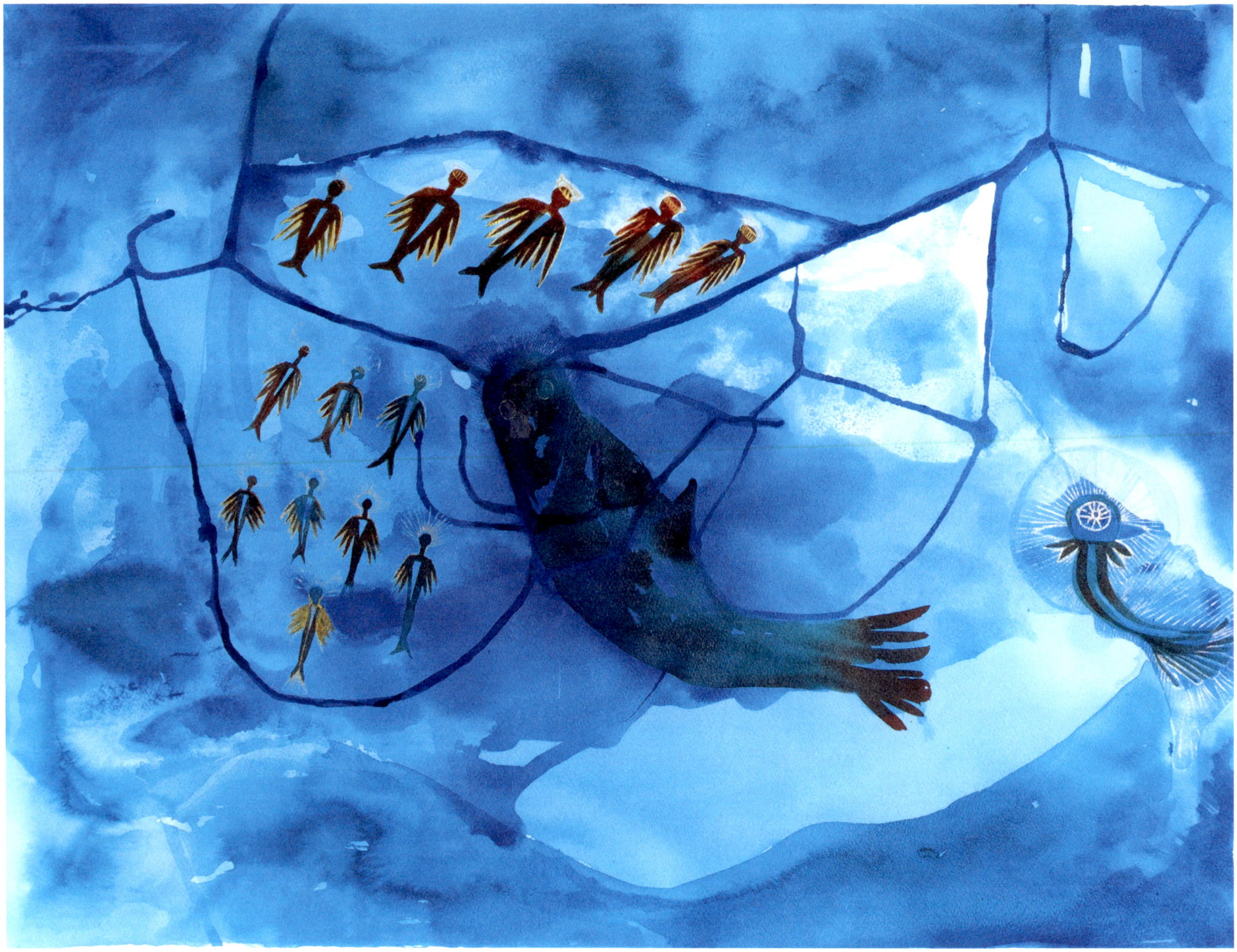

PLATE 76 *Floating between Temperature Zones*, from the Un Pedazo de Mar series, 2019

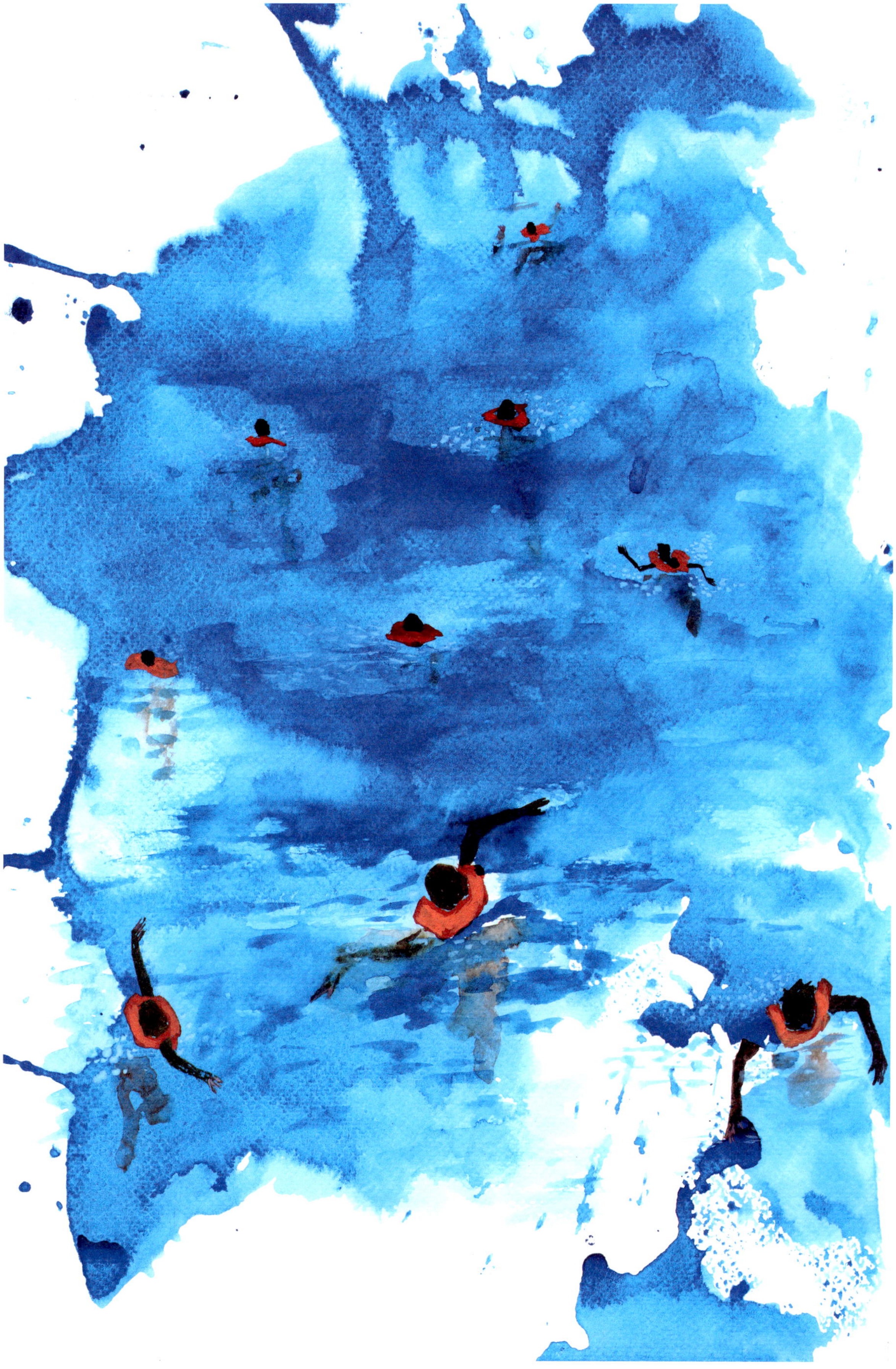

PLATE 77 *Untitled*, from the Un Pedazo de Mar series, 2019

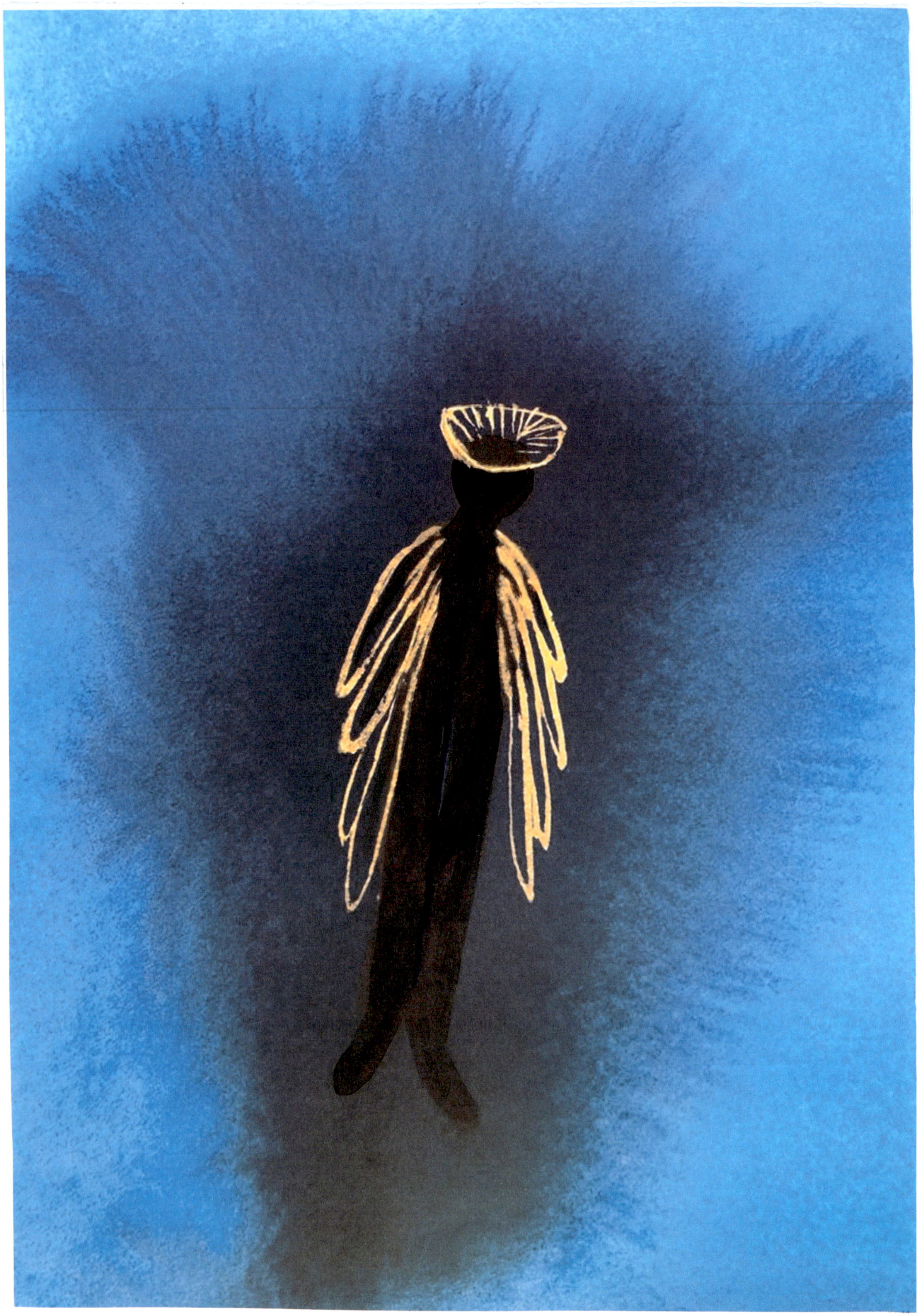

PLATE 78 *Descending Angel*, from the Un Pedazo de Mar series, 2019

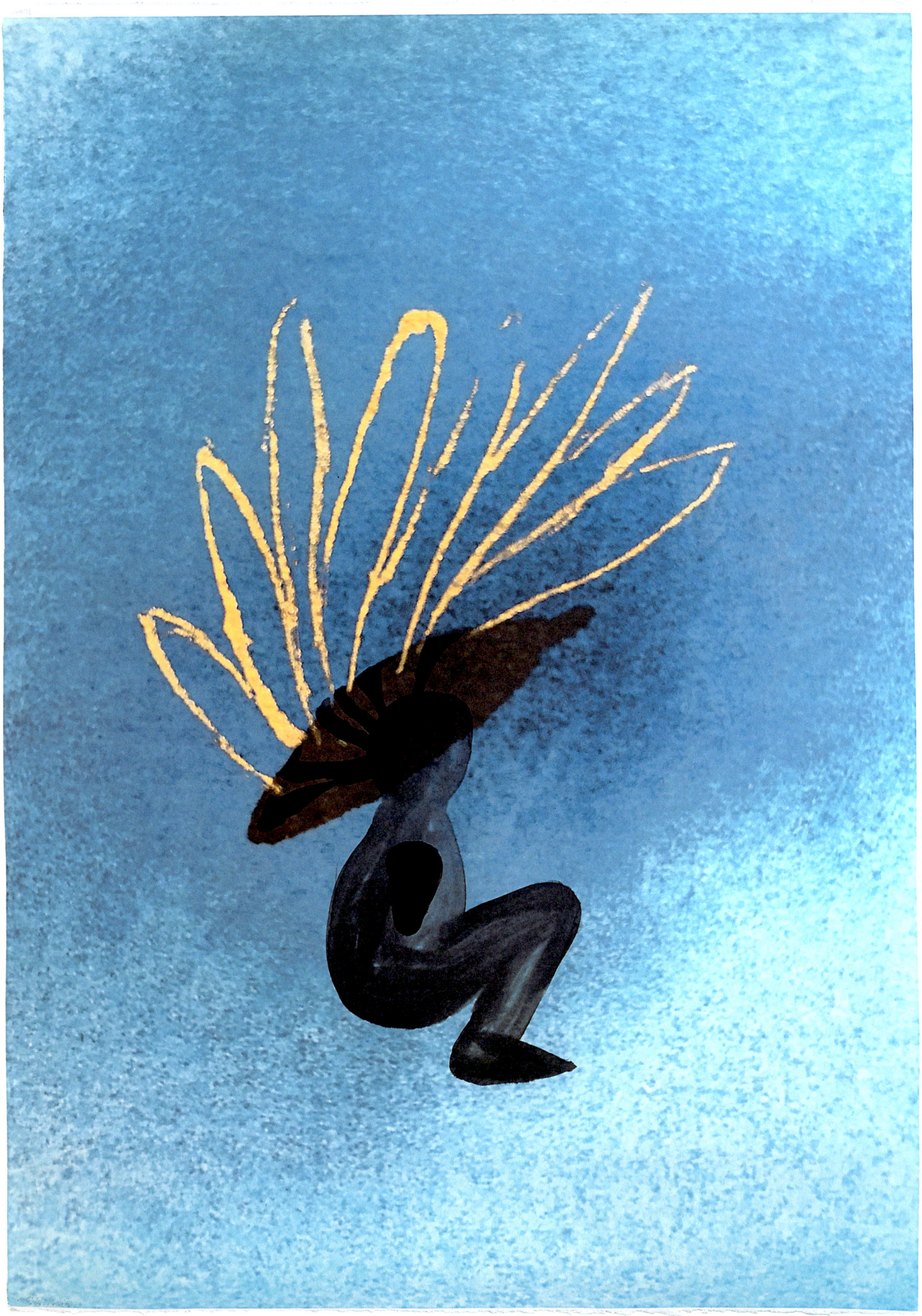

PLATE 79 *Descending Angel 2*, from the Un Pedazo de Mar series, 2019

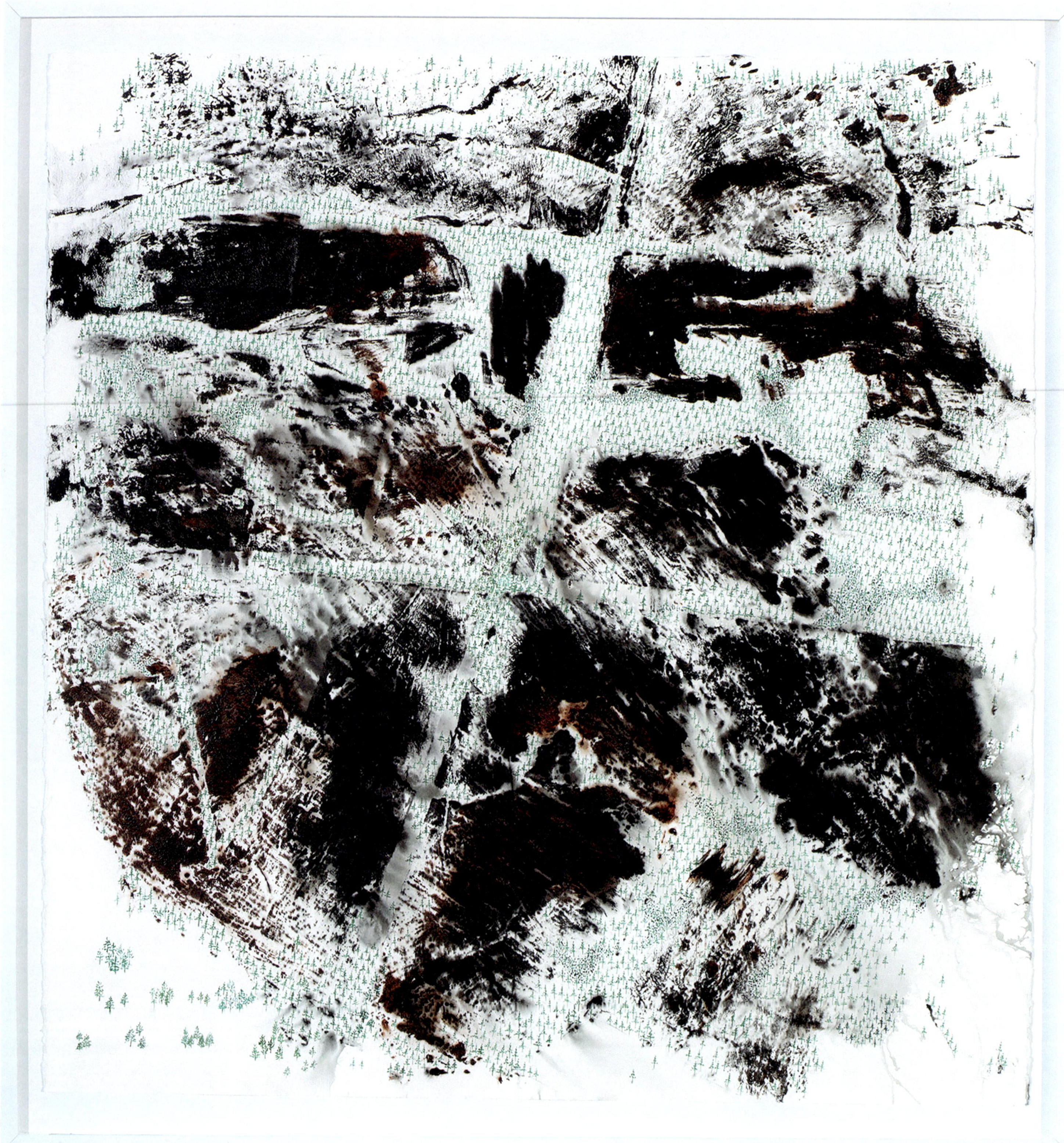

PLATE 80 *Because the human body is a tree, Spring Awakening II*, 2019–20

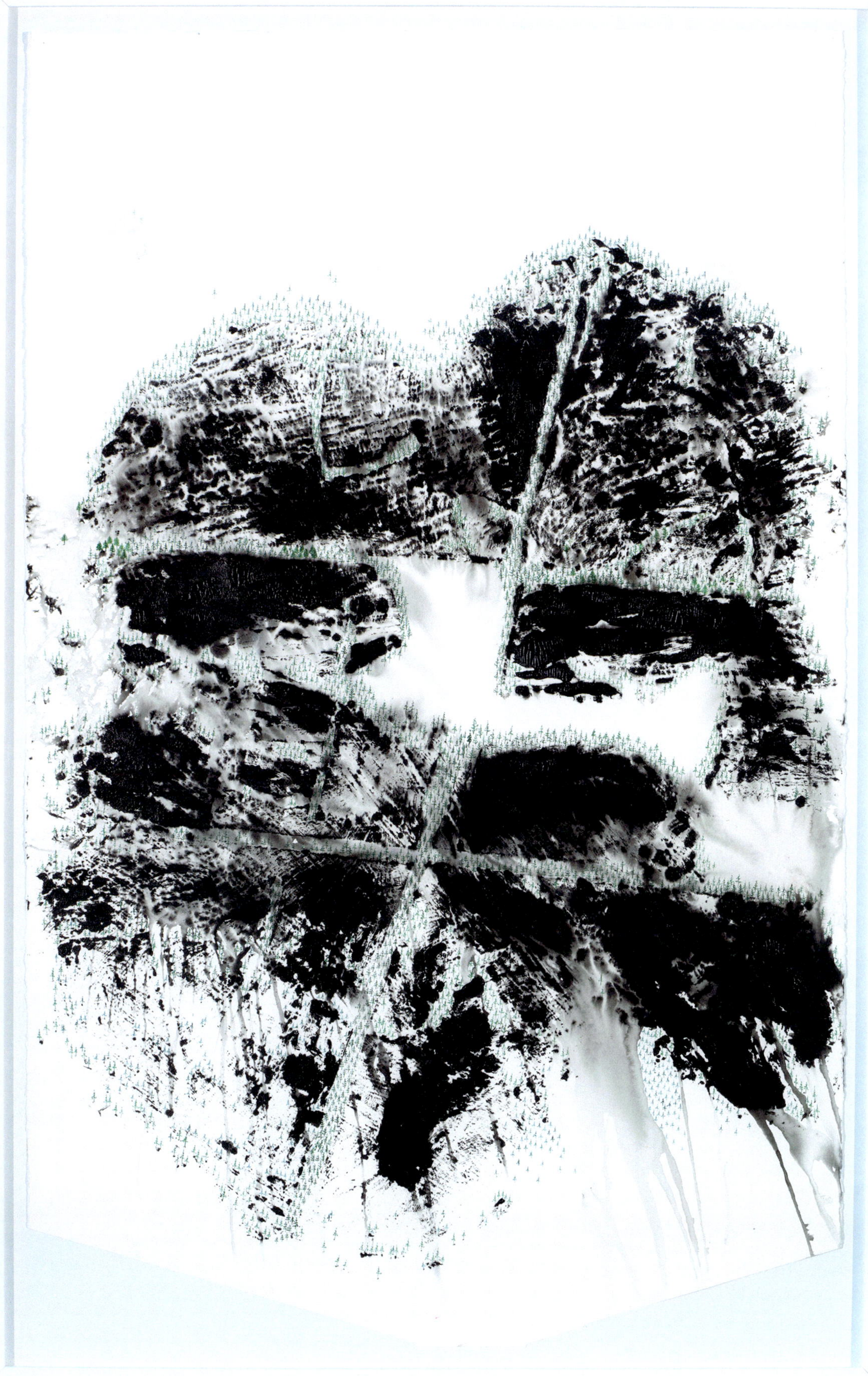

PLATE 81 *Because the human body is a tree, Spring Awakening III*, 2019–20

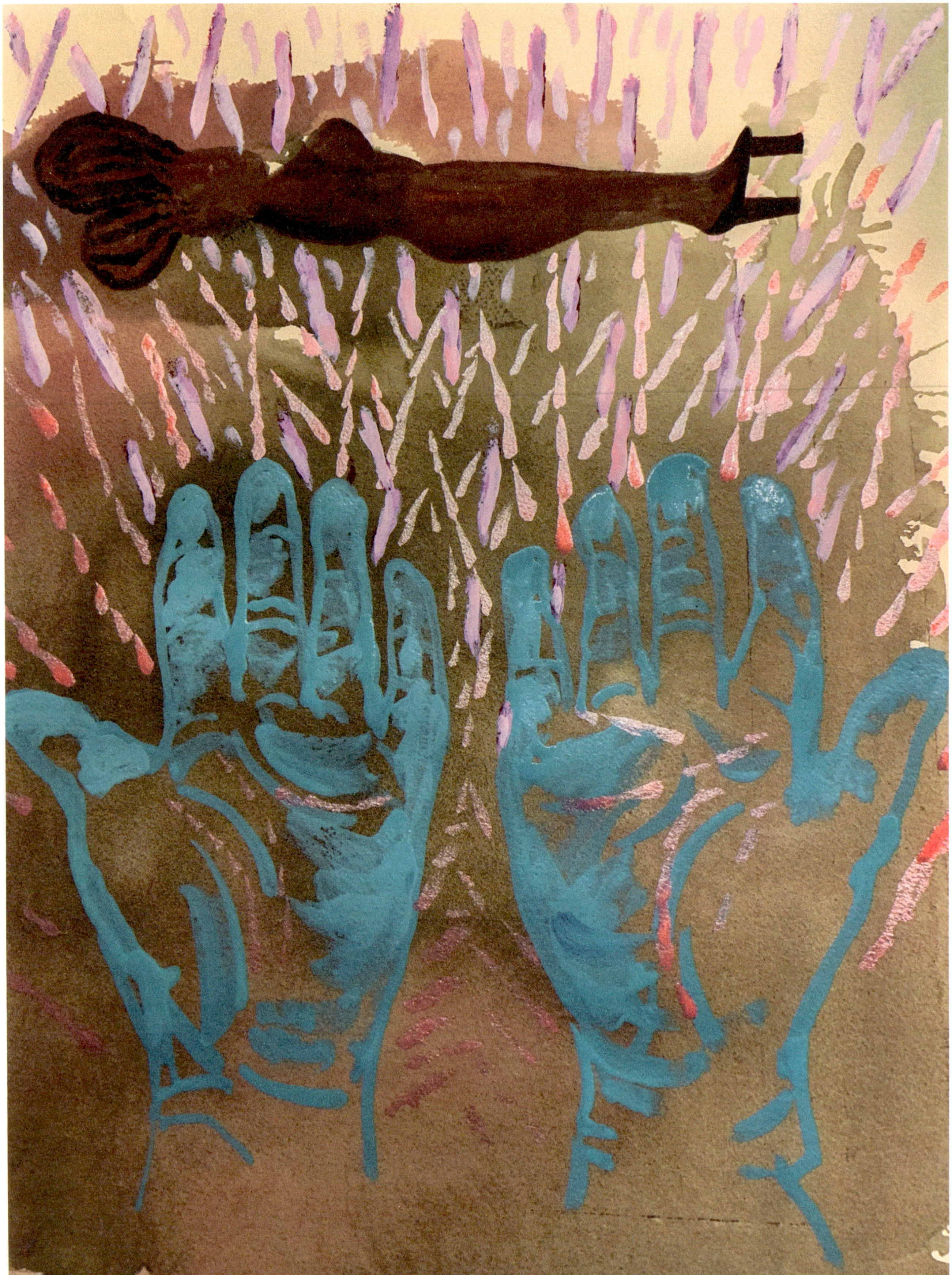

PLATE 82 *Miasma #1*, 2020

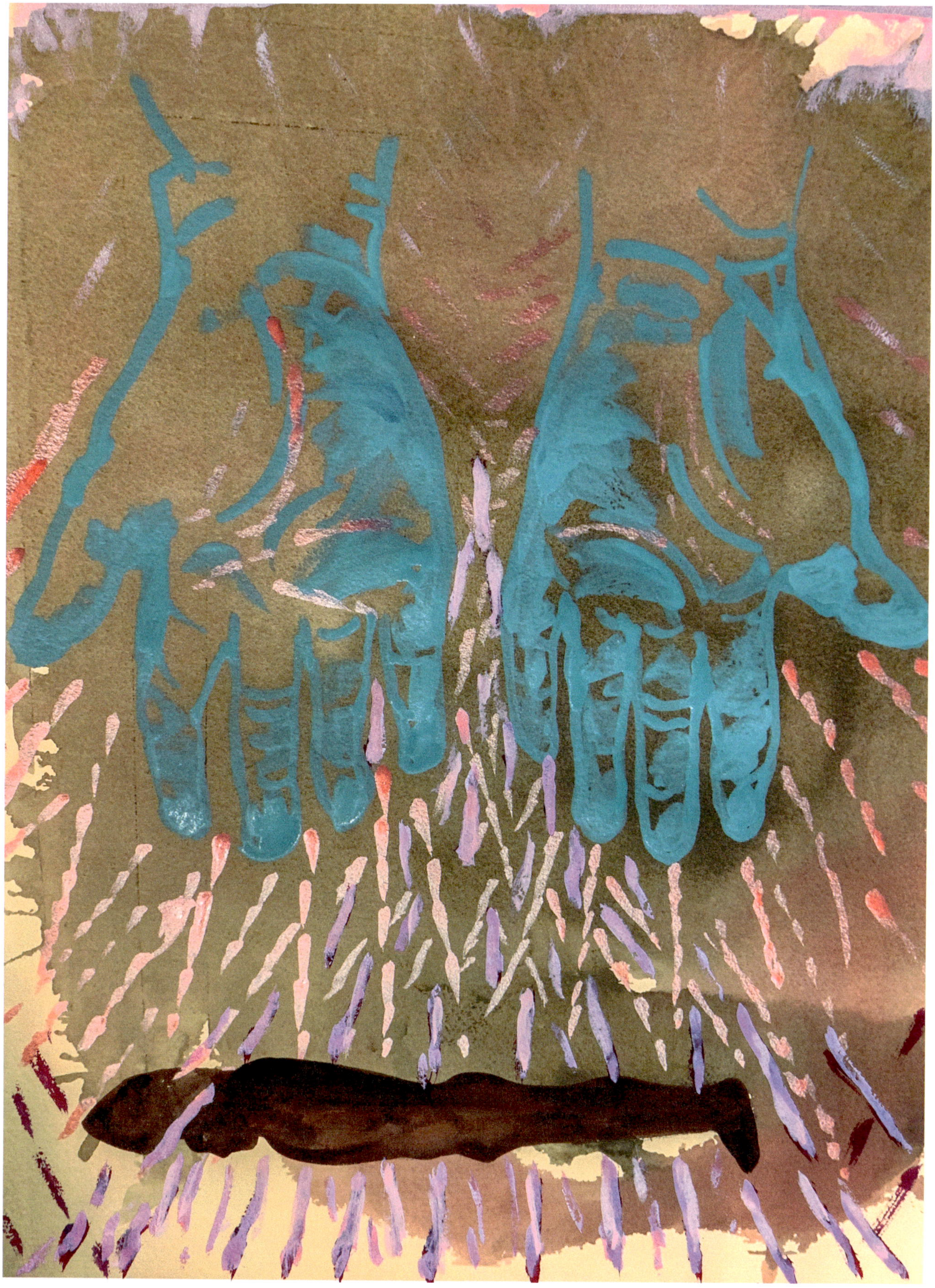

PLATE 83 *Miasma #2*, 2020

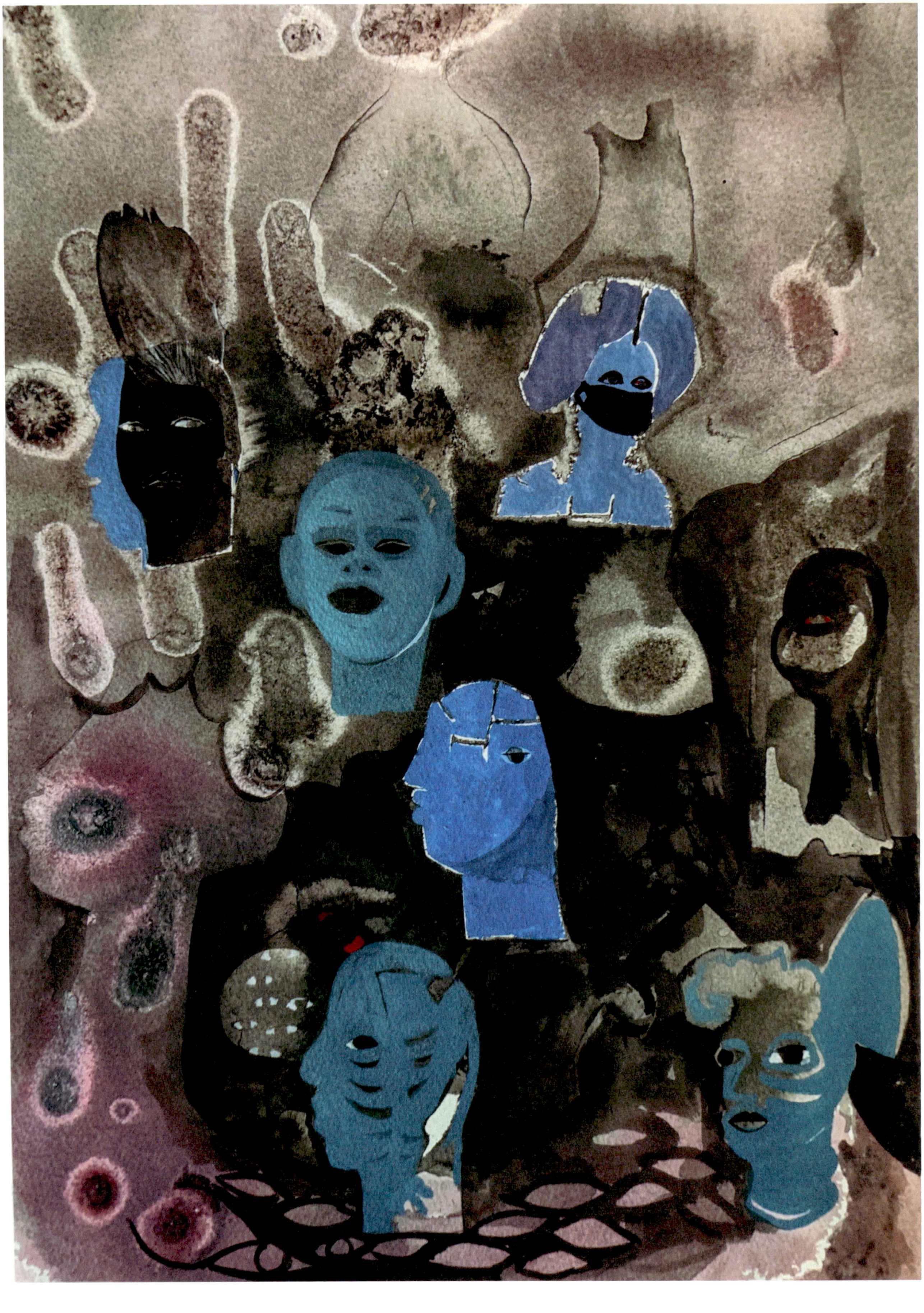

PLATE 84 *Miasma #5*, 2020

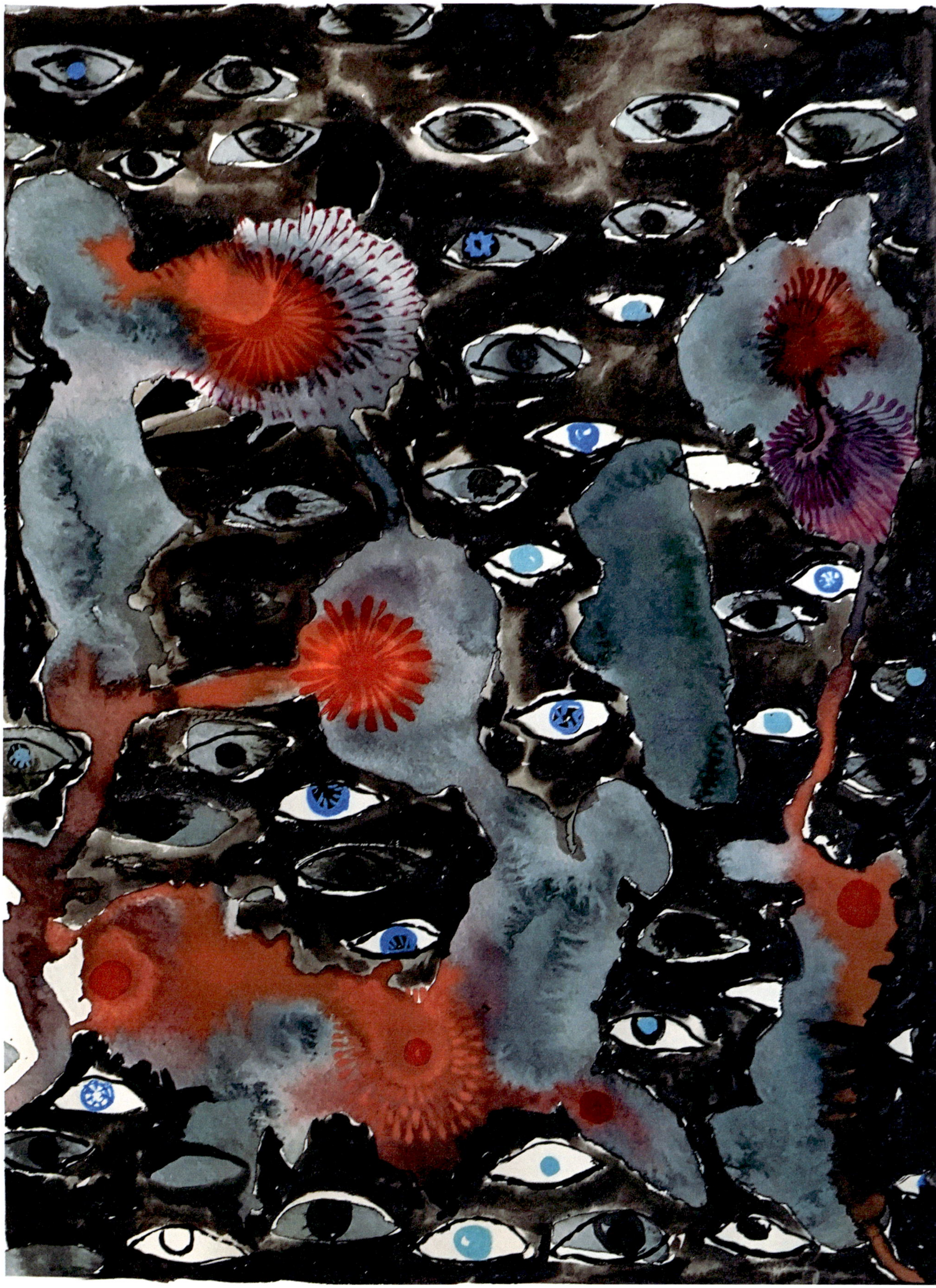

PLATE 85 *Miasma #7*, 2020

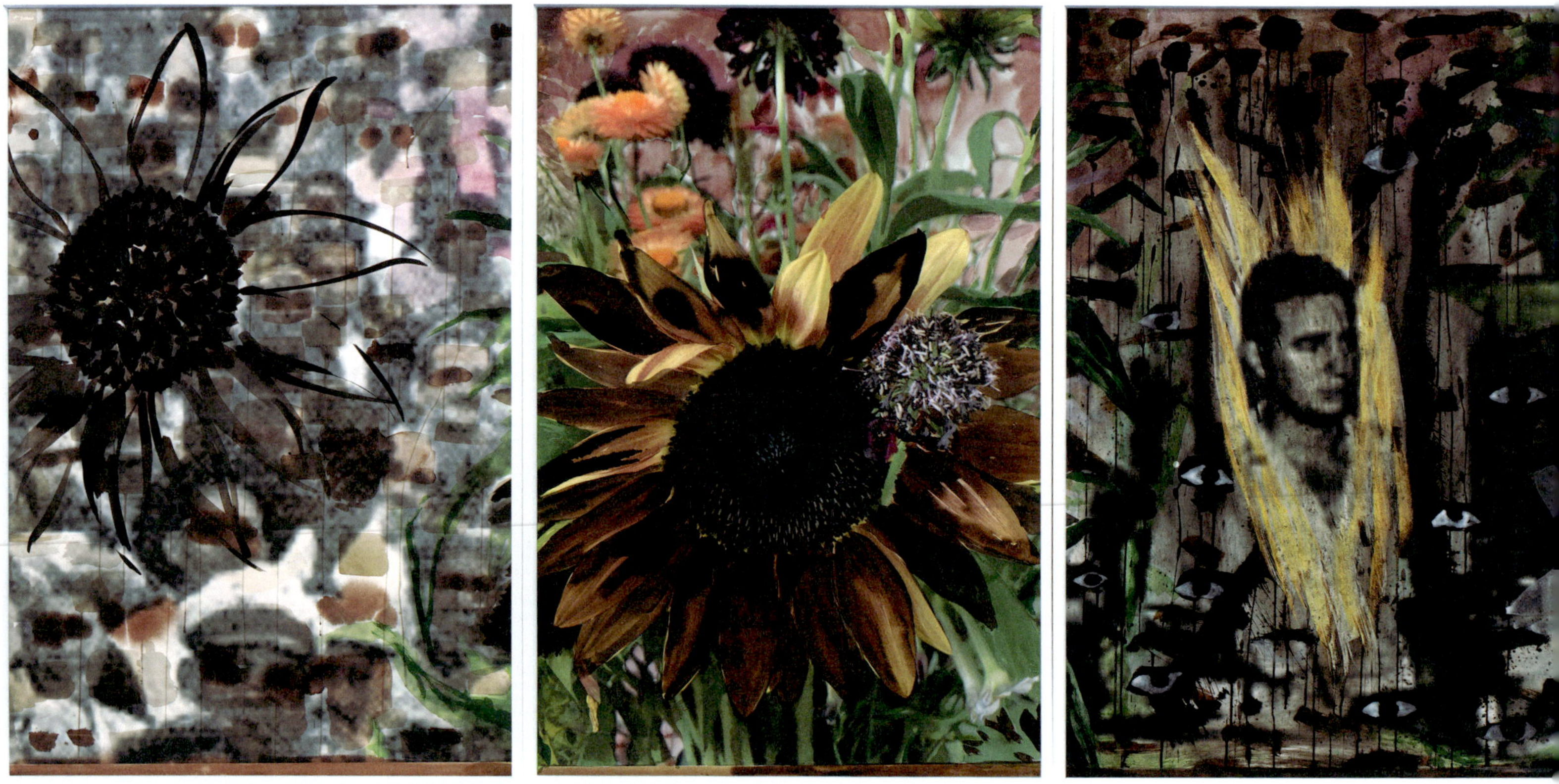

PLATE 86 *Carta Natal 7/26/1953, 7/22/1959, 7/13/1989, 7/11/2021*, 2021

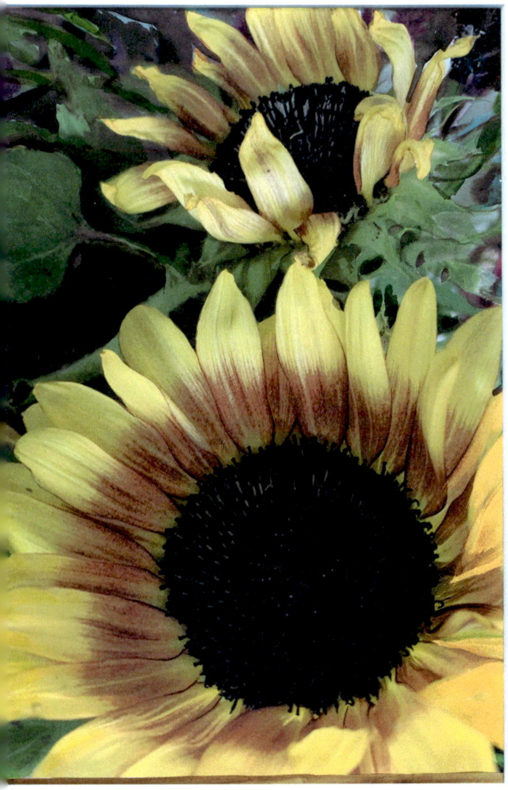

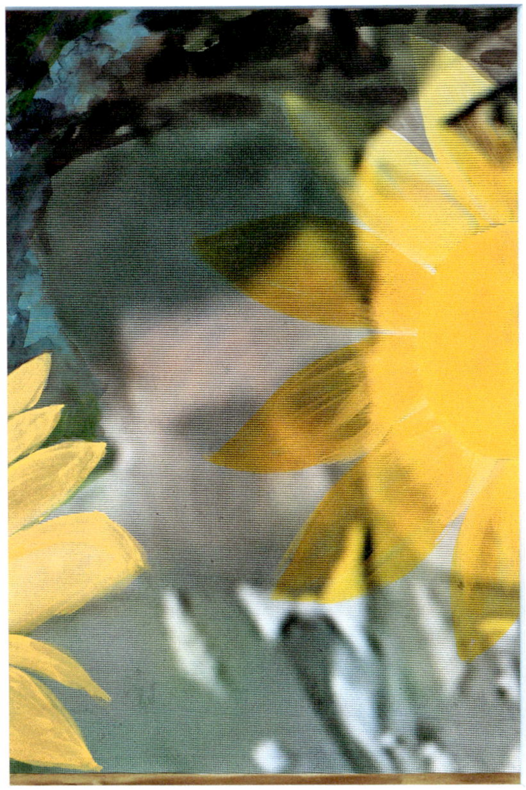

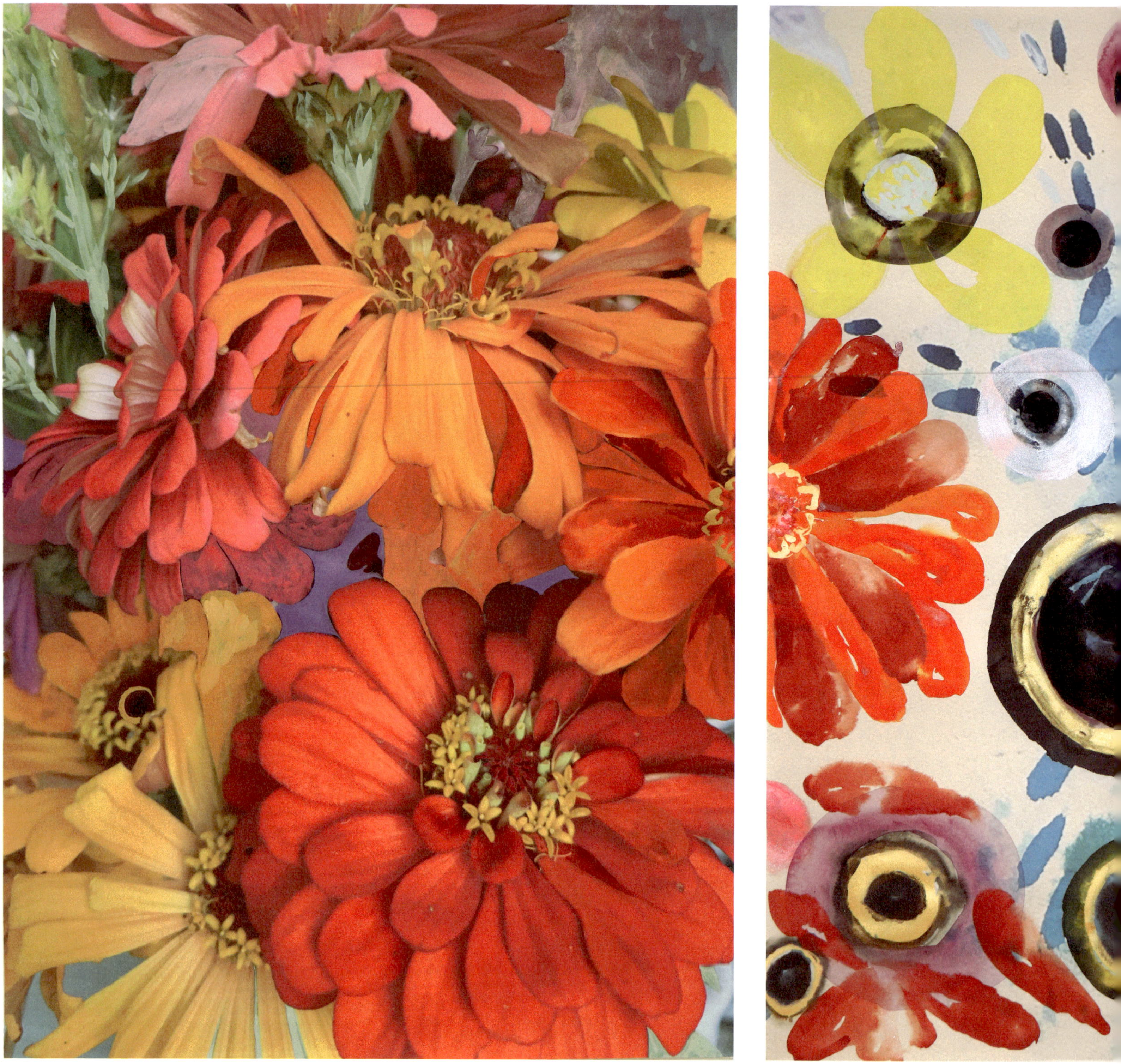

PLATE 87 *Butterfly Eyes (for Breonna Taylor)*, 2021

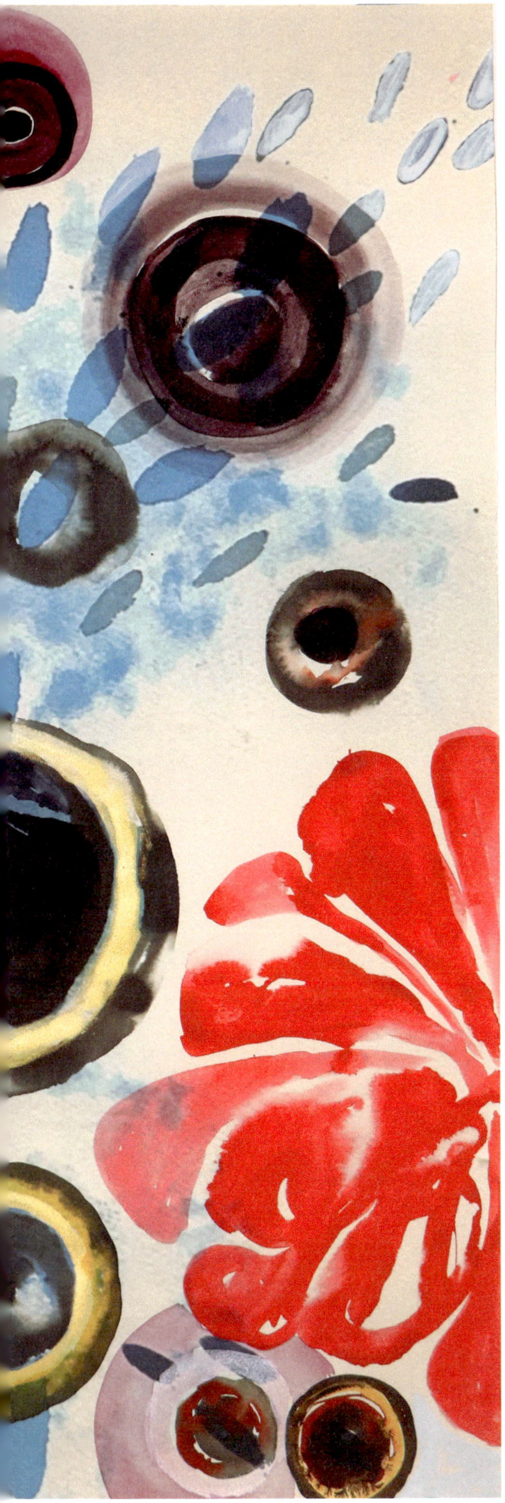

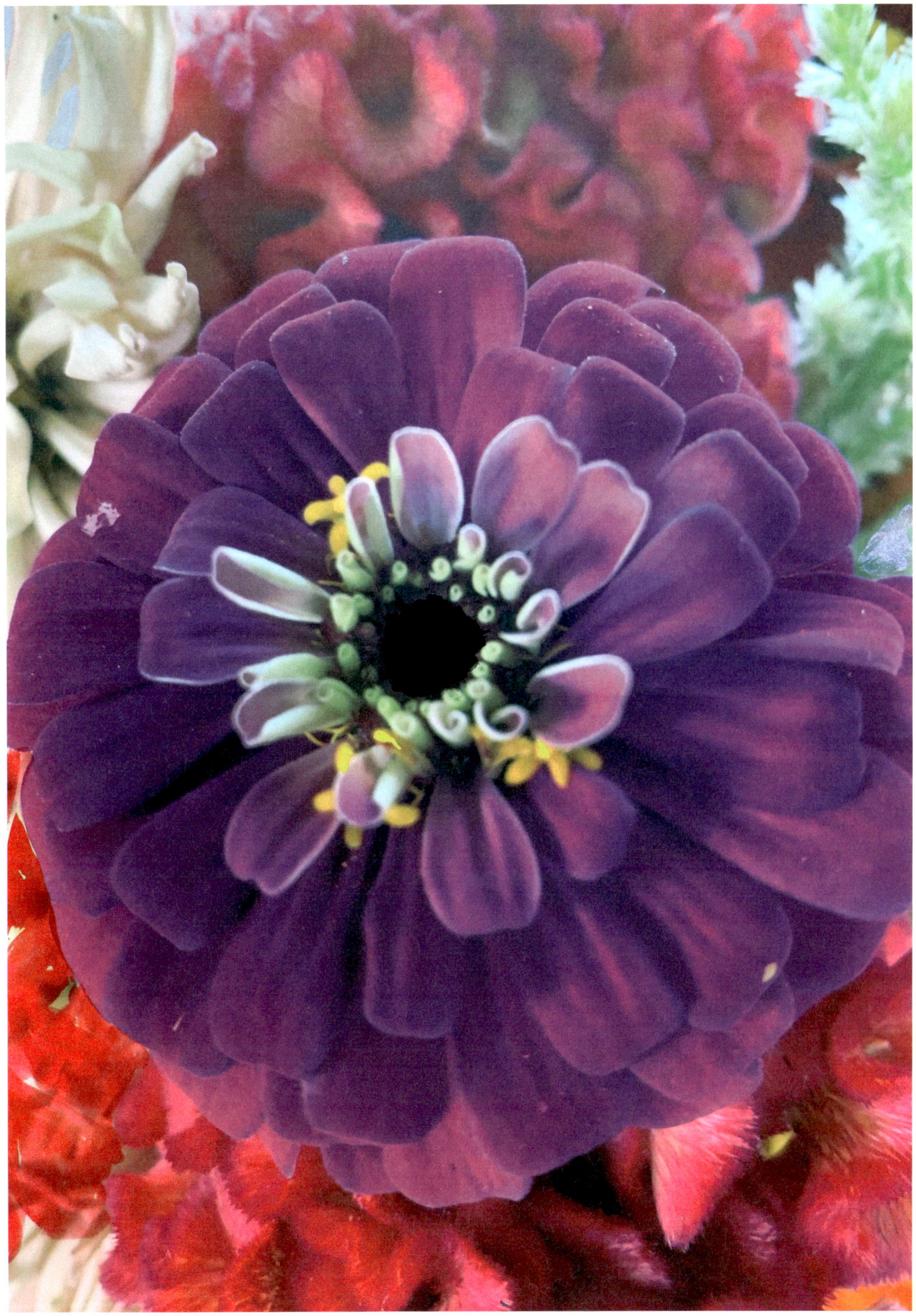

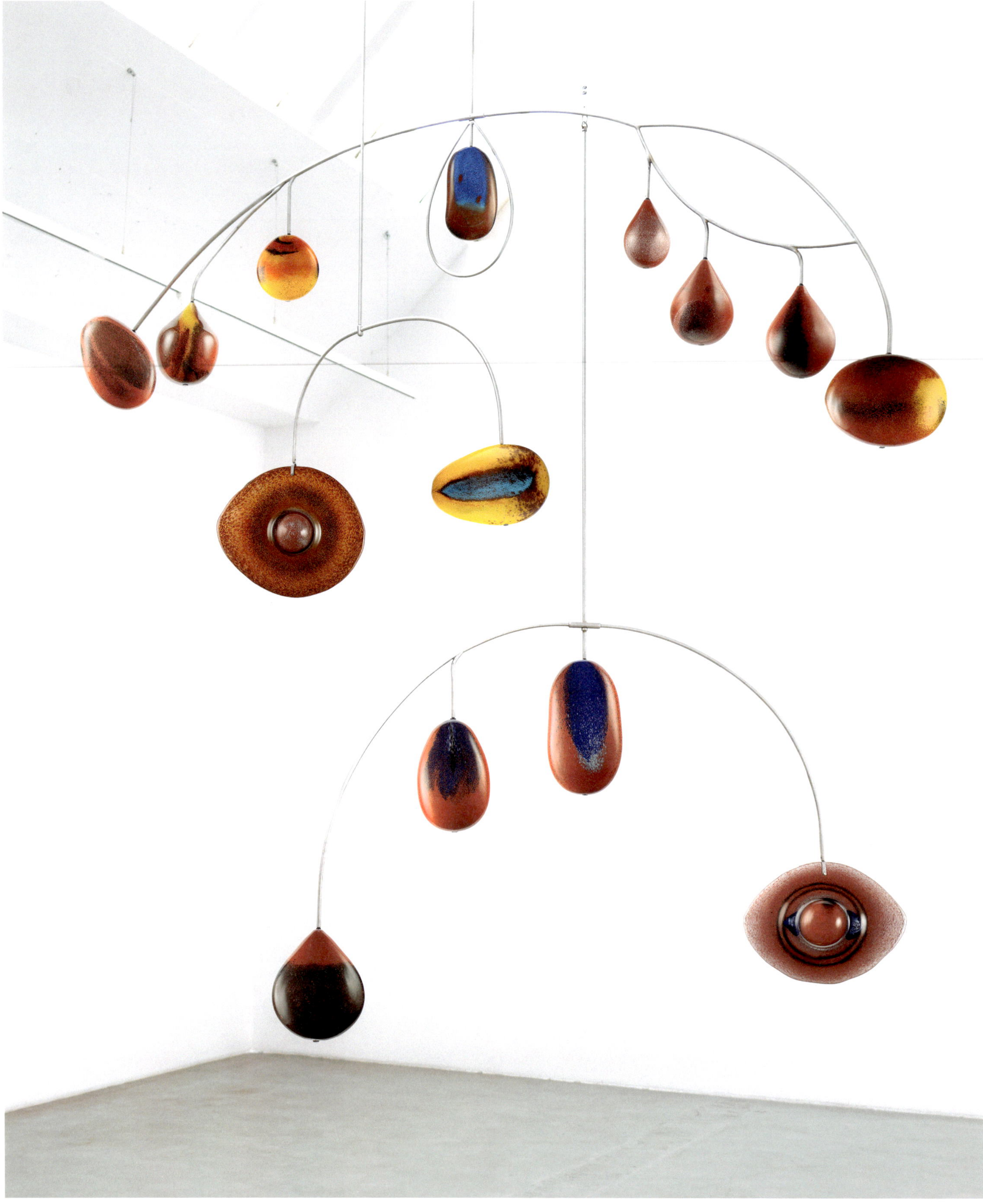

PLATE 88 *Mobile #2*, from The Rise of the Butterflies series, 2021

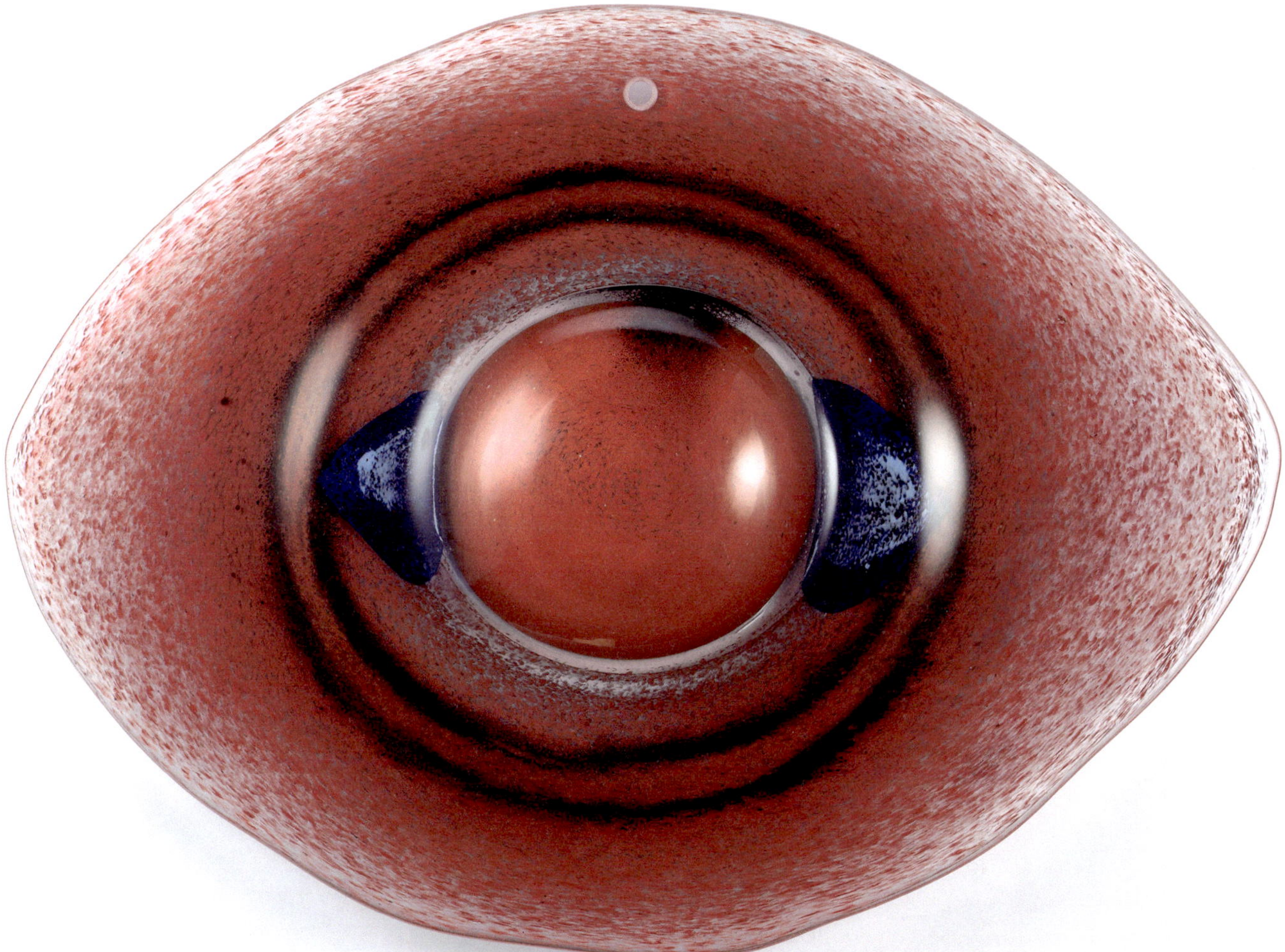

PLATE 89 *Mobile #2*, detail from The Rise of the Butterflies series, 2021

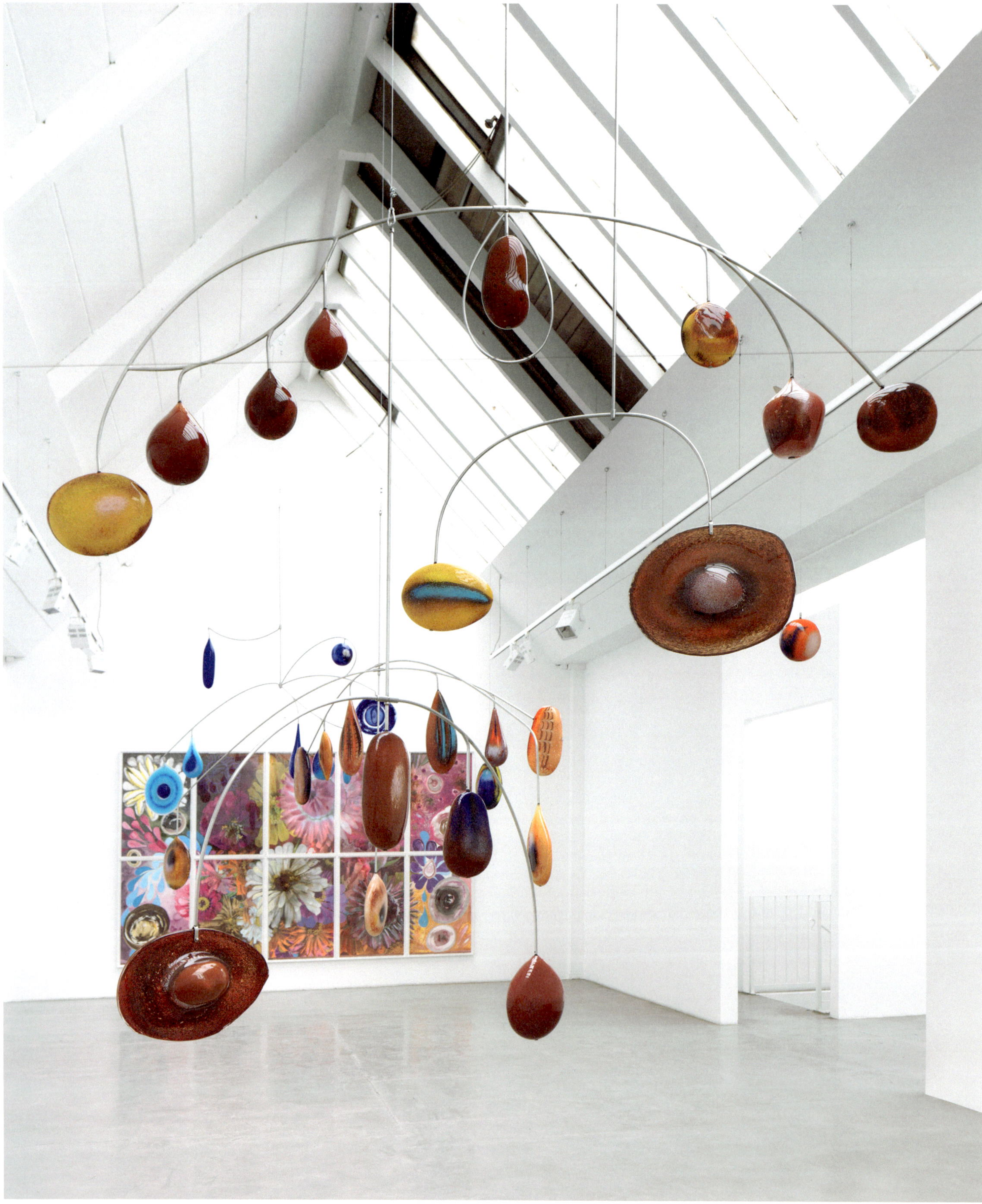

PLATE 90 Installation view, showing *Mobile #2* (front) and *Mobile #1* (middle), from The Rise of the Butterflies series, 2021

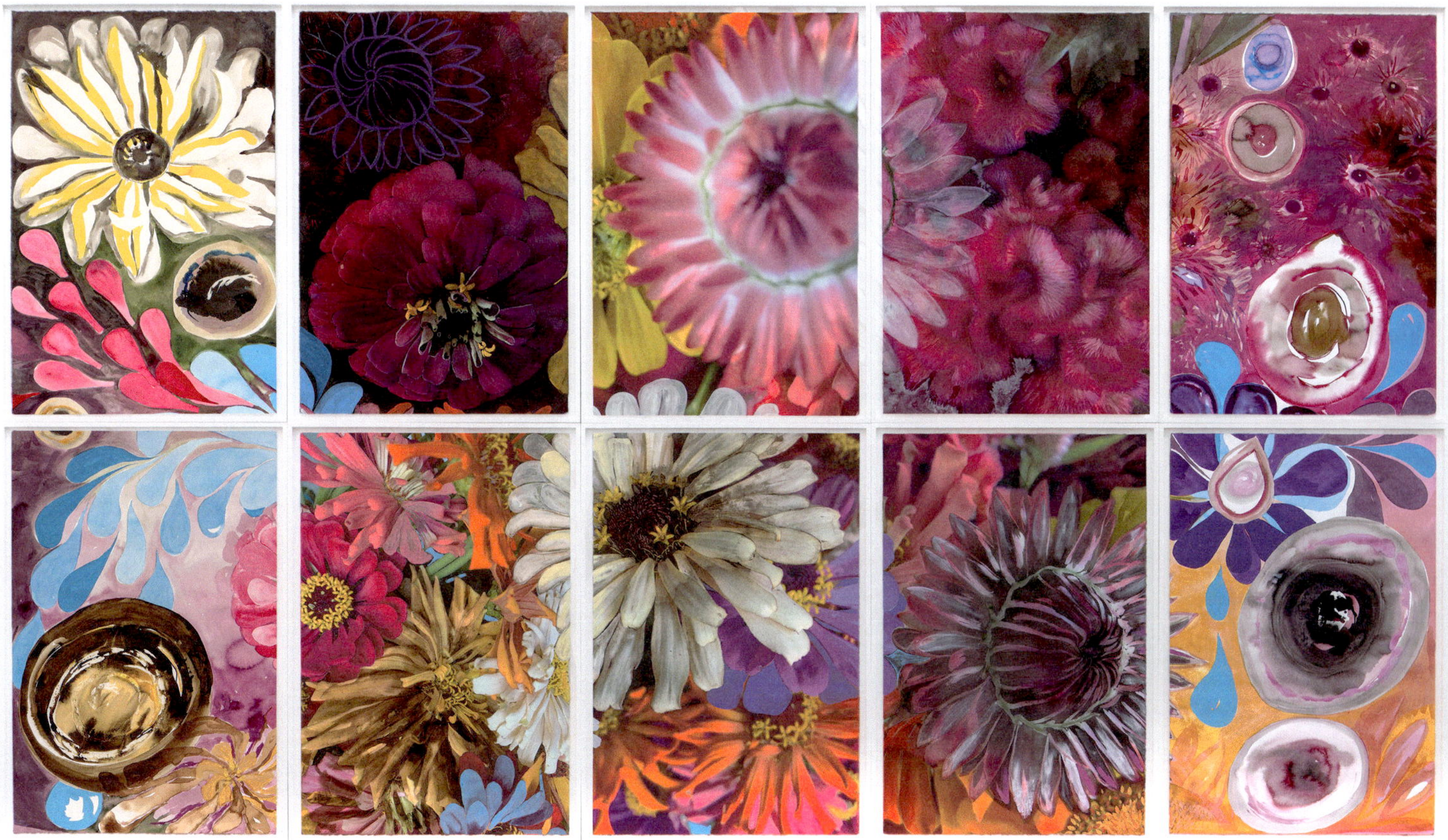

PLATE 91 Untitled, from The Rise of the Butterflies series, 2021

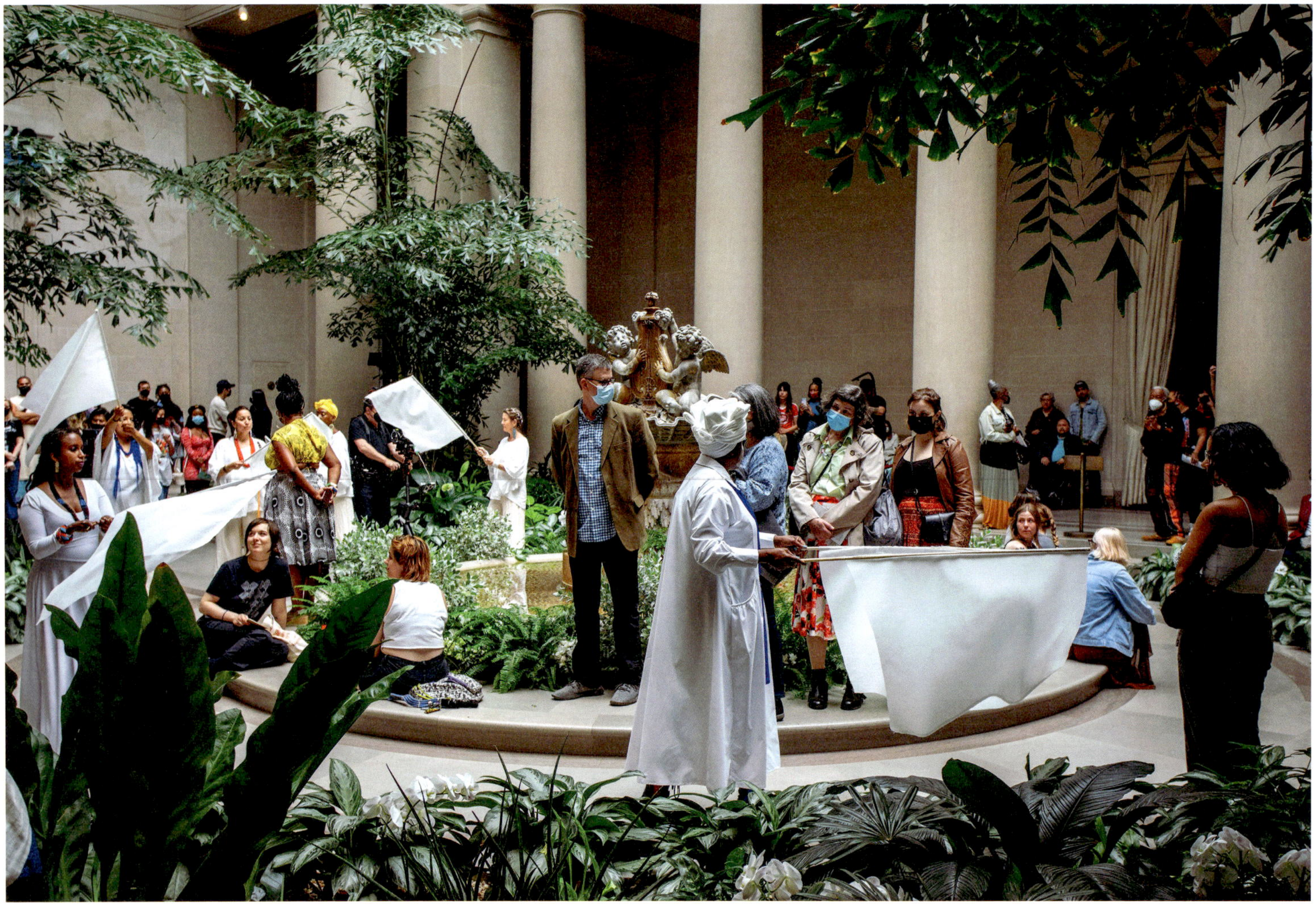

PLATE 92 *When We Gather*, performance, 2022

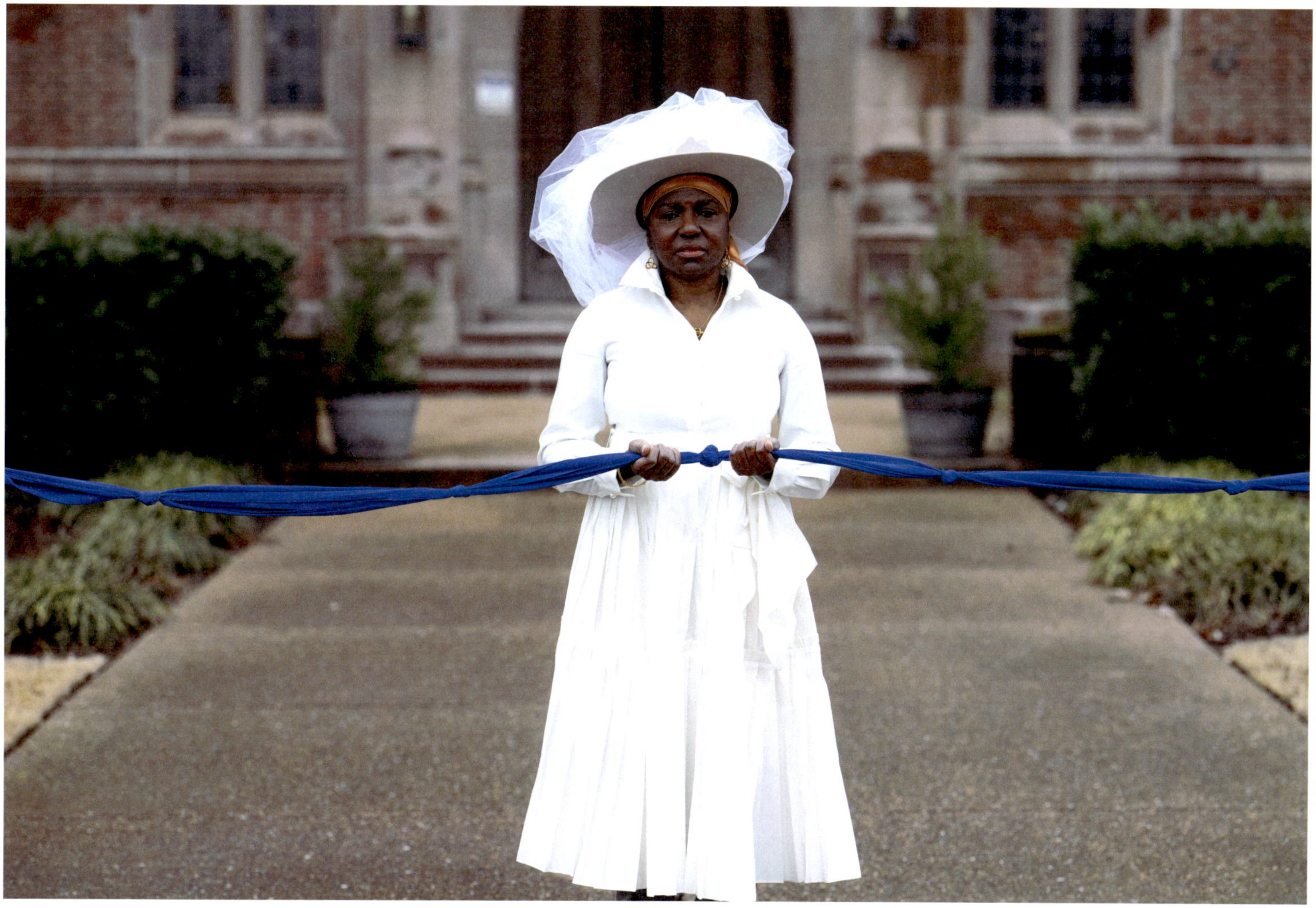

PLATE 93 *When We Gather*, performance and video, 2021

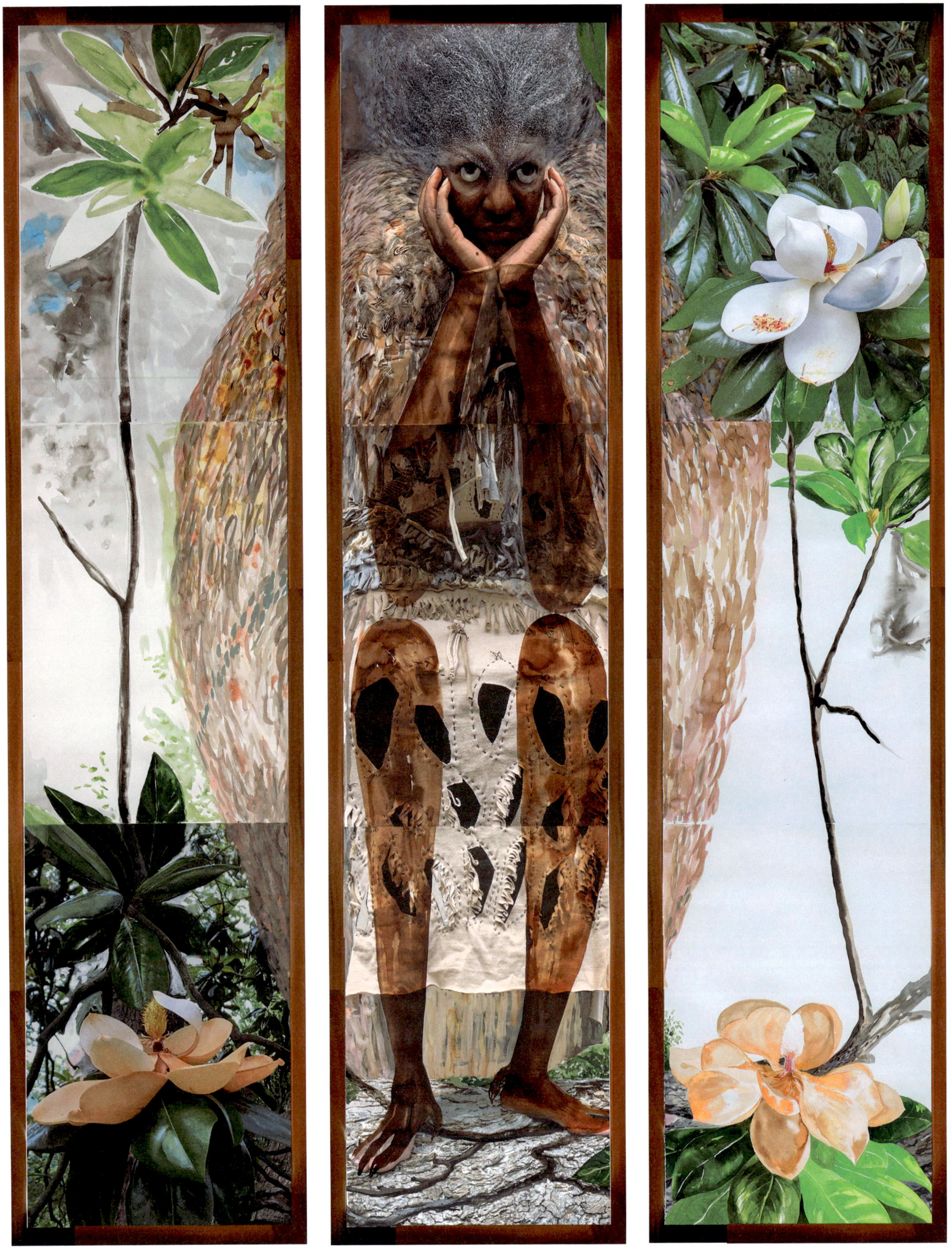

PLATE 94 *Secrets of the Magnolia Tree*, 2021

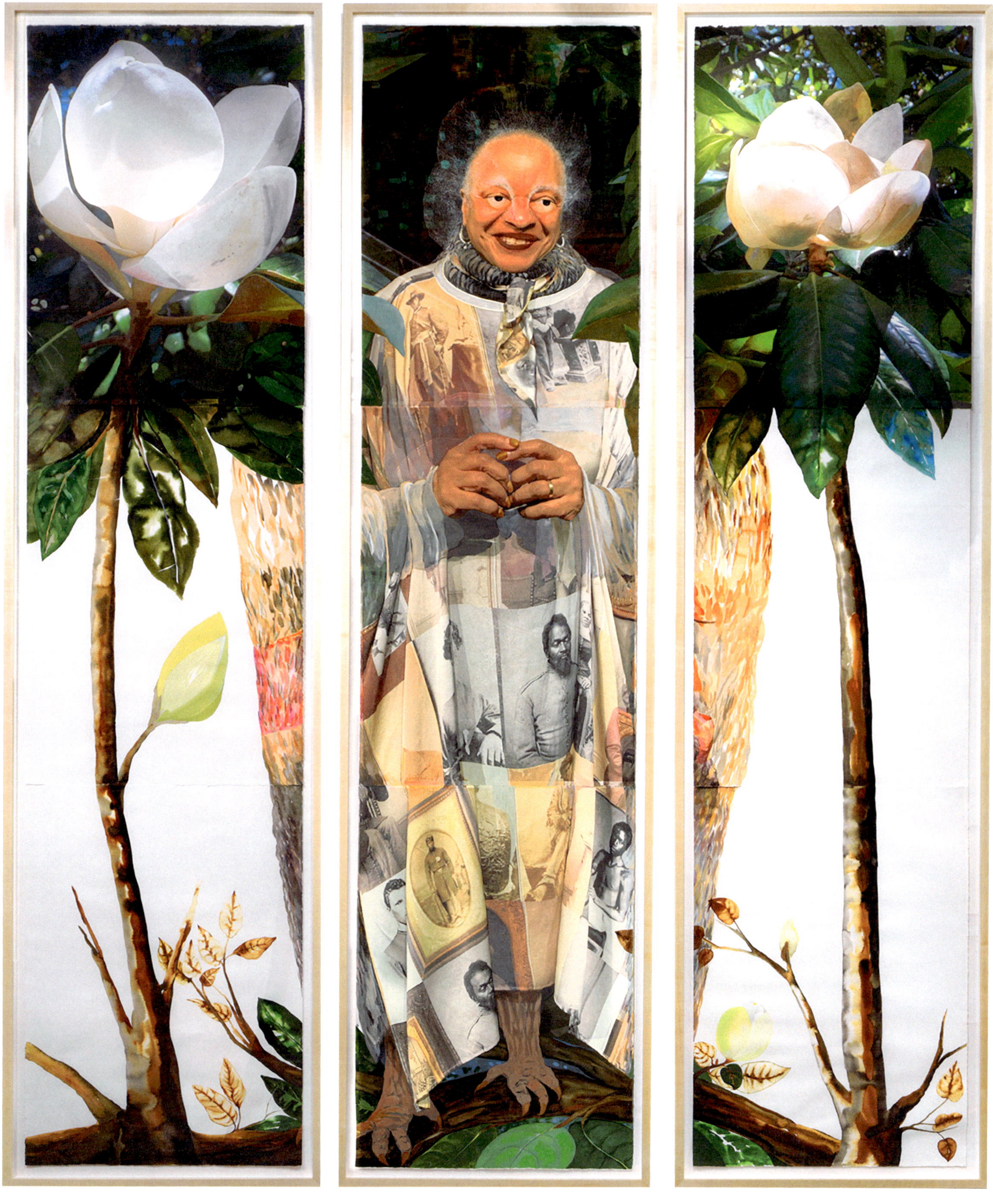

PLATE 95 *Deb Luminosity*, from the Secrets of the Magnolia Tree series, 2022

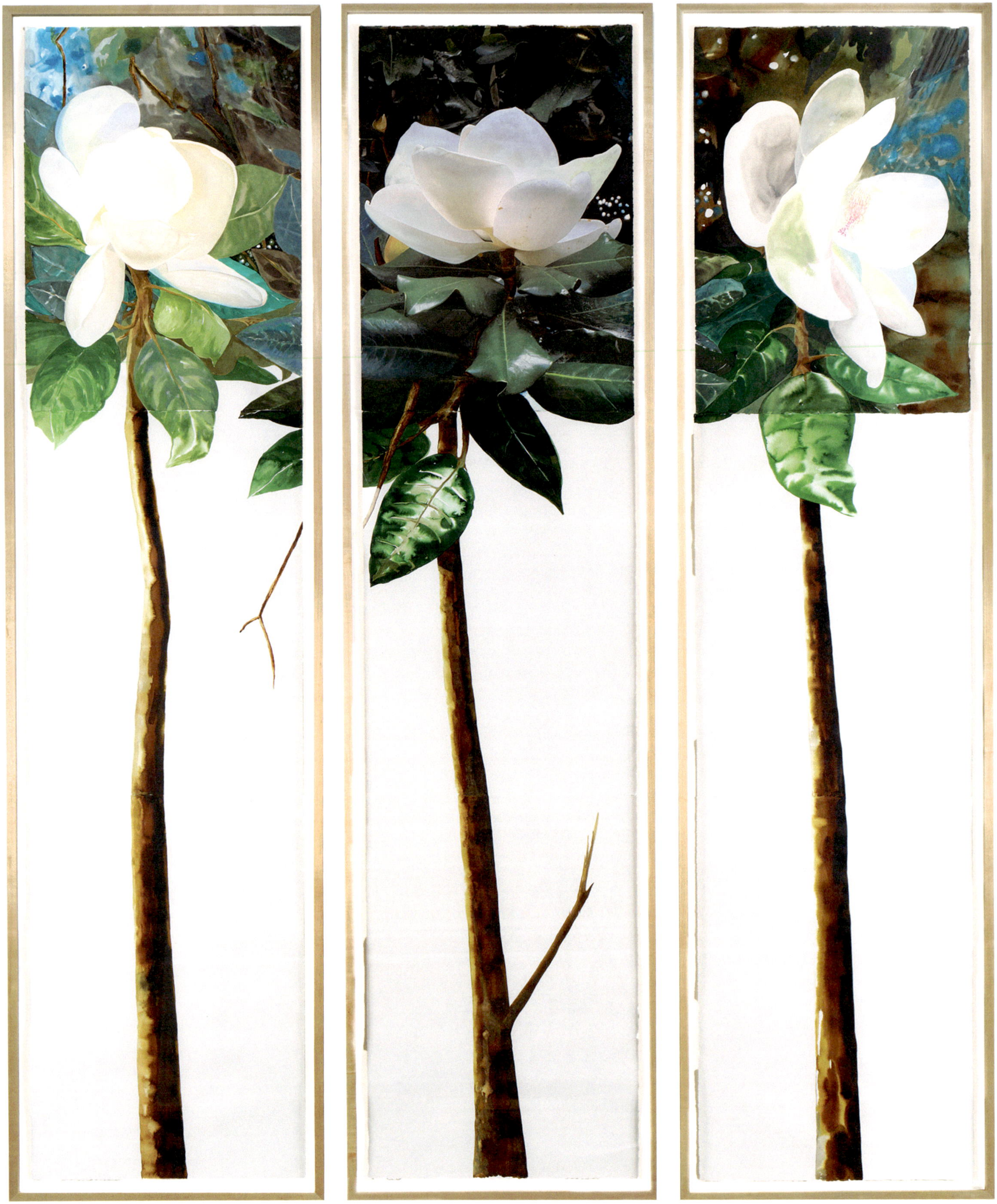

PLATE 96 *Forest of Solitude*, from the Secrets of the Magnolia Tree series, 2022

PLATE LIST

NOTE TO THE READER

Campos-Pons has approached titling in different ways during different parts of her career. Early titles are often in Spanish with English translations in parentheses; later works tend to use both English and Spanish titles (indicated by a slash) or solely English or Spanish. Titles are styled here as determined by the artist.

Many institutions and collectors, as well as the artist herself, refer to Campos-Pons's dye diffusion transfer prints as Polaroids, their proprietary name. For accessibility, we likewise use the commonly known term. Campos-Pons sometimes considers the full sheet of the Polaroid the artwork, leaving the dripping emulsion visible. Likewise, some works are presented framed and some unframed, so some captions do not include framed dimensions. This flexibility and specificity to series and context reflects Campos-Pons's multivalent approach as an artist.

PLATE 1 *Soy Una Fuente (I Am a Fountain)*, 1990
Mixed-media installation: oil on board, clay tablets
Dimensions variable, approx. 299.7 x 241.3 cm (118 x 95 in.)
Detroit Institute of Arts

PLATE 2 *Umbilical Cord*, 1991
Mixed-media installation: marble, carved wood, wire, fabric, soil, color photo prints
99.1 x 335.3 cm (39 x 132 in.)
Boston, Museum of the National Center of Afro-American Artists

PLATE 3 *Carta Natal (Birth Certificate)*, 1991
Mixed-media installation: marble, woodcuts, amate (bark) paper, carved wood, etched glass
Approx. 78.7 x 599.4 cm (31 x 228 in.)
Northampton, Massachusetts, Smith College Museum of Art, purchased with the Dorothy C. Miller Class of 1925 Fund

PLATE 4 *Baño Sagrado (Rite of Initiation, Sacred Bath)*, 1991
Single-channel video by Campos-Pons with sound by Neil Leonard
Video: single-channel video (color, sound, 31:37 min., transferred to video from Super 8 film); sound: composition for alto saxophone, bells, clay flute
Originally commissioned by Western Front, Vancouver
Courtesy of the artists

PLATE 5 *TRA*, 1991
Marble, wood, glass, soil, and color prints of black-and-white film transferred to canvas
Dimensions variable, each panel approx. 185 cm (73 in.) tall
Installation view, *If I Were a Poet*, Gallery Wendi Norris off-site exhibition, San Francisco, 2018
Washington, DC, Smithsonian American Art Museum, Museum purchase in part through the Smithsonian Latino Initiatives Pool, administrated by the Smithsonian Latino Center, 2022.62A-N

Tablet at left: *travesía* / FUE UN LARGO VIAJE INVOLUNTARIO como arrancar un árbol y dispersar sus raices NO TODOS LLEGARAN nosotros somos los hijos de algunos que solo recuerdan DONDE COMENZO SU DOLOR.
travesía (crossing; "It was a long involuntary journey / like ripping up a tree and scattering its roots. / Not everyone made it. / We are the children of those that remember only / where their pain began.")

Tablet at center: *trata* / AL LLEGAR UN SITO AJENO ser vendidos canjeados maltratados sus brazos espiritu sus pulmones y su sangre la energía para construir y proteger LA RIQUEZA DE SUS OPRESORES
trata (trade; "To arrive at a strange place / To be sold, exchanged, abused. Their arms, spirit, their lungs and their blood / the energy to build and to protect / the wealth of their oppressors.")

Tablet at right: *tragedia* / HOY MILLONES SIGUEN PADECIENDO en cualquier lugar que esten POBREZA DELINCUENCIA MARGINALISMO pocos grupos humanos han sido como el nuestro tan DESPRECIADOS Y USADOS.
tragedia (tragedy; "Today millions keep on suffering / wherever they are: / poverty, marginalism, delinquency. Few human groups have been as despised and used as ours."

PLATE 6 Performance with *The Seven Powers Come by the Sea*, 1992
Performance documentation, Institute of Contemporary Art, Boston, September 9, 1992
Mixed-media installation: carved wood, black-and-white photographs in frames, paint on paper
Each section: approx. 182.9 x 76.2 x 7.6 cm (70 x 30 x 3 in.)

PLATE 7 *Oh... the Isms, Footprints of a Journey*, 1992
Mixed media: wood, blood, shaved foam, enamel, glass, Plexiglas
Each pedestal: 111.4 x 53.3 x 53.3 cm (43 5/8 x 21 x 21 in.); each vitrine: 53.3 x 53.3 x 53.3 cm (21 x 21 x 21 in.); 162.6 x 221 x 53.3 cm (64 x 87 x 21 in.) overall
NSU Art Museum Fort Lauderdale, gift of the artist 95.37

Left: *Llamamos a los muertos / ellos responden / llamamos a los vivos / no responden*
(We call to the dead / they answer / we call to the living / they do not answer)

Center: *Historia / posthistoria / colonialismo / postcolonialismo / nacionalismo / chovinismo / modernismo / machismo / postmodernismo / pluralismo / individualismo / racismo / oportunismo / multiculturalismo / etc.*
(History / posthistory / colonialism / postcolonialism / nationalism / chauvinism / modernism / machismo / postmodernism / pluralism / individualism / racism / opportunism / multiculturalism / etc.)

Right: *Mejor sería adorar a la muerte / y abandonar a nuestros dioses / cuando la muerte mata a la gente / en*

que estan ocupados nuestros dioses (It would be better to worship death / and abandon our gods / when death kills people / what are our gods busy with)

PLATE 8 *History of a People Who Were Not Heroes: A Town Portrait*, 1994
Installation by Campos-Pons with sound by Neil Leonard
Sculpture: wood, glass, steel, clay tablets, black-and-white photographs, three-channel video (color, sound, approx. 9:10 min. each); sound: two-channel electroacoustic composition
Boston, Museum of Fine Arts, museum purchase with funds donated by members of the 2017–2018 Contemporary Art Visiting Committee in honor of Jen Mergel, Robert L. Beal, Enid L. Beal, and Bruce A. Beal, Senior Curator of Contemporary Art (2010–2017), and the Arthur Tracy Cabot Fund, Linde Purchase Fund for Contemporary Art, and Michael D. Wolk Fund for New Media, 2022.5

PLATE 9 *The Seven Powers*, 1994
Cibachrome prints with overpainting, black-and-white photographs in frames
Dimensions variable
Grand Forks, North Dakota Museum of Art, Gift of Jorge and Martha Schneider

PLATE 10 *The Herbalist's Tools*, 1994
Installation by Campos-Pons with sound by Neil Leonard
Sculpture: acrylic on wood, photographs, aluminum casserole pans, cornmeal, machetes, etched glass bowls, pressed wood, live plants, fresh herbs; sound: two-channel electroacoustic composition
Dimensions variable
Installation view, *María Magdalena Campos-Pons: Everything Is Separated by Water*, Indianapolis Museum of Art, 2007
Originally commissioned by Maryland Institute College of Art, Baltimore

PLATE 11 *When I Am Not Here / Estoy Allá*, 1994
Polaroid Polacolor Pro photograph
Unframed: approx. 61 x 50.8 cm (24 x 20 in.)
Hanover, New Hampshire, Hood Museum of Art, Dartmouth, purchased through the Contemporary Art Fund, 2009.12

PLATE 12 *When I Am Not Here / Estoy Allá*, 1994
Triptych of Polaroid Polacolor Pro photographs
Unframed: approx. 61 x 50.8 cm (24 x 20 in.) each; framed: approx. 61 x 55.9 x 6.4 cm (24 x 22 x 2 1/2 in.) each; approx. 198 x 55.9 x 6.4 cm (78 x 22 x 2 1/2 in.) overall
Bentonville, Arkansas, Crystal Bridges Museum of American Art, 2021.7

PLATE 13 *Identity Could Be a Tragedy*, from the When I Am Not Here / Estoy Allá series, 1995–96
Composition of six Polaroid Polacolor Pro photographs
Unframed: approx. 61 x 50.8 cm (24 x 20 in.) each; framed: approx. 66 x 55.9 cm (26 x 22 in.) each; approx. 132 x 167.7 cm (52 x 66 in.) overall
Massachusetts, Worcester Art Museum, Eliza S. Paine Fund, 2003.4

PLATE 14 *When I Am Not Here / Estoy Allá, Tríptico I*, 1996
Triptych of Polaroid Polacolor Pro photographs
Unframed: approx. 61 x 50.8 cm (24 x 20 in.) each; framed: approx. 68.5 x 58.4 x 6.4 cm (27 x 23 x 2 1/2 in.) each; approx. 100 x 238.2 x 6.4 cm (39 1/4 x 93 3/4 x 2 1/2 in.) overall
West Palm Beach, Florida, Norton Museum of Art, Purchase, R. H. Norton Trust, 99.92.1-3

PLATE 15 *When I Am Not Here / Estoy Allá, Tríptico I (remade)*, 1996/2013
Triptych of Polaroid Polacolor Pro photographs
Unframed: approx. 61 x 50.8 cm (24 x 20 in.) each; framed: approx. 66 x 55.9 x 6.4 cm (26 x 22 x 2 1/2 in.) each; approx. 66 x 167.7 x 6.4 cm (26 x 66 x 2 1/2 in.) overall
Collection Pérez Art Museum Miami, gift of Jorge M. Pérez

PLATE 16 *Abridor de Caminos (The One Who Opens the Path)*, 1997
Composition of ten Polaroid Polacolor Pro photographs
Unframed: 73.7 x 55.9 cm (29 x 22 in.) each; approx. 147.4 x 279.5 cm (58 x 110 in.) overall
Boston, Polaroid Collection

PLATE 17 *Red Composition*, from the Los Caminos (The Path) series, 1997
Triptych of Polaroid Polacolor Pro photographs
Framed: approx. 94 x 73.7 x 5 cm (37 x 29 x 2 in.) each; approx. 94 x 221 x 5 cm (37 x 87 x 2 in.) overall
Collection of Wendi Norris

PLATE 18 *Red Composition* from the Los Caminos (The Path) series, 1997
Triptych of Polaroid Polacolor Pro photographs
Unframed: 61 x 50.8 cm (24 x 20 in.) each; framed: approx. 82 x 56 x 5 cm (32.3 x 22 x 2 in.) each; approx. 82 x 168 x 5 cm (32.3 x 66 x 2 in.) overall
Los Angeles, J. Paul Getty Museum, 2022.55

PLATE 19 *Susurro (Whispers)*, 1997
Diptych of Polaroid Polacolor Pro photographs
Unframed: 73.7 x 55.9 cm (29 x 22 in.) each
Boston, Polaroid Collection

PLATE 20 *History of a People Who Were Not Heroes: Spoken Softly with Mama*, 1998
Installation by Campos-Pons with sound by Neil Leonard
Sculpture: embroidered silk and organza over ironing boards with photographic transfers, embroidered cotton sheets, *pâte de verre* irons and trivets, wooden benches, six projected video tracks; sound: four-channel non-repeating electroacoustic composition
Overall: 853.4 x 866.1 cm (336 x 341 in.)
Ottawa, National Gallery of Canada, purchased 1999

PLATE 21 *History of a People Who Were Not Heroes: Meanwhile the Girls Were Playing*, 1999–2000
Installation by Campos-Pons with sound by Neil Leonard
Sculpture: metallic organdy, silk, embroidered fabric, *pâte de verre* flowers, four projected video tracks (approx. 3:30 min. each); sound: four-channel non-repeating electroacoustic composition
Gallery Wendi Norris

PLATE 22 *The Right Protection*, 1999
Polaroid Polacolor Pro photograph
Unframed: approx. 61 x 50.8 cm (24 x 20 in.)
Collection of Francesca Biancacci and Fabio Sbianchi

PLATE 23 *Untitled (The Right Protection)*, 1999
Lithograph with colored paper pulp additions, edition of fourteen
51.4 x 44.5 cm (20 1/4 x 17 1/2 in.)
Published by Rutgers Center for Innovative Printmaking
New York, Museum of Modern Art, Howard Johnson Fund, 219.2002

PLATE 24 *Nesting II*, 2000
Triptych of Polaroid Polacolor Pro photographs
Unframed: 61 x 50.8 cm (24 x 20 in.) each; framed: approx. 82 x 168 x 5 cm (32 1/4 x 66 x 2 in.) overall
Nashville, Hess Collection

PLATE 25 *Nesting IV*, 2000
Composition of four Polaroid Polacolor Pro photographs
Unframed: approx. 83.8 x 63.5 cm (29 x 25 in.) each; approx. 83.8 x 254 cm (33 x 100 in.) overall
Boston, Museum of Fine Arts, The Living New England Artists Purchase Fund, created by The Stephen and Sybil Stone Foundation, 2001.271.1-4

PLATE 26 *Replenishing*, 2001
Composition of seven Polaroid Polacolor Pro photographs
224.79 x 167.64 cm (88.5 x 66 in.) overall
Collection Pérez Art Museum Miami, museum purchase with funds provided by PAMM's Collectors Council

PLATE 27 *Elevata*, 2002
Composition of sixteen Polaroid Polacolor Pro photographs
Framed: approx. 296 x 264.2 cm (116 1/2 x 104 in.) overall
Indianapolis Museum of Art, purchased through the IMA Business Group Art Acquisition Fund, 2004.154A-P

PLATE 28 *Classic Creole*, 2003
Composition of twelve Polaroid Polacolor Pro photographs
Unframed: approx. 182.9 x 279.4 cm (72 x 110 in.)
Gallery Wendi Norris

PLATE 29 *The Calling*, 2003
Diptych of Polaroid Polacolor Pro photographs
Framed: approx. 61 x 111.8 cm (24 x 44 in.) overall
Collection of Jonathan and Barbara Lee

PLATE 30 *One Thousand Ways to Say Goodbye / Mil maneras para decir adiós / Threads of Memory*, 2003
Installation by Campos-Pons with sound by Neil Leonard
Sculpture: cast cut polymer resin, mild steel, rebar; five-channel video (7 min.); sound: two-channel electroacoustic composition
Dimensions variable
Installation view, *One Thousand Ways to Say Goodbye*, Henie Onstad Art Center, Høvikodden, Norway, 2003

PLATE 31 *Constellation*, 2004
Composition of sixteen Polaroid Polacolor Pro photographs
Unframed: approx. 244 x 203.2 cm (96 x 80 in.) overall
Washington, DC, Smithsonian American Art Museum, museum purchase through the Luisita L. and Franz H. Denghausen Endowment, 2013.23A–P

PLATE 32 *The Magician's Tools*, 2004
Composition of fifteen Polaroid photographs
Unframed: approx. 61 x 50.8 cm (24 x 20 in.) each; approx. 182.9 x 304.8 cm (72 x 120 in.) overall
Collection Pérez Art Museum

Miami, promised gift of Jorge M. and Darlene Pérez

PLATE 33 *Backyard Dreams #8*, 2005
Inkjet print on watercolor paper on aluminum
160 x 175 cm (63 x 69 in.)
Galleria Giampaolo Abbondio

PLATE 34 *El Nacimiento de la Flor de Cardi*, 2006
Gouache, watercolor pencil, watercolor, ink, woven threads, and gold leaf on archival paper
Approx. 251.5 x 144 cm (99 x 56 3/4 in.)
Collection of Debbie and Mitchell Rechler

PLATE 35 *A Reason Why Janet Jackson Should Move to the Veneto Region: A Wardrobe Malfunction Early on Goes Unnoticed*, 2006
Gouache, watercolor pencil, watercolor, and fabric on archival paper
Approx. 211 x 153 cm (83 x 60 1/4 in.)
Galleria Giampaolo Abbondio

PLATE 36 *Pied-à-terre, Everyone Needs His Oba Oba*, 2006
Gouache, watercolor pencil, watercolor, ink, and woven threads on paper
Approx. 212 x 152.5 cm (83 1/2 x 60 in.)
Private collection

PLATE 37 *Invocazione alla Questura - Rita of Nigeria*, 2006
Gouache, watercolor pencil, watercolor, and fabric on archival paper
Approx. 111 x 181 cm (43 3/4 x 71 1/4 in.)
Galleria Giampaolo Abbondio

PLATE 38 *Il pane è vita. Zucchero and company are good*, 2006
Album cover, ink, watercolor, silver leaf, and collected paper wrappers affixed to archival watercolor paper
113 x 152 cm (44 1/2 x 59 7/8 in.)
Galleria Giampaolo Abbondio

PLATE 39 *Juxtaposition #1*, 2006
Inkjet print on paper
83 x 63 cm (32 4/8 x 24 3/4 in.)
Galleria Giampaolo Abbondio

PLATE 40 *Juxtaposition #3*, 2006
Inkjet print on paper
93.5 x 63 cm (36 3/4 x 24 3/4 in.)
Galleria Giampaolo Abbondio

PLATE 41 *Madonna Pellegrina - La Viajera*, 2006
Installation and video by Campos-Pons with sound by Neil Leonard
Carved wood, golden leaf, varnished aluminum grid, video projection (color, sound, 4:50 min.)
Sculpture: 124.5 x 996 x 2 cm (49 x 392 1/8 x 3/4 in.)
Galleria Giampaolo Abbondio

PLATE 42 *Habilitation, Mojitos, and Crocodile's Tears*, 2006
Performance by Campos-Pons with sound by Neil Leonard
Performance and spoken word: Campos-Pons and Neil Arcadio Leonard-Campos; music: Neil Leonard (alto/soprano saxophones composition), Gabi Sasson (laptop/turntable electro compositions), Ernestico Rodriguez (Cuban percussion)
Documentation of performance, Galleria PACK, Milan, June 2006

PLATE 43 *De Las Dos Aguas (Of the Two Waters)*, 2007
Composition of twelve Polaroid Polacolor Pro photographs
Framed: approx. 68.6 x 58.4 cm (27 x 23 in.) each; approx. 203.2 x 228.6 cm (80 x 90 in.) overall
NSU Art Museum Fort Lauderdale, Florida, promised gift of David Horvitz and Francie Bishop Good

PLATE 44 *My Mother Told Me I Am Chinese: China Porcelain*, installation and preparatory sketches for the vases, 2008
Installation by Campos-Pons with sound by Neil Leonard
Sculpture: hand-painted Chinese porcelain, Plexiglas shelf, single-channel video projection (color, sound, 5:48 min.); sound: two-channel electroacoustic composition; sketches: ink and watercolor on watercolor archival paper
Approx. 228.6 x 231.1 x 139.7 cm (90 x 91 x 55 in.)

PLATE 45 *Blue Refuge*, 2008
Composition of nine Polaroid Polacolor Pro photographs
Approx. 213.6 x 186.6 cm (84 x 73 1/2 in.) overall
Lincoln, Massachusetts, deCordova Sculpture Park and Museum, museum purchase with funds provided by members of the deCordova Collections and Exhibitions Committee and the Frederick P. Walkey Fund, gift of the Stephen and Sybil Stone Foundation, 2009

PLATE 46 *Voyeurs and Beholders of…*, 2008/2015
Composition of fifteen Polaroid Polacolor Pro photographs
Approx. 61 x 50.8 cm (24 x 20 in.) each
Gallery Wendi Norris

PLATE 47 *Dreaming of an Island*, 2008
Composition of nine Polaroid Polacolor Pro photographs
Framed: approx. 217.2 x 192.4 cm (85 1/2 x 74 3/4 in.) overall
The Watch Hill Collection

PLATE 48 *Thinking of It*, 2008
Watercolor, gouache, ink, and Prismacolor on paper
Approx. 185 x 131 cm (73 x 55 in.)
Shelly and Donald Rubin private collection

PLATE 49 *After Duchamp*, 2010
Composition of nine Polaroid Polacolor Pro photographs
Approx. 61 x 50.8 cm (24 x 20 in.) each; overall: 228.6 x 179.1 cm (90 x 70 1/2 in.)
Bernice Steinbaum Gallery

PLATE 50 *Shooting Stars for Fallen Soldiers*, 2010
Composition of twelve Polaroid Polacolor Pro photographs
Approx. 60.7 x 50.8 cm (24 x 20 in.) each; 183 x 203 cm (72 x 80 in.) overall
Cambridge, Massachusetts, Harvard Art Museums, Fogg Museum, gift of Polaroid Corporation

PLATE 51 *Sugar/Bittersweet*, 2010
Mixed-media installation: wood stools, metal spears cast glass, sugar, video projection
Dimensions variable
Installation view, *Sugar: María Magdalena Campos-Pons*, Smith College Museum of Art, Northampton, Massachusetts, 2010
Cambridge, Massachusetts, Ethelbert Cooper Gallery of African and African American Art, Harvard University, gift of Richard D. Cohen
Courtesy Smith College Museum of Art

PLATE 52 *The Warrior Reservoir*, 2010–11
Made in collaboration with Neil Arcadio Leonard-Campos
Watercolor, ink, and Prismacolor on cotton fiber, amate (bark), and handmade paper with ribbon and African totems and spears
Approx. 204.5 x 332.7 cm (80 1/2 x 131 in.) overall
Nashville, Vanderbilt University Fine Arts Gallery, gift from Dr. and Mrs. William Ewers, with additional support provided by Janice D. Forsythe Memorial Fund, the Julian Haddock Fine Arts Memorial Fund, and the Thomas Brumbaugh Fund

PLATE 53 *The One That Carried the Fire*, 2011
Human hair and watercolor on archival paper
Composition of three panels, 86.4 x 233.7 cm (34 x 92 in.) each
Collection of June Michel McCormack

PLATE 54 *El Mensajero*, 2011
Composition of twelve Polaroid Polacolor Pro photographs
Approx. 60.7 x 50.8 cm (24 x 20 in.) each; 183 x 203 cm (72 x 80 in.) overall
Courtesy of Kathryn and Craig Hall's Personal Collection, Dallas, Texas

PLATE 55 *Cuba Walk*, 2012
Single-channel video (color, sound, 4:01 min.) by Campos-Pons and Neil Leonard
Camera and video editing by Neil Leonard; shot on the Malecón, Havana

PLATE 56 *Llegooo! FeFa!*, 2012
Installation by Campos-Pons and Neil Leonard
Sculpture: found glass, found wood, fresh-baked bread, plastic-wrapped goods, single-channel video (color, sound, 9 min.); sound: two-channel non-repeating sound composition based on field recordings of Cuban street criers (*pregoneros*)
Dimensions variable
Dual commission by Campos-Pons and Neil Leonard
Installation view, 11th Havana Biennial, Wifredo Lam Center of Contemporary Art, Havana, 2012

PLATE 57 *Llegooo! FeFa!*, 2012
Processional performance by Campos-Pons and Neil Leonard
Sound: saxophone and Cuban street criers *(pregoneros)*
Presented by Detras del Muro, Malecon, Havana, Cuba
Curated by Juanito Delgado
Dual commission by Campos-Pons and Neil Leonard

PLATE 58 *Songs of Freedom*, 2013
Composition of six Polaroid Polacolor Pro photographs
Approx. 61 x 50.8 cm (24 x 20 in.) each
Galleria Giampaolo Abbondio

PLATE 59 *53+1=54+1=55 / Letter of the Year*, 2013
Installation by Campos-Pons and Neil Leonard
Sculpture: 100 rattan bird cages, 55 media players for audio and video, 80 bamboo sticks, 18 custom-designed audio speakers, 18-channel non-repeating sound composition based on field recordings of Cuban street criers (*pregoneros*)
Dual commission by Campos-Pons and Neil Leonard
Installation view, Cuban Pavilion, 55th Venice Biennale, June 1–November 24, 2013

PLATE 60 *FeFa*, 2013
Processional performance by Campos-Pons and Neil Leonard in Piazza San Marco, Venice

Sound: Neil Leonard (soprano saxophone, composition) with Jason Lim (violin), Feliciano Arango (bass, voice, percussion, composition), Eugenio Arango (voice, percussion), and Cristina Arango (voice, percussion)
Dual commission by Campos-Pons and Neil Leonard for the Cuban Pavilion, 55th Venice Biennale, Italy

PLATE 61 *Freedom Trap*, 2013
Polaroid Polacolor Pro photograph
Approx. 61 x 50.8 cm (24 x 20 in.)
Gallery Wendi Norris

PLATE 62 *Freedom Trap*, 2013
Polaroid Polacolor Pro photograph
Approx. 61 x 50.8 cm (24 x 20 in.)
Gallery Wendi Norris

PLATE 63 *The Flag Year 13. Color Code Venice*, 2013
Polaroid Polacolor Pro photograph
235 x 170.2 cm (92 1/2 x 67 in.)
Medford, Massachusetts, Tufts University, partial gift of Kenneth A. Aidekman A75, Family Foundation, 2014.01.A–I

PLATE 64 *Habla La Madre*, 2014
Opening procession for *Carrie Mae Weems LIVE: Past Tense/Future Perfect*, Solomon R. Guggenheim Museum, New York, April 25, 2014
Processional performance by Campos-Pons and Neil Leonard
Spoken word: Campos-Pons and Natasha Diggs; music: Neil Leonard (bass clarinet, composition), Jen Baker (trombone), Monique Buzzarté (trombone), Dick Griffin (trombone), Kiane Zawadi (euphonium), Elena Kakaliaguo (French horn), Jay Rozen (tuba), Joseph Daley (tuba), Oriente Lopez (percussion, flute), and Roman Díaz (bata, voice); duration: approx. 30 min.
Dual commission by Campos-Pons and Neil Leonard for the Guggenheim Museum

PLATE 65 *Finding Balance*, 2015
Composition of twenty-eight Polaroid Polacolor Pro photographs
Approx. 268 x 404.4 cm (105 1/2 x 159 1/4 in.) overall
Miami, Jorge M. Pérez Collection

PLATE 66 *Alchemy of the Soul, Elixir for the Spirits*, 2015
Installation by Campos-Pons and Neil Leonard
Sculpture: blown glass, cast glass, steel, cast resin, silicone, acrylic, polyvinyl chloride tubing, water, and rum essence; sound: ten-channel composition featuring Leonard's saxophone, Cuban field recordings, and chants by Los Muñequitos de Matanzas; duration: 11 min.
Dimensions variable
Dual commission by Campos-Pons and Neil Leonard for the Peabody Essex Museum
Installation view, *Alchemy of the Soul: María Magdalena Campos-Pons*, Peabody Essex Museum, Salem, Massachusetts, 2016

PLATE 67 *Catch of the Day #1*, from the Extreme Weather, Captiva series, 2016
Ink, watercolor, hair, and gouache on archival paper
100 x 65 cm (39 3/8 x 25 1/2 in.)
Galleria Giampaolo Abbondio

PLATE 68 *Jungle*, from the Extreme Weather, Captiva series, 2016
Fruit pulp and ink on embossed archival paper
108.5 x 75.5 cm (42 3/4 x 29 3/4 in.)
Galleria Giampaolo Abbondio

PLATE 69 *La Ira de Chango & Zeus*, from the Extreme Weather, Captiva series, 2016
Mixed media on archival paper
106.5 x 75.5 cm (42 x 29 3/4 in.)
Galleria Giampaolo Abbondio

PLATE 70 *Identified*, 2016
Performance by Campos-Pons and Neil Leonard
Performance documentation at National Gallery, Washington, DC, May 14, 2016
Performance/spoken word: Campos-Pons, Monifa Love, Dell Hamilton, Helina Metaferia, and Natasha Diggs; sound for ensembles in discrete galleries: Kogod Courtyard: saxophone, trumpet, keyboard, three congas; spiral stairway from first to second floor: jazz orchestra; third-floor gallery: three vocalists, three bata, one percussionist
Music: Neil Leonard (soprano and alto saxophones, electronics, composition), Terrence Blanchard (trumpet), Oriente Lopez (percussion/flute/piano), Rámon Garcia "Sandy" Pérez (percussion, voice), Lázaro Cárdenas Batel (percussion, voice), Vanessa Lindberg (voice), Oscar Rousseax (percussion, voice), Randy Rosso (percussion, voice), Ernesto Gattel (percussion), Frank "Squirrel" Williams (percussion), Duke Ellington School Jazz Band directed by Ike Daniels; duration: approx. 40 min.
Dual commission by Campos-Pons and Neil Leonard for the Smithsonian Institution National Portrait Gallery, Washington, DC

PLATE 71 *Matanzas Sound Map*, 2017
Installation by Campos-Pons and Neil Leonard
Sculpture: cast glass, blown glass, handmade paper, coconut tree bark,

coconut shells, Calea stone; sound/video: single-channel video (color, sound, 16 min.), sound composition comprising alto saxophone, Cuban field recordings, and voices by Los Muñequitos de Matanzas
Dimensions variable
Dual commission by Campos-Pons and Neil Leonard for Documenta 14, Athens
Gallery Wendi Norris

PLATE 72 *Angels' Trumpets, Devils' Bells*, 2019
Mixed media on archival paper
Composition of nine panels, 101.6 x 66 cm (40 x 26 in.) each
Gallery Wendi Norris

PLATE 73 *She Always Knew of the Space in Between*, 2019
Gouache, watercolor, graphite, acrylic ink, and peacock feather on archival paper
160 x 81.3 cm (63 x 32 in.) each; approx. 160 x 406.4 cm (63 x 160 in.) overall
Gallery Wendi Norris

PLATE 74 *Wet All Day*, from the Un Pedazo de Mar series, 2019
Watercolor, gouache, and ink on archival paper
Unframed: 111.7 x 81.9 cm (44 x 32 1/4 in.); framed: 119.4 x 83.8 cm (47 x 33 in.)
Gallery Wendi Norris

PLATE 75 *An Army of Angels*, from the Un Pedazo de Mar series, 2019
Gouache, watercolor, graphite, and ink on paper
109.2 x 76.2 cm (43 x 30 in.)
The Melo-Gaenslen Collection

PLATE 76 *Floating between Temperature Zones*, from the Un Pedazo de Mar series, 2019
Gouache, watercolor, graphite, and ink on paper
64.3 x 83.8 cm (25 1/4 x 33 in.)
Leah Bennett, private collection

PLATE 77 *Untitled*, from the Un Pedazo de Mar series, 2019
Gouache, watercolor, graphite, and ink on paper
76.2 x 55.9 cm (30 x 22 in.)
Galleria Giampaolo Abbondio

PLATE 78 *Descending Angel*, from the Un Pedazo de Mar series, 2019
Digital print, gouache, watercolor, graphite, and ink on paper
76.2 x 55.9 cm (30 x 22 in.)
The Carl M. Freeman Foundation

PLATE 79 *Descending Angel 2*, from the Un Pedazo de Mar series, 2019
Digital print, gouache, watercolor, graphite, and ink on paper
101 x 76 cm (40 x 30 in.)
The Carl M. Freeman Foundation

PLATE 80 *Because the human body is a tree, Spring Awakening II*, 2019–20
Ink and watercolor on watercolor paper
119.4 x 114.5 cm (47 x 45 in.)
Galleria Giampaolo Abbondio

PLATE 81 *Because the human body is a tree, Spring Awakening III*, 2019–20
Ink and watercolor on watercolor paper, 106.5 x 114.5 cm (42 x 45 in.)
Galleria Giampaolo Abbondio

PLATE 82 *Miasma #1*, 2020
Ink and watercolor on archival paper
74 x 55.9 cm (29 1/8 x 22 in.)
Galerie Barbara Thumm

PLATE 83 *Miasma #2*, 2020
Ink and watercolor on archival paper
74 x 55.9 cm (29 1/8 x 22 in.)
Galerie Barbara Thumm

PLATE 84 *Miasma #5*, 2020
Ink and watercolor on archival paper
74 x 55.9 cm (29 1/8 x 22 in.)
Miami, Jorge M. Pérez Collection

PLATE 85 *Miasma #7*, 2020
Ink and watercolor on archival paper
74 x 55.9 cm (29 1/8 x 22 in.)
Miami, Jorge M. Pérez Collection

PLATE 86 *Carta Natal 7/26/1953, 7/22/1959, 7/13/1989, 7/11/2021*, 2021
Mixed media: archival digital inkjet prints, watercolor, ink, gouache, and gum arabic on archival paper
Five panels, 111.5 x 76 cm (43 7/8 x 30 in.) each; 111.5 x 380 cm (43 7/8 x 149 5/8 in.) overall
Galleria Giampaolo Abbondio

PLATE 87 *Butterfly Eyes (for Breonna Taylor)*, 2021
Mixed media: archival digital inkjet prints, watercolor, ink, gouache, and gum arabic on archival paper
Three panels, 104.1 x 73.7 cm (41 x 29 in.) each
Louisville, Kentucky, Speed Art Museum

PLATE 88 *Mobile #2*, from The Rise of the Butterflies series, 2021
Mouth-blown Murano glass and stainless steel
Approx. 420 x 330 x 180 cm (165.3 x 129.9 x 70.9 in.), edition of three
Galerie Barbara Thumm

PLATE 89 *Mobile #2*, detail from The Rise of the Butterflies series, 2021
Mouth-blown Murano glass and stainless steel

Galerie Barbara Thumm, Berlin, 2021
Galerie Barbara Thumm

PLATE 90 Installation view, showing *Mobile #2* (front) and *Mobile #1* (middle), from The Rise of the Butterflies series, 2021
Mouth-blown Murano glass and stainless steel
Each mobile approx. 420 x 330 x 180 cm (165.3 x 129.9 x 70.9 in.), edition of three
Galerie Barbara Thumm

PLATE 91 Untitled, from The Rise of the Butterflies series, 2021
Mouth-blown Murano glass and stainless steel
Approx. 200 x 250 x 200 cm (78 3/4 x 98 3/8 x 78 3/4 in.), edition of three
Galerie Barbara Thumm

PLATE 92 *When We Gather*, 2022
Performance documentation, National Gallery, Washington, DC, April 30, 2022
Commissioned by the National Gallery of Art, Washington, DC
Campos-Pons with Dell Marie Hamilton, Jana Harper, Sue-Ann Letta Forde, Stephanie Mercedes, Helina Metaferia, and Jessica Sandhu
Executive producers Wendi Norris and Virginia Shore; producers Greta Knutzen, Gabi Madsen, and Andrea Yu-Chieh Chung
The performance was made possible by major support from the Phyllis & Jerome Lyle Rappaport Foundation and a grant from the Alice L. Walton Foundation. Additional generous support was provided by the Carl M. Freeman Foundation, Craig and Kathryn Hall, and Leah R. Bennett

PLATE 93 *When We Gather*, 2021
Performance and video (color, sound, 5:43 min.)
Campos-Pons with Okwui Okpokwasili and LaTasha N. Nevada Diggs, with the participation of Dell Marie Hamilton, Jana Harper, Samita Sinha, and Lisa E. Harris
Directed by Codie Elaine Oliver
Courtesy of Gallery Wendi Norris and María Magdalena Campos-Pons

PLATE 94 *Secrets of the Magnolia Tree*, 2021
Watercolor, ink, gouache, and digital printing on paper on three panels
Approx. 335.3 x 228.6 cm (132 x 90 in.) overall
New York, Museum of Modern Art, Latin American and Caribbean Fund and gift of Ronnie Heyman, 2022

PLATE 95 *Deb Luminosity*, from the Secrets of the Magnolia Tree series, 2022
Watercolor, ink, gouache, and digital printing on paper on three panels
Approx. 335.3 x 228.6 cm (132 x 90 in.) overall
Princeton University Art Museum

PLATE 96 *Forest of Solitude*, from the Secrets of the Magnolia Tree series, 2022
Watercolor, ink, gouache, and digital printing on paper on three panels
Approx. 335.3 x 228.6 cm (132 x 90 in.) overall
Gallery Wendi Norris

FURTHER READING

This publication builds on the important scholarship of curators and academics who have explored María Magdalena Campos-Pons's multifaceted practice. Here, readers can find additional resources and writings to continue their own exploration. In particular, the 2007 exhibition catalogue *Everything Is Separated by Water* provides the foundation on which this publication builds; it is from Lisa D. Freiman's extensive research and Okwui Enwezor's generative scholarship that this work continues.

Since the publication of *Everything Is Separated by Water* sixteen years ago, greater attention has been paid to the resonance of art from the Caribbean and the African diaspora. We carry this work forward with gratitude to the scholars who have expanded our conceptualization of the "diasporic archive" from what Enwezor describes as "the narrow context of racial identity" to one that acts as "a vehicle for freeing the imagination of contemporary art and its resilient embedment in classical Western art" (65).

ARTICLES

Bell, Lynne. "History of People Who Were Not Heroes: A Conversation with María Magdalena Campos-Pons." *Third Text* 12, no. 43 (Summer 1998): 33–42.

Berger, Sally. "María Magdalena Campos-Pons, 1990–2001." In *Authentic/Ex-Centric: Conceptualism in Contemporary African Art*, edited by Salah Hassan and Olu Oguibe, 122–42. Venice: La Biennale de Venezia, Forum for African Arts, 2001.

DeLoughrey, Elizabeth, and Tatiana Flores. "Submerged Bodies: The Tidalectics of Representability and the Sea in Caribbean Art." In *Liquid Ecologies in Latin American and Caribbean Art*, edited by Lisa Blackmore and Liliana Gómez, 132–65. New York: Routledge, 2020.

Ferrer, Elizabeth. "Staging Self, Narrating Culture." In *Latinx Photography in the United States: A Visual History*, 83–104. Seattle: University of Washington Press, 2020.

Finley, Cheryl. "Schematics of Memory." *small axe* 35 (July 2011): 96–116.

Freiman, Lisa D. "María Magdalena Campos-Pons: Circling Campos-Pons." In *Unpacking Europe: Towards a Critical Reading*, edited by Salah Hassan and Iftikhar Dadi, 314–19. Rotterdam: Museum Boijmans Van Beuningen and Nai, 2002.

González, Flora M. "Possession and Altar Making: Reconstruction of Memory as Artistic Performance in the Multimedia Installations of María Magdalena Campos-Pons." *Cuban Studies* 31 (2000): 102–17.

Green Fryd, Vivien. "'Between What Is Home': María Magdalena Campos-Pons's 'Artistic Circuits' in the 'In-Between' Spaces of Matanzas, Cuba and Nashville, Tennessee." Unpublished article, Vanderbilt University, 2022.

Hart, David C. "Memory and the Installation Art of María Magdalena Campos-Pons." PhD diss., University of North Carolina at Chapel Hill, 2005.

Herzberg, Julia P. "Ritual in Performance." In *NeoHooDoo: Art for a Forgotten Faith*, edited by Franklin Sirmans, 54–67. Houston: Menil Foundation, 2008.

Leonard, Neil. "True Bread: The Sounds of Change in Cuba." *Leonardo Music Journal* 25 (2015): 95–96.

Lewis-Cappellari, Sarah, and María Magdalena Campos-Pons. "On the Art of Alchemy and Unfolding Desires: A Conversation with María Magdalena Campos-Pons." *Theatre Journal* 72, no. 3 (September 2020): E1–7.

Luis, William. "Art and Diaspora: A Conversation with María Magdalena Campos-Pons." *Afro-Hispanic Review* 30, no. 2 (Fall 2011): 155–56.

Martín-Sevillano, Ana Belén. "Crisscrossing Gender, Ethnicity, and Race: African Religious Legacy." *Cuban Contemporary Women's Art in Cuban Studies* 42 (2011): 136–54, 268.

Paravisini-Gebert, Lizabeth. "Gatherings: María Magdalena Campos-Pons and the Art of Recovery." *Caribbean Rasanblaj* 12, no. 1 (2015), https://hemisphericinstitute.org/en/emisferica-121-caribbean-rasanblaj/12-1-review-essays/e121-review-campos-pons.html.

Thompson, Barbara. "Decolonizing Black Bodies: Personal Journeys in the Contemporary Voice." In *Black Womanhood: Images, Icons, and Ideologies of the African Body*, edited by Barbara Thompson and Ifi Amadiume, 279–311. Seattle: University of Washington Press, 2008.

Wallace-Sanders, Kimberly. "The Body of a Myth: Embodying the Black Mammy Figure in Visual Culture." In *Black Womanhood: Images, Icons, and Ideologies of the African Body*, edited by Barbara Thompson and Ifi Amadiume, 163–179. Seattle: University of Washington Press, 2008.

Zavala, Adriana. "Blackness Distilled, Sugar and Rum: María Magdalena Campos-Pons's *Alchemy of the Soul, Elixir for the Spirits*." *Latin American and Latinx Visual Culture* 1, no. 2 (2019): 8–32.

BOOKS

Alexander, M. Jacqui. *Pedagogies of Crossing*. Durham, NC: Duke University Press, 2006.

Cavallarin, Martina, and Sergio Risalti. *Sono Qui: María Magdalena Campos-Pons*. Milan: Galleria PACK, 2006.

Chang, Alexandra. *Circles and Circuits: Chinese Caribbean Art*. Durham, NC: Duke University Press, 2018.

Farris Thompson, Robert. *Flash of the Spirit: African and Afro-American Art and Philosophy*. New York: Random House, 1983.

Flores, Tatiana, and Elizabeth DeLoughrey. *María Magdalena Campos-Pons: Sea and Self*. Milwaukee: Haggerty Museum of Art, Marquette University, 2021.

Flores, Tatiana, and Michelle A. Stephens, eds. *Relational Undercurrents: Contemporary Art of the Caribbean Archipelago*. Long Beach, CA: Museum of Latin American Art, 2017.

Freiman, Lisa D. *María Magdalena Campos-Pons: Everything Is Separated by Water*. Indianapolis: Indianapolis Museum of Art; New Haven, CT: Yale University Press, 2007.

Garcia Triana, Mauro, and Pedro Eng Herrera. *The Chinese in Cuba, 1847–Now*. Lanham, MD: Lexington Books, 2009.

Greene, Nikki A. *Grime, Glass, and Glitter: The Body and the Sonic in Contemporary Black Art*. Durham, NC: Duke University Press, forthcoming.

Hassan, Salah M., and Cheryl Finley, eds. *Diaspora, Memory, Place: David Hammons, María Magdalena Campos-Pons, Pamela Z*. Munich, New York: Prestel, 2008.

López, Kathleen. *Chinese Cubans: A Transnational History*. Chapel Hill: University of North Carolina Press, 2013.

Mercer, Kobena. *Travel and See: Black Diaspora Art Practices since the 1980s*. Durham, NC: Duke University Press, 2016.

Nash, Jennifer. *Black Feminism Reimagined*. Durham, NC: Duke University Press, 2019.

Neon Queen Collective. *Notes on Sugar / Like the Lonely Traveler: María Magdalena Campos-Pons*. Austin, TX: Neon Queen Collective and Wendi Norris Gallery, 2018.

Ossa, Luisa Marcela, and Debbie Lee-DiStefano. *Afro-Asian Connections in Latin America and the Caribbean*. Lanham, MD: Lexington Books, 2019.

Raiford, Leigh, and Heike Raphael-Hernandez, eds. *Migrating the Black Body: The African Diaspora and Visual Culture*. Seattle: University of Washington Press, 2017.

Weiss, Rachel. *To and From Utopia in the New Cuban Art*. Minneapolis: University of Minnesota Press, 2011.

WEBSITES

Bernal Roque, Dayara. "María Magdalena Campos-Pons + Neil Leonard." In *Artists' Prospectus for the Nation*, trans. Rebeca Hey-Colón, July 2013, http://www.artistsincontextprospectus.org/2013/07/23/maria-magdalena-campos-pons-neil-leonard/.

Images, clips, and information related to the performance and film *When We Gather* (2022) are accessible through the project website: http://www.whenwegather.org/.

Images, essays, and interviews related to Campos-Pons's multimedia installation *Alchemy of the Soul, Elixir for the Spirit* (2015) are accessible through the Peabody Essex's exhibition website: Joshua Basseches and Esther Allen, "Alchemy of the Soul," Peabody Essex Museum, 2016, http://alchemy.pem.org.

"A History of Indentureship." Ameena Gafoor Institute for the Study of Indentureship and Its Legacies, 2022, https://ameenagafoorinstitute.org/a-history-of-indentureship.

INDEX

Italicized plate and page numbers refer to illustrations.

ILLUSTRATION CREDITS

All artworks by María Magdalena Campos-Pons are © María Magdalena Campos-Pons. Unless otherwise noted, all images are courtesy of María Magdalena Campos-Pons.

Plates 1, 2, 3, 6: Images courtesy of the Indianapolis Museum of Art at Newfields

Plate 5: Image courtesy of the artist and Gallery Wendi Norris, San Francisco / Photo: Maciek Janicki

Plate 7: Image courtesy the NSU Art Museum

Plates 10, 20, 21, 56: Images courtesy of María Magdalena Campos-Pons / Sound by Neil Leonard

Plate 11: Image courtesy of María Magdalena Campos-Pons and Peg Alston/Peg Alston Fine Arts, Inc.

Plate 13: Photos courtesy of the Worcester Art Museum

Plates 17, 25, 28, 31, 44, 46, 50, 53, 54, 61, 62, 65, 72–79, 93, 94: Images courtesy of María Magdalena Campos-Pons and Gallery Wendi Norris, San Francisco

Plates 22, 24, 33–41, 43, 55, 58, 60, 67–69, 80, 81: Image courtesy of María Magdalena Campos-Pons and Galleria Giampaolo Abbondio, Milano

Plate 23; fig. 3: Digital Images © The Museum of Modern Art / Licensed by SCALA / Art Resource, NY

Plate 30: Image courtesy of the artist and Selene Wendt

Plate 42: Image courtesy of María Magdalena Campos-Pons and Galleria Giampaolo Abbondio, Milano / Photo: Gianmaria Conti

Plate 45: Courtesy of the deCordova Sculpture Park and Museum, The Trustees of Reservations

Plate 48: Image courtesy of Shelley and Donald Rubin Private Collection

Plate 49: Image courtesy of Bernice Steinbaum Gallery

Plate 51: Image courtesy of María Magdalena Campos-Pons and Smith College Museum of Art / Photo: Stephen Petegorsky / Notebook drawings courtesy of María Magdalena Campos-Pons

Plate 52: Image courtesy of María Magdalena Campos-Pons and Vanderbilt Fine Arts Gallery / Photo: John Schwelkert

Plate 59: Image courtesy of Galleria Giampaolo Abbondio / Photo: Riccardo Gay Lugar

Plate 63: Image courtesy of Tufts / Photo: Alonso Nichols

Plate 64: Solomon R. Guggenheim Museum

Plate 66: Image courtesy of Peabody Essex Museum / Photo: Peter Vanderwarker

Plate 70: Image courtesy of Nikki A. Greene

Plate 71: Images courtesy of María Magdalena Campos-Pons and Documenta / Audio and video courtesy of Neil Leonard

Plates 82, 83, 91: Images courtesy of María Magdalena Campos-Pons and Galerie Barbara Thumm

Plates 88, 89, 90: Images courtesy of María Magdalena Campos-Pons and Galerie Barbara Thumm / Photos: Jens Ziehe

Plate 92: Image courtesy of María Magdalena Campos-Pons and Gallery Wendi Norris, San Francisco / Photo: Mariah Miranda

Fig. 4: © 2022 Remedios Varo, Artists Rights Society (ARS), New York / VEGAP, Madrid

Fig. 6: Courtesy of Selene Wendt

Fig. 9: © Abelardo Morell

Fig. 10: © Carrie Mae Weems / Courtesy of the artist and Jack Shainman Gallery, New York / Image courtesy of Modern Art Museum of Fort Worth

Figs. 11, 13, 14, 15: Baker Library Special Collections, Harvard Business School

Fig. 12: © 2022 Dara Birnbaum / Courtesy of Dara Birnbaum and Electronic Arts Intermix (EAI), New York

Fig. 16: © María Magdalena Campos-Pons / Photo: © President and Fellows of Harvard College

Fig. 17: Cuban Film Poster Collection, Special Collections Research Center, William & Mary Libraries

Fig. 18: © Gallerie dell'Accademia di Venezia / su concessione del Ministero della Cultura

Fig. 20: Gallery Wendi Norris, San Francisco

Fig. 21: © 2023 Lorraine O'Grady / Artists Rights Society (ARS), New York / Image courtesy of Alexander Gray Associates

Fig. 22: © Nick Cave / Courtesy of the artist and Jack Shainman Gallery, New York / Photo: James Prinz Photography

Fig. 23: © The Lisette Model Foundation, Inc. (1983). Used by permission

Fig. 24: © Ryan Hodgson-Rigsbee

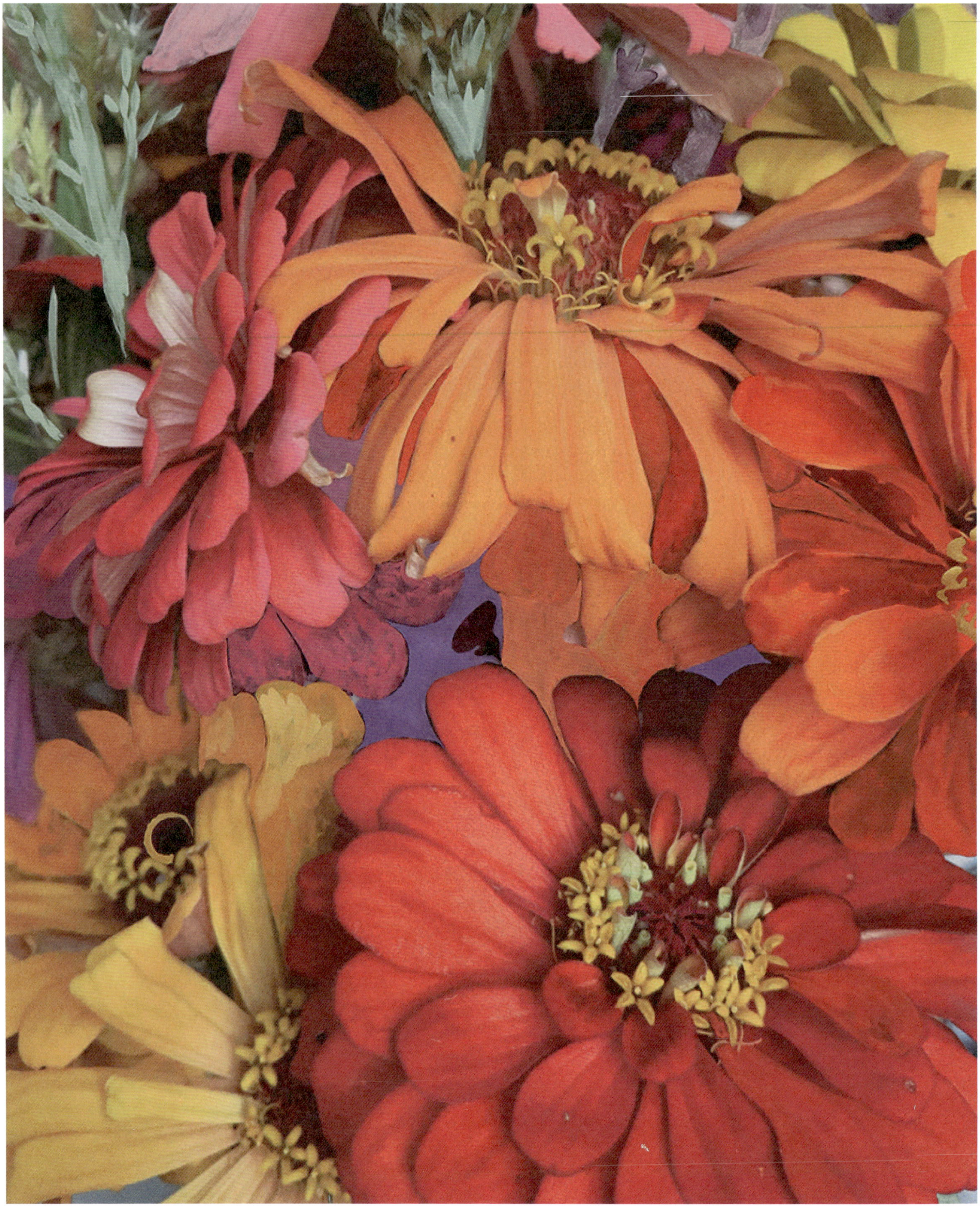